BELIEVERS UNDER

MW00929310

Many today want to assert that the inward direction of the indwelling Holy Spirit applying the law of love is the sum and essence of the law of Christ. I think David Gay's book, **Believers Under the Law of Christ**, *thoroughly refutes this view and proves that the commandments of Jesus and the exhortations of the New Testament writers are the very foundation of the law of Christ.*
Wayne Hinton, Administrator Discover New Covenant Theology Facebook Group

I have skimmed through this download. I agree with my whole heart that God the Holy Spirit ALWAYS and ONLY works in concert with his written word in the life of the believer – first in bringing him to Christ, then onward to conformity to Christ.
Mark D.Pierson

After some thought and in a spirit of conciliation, this [the Introduction] is the best résumé in a few lines I have been led to.
Tom Mitchell

A book that in my opinion that is sorely needed at this time. It is better to correct error at its inception than try to correct it after it gains a foothold. This book does that. The men of God down through the ages on whose shoulders we stand: What say they? I'm looking forward to reading the finished product.
Chuck Hoskins

David Gay's collection of works concerning the believer and the law of Christ deals with one of the most pertinent issues concerning the sanctification of the believer. His superior exegesis of the Scripture shows us the reality that believers are... not lawless, [but]that the rule of life is ultimately in the law of Christ.
Auston Duggins

Bro. David Gay has done it again. **Believers Under the Law of Christ** *is a thoroughly biblical work that addresses one of NCT's most crucial areas – the law of Christ & the believer's relationship to it. Can it be that in our zeal to remain biblically consistent when it comes to the Mosaic law-covenant that some may have gone too far? That will be for you to judge. David has provided the new-covenant believer with a great examination of that very question.*
Bro. Paul A.Kaiser, Pastor, New Covenant Baptist Church, Sacramento, California

David Gay's ministry has been instrumental in the lives of many Christians who have come to understand and enjoy the freedom they have received in Christ from the bondage of the law of Moses as taught by Reformed/Covenant Theology. Now, in this new volume, David sets out to prevent the derailing of the NCT movement. Within its own ranks are those who would swing the pendulum into the extreme opposite direction of another error. At stake is the place Scripture holds in the law of Christ, the saints' relationship to that law, as well as the believers role in his sanctification. As always, David's work is solidly constructed with a framework of Scripture that is thorough and compelling. This is a must-read for any who desire to have a biblical understanding of the law of Christ in the life of those in the new covenant.

Christopher Fales

Historically, following a revival in the 'Doctrines of Grace', paths start to diverge, one road emphasising the believer's duty and the God-ordained means of sanctification, and the other the internal work of the Spirit and our union with Christ. Attempts to bridge the gap in the past have fallen short either because they fail to give priority to the new-covenant reign of the Spirit and Christ as the new lawgiver, or focus at the other extreme on a nearly, if not exclusive, emphasis on the mystical work of the indwelling Spirit. David Gay labours to show how the psalmist and the apostle are both right, how 'law' in the New Testament can be seen as both 'a delight to the heart' (Ps. 19) as well as 'the old way of the written code' (Rom. 7:1-6). It is a challenging study, but one that I highly recommend.

Dr J.David Gilliland, Providence Theological Seminary

*David Gay's book, **Believers Under the Law of Christ**, is a collection of his articles, written for the very purpose of helping believers to leave the desert (the law of Moses) and to lead them into the promised land filled with milk and honey (the law of Christ). 'For my yoke is easy, and my burden is light' (Matt. 11:30). **Believers Under the Law of Christ** has been very helpful to me [Peggy]. I like having the articles conveniently collected and organised in one book that confirms my thinking as to practical new-covenant living, gives definition to what were for me some hazy areas, and brings fresh and further consideration to aspects of my union with Christ − of all he has accomplished through his amazing love and grace!*

Ace and Peggy Staggs

A great book from brother David Gay clarifying a new-covenant-theology perspective on the law of Christ and the believers need of outward commands as well as the inward Spirit. He goes on to show us where a denial of the law of Christ as outward commands is something that Scripture never does with the institution of this new law.
Justin Gardner

Brother David H.J.Gay has remained biblical and responsible to the reality of an active faith. This proper emphasis of the inseparable truths of 'walking by faith' and 'walking worthy' of such a calling gets to the heart of the believers attitude toward sin.
Brian W.Grimes

Books by David H.J.Gay referred to in this volume:

Assurance in the New Covenant.

Battle for the Church 1517-1644 (second edition).

Christ Is All: No Sanctification by the Law.

Eternal Justification: Gospel Preaching to Sinners Marred by Hyper-Calvinism.

Fivefold Sanctification.

Four 'Antinomians' Tried and Vindicated: Tobias Crisp, William Dell, John Eaton and John Saltmarsh.

No Safety Before Saving Faith.

Positional Sanctification: Two Consequences.

Psalm 119 and The New Covenant.

Sabbath Notes & Extracts.

Sabbath Questions: An open letter to Iain Murray.

Septimus Sears: A Victorian Injustice and Its Aftermath.

The Glorious New-Covenant Ministry.

*The Gospel Offer **is** Free (second edition).*

The Priesthood of All Believers.

Believers Under The Law Of Christ

Speaking the truth in love... Therefore... let each one of you speak the truth with his neighbour, for we are members one of another

Ephesians 4:15,25

They received the word with all eagerness, examining the Scriptures daily to see if these things were so

Acts 17:11

David H.J.Gay

BRACHUS

BRACHUS 2015
davidhjgay@googlemail.com

Scripture quotations come from a variety of versions

All my books, kindles, sermons, audio books, articles and videos
can be found by searching the internet under David H.J.Gay

Contents

Introduction

Ever since the Reformation, knowingly or not, the overwhelming majority of evangelicals[1] have held a view of the Mosaic law (if they have had any view at all) which has been formed largely by John Calvin's doctrine of its threefold use; namely, that the law (that is, the law reduced to the ten commandments, the so-called 'moral law') restrains sin, prepares sinners for Christ, and serves as both the whip and the perfect rule for the believer's progressive sanctification.[2]

During the 1980s, however, things began to change. God raised up an increasing number of teachers who, going directly to Scripture unfiltered by the Reformed Confessions, began to expound the full glories of Christ in the new covenant. The succeeding years have witnessed an explosion in the amount of valuable material on this vital subject. And this recovery – I use the word advisedly – of the biblical theology of the new covenant, has been an enormous blessing to an increasing number of believers. The Holy Spirit surely has been at work, and many can testify to the scriptural liberation, assurance and sense of joy they have found in Christ and his gospel through this resurgence of what has become known as new-covenant theology.

In recent years, however, as has happened before during the long history of the church, some have allowed the pendulum to swing too far; indeed, some have encouraged it to swing too far.

---

[1] But not all; there have been 'new-covenant theologians' of one sort or another through all those centuries, and before. See my 'New Kid on the Block?' New-covenant theology is, of course, biblical.

[2] The sinner, on coming to faith, is united to Christ and is justified and positionally sanctified. Thus, in God's sight, in Christ he is accounted or made righteous, free of sin and condemnation, and perfectly separated unto God. See, for instance, 1 Cor. 1:2,30; 6:11; Eph. 5:25-27; Heb. 10:10-18; 13:12. In his Christian life, he has to work out his perfection in Christ, and he will be moved to do so by the Spirit under the direction of Scripture; this is his progressive sanctification or holiness of life. But this, alas, is imperfect. The believer will only be absolutely sanctified in the eternal state. See my *Fivefold*.

We recognise the danger, do we not? When people discover what is to them a new idea, they often become over-zealous and over-emphasise the point. I certainly feel the temptation! In recent years, alas, some who have discovered the distinction between law and gospel have stressed it to the detriment of other aspects of truth.

Rightly rejecting the believer's bondage under the Mosaic law as found in Calvin's teaching, and rightly emphasising the believer's liberty in Christ, the inward writing of God's law – the law of Christ – on the heart, along with the power of the indwelling Spirit, some new-covenant theologians have so stressed these glories that they have been in danger of playing down other – equally scriptural – aspects of the believer's life in the new covenant. By stressing the believer's liberty and laying too little stress on 'law' in 'the law of Christ',[3] by emphasising the Spirit's work at the expense of the believer's obligation, duty and accountability for determined and voluntary obedience to Scripture, and by stressing the inward written law of God and the work of the Spirit, while at the same time asserting that the written Scriptures are not an integral part of Christ's law, they have ended up in an unscriptural place.[4]

In addition, and in tandem with this, some deny the concept of progressive sanctification. They virtually make justification and sanctification one and the same.[5] This is a serious mistake. For Scripture teaches us that believers are not only justified and positionally sanctified, but that they must be progressively sanctified; that is, they must be transformed into Christ-likeness in their actual lives. Take just one passage to make the point. Peter, addressing believers, commanded them:

---

[3] Or none at all, even denigrating the concept.

[4] Consider this from one advocate: 'The spirit has pre-eminence over the written word, or the letter'. Even if we replace 'spirit' with 'Spirit' it sounds little better! Do not miss the confusion in the unscriptural link between 'the written word' and 'the letter'; indeed, their virtual equivalence. This is wrong. I will deal with it.

[5] If not making regeneration, justification and sanctification one and the same. They are connected but distinct. See my *Fivefold* pp35-39.

Therefore, preparing your minds for action, and being sober-minded, set your hope fully on the grace that will be brought to you at the revelation of Jesus Christ. As obedient children, do not be conformed to the passions of your former ignorance, but as he who called you is holy, you also be holy in all your conduct, since it is written: 'You shall be holy, for I am holy' (1 Pet. 1:13-16).

As John Gill said, this refers to:

...external holiness, holiness of life and conversation, in all the parts and branches of it, both with respect to God and men, in matters both of religion and civil life... To be holy in this sense is an imitating of God, a copying of him... walking worthy of him, who has called us to his kingdom and glory, and walking worthy of that calling wherein we are called, and a following of God, as dear and obedient children, and what is according to his will, and what he directs unto and requires.

Believers must not be 'conformed' (either passively or actively) to their pre-conversion way of life, but they must 'prepare their minds for action' and so be transformed (compare Romans 12:2) to be holy in likeness to God himself. Take the word 'holy', *hagios*. God is 'holy' (1 Pet. 1:15-16), and believers – or, rather, saints, those who have been sanctified by the Spirit (1 Pet. 1:2) (*hagiasmō*) – have to be 'holy' (*hagioi*) because God is 'holy' (*hagion* and *hagios*). So the sanctified have to be sanctified, the 'holified' have to be 'holified'; that is, the positionally sanctified have to be progressively sanctified. And as for the progressive nature of this sanctification, see how Peter takes his concept of believers being 'obedient children' (1 Pet. 1:14) having been regenerated (1 Pet. 1:23), and almost immediately develops it in terms of their growth and continual edification:

Put away all malice and all deceit and hypocrisy and envy and all slander. Like newborn infants, long for the pure spiritual milk, that by it you may grow up into salvation – if indeed you have tasted that the Lord is good. As you come to him, a living stone rejected by men but in the sight of God chosen and precious, you yourselves like living stones are being built up as a spiritual house, to be a holy priesthood, to offer spiritual sacrifices acceptable to God through Jesus Christ (1 Pet. 2:1-5).

This is what I understand by progressive sanctification.[6]

All this, I fear, is under threat. The debate centres on the role of the Scriptures in the law of Christ, whether the believer is under that law, and whether the believer is passive or active in his progressive sanctification, if, indeed, such a thing exists. For my part, I assert that the believer *is* under the law of Christ, that the Scriptures *are* at the heart of that law, that progressive sanctification *is* both a reality and a necessity, and that the believer *is* responsible and accountable for it. In saying this, I do not, of course, deny the essential power of the Spirit to produce this progressive sanctification. Moreover, this power of the Spirit is not only necessary for the believer's progressive sanctification; in the provisions of the new covenant, Christ gives his Spirit to all his elect. As they are regenerated by the Spirit, united to Christ by faith, justified and positionally sanctified, they are transformed, given a new heart, mind, spirit and will to love and serve Christ by obeying his commands. And this ensures their fruitfulness to the glory of God. See, for instance, Ezekiel 36:25-27; Romans 6:1 – 7:6; 8:1-17.

I freely admit that 'the law of Christ', as a phrase, is rare in Scripture,[7] and that Christ and the apostles do not often speak in terms of 'law' when addressing believers. But this is not the end of the story. How about 'command', 'commandment', 'rule' and 'instruct'? And when the apostles use 'ought' or 'let', when they 'beseech', 'insist', 'implore', 'exhort' or 'urge', make no mistake: they are commanding! And none of this begins to exhaust the countless imperatives which come thick and fast from the apostles. Nobody can read the New Testament and be left in any doubt that believers are men and women under authority – the authority of Christ, revealed in Scripture by the Spirit through the apostles.

---

[6] Compare, for instance, Rom. 6:19,22; 12:1-2; Eph. 4:17ff; 1 Thess. 4:3-4,7; 5:23; Heb. 10:10,14; 12:14; 2 Pet. 3:17-18. For the argument, see my *Fivefold*; *Positional*.

[7] But the same may be said of 'the ten commandments', 'the new covenant' and 'the Lord's supper'.

With regard to the objection over the rarity of the phrase, 'the law of Christ', in Scripture, let me quote the answer I gave in my *Christ is All*:

The phrase, 'the law of Christ', appears but once in Scripture.[8] So it does. In Galatians 6:2. But very close parallels appear in other places: 'The law of the Spirit of life in Christ Jesus' (Rom. 8:2); 'under law towards Christ' (1 Cor. 9:21) or 'Christ's law' (NIV)... 'The ten commandments' appears as a phrase but three times in the Bible, and 'new covenant' but four. What conclusion should we draw from *that*? We are told 'we have the mind of Christ', but once (1 Cor. 2:16). The same goes for 'the Spirit of Christ' (Rom. 8:9), 'the sufferings of Christ' (2 Cor. 1:5), 'a letter of Christ' (2 Cor. 3:3), 'the gospel of the glory of Christ' (2 Cor. 4:4), 'the power of Christ' (2 Cor. 12:9), 'the word of Christ' (Col. 3:16),[9] 'partakers of Christ' (Heb. 3:14), and so on. I am not for a moment suggesting that these phrases are not important, that their equivalent does not appear elsewhere, or – above all – that the ideas they encapsulate are not written large in Scripture. I am simply showing that this first objection to 'the law of Christ' is puerile. I am also claiming that although 'the law of Christ', as a phrase, is rare, its principles dominate the New Testament. For those who are still hesitant, many things which, though not *explicitly* stated in Scripture, are, nevertheless, true. They can be – and are – properly deduced from Scripture. After all, words and phrases such as 'the trinity', 'unconditional election', 'particular redemption', 'the righteousness of Christ' or 'Christ's righteousness', 'the free offer', 'duty faith', 'believer's baptism', 'progressive sanctification', 'church membership' and 'closed communion' don't appear at all in Scripture. What are we to deduce from *that*? Surely, we should ask that whether or not the phrase appears in Scripture, does the idea?... Many... will quite happily use such phrases as 'personal Saviour', 'open-air work', 'quiet time', 'pastoral ministry', 'theological college', 'Bible college' or 'seminary', 'Sunday school', 'mission' or 'missionary', 'evangelism', 'covenant of works', 'covenant of grace', and 'Confession of faith', perhaps without realising that they appear nowhere at all in Scripture. Do they all appear in Scripture as

---

[8] How many times did Paul use the phrase 'the law of Moses'? Once only (1 Cor. 9:9).

[9] But see Rom. 10:17 (NIV, NASB); 'the word of God' (NKJV).

concepts? [The answer is No!] To sum up: What now of the objection about the infrequency of 'the law of Christ'? What is more, this phrase *does* appear in Scripture. So, if what I have said about it is wrong, what *does* it mean?

Of course, 'liberty' and 'freedom' are powerful aspects of the new covenant, *but 'duty', 'obligation', 'command' and 'law' are no less*. To accommodate the words of Christ in Matthew 23:23, those I am writing against should have stressed the one and not neglected to give equal weight to the other.[10]

Before I go on, let me repeat what I have just said, so important is it. In this book I am stressing the believer's responsibility to live a godly life under the law of Christ as revealed in Scripture; that is my purpose in writing at this time. But in doing this, I am not in the least going back on what I have said on countless other occasions; the motive, the spring and spur for this holiness of life is the person and work of Christ in the power of the Spirit. Scripture makes it as plain as plain can be that it is as believers set their minds and hearts on Christ that they are enabled by the Spirit to live to the glory of God. The spiritual life is not produced by rule and fear under the Mosaic law (*à la* Calvin with his whip). See, for example, 2 Corinthians 3:18 and Colossians 3:1-17. And that is but two of scores and scores of examples I could choose to make the point. Even so, where do we find the teaching, the instruction, the command that we should set our hearts on Christ? In Scripture, of course! And that is why I deplore any move – however slight – away from maintaining that Scripture is central to the law of Christ. I want to do all I can to ensure that there is not the slightest shift in the biblical balance

---

[10] 'Contrary to much teaching that wants to pit relationship against word and obedience, the inspiration and application of the written word is no less a work of God and the Spirit than the expression of his indwelling presence' (David J.Gilliland: 'New Covenant Theology: Is There Still a Role for the Imperatives?', being a paper at the Providence Theological Seminary Doctrinal Conference, 2011, p8). See the entire paper. Gilliland returned to the subject a year later, broadening the discussion, in 'The New Heart, The New Covenant, and Not So New Controversies: A Critique of the Modern "Grace Movement"', being a paper at the Providence Theological Seminary Doctrinal Conference, 2012.

between, on the one hand, the inward work of the Spirit within believers, and, on the other, the external Scriptures. It is both.

C.H.Spurgeon did not get everything right on all things all the time, but he certainly knew the scriptural balance between the internal and the external, between the Spirit and the Scriptures. Listen to him on the internal work of the Spirit enabling the believer to live experientially in union with Christ:

> I do not know a better epitome of Christian experience than this. This is the daily walk of a true child of God. If he lives after any other sort, then he lives not a Christian's life at all! Christ living in us, ourselves living upon Christ and our union to Christ being visibly maintained by an act of simple faith in him – this is the true Christian's life.[11]

Excellent! The maintenance of the spiritual life is down to the believer's union with Christ. So said Spurgeon. I agree! But now listen to him on the external, the Scriptures. When preaching on 'To the law and to the testimony; if they speak not according to this word, it is because there is no light in them' (Isa. 8:20), Spurgeon declared:

> When men leave the sacred book of revelation, ah! my friends, where do they go? We find that in Isaiah's time they went to strange places... Oh! that we may each of us be more wise, that we may not forsake the good old path, nor leave the way that God has prepared for us... Search the Scriptures, for in them you think you have eternal life, and these are they that testify of Jesus Christ. I feel at this particular crisis of religious affairs, it is imperative upon the Christian minister to urge his [hearers] to hold fast the doctrines of the truth – the words of God... What better advice can the minister give in such times as these? To what book shall he commend his hearers? How shall he keep them fast? Where is the anchor which he shall give them to cast into the rocks? or where the rocks into which they should cast their anchor? Our text is a solution to that question. We are here furnished with a great answer to the inquiry: 'To the law and to

---

[11] Exposition of Gal. 2:19-20, sermon number 2370. This, of course, is by the Spirit (Gal. 3:1-5). Remember, verse and chapter divisions are not inspired but are imposed, and often artificial and misleading.

the testimony; if they speak not according to this word, it is because there is no light in them'...

Remember, also, to bring the preachers of the gospel to this standard... Some men always believe like the last speaker... The reason [for] that is because the mass of people do not lay hold upon what is said, but upon how it is said: and if it is said smartly, said prettily, and said forcibly, that is enough for them, though it be a lie... Now, the Christian... does not care about how the man says it; it is the thing that is said that he cares about. All he asks is: 'Did he speak the truth?'... It is not what I say, but what my God says, that you are demanded to receive. Put myself and put all my brethren into the sieve; cast us each into the fire; put us into the crucible of truth; and what is not according to God's word must be consumed like dross.

There is another class of men quite contrary to those I have referred to. These men are their own preachers; they believe no one but themselves... These persons, if they hear a truth preached, judge of it not by the Bible, but by what they think the truth ought to be... Bring, then, I beseech you, your own thoughts and your own sentiments to the touchstone of the truth; for 'if they speak not according to this word, it is because there is no light in them'. And just do the same with all books that you read... It is God's word that breaks the fetters and sets the prisoner free; it is God's word instrumentally that saves souls; and therefore let us bring everything to the touchstone. 'To the law and to the testimony; if they speak not according to this word, it is because there is no light in them'.[12]

In short, as Spurgeon put it: 'Search all questions, try all by the word of God'.[13]

And finally:

It is not the letter which saves the soul; the letter kills many senses, and never can it give life. If you harp on the letter alone you may be tempted to use it as a weapon against the truth, as the Pharisees did of old, and your knowledge of the letter may breed pride in you to your destruction. It is the spirit, the real inner meaning, that is sucked into the soul, by which we are blessed and sanctified. We become saturated with the word of God, like Gideon's fleece, which was wet with the dew of

---

[12] Sermon number 172.
[13] Sermon number 15.

heaven; and this can only come to pass by our receiving it into our minds and hearts, accepting it as God's truth, and so far understanding it as to delight in it. We must understand it, then, or else we have not read it aright.

Having issued that vital warning, Spurgeon came to this:

Love your Bibles. Keep close to your Bibles... Oh, love your Bibles and search them! Take them to bed with you, and when you wake up in the morning... Oh, cling you to Scripture. Scripture is not Christ, but it is the silken clue which will lead you to him. Follow its leadings faithfully... When you have received regeneration and a new life, keep on reading, because it will comfort you. You will see more of what the Lord has done for you. You will learn that you are redeemed, adopted, saved, sanctified. Half the errors in the world spring from people not reading their Bibles... It will be for your nourishment, too. It is your food as well as your life. Search it and you will grow strong in the Lord and in the power of his might. It will be for your guidance also. I am sure those go most right who keep closest to the book.[14]

As I say, Spurgeon got the balance between the inward and the outward, between the Spirit and the Scriptures, right. It is not one or the other; it is both.

I am grieved that it is necessary for me to write about what I see as a threat to this vital principle of the scriptural union between the internal and the external. But write I must. Warm sentiment is no protection against error. Yes, it is 'nicer' to be 'positive', and there is nothing new in the demand for 'smooth [or pleasant] things' (Isa. 30:10),[15] but sometimes the alarm has to be sounded. I am persuaded that this is one such occasion.

---

[14] Sermon number 1503.

[15] See also 1 Kings 22:8,13-14; Jer. 6:14; 23:17; Amos 7:10-13; Rom. 16:18; 2 Tim. 4:3-4. Christ was not wanted was he? See Luke 8:37; 13:31. I can feel the anguish in the apostle's words: 'Have I then become your enemy by telling you the truth?' (Gal. 4:16). John Gill: Paul 'spoke publicly, plainly, honestly, fully, and faithfully, boldly, constantly, and with all assurance, consistently, and in pure love to their souls, and yet it brought on him their anger and resentment. Telling the truth in such a manner often brings many enemies to the ministers of Christ – not only

I acknowledge that those I write against would endorse all I have just quoted from Spurgeon, but even so it is the tendency of their doctrine that carries the threat I speak about. And I am thinking of the long-term consequences.

How has this threat come about? I suggest, in part at least, it is because of a faulty exegesis of a handful of major passages of Scripture. And I lay weight on 'passages'. Proof-texting is useless for coming to a sound exegesis; the context and the big picture are vital.[16] The advocates of this new view founder not only on the minutiae of key verses, but in failing to give sufficient weight to the context of those verses. In particular, they miss the big picture.

What I am talking about is not an abstruse nicety, fit only for those who like a good theological knockabout. *Every* believer must be thoroughly grounded in the biblical principles which govern his life in Christ. This is essential. The fact is, I fear that the consequences of the mistake I am addressing, if allowed to go uncorrected, will be very serious. I dread the thought that, if this new teaching gains ground, coming generations may repeat the calamities of former years and fall into the twin errors of antinomianism and perfectionism, or else get close to the old Keswick mantra of 'Let go, and let God', quietism[17] or Situation Ethics when talking about progressive sanctification – if, indeed, progressive sanctification is still on the agenda!

As Douglas J.Moo put it:

At the opposite extreme from moralism [here, sanctification by our own efforts] is what we might call the 'magical' view of the

---

[among] the men of the world, profane sinners, but professors of religion, and sometimes such who once loved and admired them'.

[16] Let me illustrate the danger of ignoring context. Infant baptisers, wrenching 1 Cor. 7:14 out of its context, build an enormous castle in the air. But as the context makes clear, in a marriage under the circumstances envisaged by the apostle a believer may rest assured that his children are not tainted, are not inferior, and carry no stigma. It has nothing to do with the spiritual standing of the infant in the sight of God, and has not the remotest connection with baptism. Above all, it offers no justification whatsoever for baby sprinkling.

[17] 'Abandonment of the will as a form of religious mysticism'.

Christian life... We find sincere and dedicated believers who fall into this trap. They write books and present seminars, all with the basic thrust that the key to the victorious Christian life is simply letting our new redeemed natures take their course. 'Let go, and let God' is the slogan. The indicative [what God tells us he has done] is given pride of place in this approach, and is often presented as an alternative to legalism or moralism.[18] But the magical view gives insufficient emphasis to the reality of the imperative [what God commands us to do]. God commands us to act, and the very fact that Paul's letters are peppered with commands shows that obedience is not automatic... Thus we need to listen to and respond to the commands of Scripture. Particular trouble is the tendency of Christians to think that the indicative is all they need... Paul goes on to make clear that our enjoyment of eternal life is contingent on our obedience (Rom. 8:12-13).[19]

Furthermore, I can see close similarities between this new teaching in connection with progressive sanctification and the fundamental error in the hyper-Calvinistic view of conversion, with its denial of duty faith.

As for the long term consequences, I reject any suggestion that I am making a fuss about nothing. When a train passes over points, it takes one route or another, and, depending on which track (or 'road' as the professionals call it) the train takes, the passengers will end up in very different places. But at the points, the difference will be minuscule. Let me try another illustration. When on the high moors, I have often stepped across damp patches in the moss, so small that it would be an exaggeration to call them anything other than moist peat, driblets at most. But within a few miles, those driblets will become a deep, wide and fast flowing tidal river leading to the ocean. Large oaks come from small acorns. Do I need to spell the lesson out? Apparently I do.

---

[18] One advocate of the new view asked how I would like it if somebody said: 'Your view is narrowly law-focused and leads to legalism and a law-keeping religion devoid of Christ'. When challenged by a third party, he said he was speaking 'hypothetically'.

[19] Douglas J.Moo: *The NIV Application Commentary: Romans*, Zondervan, Grand Rapids, 2000, p216.

What is more – in this regard, perhaps above all – we surely realise that it is not only what we say, but what people think we say, what people hear, that counts. What people bring to our words, and then take away with them, carries more weight than what we intend to say. In my works, I do all I can to prevent any mistake here. Sad to say, the proponents of this new view do not seem sufficiently to weigh these two points – the large consequences which stem from small beginnings, and the power of unguarded words. In some cases, they do not even seem to see their likelihood!

So critical is this matter, I say it again, I feel obliged to do what I can to uphold the scriptural balance at the heart of the new covenant, one which plays a vital role in the believer's progressive sanctification; namely, the balance between the Spirit and the Scriptures. Indeed, the balance (inadequate word!) is between Christ the Word (John 1:1-2,14; Rev. 19:13), the Spirit-breathed word in Scripture (Matt. 4:4; 2 Tim. 3:16), and the life-giving words of Christ by the Spirit (John 6:63,68). Balance? Nothing must be allowed to mar *the union* between Christ, the Spirit and the Scriptures.

As Joseph Hart put it:

> *Say, Christian, would'st thou thrive*
> *In knowledge of thy Lord?*
> *Against no Scripture ever strive,*
> *But tremble at his word.*
>
> *The Scriptures and the Lord*
> *Bear one tremendous name;*
> *The written and the incarnate Word*
> *In all things are the same.*

Hence this book.

Let me explain how I propose to go about my task.

I gather together a series of my articles on the law and the believer, the most important of which for my present purpose is 'Believers Under the Law of Christ'. I follow this with 'One Command or Many in One?', 'The Obedience of Faith', 'Hans Denck: The Inner and the Outer Word', 'Antinomianism

Introduction

Reformed and Mystical' and 'Christ the Covenant?' – all written in response to the tone of a number of Facebook posts which were advocating the new position. These six articles form the first section of this present volume. In these articles, I refer to some of my other pieces on both the law of Moses and the law of Christ, and these make up the rest of the book. Thus I arrive at my threefold division:

The Argument

The Law of Moses

The Law of Christ

Alas, my chosen method inevitably means that this book is somewhat disjointed, incomplete and not so well-structured as it ought to be, with a measure of overlapping material. Nevertheless, accepting these drawbacks, I hope the benefit of gathering these articles in one volume might make a contribution, however small, to the maintenance of the biblical position on the believer and the law of Christ. I certainly pray it may be so.

One last thing. I can well imagine a reader scratching his head and wondering what this is all about. Why this fuss? Hasn't a cat got four legs? Yes. Does it need 350 pages to prove it? No. So why does it take that many pages to prove something so self-evident as the fact that the believer is under the law of Christ, with the Scriptures at the heart of that law? I agree! It doesn't! When I open my Bible and read of the comparison and contrast between Moses and Christ (Deut. 18:15-18; John 1:17), and when, in reading of how Jesus went up 'on the mountain', where 'he opened his mouth and taught' (Matt. 5:1-2), I can hear unmistakable echoes of Moses ascending Mount Sinai to receive his law from God for Israel, and when I read of Jesus saying: 'You have heard that it was said to those of old... but I say to you... (Matt. 5:21-22,27-28,31-32,33-34,43-44), and when I read the way in which Matthew rounds off that discourse (Matt. 7:28-29), and when I read of Jesus, addressing his disciples in his final great discourse which is so full of his commandments (John 12:47-50; 13:1 – 16:33), saying: 'A new commandment I give to

23

you' (John 13:34), and when I meet countless apostolic commands to me as a believer in the post-Pentecost Scriptures, and when I read of 'the endurance of the saints' – 'those who keep the commandments of God and hold to the testimony of Jesus', 'those who keep the commandments of God and the faith of Jesus' (Rev. 12:17; 14:12)... then I need no more. If Jesus, the greater Moses of the new covenant, issues his commandments, his law, to his people, then it really does indeed seem self-evident that believers must be, can only be, under the law of Christ. And where shall we find that law? The very fact that all these statements have come from Scripture would seem, once again, to make the answer self-evident. So, reader, if this paragraph convinces you that the believer *is* under the law of Christ, and that the Scriptures *are* at the heart of his law, and that the believer *is* responsible and accountable for obedience to Christ in that law by his Spirit, then you really have no need to plough through the next 340 pages proving that this particular cat does, after all, have four legs.

The Argument

In this section, I exegete key verses (Romans 6:14; 1 Corinthians 9:19-23; Galatians 5:1 – 6:2; 1 John 3:4) in their context to show that the believer is under the law of Christ. I then show that Christ's new commandment encapsulates all the new-covenant commands found in Scripture. I follow this by a look at 'the obedience of faith', arguing that the believer is not passive in the matter of progressive sanctification. He himself, not the Spirit or Christ, is responsible and accountable for obedience to the law of Christ. Three articles follow, each dealing with the mystical approach to the law of Christ and progressive sanctification.

Believers Under the Law of Christ

Synopsis

Some new-covenant theologians, dissenting from mainstream new-covenant theology, teach that believers are not under the law of Christ. In tandem with this, they also say that the Scriptures are not an integral part of Christ's law. These two points are inextricably linked. In this article, I seek to prove that these men are wrong, that their case depends on faulty exegesis of certain key texts of Scripture. Indeed, on some of these texts, they adopt, or at least favour, a translation not found in any modern major version of the Bible. Finally, I argue that the consequences of this faulty exegesis are severe.

Introduction

Todd Braye, for instance, has published two papers: 'Law of Christ' (2nd June 2015) and 'Five Reasons Why I Object to Classic NCT's Definition of the Law of Christ' (6th March 2012), in which he is explicit: believers are not under the law of Christ; the Scriptures are not part of the law of Christ; the law of Christ is entirely inward and spiritual.[1] Braye states:

> We all understand that, as Christians, 'we are not under law' (Rom. 6:14). Christ died to set us free from the law in its totality (Gal. 5:1). I take Paul to mean exactly that. We are not under law, any covenantal law.

Responding to my enquiry, Braye confirmed this:

> I do not think we are under the law of Christ. I do not think we are under law! I think the obedient Christian is ruled by the promised Spirit, not law. I think the Christian is a '*doulos Christou*' and obeys his word. But that is not the same as being under a new external law, however spun.

---

[1] Braye, of course, is not alone in this. Several members of the Facebook group, New Covenant Grace, are very much in sympathy with him on this issue.

Even so, in his articles he affirms:

> We all understand and embrace the necessity of obedience to Christ. This is an inside-out obedience which is actual and verifiable. I do not advocate libertinism or moral licence. ALL Scripture is profitable for... correction, reproof, and 'training in righteousness'. Discipleship is nothing more or less than baptising believers, and teaching them to obey everything Christ commanded. I repeat: obedience to Christ is necessary. And that means, *ipso facto*, obeying the law of Christ.

But what is the role of the Scriptures?

> What then of commands written in ink on a page? I am truly happy to have them. They are gifts to us. What are [*sic*] their role? The apostle tells us that all Scripture is profitable for doctrine, reproof, correction, and training in righteousness. Could we not leave it at that?... New-covenant imperatives and commands are not the law of Christ, but simply express what is in accordance with that law, *i.e.* the indwelling Christ in/by [*sic*] his Spirit.

In expressing such views, as Braye himself admits, he is rowing against the 'established' tide of new-covenant theology. As he puts it, he disagrees with:

> Classic new-covenant theology [which] defines the law of Christ in terms of the commandments of Christ and his apostles found in the New Testament, written on the pages of Scripture, written in ink. It's defined, therefore, as something external, outside the believer.

So, his own conclusion is:

> Where is the law of Christ?... I say: 'The law is written on my heart. [Christ] is engraved there, because "God sent the Spirit of his Son into our hearts" (Gal. 4:6), and Christ "lives in me" (Gal. 2:20). As Ezekiel of old wrote: "...I will put my Spirit within you, and cause you to walk in my statutes..." (Ezek. 36:27)'.

> The law of Christ is the indwelling Christ, written upon the hearts of believers in [*sic*] his Spirit. It is not external, but internal, not in the form of code, but a person. New-covenant members are conformed to a person, not to an external code, or list of imperatives.

While there is much that I agree with in both Braye's papers, much that is heart-warmingly scriptural – the emphasis on the inward work of the Spirit, the believer's liberty in Christ, the believer's conformity to Christ, and so on – nevertheless, on these vital points – whether or not the believer is under the law of Christ as a law, and whether or not the Scriptures are an integral part of the law of Christ – I strongly disagree with him. I am convinced that his exegesis is wrong. I go further. Braye's faulty exegesis must not gain ground. If it does, the consequences will be very severe indeed. We are talking about something that is crucial, at the very heart of the new covenant, something I know that Braye is also convinced of.

The evidence is strong that those who disagree with me on this point will insist that I, and others like me, are in some way playing down the work of the Spirit in the heart of the believer in this day of the new covenant, that we are returning to something very much like the age of Moses, and that we are trying to live the spiritual life in a legal way, urging fleshly obedience to a list of rules. I must, therefore, try to make my position as plain as I can.[2] Although I have said such things repeatedly throughout my works, I say it again here:

The new covenant is radically different to the Mosaic covenant in its nature. It is not merely outward. One of the great provisions of the new covenant is that Christ writes his law, by his Spirit, not only in the Scriptures, but in the heart of every believer. Every believer is taught by the Spirit. Christ is formed in the heart of every believer. The Spirit motivates and empowers the child of God to willing, not slavish, obedience to Christ, obedience to Christ as revealed in Scripture, out of love for him, and not from tormenting fear of punishment.

---

[2] In fact, the criticism can get even more bizarre. Take one of the aforementioned Braye's supporters, who, when talking of the work of the Spirit and the commands of Christ, challenged those of us who take the stance I do here: 'Why will [you] persist in "tearing apart what the Lord has joined together"?' I replied: 'This is precisely what some of us see you and others doing. Admit that the Spirit and the Scriptures are in harness at the heart of the law of Christ, and this debate is over. It is you and others who "tear them apart"'.

31

All that, and more like it, is taken for granted in this article. Taken for granted? I *glory* in it! So when I contend for the centrality of the Scriptures within the law of Christ, I do so with the absolute understanding that this is completely and utterly in harness with the Spirit in the believer's heart.

Now to go on.

I draw attention to some warning flags concerning his exegesis, flags raised by Braye himself. As he so clearly states, he disagrees with 'classic new-covenant theology', taking a view in contrast to that expressed by several named writers of weight.[3] This does not necessarily mean that he is wrong, but it ought to give his readers serious pause for thought. What is more, on certain key texts (Galatians 6:2 and 1 Corinthians 9:19-21) he favours a translation which is found in none of the major Bible versions.[4] While Braye's suggested changes to the usual translation in these key texts do not automatically rule out his conclusion, they give further ground for serious pause for thought. What is more, I fail to see how he can assert that believers have to 'obey everything Christ commanded. I repeat: obedience to Christ is necessary. And that means, *ipso facto*, obeying the law of Christ', and yet, at the same time, say that believers are not under Christ's law, and that the Scriptures are not part of that law. Braye, it seems to me, is self-contradicting at this point.

---

[3] I exclude myself from this encomium, though he does name me, for which I sincerely thank him.

[4] This reminds me of Jonathan F.Bayes' defence of the citadel of his own work, *The Weakness of the Law: God's Law and the Christian in New Testament Perspective*, Paternoster Press, Cumbria, 2000, in which he propounded the covenant-theology view of the law. I refer to the way Bayes dealt with Rom. 8:1-4. He could only do this by proposing a series of changes to the text. I concluded what I said in response to Bayes on this point: 'In this sophisticated way, the plain teaching of the apostle is turned on its head. I, for my part, will stick with the almost-universally held text. Besides, both the immediate context of Rom. 5 – 8, and the analogy of faith, support the usual translation against that proposed by Bayes. And the context is always king!'

This is how I propose to go about making good my claim that Braye's exegesis is faulty, and that this inevitably leads to a wrong conclusion. I will look at the vital texts; namely, Romans 6:14, 1 Corinthians 9:19-23, Galatians 5:1 and 6:2, and, finally, 1 John 3:4.[5] From these passages, I hope to show that it is perfectly right and proper to speak of the believer being under the law of Christ. This, it seems to me, is my great task in this article. For if it can be established that the believer is, indeed, under the law of Christ, then the question naturally arises: Where shall we find that law? It has to be objective. Where is it? There can only be one answer. In Scripture! Thus it is imperative for me to try to storm the citadel, as it were, and prove, from Scripture, that the believer *is* under the law of Christ. As I have said, the citadel having been gained – namely, that the believer is under the law of Christ – then the fact that the commands of Christ and the apostles[6] are an integral part of the law of Christ, must, as a matter of course, follow. Braye's assertion that believers have to obey Scripture, it seems to me, concedes the point. Scripture is the arbiter. In other words, Scripture is the believer's rule; Scripture is the believer's law.

Before getting into the detail of individual texts, however, we should look at the big picture. That is to say, before we get involved in the minutiae of specific verses and passages,[7] let us remember that the overwhelming majority of the first readers of those passages were not readers at all. Could they all read? In any case, none of them possessed a copy of the apostolic letters in question. They were hearers, listening, almost certainly, to one man reading the one copy of an individual letter. How did they *hear* the words? What impression did they take away with them? They did not have the opportunity that we have – to take out our

[5] I choose the latter partly because it is a crucial text in this debate, and partly because at least one of the advocates of Braye's view takes a view of the verse which is supported by none of the major modern versions, and, as a consequence, comes to a wrong view of the passage.
[6] Who, of course, include the old covenant as a paradigm. See my 'The Law the Believer's Rule?'
[7] As will be obvious, I am not dismissing detailed examination of specific texts.

personal copy, pore over every nuance at our leisure, consult parallel places, and so on. What I am saying is that we must not miss the wood for the trees. What is the general impression, the overall picture, that we discover in the post-Pentecost Scriptures? Clearly, it is one of believers being called to obedience, in the power of the Spirit of God, to apostolic commands, the apostles addressing believers as responsible and accountable men and women obliged to obey the instructions they are being given in Scripture, all to the glory of God in Christ by the Spirit. In short, speaking for myself, the New Testament gives me the impression – to put it no stronger – that the believer is under Christ's law, rule, reign, headship, lordship and governance, administered through the apostles by the Spirit in the Scriptures, the believer having had that law written in his heart by the Spirit. And this law is more penetrating than Moses' law. Yes, it is so![8]

Of course, I admit at once that the phrase 'under the law of Christ' does not appear in Scripture, but this is the merest quibble; the same could be said of not a few words and phrases which are common currency among us. And rightly so.[9] The question is, is the principle, the concept, scriptural? I hope to prove that the passages I have mentioned, in their context, establish beyond all doubt that the believer *is* under the law of Christ.

Christ is King (Ps. 2:6; 45:6; Matt. 28:18-20; John 12:15; 18:37; Acts 2:30-31; Heb. 1:8). A king does not reign unless he issues his rule. The glory of the new covenant is that King Jesus reigns and rules his people by his word, having, by his Spirit, written his law in their heart, and moving them and enabling them to submit willingly to his 'gentle' (Matt. 11:28-30) reign. That great messianic psalm (it is quoted more than any psalm in the New Testament) could not be plainer; Christ rules a willing people:

---

[8] See my 'The Penetrating Law of Christ'. I will return to this.
[9] 'New covenant' appears only three times, 'justification by faith alone' never, 'the law of Christ' once, 'the Lord's supper' once, 'the ten commandments' twice, 'the righteousness of Christ' never, and so on.

The LORD says to my Lord: 'Sit at my right hand, until I make your enemies your footstool'. The Lord sends forth from Zion your mighty sceptre. Rule in the midst of your enemies! Your people will offer themselves freely on the day of your power (Ps. 110:1-3).

And, I assert, Christ rules them, not only inwardly by his Spirit in their heart, but by his Spirit in his written word. That is to say, although I agree with Braye that the Scriptures are useful (profitable) (2 Tim. 3:16-17), nevertheless this is not the last word on the subject. For a start, the Scriptures are useful for *instruction*, and, moreover, instruction in, and including, *paideia*, 'the whole training and education of children, employing commands and admonitions, reproof and punishment, correcting mistakes, curbing passions, including chastisement and chastening for their amendment'.[10] The law of Christ does not stop at the inward work of the Spirit, leaving the Scriptures as something useful, something alongside and supportive of, but not absolutely essential to, the inward work of the Spirit. Far from it! Yet, according to Braye, the commands and imperatives of the new covenant are not part and parcel of the law of Christ. I assert the opposite: the law of Christ comprises the presence of the inward Spirit *and* the external Scriptures, the Spirit *and* the word, in harness, right at its very heart. They cannot be divorced. They must not, in any way, be divorced. Indeed, we must never teach in such a way that anybody could think there is the slightest gap between the inward and outward work of the Spirit – in the heart and in the written word. All this I see as the overall big picture of the New Testament.

And this leads me to the conclusion that it is right and proper for believers to talk of 'law' and 'commands' and 'rule' in the new covenant. Moreover, I will argue that it is essential for believers to think, speak and act in this way. Not to do it will, as I have said, lead to dire consequences.

---

[10] See Thayer.

35

One final point. Since I want to keep this article in bounds, I will confine my remarks to the essentials.[11] For my full argument, the reader should consult my *Christ Is All: No Sanctification by the Law*, including the relevant extracts.[12]

Romans 6:14

> Sin will have no dominion over you, since you are not under law but under grace (Rom. 6:14).

At first glance, these words seem to teach, as Braye asserts, that the believer is delivered from law, all covenantal law; indeed, from all law altogether. But 'first glance' is not the way to discover the meaning of Scripture. The context is king. And that context flatly refutes the notion that the believer is not under any covenantal law. Throughout Romans 5:12 – 7:6, the apostle is clearly speaking of the law of Moses. I submit that the context further shows that while the believer is most definitely delivered from the law of Moses, he, equally definitely, is now under Christ's law. I summarise the leading points:

The lack of the article – 'law' and not 'the law' – makes no difference. It probably strengthens the point.[13]

Paul has already established that all men are under one law or another (Rom. 2:12-15).[14]

Throughout the passage, Paul is speaking of the Mosaic law.

Having spoken of justification in the earlier part of Romans, in Romans 6 the apostle has now moved on to speak of progressive sanctification.

Do not miss the eschatological 'but now' (or, in the context, 'now') which comes in this context, as it does again and again in

---

[11] Even so, on re-reading this prior to publication, I find that my remarks have been extended to an inordinate length. I apologise. It is only the seriousness of the matter that has driven me to such a length.

[12] Especially, but not exclusively, pp211-278,481-527.

[13] See my 'What Is the Law?'

[14] See my 'All Men Under Law'.

Romans – indeed, throughout the New Testament (Rom. 3:21; 5:9,11; 6:22; 7:6; 8:1; 11:30; 11:31 (second 'now' in NIV, NASB); 16:26; see also John 15:22,24; Acts 17:30; 1 Cor. 15:20; Gal. 4:9; Eph. 2:12-13; 5:8; Col. 1:26; Heb. 8:6; 9:26; 12:26; 1 Pet. 2:10). It is the *eschatological* 'but now' which is at the root of the apostle's argument from Romans 5:12 and on. We have moved out of the old age, the age of the old covenant, into the new age, the age of the new covenant. This is the basis of the apostle's argument here.

Coming to the individual experience, having spoken of the believer's union by faith to Christ at conversion (Rom. 6:1-13), and having made his statement – 'Sin will have no dominion over you, since you are not under law but under grace' (Rom. 6:14) – the apostle immediately moves into two illustrations; slavery and marriage. The believer has a new slave master. He is no longer a slave to sin; he is now Christ's slave (Rom. 6:15-23). The believer is no longer married to the law, the law of Moses; he is married to Jesus Christ, he belongs to him (Rom. 7:1-6). Both illustrations, in the context, speak of rule, reign, headship, lordship and governance; in short 'law'.[15] While the phrase 'the law of Christ' is not used in the context of Romans 6:14, whatever else is the apostle speaking about? He is speaking of Christ as the believer's ruler, master, head, lord, governor, husband – one who exercises his rule by his law. The slavery illustration surely speaks for itself; for the husband illustration, see Ephesians 5:22-24; Colossians 3:18; Titus 2:5; 1 Peter 3:1. Nothing could be clearer: the believer is no longer under the rule, the reign, the headship, the lordship, the governance of Moses

---

[15] And we know that marriage is a covenant (Mal. 2:14; see also Prov. 2:17). The wife is under the covenantal law of marriage to her husband. Anticipating what is to come, let me have a word about an objection I have seen raised; namely, that slaves do not have written contracts, do not consult a book of rules. With respect, this is a quibble, pushing the illustration too far. Something similar could be done with the marriage illustration – the wrong person has died! As always with illustrations we must get the main point. And the main point here is that the believer is *under* the rule of Christ. In any case, slavery-law, written slavery-law, was enshrined in the old covenant, as well as other cultures in antiquity.

and his law, but he is under the rule, the reign, the headship, the lordship, the governance of Christ; in short, he is under the law of Christ.

To be under the law, whether the Mosaic or pagan, is to be under the dominion of sin. To be under grace is to be liberated from the rule of the law, whether the Mosaic or pagan, released from the dominion of sin (Rom. 6:14; 7:6).

None of this rules out the fact that the believer is under the law of Christ. Rule it out! It establishes it! The law that Paul speaks of in Romans 6 and 7, the law that the believer is free of, is the law of Moses, the law of sin and death (Rom. 8:2), and the law that has set him free from that law is 'the law of the Spirit of life... in Christ Jesus' (Rom. 8:2). Clearly the believer is under that law! When Paul says: 'Now we are released from the law, having died to that which held us captive, so that we serve in the new way of the Spirit and not in the old way of the written code' (Rom. 7:6), he is telling believers that they are no longer in the old age but in the new. In the old age, men served under an external code in the 'old way'. In the new age, believers serve – yes they do 'serve' – in the new way, in the power, energy and life of the Spirit, under the law of the Spirit of life in Christ Jesus; in short, under the law of Christ. They 'serve', said Paul, using *douleuō*, 'to obey commands, to render service due, to be a slave'.[16]

I do not see how the apostle could have been more explicit:

> Thanks be to God that you who were once slaves of sin have become obedient from the heart to the standard of teaching to which you were committed, and, having been set free from sin, have become slaves of righteousness. I am speaking in human terms, because of your natural limitations. For just as you once presented your members as slaves to impurity and to lawlessness leading to more lawlessness, so now present your members as slaves to righteousness leading to sanctification (Rom. 6:17-19).

'Obedient from the heart to the standard of teaching to which you were committed'. Where are believers supposed to find that 'standard of teaching'? Do they know it by the Spirit writing it in

---

[16] See Thayer.

their heart? Do they know it by the external word? Or is it a happy combination of both? I say it is that happy combination. But I also assert that Paul was here stressing the written word, the Scriptures, especially the apostolic instruction in and through those Scriptures, even as he was contributing to them. And this, I am convinced, is all part and parcel of the law of Christ which the believer is under.

The apostle enforces all this by what he goes on to say in Romans 8:

> There is therefore now no condemnation for those who are in Christ Jesus. For the law of the Spirit of life has set you free in Christ Jesus from the law of sin and death. For God has done what the law, weakened by the flesh, could not do. By sending his own Son in the likeness of sinful flesh and for sin, he condemned sin in the flesh, in order that the righteous requirement of the law might be fulfilled in us, who walk not according to the flesh but according to the Spirit. For those who live according to the flesh set their minds on the things of the flesh, but those who live according to the Spirit set their minds on the things of the Spirit. For to set the mind on the flesh is death, but to set the mind on the Spirit is life and peace. For the mind that is set on the flesh is hostile to God, for it does not submit to God's law; indeed, it cannot. Those who are in the flesh cannot please God (Rom. 8:1-8).

Let me pause. The man in the flesh cannot please God; he cannot submit to his law, he will not submit to it, because he hates both the lawgiver and his law. The things of God are not only foolishness to him (1 Cor. 2:14); they are hateful to him. But when that man is transformed from being a man 'in the flesh' into a man 'in the Spirit' – that is, when God delivers him from the realm of darkness, and transfers him into the kingdom of Christ (Col. 1:13), clearly, as a man who is now in the Spirit, under Christ's reign, he can please God, he will please God. How? When he was a man in the flesh he showed his hostility to God by refusing to submit to his law. Now, as a man in the Spirit, he shows his love for God by submission to it; that is, he delights in God's law, he obeys God's law. Does he do it in his own power? Not at all! The context is clear. It is the indwelling Spirit who turns this man from rebellion to submission, enabling him to 'walk... according to the Spirit'. When he was in the flesh, the man hated God's law; now that he is in the Spirit, he echoes David's words: he loves God's law (Ps. 119:97).[17]

The underlying argument here, of course, is eschatological, not merely personal or individual. It is true in the personal sense, it goes without saying, gloriously true, but the basic fact remains that whereas, as a man in the flesh, he belonged to the age of the old covenant,[18] now, as a man in the Spirit, he belongs to the age of the new covenant. And the effect of this transfer is shown, as Paul states here, either by rebellion or submission to God's law. As the apostle goes on to declare: 'You... are not in the flesh but in the Spirit, if [since] in fact the Spirit of God dwells in you. Anyone who does not have the Spirit of Christ does not belong to him' (Rom. 8:9). But the believer, since he is a new man in the Spirit, does belong to Christ, he is married to Christ (Rom. 7:4).[19] Thus the believer will submit to Christ under his law, submit as a willing slave of Christ, and joyfully submit to him as a wife to her husband (Eph. 5:22-24; Col. 3:18; Tit. 2:5; 1 Pet. 3:1).

The great question is: What is the law of God in these two ages? The law in the first age was the law of Moses. But what law does the believer, the man in the Spirit, submit to? The answer is obvious: the law of Christ. The law of God in the old covenant was the law of Moses; the law of God in the new covenant is the law of Christ.[20] In the context starting at Romans 5:12, the law for the believer must be, can only be, the law of Christ. The man, having died to the law of Moses, is now under Christ as his slave and his husband-head, with the result that he is under Christ's law. Paul takes this absolutely for granted here in order to lay stress on the believer's obedience to Christ's law. This is the apostle's purpose – not merely to inform the believer that he is under the law of Christ. That can be taken as given.

---

[17] See my *Psalm 119*.

[18] In eschatological terms, the unconverted still do.

[19] Note how 'belong' is used in Rom. 7:4 (ESV, NIV) and Rom. 8:9 (ESV, NIV, NASB) even though translating two different Greek words. Why? Because this conveys the proper sense.

[20] I make this point repeatedly throughout my *Christ*. See especially pp214-219,483-487.

What the apostle is looking for is the believer's obedience to that law. Obedience is his point.

And all this, of course, explains the seeming contradiction between Romans 6:15-23 (believers are slaves) and Romans 8:15 (believers do not serve as slaves). Believers are free of the law of Moses, they do not serve Christ in the flesh under the old law, under 'the written code' (Rom. 7:6), but they are slaves of Christ, under his law, and serve him by the Spirit. And this is perfect freedom.

In short, Braye's categorical deduction that the believer is not under any covenantal law – specifically, the law of Christ – is wrong. Romans 6:14, in its context, proves that the opposite is the case. The believer, united to Christ, being a slave to Christ, and married to Christ, is under Christ's rule, reign, headship, lordship and governance; in short the believer is under the law of Christ. I know the phrase 'the law of Christ' is not used in the context, but, I ask again, what else is the apostle talking about? What else can he be talking about?

In appending some extracts from others, I do not use their words to *prove* what I say; the context does that. I start with Thomas R.Schreiner:

> The phrase 'under law' (*hupo nomon*) occurs eleven times in Paul (Rom. 6:14-15; 1 Cor. 9:20 [4 times]; Gal. 3:23; 4:4-5,21; 5:18). It is immediately evident that the phrase is particularly important in Galatians since Paul uses it there most often... The phrase should be interpreted in terms of redemptive history. The old era of redemptive history refers to the time period when the Mosaic covenant was operative... To be under the law refers to the old era of salvation history, to the time period of the [Mosaic] law... Jesus Christ is the exception that proves the rule, for he was the only one who lived under the law and kept the law (Gal. 4:4-5). Consequently, through his atoning death, he was able to liberate those under the law from the power of sin. The fullness of time – the fulfilment of God's redemptive purposes in Christ – spells the end of the [Mosaic] law's reign. Indeed, Paul turned the tables on his Jewish opponents. He promised in Romans 6:14 that 'sin will have no dominion over you'. And why is it the case that sin will not rule over believers? Paul's answer on first glance is rather surprising 'since you are

not under law but under grace'. However, if the line of thought I have traced in the answer to this question has been followed, the Pauline response is actually perfectly sensible. Sin exercises control over those who live under the law [any law other than the law of Christ], and this truth is confirmed by Israel's history under the Mosaic covenant and the [Mosaic] law. Therefore, the power of sin is broken for those who are no longer under the old era of salvation history – for those who live in the new era inaugurated by Christ. It is those who are under the dominion of the [Mosaic] law who are enslaved to sin, not those who enjoy the grace of Jesus Christ. Romans 6:14-15 promises liberation from the tyranny and mastery of sin for those who live in the new era of redemptive history... [Hence] Paul's use of the phrase 'under law' should be understood in redemptive-historical terms. Those who are under the law are also under the dominion and authority of sin. The history of Israel under the Mosaic covenant confirms the truth that those who lived under the [Mosaic] law were subject to sin's mastery. Paul proclaims that believers are no longer under the [Mosaic] law. A new era of salvation history has been inaugurated... The [Mosaic] law has been abolished now that Christ has come. Believers are no longer under the [Mosaic] law.[21]

And now for Douglas J.Moo[22] on Romans 6:14:

These words are to be understood of a promise that is valid for every believer at the present time: 'Sin shall certainly not be your lord – now or ever!'

The promise is confirmed by the assurance that 'you are not under law but under grace' [Rom. 6:14 linked to Rom. 3:19-21,27-28; 4:13-15; 5:13-14,20 and, especially Rom. 5:20 and 7:1-6].

As in all these references, *nomos* here must be the Mosaic law, the *torah*.

---

[21] Thomas R.Schreiner: *40 Questions About Christians and Biblical Law*, Kregel, 2010, pp73-75.
[22] I am glad to quote Moo since he is a thoroughly competent witness, an acclaimed witness, one who is highly respected. But at certain key points he is too cautious, even weak, as I will indicate. The truth is, his very reticence in those areas gives added weight to my use of him.

Paul [makes] release from the law [of Moses] a reason for the Christian's freedom from the power of sin: as he has repeatedly stated, the Mosaic law has had a definite sin-producing and sin-intensifying function; it brought 'knowledge of sin' (Rom. 3:20), 'wrath' (Rom. 4:15), 'transgression' (Rom. 5:13-14), and an increase in the severity of sin (Rom. 5:20). The law, as Paul puts it in 1 Corinthians 15:56, is 'the power of sin'. This means, however, that there can be no final liberation from the power of sin without a corresponding liberation from the power and lordship of the law [of Moses]. To be 'under law' is to be subject to the constraining and sin-strengthening regime of the old age; to be 'under grace' is to be subject to the new age in which freedom from the power of sin is available.

[Of course:] We cannot conclude from this verse that the believer has no obligation to any of the individual commandments... Still less... that Christians are no longer subject to 'law' or 'commandments' at all – for *nomos* here means *Mosaic* law, not 'law' as such.[23]

Moo on Romans 6:17-19:

Paul wants to make [it] clear that becoming a Christian means being placed under the authority of Christian 'teaching', that expression of God's will for New Testament believers... Paul would then imply that Christians, while no longer 'under the Mosaic law', are nevertheless bound by an authoritative code of teaching.[24]

Moo's use of 'imply' is too weak. Paul statement is categorical. As I said before, I do not see how the apostle could have been more explicit:

Thanks be to God that you who were once slaves of sin have become obedient from the heart to the standard of teaching to which you were committed, and, having been set free from sin,

---

[23] Douglas J.Moo: *The Epistle to the Romans*, William B.Eerdmans Publishing Company, Grand Rapids, 1996, pp387-390; 'The Law of Moses or the Law of Christ', *Continuity and Discontinuity: Perspectives on the Relationship between the Old and New Testaments*, John S.Feinberg (editor), Crossway Books, Westchester, 1988, pp210-211, emphasis his.

[24] Moo: *Romans* pp401-402.

have become slaves of righteousness... so now present your members as slaves to righteousness leading to sanctification (Rom. 6:17-19).

Moo on Romans 7:

> The main topic... is the Mosaic law. [Rom. 7:1-6] contains the main point that Paul wants to make in this chapter... It is almost certain... that Paul here refers to the Mosaic law.

> Paul argues that a person's bondage to the law [of Moses] *must* be severed in order that he or she may be put into a new relationship with Christ... Death severs relationship to the law... But... not only... does Paul... illustrate the general principle that 'a death frees one from the law'... he also sets up the theological application... in which severance from the law [here, of Moses] enables one to enter a new relationship.[25]

Moo, commenting on Romans 7:4, spoke of the apostle's preceding argument which, Moo (too weakly) said, suggests:

> ...that, as in Romans 6:14, Paul in Romans 7:4 is viewing the law as a 'power' of the 'old age' to which the person apart from Christ is bound. The underlying conception is again salvation-historical, as is suggested by the 'letter'/'Spirit' contrast in Rom. 7:6. Just as, then, the believer 'dies to sin' in order to 'live for God' (Rom. 6), so he or she is 'put to death to the law' in order to be joined to Christ. Both images depict the transfer of the believer from the old realm to the new. As long as sin 'reigns', God and righteousness cannot; and neither, as long as law 'reigns', can Christ and the Spirit.[26]

Moo, writing later in Romans:

> Against those who might object that the abandonment of the law [of Moses] as a code of conduct (Rom. 6:14; 7:1-6) leads to licence, Paul argues that the gospel itself provides sufficient ethical guidance for Christians. Through the renewal of the mind that the gospel makes possible, Christians can know and do the will of God (Rom. 12:2), and by following the dictates of love,

---

[25] Moo: *Romans* pp409-414.

[26] Moo: *Romans* pp414-416. See my 'The Law Written'; 'The Law on the Believer's Heart'.

they can accomplish all that the law [of Moses] itself demands of them (Rom. 13:8-10).[27]

Yes, but yet again, Moo is weak. The Spirit *accomplishes* all this; he does more than make it 'possible'. This is one of the great glories of the new covenant; the Spirit really does motivate and enable the believer to be obedient. Further, we need to be clear: the gospel does provide guidance for the believer, yes. But how can we know what this gospel is? Directly by the Spirit or by the Spirit interpreting and applying Scripture? The very fact that the apostle is teaching this, and teaching it through writing, would seem to suggest, to put it no stronger, that it must be the latter; it can only be the latter. And, finally, this instruction is not merely 'guidance', 'advice', 'suggestion', only 'good' or 'valuable'. It is Christ's *law*, and the believer must obey it.

In short, on Romans 6:14, I submit, Braye is wrong. The believer *is* under the law of Christ.

1 Corinthians 9:19-23

For though I am free from all, I have made myself a servant to all [men], that I might win more of them. To the Jews I became as a Jew, in order to win Jews. To those under the law I became as one under the law (though not being myself under the law) that I might win those under the law. To those outside the law I became as one outside the law (not being outside the law of God but under the law of Christ) that I might win those outside the law. To the weak I became weak, that I might win the weak. I have become all things to all people, that by all means I might save some. I do it all for the sake of the gospel, that I may share with them in its blessings (1 Cor. 9:19-23, ESV).

Let me quote the pertinent words in other versions:

I am not free from God's law but am under Christ's law (NIV).
Not being without the law of God but under the law of Christ (NASB).
Under the law to Christ (AV).

---

[27] Moo: *Romans* p746. Note his reference to James D.G.Dunn's 'the kind of life expected' of believers.

I have quoted the entire paragraph because it is essential to get the context. The real issue of the passage is evangelism. The passage is not primarily a discourse on law, but on how to reach sinners with the gospel. So whatever we deduce from the passage, we need to bear in mind that Paul was not setting out to make a definitive statement on 'law'. That being said, clearly 'law' plays a vital part in this paragraph. But why did Paul raise – not merely mention – 'law', when he was really talking about his approach to sinners? Why raise such an abstruse topic at this point?

Because he knows that all men are under law,[28] in one form or another, as he so clearly stated in Romans 2:12-15; that is, because he knows that all men are slaves to one master or another, subject to their master's law. Slavery is the fundamental issue here. All men, I say again, are slaves. In Christ, that slavery is perfect freedom (Rom. 8:21; 2 Cor. 3:17; Gal. 5:1,13); outside of Christ that slavery is utter bondage (2 Pet. 2:19), and condemnation (2 Cor. 3:6-11). And the preaching of the gospel, the preaching of Christ (1 Cor. 2:2; 9:16; 2 Cor. 4:5), leading to conversion, is designed by God to deliver sinners from all forms of bondage, and bring them into glorious freedom in Christ (Luke 4:18; John 8:31-36). So that is why Paul raised the question of 'law' here. 'Law' leading to slavery is at the root of the problem.[29]

'Am I not free?' thundered the apostle, right at the start of the chapter. Of course he is! But... he is willing to become a slave in order to[30] reach men with the gospel: 'Though I am free from all,

---

[28] God always deals with men under law. All men are under law. God has ensured it thus by creation (Rom. 2), then with the Jews at Sinai, then with believers in Christ. As before, see my 'All Men Under Law'.

[29] There is a close parallel in Rom. 7:1-6. See my 'Who's Your Husband?' Similarly, see Heb. 12:18-24. In opening a sermon on this passage, I asked the question: 'Which mountain are you living on?' This was especially apposite since I was preaching in a relatively flat area of the UK. I was, of course, speaking spiritually. Here the question is: 'What law are you under? Who's your bond-master?' See my 'Three Questions in One'.

[30] Do not miss the repeated *hina*, 'in order that', seven times in verses 19-23, taking the form (though not the content) of a chiasm, a writing style that uses a repetitive pattern for clarification and/or emphasis.

I have made myself a servant to all [men]'. Actually, it is stronger than this: Paul was willing to become a slave, *edoulōsa*, to enter into slavery, bondage (see NIV, NASB), in order to reach men with the gospel.

The apostle was defending his ministry, especially the seeming inconsistency of his behaviour, in face of the abuse he received for it (1 Cor. 9:3). As he explained, he was willing to do all he could to reach all men with the gospel, even to the extent of putting himself into slavery, although this made him appear inconsistent to others. Men are divided into two: Jews and Gentiles. The Jews have the law of Moses; they are under the law of Moses. The Gentiles do not have the law of Moses; they are not under the law of Moses, but they are under their own law. Very well. As the apostle explained, in order to reach the Jews, 'those under the law [of Moses], I became as one under the law [of Moses]', even though he himself was not under the law of Moses. To reach the Gentiles, 'those outside the law [of Moses], I became as one outside the law [of Moses]', even though he himself was *not* outside the law of God. In all this, contrary to appearances, Paul was acting consistently.

Do not miss the word play.[31] When he was trying to reach Gentiles, Paul was willing to become *anomos*. But this did not make him *anomos*! What? No, indeed! The apostle was willing to become *anomos* (literally, here, act as one not under law; that is, not under Jewish law, the law of Moses), but this did not make him *anomos* (literally here, either lawless or law-less; that is, he was still under law, still obliged to keep the law that he was under).[32] Throughout the passage he was talking about legal obligation, slavery. Even though he was acting as if he were free of law, treating law with cavalier abandon, playing fast and loose with law, he was, in truth, under law all the time. So much so, he

---

[31] Scripture is full of word play (see Mic. 1:8-16; Matt. 16:18; Rom. 3:27; 8:2-4; 9:6; 1 Cor. 9:19-23; 11:3-16; Gal. 3:24 with 5:18; Gal. 6:2,16; Phil. 3:3; 2 Thess. 3:11 (NIV); Philem. 10-11, and so on).

[32] See below on 1 John 3:4, where *anomos* will play a vital part yet again.

immediately went on to explain what law it was that he was under throughout.[33]

Though I have kept to the past tense – as did the apostle – the fact is we must read it in the present tense.[34] This is the apostle's settled position in the new covenant. That is what he is saying. And, clearly, in the new covenant, the apostle is not under the law of Moses, but, even so, he is still in a law relationship with God. Indeed he is under law to God. As all the major versions express it, he is under the law of Christ. The law of God in the new covenant is the law of Christ.[35] And Paul is under it. And all this applies to every believer today.

Now, although all the major versions use 'under the law of Christ' or its equivalent, Paul did not actually use *hupo nomon*, 'under law', but *ennomos*, 'in law'. So why do all the major translations, without exception, use '*under* law'? Because that is precisely what Paul is saying! I have already touched on the apostle's love of word play. Is it possible that Paul is engaging in more of it here – between *ennomos*, 'in law' and 'in Christ'? I think it very likely. In fact, I am sure of it. And to be 'in Christ', as I explained from Romans 6, is to be united to Christ. And part of this union with Christ is to be united to him as slave-master and husband, to be under Christ's rule, reign, headship, lordship and governance; in short, to be under the law of Christ. Therefore it is perfectly correct – indeed, necessary – to speak of the believer being 'under the law of Christ' in 1 Corinthians 9. The major versions all agree. This is precisely what Paul is saying in the context.

Paul had already told the Corinthians that believers are slaves of Christ: 'For he who was called in the Lord as a bondservant is a freedman of the Lord. Likewise he who was free when called is

---

[33] Incidentally, given the lawless behaviour of the believers at Corinth, it is not difficult to see why Paul is stressing this point so vehemently here.

[34] Actually, 'made myself a slave' (verse 19) and 'became' (verse 20) are in the aorist – one act with lasting result. See Gordon D.Fee: *The First Epistle to the Corinthians*, in *The New International Commentary on the New Testament*, William B.Eerdmans Publishing Company, Grand Rapids, reprinted 1991, pp427-428.

[35] See my *Psalm 119*; '"The Law" in "the Law of Christ"'.

a bondservant of Christ' (1 Cor. 7:22). The apostle used *doulos*, the very word he used in Romans 6. The Corinthians would have got the point, even as they listened to the apostle's words (1 Cor. 9:19-23) being read to them. Slavery is the underlying theme of the paragraph in question. Believers are slaves of Christ. This can only mean that they are under his rule, governance and law.

C.K.Barrett translated 1 Corinthians 9:21 thus:

> I became as if I were outside the law (though I am not free of legal obligation to God but under legal obligation to Christ)...

He commented:

> This is one of the most difficult sentences in the [letter], and also one of the most important, for in it Paul shows how the new relation to God which he has in Christ expresses his debt of obedience to God... He is not free of legal obligation to God (*anomos theou*) but under legal obligation to Christ (*ennomos Christou*).

Barrett then spoke of 'the difficulty in which Paul found himself':

> He must direct the Corinthians' obedience in the way of Christ, but he must do this without permitting Christianity to become a new law... He does not say that he is 'under the law of the Messiah' (*hupo ton nomon tou Christou*). Yet he is not 'God's lawless one' (*anomos theou*)... He is 'Christ's law-abiding one' (*ennomos Christou*)... He is not related to God by legal observance, but by grace and faith, and in Christ, only; but precisely in this non-legal relationship he is Christ's slave, who owes absolute obedience not to a code (though on occasion [too weak, DG], and with due caution, he can give precepts to his followers), but to Christ as a person, and to the absolute principle of universal love, which Christ both taught and exemplified.[36]

I have just hinted at the Corinthians having to hear these words. For that is the fact of the matter. We should bear in mind that the Corinthians would have heard these words read aloud to them in

---

[36] C.K.Barrett: *The First Epistle to the Corinthians* (second edition), A&C Black, London, 1971, pp212-214. The law of Christ is not a list of rules but, as Barrett agrees (but too weakly, alas), the believer is under Christ's commands by the apostles through the Spirit in Scripture.

the first instance. What would they have taken away from that hearing? We don't have to guess! Read the passage aloud and see. Men are under law, both Jew and Gentile. All men are. The issue is, what is the law in question? The believer is not under the old law, the law of Moses. But neither is he outside or removed from law, free from all law. He is not law-less. The question is, what law is the believer under? That is the question. He is under law, but what law? The law of Christ. The believer's law is the law of Christ. As Femi Adeyemi put it:

> *Christou* is [a] genitive of source, which indicates that this law comes from Christ. In verses 20-21 Paul drew a clear distinction between the Mosaic law and what he called 'the law from Christ'.[37]

In looking first at the big picture, I am not suggesting we should ignore the minutiae of the words. Far from it. Indeed, I am now about to look at the exact words of the apostle.

It might be that *ennomos* has a nuance very slightly different to *hupo nomon*, but it is only a shade of a difference. In any case, the concept of being subject to law, keeping within the law, closely related to the Lord by law, is strengthened by the nuance. It is a far more intimate relationship than merely being 'under' the law of Christ. As Gordon D.Fee translated it, it speaks of being 'subject to law'.[38] I see the nuance reflecting the marriage aspect of the believer's union with Christ, rather than its slavery aspect. Believers are not only under Christ's law; they are in-lawed to Christ. Let me explain.

According to Joseph Henry Thayer, *ennomos* means 'bound to the law, bound by the law', while *en*, in this context, speaks 'of a person to whom another is wholly joined, and to whose power and influence he is subject... So used in the writings of Paul and of John particularly of intimate relationship with God or with

---

[37] Femi Adeyemi: 'The New Covenant Law And The Law Of Christ' in *Bibliotheca Sacra* (Oct.-Dec. 2006) pp440-441. See Daniel B.Wallace: *Greek Grammar Beyond The Basics*, Zondervan, Grand Rapids, 1996, p113.
[38] Fee p430.

Christ, and for the most part involving contextually the idea of power and blessing resulting from that union'.

According to W.E.Vine, *ennomos* means '"lawful, legal", literally "in-law", or, strictly, "what is within the range of law", [and] is translated "lawful" (Acts 19:39) of the legal tribunals in Ephesus. Or "under law" in relation to Christ (1 Cor. 9:21)... not merely the condition of being under "law", but the intimacy of a relation established in the loyalty of a will devoted to his Master'.

In addition, take *teleō*, 'to do just as commanded, to accomplish, fulfil' (Thayer), including: 'It is accomplished' (John 19:30). Compare that with *enteleō*, 'to order, command to be done, enjoin' (Thayer). I say the same applies to *ennomos*.

What is more, look at Romans 2:12-15. Literally: 'For as many as without law (*anomōs*)... without law (*anomōs*)... and as many as in law (*en nomō*)...'.[39] Do not miss the *en nomō*. Not a million miles away from *ennomos*, is it? And in the context of Romans 2:12-15, when Paul spoke of those *en nomō* he was referring to Jews, those under the Mosaic law.[40] Jews were *en nomō* (the law of Moses); believers are *ennomō* (the law of Christ). Yet again, take Romans 3:19: 'Now we know that whatever the law says it speaks to those who are under the law'; literally, 'to those in the law', *tois en tō nomō*.[41]

So, yet again, I disagree with Braye – this time when he says that '"under" is not correct [but] the idea conveyed here is in-ness, not "under"'.[42] He is making a dichotomy and a distinction where none exists. Having done that, he goes on to build far too much on it, and ends up with an unbiblical conclusion; namely, that the believer is not under the law of Christ, when the opposite is the case. The believer, by reason of his union with Christ,

---

[39] *anomōs* is an adverb, though not always translated as such.

[40] Of course, those under any law who break that law will be judged by that law. But the point I am making is that *en nomō* means under law, in law, governed by law, ruled by law, subject to law. I say the same applies to *ennomos*.

[41] And so it goes on: *ek nomou*, literally 'out of law' (Rom. 4:14), or *ek tou nomou*, literally 'out of the law' (Rom. 4:16); that is, speaking of those who 'live by the law', 'adhere to the law'.

[42] 'Five Reasons'.

being 'in Christ', is in-lawed to Christ. And this means that he is
under the law of Christ, intimately bound to Christ as his loving
slave-master. The believer yields a willing obedience to his
Saviour's law. But he most definitely is under it.[43]

And there is something else we should bear in mind. This is
the only place in the entire Bible where the word *ennomos* is used
in this form. As a consequence, it would not be wise to build a
massive case on this single use, especially if it ends up flying in
the face of the context (and parallel passages) – where the slavery
involved in being 'under law' is clearly the main thrust of the
apostle's argument. Indeed, slavery is stronger than merely being
'under law'.

Moo:

> The Christian is no longer bound to the Mosaic law; Christ has
> brought its fulfilment. But the Christian *is* bound to 'God's law'
> (1 Cor. 9:20-21; *cf.* 'God's commands' in 1 Cor. 7:19 and 1 John
> *passim*). 'God's law' is not [now], however, the Mosaic law, but
> 'Christ's law' (1 Cor. 9:20-21; Gal. 6:2), because it is to Christ,
> the fulfiller, the *telos* of the law (Rom. 10:4), that the Christian is
> bound... Failure to observe this distinction [between the law of
> Moses and the law of God] has resulted in considerable
> confusion and misunderstanding.[44]

On 1 Corinthians 9:20-21, Moo:

> Paul's point... is that he as a Christian is not subject to the rule
> and authority of the Mosaic law, but he willingly gives up that
> freedom, and conforms to that law when evangelising Jews...
> Paul wants to guard against any idea that he has no more
> obligations to the law of God. Indeed, while not being 'under the
> law', he recognises a continuing obligation to 'God's law', in the
> form of 'Christ's law' (the Greek is *ennomos Christou*). The
> conceptualisation of this text provides as neat a summary of my
> view [Moo's, and mine – DG] of the law as the New Testament

---

[43] I am convinced that those I oppose here make a mountain out of the
molehill of the absent *hupo*. As I have said, in 1 Cor. 9 Paul is speaking
of the believer under the law of Christ but avoiding the pitfall of likening
that law to the law of Moses. But, as I say, he is not really arguing about
the law in 1 Cor. 9, but talking about evangelism.

[44] Moo: 'The Law' pp217-218, emphasis his.

affords. It suggests that 'God's law' comes to his people in two forms: to Israel in the form of 'law', *torah*, and to Christians in the form of 'Christ's law'. Here we find the 'new-covenant theology' emphasis on two contrasting covenants worked out in terms of two different 'laws'. But the key question remains: How different are they?

To answer this question, [Moo said], we return to Galatians [in particular, to Gal. 5:13 – 6:2]. To recapitulate: ...The teaching of the New Testament on the matter of the law of God is neatly summarised in the distinctions that Paul draws in 1 Corinthians 9:20-21: the law of Moses, the *torah* ('law' simply), was given to the people of Israel to govern them until the coming of the Messiah; since his coming, the people of God are governed by the 'law of Christ'. Biblical law, in other words, is firmly attached to the temporal two-covenant structure that is the hallmark of 'new-covenant theology'.[45]

In short, 1 Corinthians 9:19-23 teaches that the believer *is* under the law of Christ.

Galatians 5:1

The context is king. In the allegory of Sarah and Hagar (Gal. 4:21-31), we are expressly told that the law on Mount Sinai was a covenant of bondage, in contrast to another covenant (Gal. 4:21,24-27); namely, the Abrahamic covenant fulfilled in the new. The covenant represented by Hagar is the law, the Mosaic covenant. Writing to those who desired 'to be under the law' – that is, the Mosaic law – Paul directed his argument against the Judaisers who wanted believers to go under that covenant. That covenant, being a covenant of bondage, he would have none of it:

For freedom Christ has made us free; stand fast therefore, and do not be entangled again with a yoke of bondage (Gal. 5:1, footnote).

It was for freedom that Christ set us free; therefore keep standing firm and do not be subject again to a yoke of slavery (NASB).

---

[45] Douglas J.Moo: 'The Covenants and the Mosaic Law: The View from Galatians', Affinity Theological Study Conference: *The End of the Law?*, February, 2009, pp20,27.

The opening note of Galatians 5 is vital. Freedom! Liberty! LIBERTY! But what is this freedom? Freedom from sin, death and the law; in particular, here, the law, the law of Moses, not excluding the possibility of pagan law (Gal. 4:8-11; Col. 2:6-23).

Do not miss the word play on 'yoke'. 'The yoke of bondage' or 'slavery' is the Mosaic law (Acts 15:10; Gal. 4:24) (or, pagan law, of course), and this is contrasted to Christ's 'easy' yoke and 'light' burden (Matt. 11:28-30), Christ's law.[46] The royal law of liberty (Jas. 1:25; 2:8), the law of Christ, is no 'yoke of bondage'!

Paul is teaching that believers cannot possibly be progressively sanctified by the law of Moses. But this is no problem. After all, believers are not under the law of Moses. His point is that they should never entertain the suggestion that they should go back to it (or to pagan law). Believers, united to Christ, are released from the law of Moses, the law of bondage, having died to it. They no longer live in the age of law, but in the age of the Spirit and grace. So don't go back to the law of Moses, that yoke of bondage!

Clearly, none of this has a word to say against the claim that the believer is under the law of Christ. Braye's categorical deduction that the believer is not under the law of Christ is wrong. Galatians 5:1 has nothing to say on that score. Nothing at all!

But we can go further. While there are risks in arguing from silence, nevertheless the fact that Paul does not rule out submitting to the law of Christ at this point is, in itself, not without significance. 'Don't go to the law of Moses', he said. 'You are free'. Now if he knew that believers are under no law whatsoever, freed from all law, why did he not go directly for the root of the tooth, and not merely content himself with the crown? What I mean is, if he had said: 'Don't listen to these Judaisers and go to the law of Moses. After all, you are free from all law. So, when I come to talk about the law of Christ in a short while, remember you are not even under that law. You are free from all

---

[46] Incidentally, do not miss the parallel with 1 John 5:3: 'This is the love of God, that we keep his commandments. And his commandments are not burdensome'. I will return to 1 John.

law, under no law, not even the law of Christ. Consequently, don't go back to any law'. How simple, how unequivocal that would have been! But he did not say anything of the sort! I don't build anything on this silence, but I notice it.

In any case, as I have shown, Paul is blunt: believers are not under Moses' law, the law of bondage, and must never listen to teachers who urge them to go under it. But that has nothing to say about the believer and the law of Christ.

Now glance at the way the apostle proceeds in Galatians 5 and 6. Having dealt with justification by faith and not by the law (Gal. 5:2-12), Paul moves on :

> For you were called to freedom, brothers. Only do not use your freedom as an opportunity for the flesh, but through love serve one another. For the whole law [of Moses] is fulfilled in one word: 'You shall love your neighbour as yourself'... But I say, walk by the Spirit, and you will not gratify the desires of the flesh... But if you are led by the Spirit, you are not under the law [of Moses]. Now the works of the flesh are evident... But the fruit of the Spirit is... And those who belong to Christ Jesus have crucified the flesh with its passions and desires. If [since] we live by the Spirit, let us also keep in step with the Spirit... Fulfil the law of Christ (Gal. 5:13 – 6:2).

The contrast, the argument, could not be clearer: the believer is no longer under the Mosaic law, but in the Spirit, and by 'walking in the Spirit', 'keeping in step with the Spirit', he must and will fulfil the law of Christ.[47] As John G.Reisinger put it: 'What does it mean to "walk in the Spirit"? Walking in the Spirit is nothing less than walking in obedience to the revealed will of God in Scripture'.[48] And that is the law of Christ. 'A natural consequence of walking in the Spirit [is that it] fulfils the law of Christ'.[49]

In light of Galatians 4:21 – 5:1, the link between 'the believer' and 'the law of Christ' is highly charged, to say the least. The Galatians would have got the point! We know the sort of thing

---

[47] Gal. 6:2 could be a statement or a command, but this is immaterial to the question in hand. See below.

[48] John G.Reisinger: *Studies in Galatians*, New Covenant Media, Frederick, 2010, pp408-409.

[49] Reisinger p432.

the Judaisers were telling them about the law of Moses: '*It is necessary* to circumcise them and *to order them to keep the law of Moses*' (Acts 15:5). The Galatians would have recognised what Paul was telling them: 'It is necessary... to keep the law of Christ'.

The word 'fulfil' (Gal. 6:2) is vital here. But before I move on to that verse, let me quote Moo with reference to what we have seen thus far:

> 'Under law' designates the status antithetical to the status of the believer. To be 'under grace', free children of God, 'led by the Spirit', means to be living in the new age of redemption, and no longer in the old age that was characterised by, and dominated by, the law... Life in the Spirit is put forward by Paul as the ground of Christian ethics, in contrast to life 'under law'.[50]

'Under law' here, in the context, clearly means 'under the Mosaic law'. The believer is not under Moses' law. But this certainly does not signify that life in the Spirit rules out being under the law of Christ! The apostle has not even mentioned the law of Christ at this stage. Moo went on:

> [But] if Christians are no longer 'under the law',[51] what will guide and empower their conduct? Paul answers in terms of the Spirit and (surprisingly, perhaps) the law [of Moses]. Christians enjoy the indwelling presence of the Spirit. By 'walking' by the Spirit (Gal. 5:16) and 'keeping in step with the Spirit' (Gal. 5:25), believers will develop those character traits that should mark God's people... In Galatians 5:14, [the apostle] proclaims that 'the entire law is fulfilled in keeping this one command: "Love your neighbour as yourself"'. How does the love command of Leviticus 19:18 'fulfil' the law? It may mean simply that [love] is so central to the law that one is not really obeying the law if love is not present. Paul highlights love, not to displace the law in any sense, but to point to its true meaning and essence. But the language of 'fulfil' suggests [it does more than suggest!] that Paul means something [far] more radical than this. Vital to understanding Paul's perspective on the law is to recognise a principal distinction in his writings between 'doing'

---

[50] Moo: 'The Law' p215.
[51] Note Moo's view, as mine, '*the* law', 'the law of Moses'.

and 'fulfilling' the law [of Moses]. Nowhere does Paul say that Christians are to 'do' the law, and nowhere does he suggest that any but Christians can 'fulfil' the law [of Moses].[52] 'Doing' the law refers to that daily obedience to all the commandments that was required of the Israelites. 'Fulfilling' the law, on the other hand, denotes that complete satisfaction of the law's demands that comes only through our identification with Christ (Rom. 8:4) and our submission to that commandment which Christ put at the heart of his new-covenant teaching: love. It is the love of others, first made possible by Christ (hence the 'new' commandment, John 13:34), that completely satisfies the demand of the law. The other reference to 'law' in this concluding section of Galatians comes in Galatians 6:2.[53]

Exactly! And 'that other reference to "law"' is, of course, in utter contrast to the law of Moses; it is the law of Christ.

Galatians 6:2

> If [since] we live by the Spirit, let us also keep in step with the Spirit... and so fulfil the law of Christ (Gal. 5:25 – 6:2).

The Judaisers were pressing the Galatian believers to keep the law of Moses, to go *under* it, and the Galatians were hankering after it. Paul, arguing his case resolutely, tells his readers that they are released from the law of Moses (along with pagan law), and must on no account go back to it. Does that leave them lawless? Not a bit of it! As he tells them, they are not under the law of Moses but must fulfil the law of Christ; in other words, that they are under the law of Christ.[54]

---

[52] We may go further. In every believer, by Christ's work, by 'the law of the Spirit of life in Christ Jesus', 'the righteous requirement of the law [of Moses] [is] fulfilled' (Rom. 8:2-4).

[53] Moo: 'Galatians' pp20-21.

[54] In what follows, as I have said, it does not matter whether we should read Gal. 6:2 as a command or a statement; on the issue in hand, it amounts to the same thing: believers are under the law of Christ. To avoid cluttering the text of my article, I will stick to 'command'. If any reader prefers it in the statement form, he can make the necessary adjustment in the article. In any case, 'let us keep in step with the Spirit' *is* a command. 'Let us' is not a suggestion!

Let me explain. By 'fulfilling the law of Christ', the apostle is, in fact, speaking of believers obeying that law. In truth, it is stronger than that, much stronger. Paul does not use *plēroō*, 'to fulfil', as did Matthew concerning Christ (Matt. 5:17), as he might well have done, since it would have been more than enough to make the point. Why would *plēroō* have done? Because Christ came to fulfil the law of Moses: 'Do not think that I have come to abolish the law or the prophets; I have not come to abolish [them] but to fulfil (*plērōsai*) [them]' (Matt. 5:17), he declared. And to do that, he had to come *under* the law of Moses: 'God sent forth his Son, born of woman, born *under* the law (*hupo nomon*)' (Gal. 4:4); in other words, Christ was under the law to submit to it, and obey and keep it. 'Fulfilling the law' inevitably involves 'being under the law'. Thus the believer is under the law of Christ and has to fulfil it; because he has to fulfil it, he must be under it.[55] In other words, *plēroō* would have been perfectly adequate for Paul's purpose.

But, in fact, he uses *anaplēroō*, 'to fill to the brim, to fully satisfy, to observe perfectly'.[56] The case could not be more strongly made. The believer is most definitely under the law of Christ, and he has to carry it out to the full, keep it thoroughly. He has to fulfil it entirely. He is obligated to obey that law. He is to copy his Master, Christ. As Christ, filled with the Spirit (Matt. 12:18; Luke 4:18; John 3:34; Acts 10:38), came under the law of Moses in order to fulfil it, so the believer has the Spirit and is under Christ's law in order to fulfil it by walking in the Spirit. 'Just as Christ' is a powerful new-covenant argument (John 13:15,34; 15:12; 17:18; Eph. 5:2,25, and so on). It underlies Galatians 5:25 – 6:2.[57]

---

[55] In Rom. 8:1-4, Paul is dealing with justification leading to progressive sanctification. But that passage does not undermine the point I have made concerning Gal. 6:2. In fact, it strengthens the claim that the law of Christ involves both the inward work of the Spirit and the Scriptures.

[56] Thayer.

[57] Christ, of course, completely fulfilled the law; believers, in their progressive sanctification, do not. Nevertheless, they must aim for perfection, full maturity, complete likeness to Christ (Matt. 5:48; 2 Cor.

Now for the obvious but frequently ignored fact: Galatians 6 is the climax of the letter. In light of this, the juxtaposition of 'the law of Christ' and 'the Israel of God' (Gal. 6:2,16), carries great weight. The old Israel was under the old law of Moses; the new Israel is under the new law of Christ.[58]

None of this, of course, in any way diminishes the absolute necessity of the inward working of the Spirit. As I say, according to the apostle, this fulfilling of the law of Christ is only possible to those who keep in step with the Spirit. Galatians 5:25 – 6:2 captures the believer's experience of the law of Christ in a nutshell. The believer, obeying Scripture (here, an apostolic command), walking in the Spirit, fulfils Christ's law. In other words, the law of Christ is not reduced to a list of external commands, with those commands having to be kept by believers in their own power! The believer's obedience is only possible by the inward work of the Spirit. Therefore, I agree with Braye, but with one important change, when he states:

> The new law differs in its very essence and nature [from the old law]. The new law is not a list of words – commands, imperatives, statutes, or instructions – expressed externally on tablets of stone (or on a page).

Here is the way I would put it:

> The new law differs in its very essence and nature [from the old law]. The new law is not *merely* a list of words – commands, imperatives, statutes, or instructions – expressed externally on tablets of stone (or on a page).

But I would go on to make sure that people got the full picture:

> But neither is it the inward work of the Spirit *without* those external commands, imperatives, statutes and instructions, or with them *tacked on the outside of* Christ's law.

As the believer keeps the apostolic command to fulfil the law of Christ, he will, since he lives by the Spirit, keep in step with the

---

13:9,11; Eph. 3:19; 4:13,21-24; Phil. 3:12-16; Col. 1:28; 4:12; Heb. 13:21; Jas. 1:4; 2 Pet. 3:18).

[58] See my *Christ* pp314-320,552-554.

Spirit (Gal. 5:25). *And it is equally true the other way round*: as he walks in the Spirit, he will obey his Master's revealed will, including his commands, as recorded and issued by the apostles in Scripture. Both dovetail perfectly. It is not either/or; it is both. The believer has the Spirit *and* is under the Scriptures, the apostolic commands; he is under those commands *and* the Spirit writes those commands in his heart.

As Graeme Goldsworthy put it:

> The sanctification of the Christian is... in one sense automatic. We cannot take hold of Christ by faith for our justification without the Holy Spirit. It is the same Holy Spirit that both enables the sinner to believe the gospel and also works in us the fruit of sanctification. In another sense, sanctification is not automatic in that the Spirit works through our minds and wills. All the admonition and exhortation in the Bible is God's way of involving us in the [progressive] sanctifying work of the Spirit. To be human is to be responsible. To be Christianly human is to respond with mind and will to the gospel with good works... [Take] Philippians 2:6-11... Here we see sovereignty and responsibility knit together in such a way that the outworking of salvation day by day – good works – is immediately the result of human effort, but ultimately the work of God in us... What Christ did for us has its outworking in all believers as sanctification. What we already are in Christ... begins to take shape in our experience as the Holy Spirit conforms us more and more to the reality which is in Christ. The Christian struggle is against the world, the flesh and the devil. When Paul concludes the Ephesian letter... (Eph. 6:10-18), he does not take up a new subject. The practical matters of daily life in a hostile world are the spiritual warfare against principalities and powers. In urging us to put on the full armour of God, Paul is not departing from the perspective that is constantly his; namely that, by standing firm and clinging to the truth of our justification, we live the life of sanctification.[59]

And then Wayne Grudem:

---

[59] Graeme Goldsworthy: 'The Gospel in Revelation' in *The Goldsworthy Trilogy*, Paternoster, Milton Keynes, reprinted 2014, pp238-239,281-282.

The role that we play in [progressive] sanctification is both a passive one in which we depend on God to sanctify us, and an active one in which we strive to obey God and take steps that will increase our sanctification... Unfortunately today, this passive role in sanctification... is sometimes so strongly emphasised that it is the only thing people are told about the path of sanctification. Sometimes the popular phrase: 'Let go, and let God' is given as a summary of how to live the Christian life. But this is a tragic distortion of the doctrine of sanctification... [There is the] active role which we are to play... There are many aspects to this active role that we are to play in [progressive] sanctification... It is important that we continue to grow both in our passive trust in God to sanctify us and in our active striving for holiness and greater obedience in our lives. If we neglect active striving to obey God, we become passive, lazy Christians. If we neglect the passive role of trusting God and yielding to him, we become proud and overly confident in ourselves. In either case, our [progressive] sanctification will be greatly deficient. We must maintain faith and diligence to obey at the same time. The old hymn wisely says: 'Trust and obey, for there's no other way to be happy in Jesus, but to trust and obey'.[60]

So I say again: The believer has the Spirit *and* is under the Scriptures, the apostolic commands; he is under those commands *and* the Spirit writes those commands in his heart. If this is not so, we shall be left judging every case of right and wrong by motive and not by action. What a terrible thought! If the law of Christ has no external Scriptures at its heart, what is the objective standard by which to judge this 'walking in the Spirit'? Have we simply to accept the rightness of any believer who retorts that the Spirit moved him to act in such and such a way? What happens to church discipline under such a system? And that is only one question.[61]

---

[60] Wayne Grudem: *Systematic Theology...*, Inter-Varsity Press, Leicester, 1994, pdf link pp655-657.

[61] How will we distinguish between the Spirit and the flesh, the Spirit and Satan? After all, we know he can disguise himself as an angel of light (2 Cor. 11:14). How will we decide between two professing believers who urge diametrically opposed courses of action, each claiming that they are led by the Spirit?

In order to illustrate the point, consider this recent written conversation. A man was questioned about what he had written:

> You said: 'If all things are lawful to Paul, all things are permitted – even sexual immorality'. What in the world did you mean by that statement? How do you reconcile this statement with your affirmation that Christians should attempt to follow and conform to the exhortations in the New Testament?

The answer came back:

> [For Paul] the ultimate arbiter is Christ in him. He does not always have time to open his Bible if he has forgotten a verse, to see what he should do! He walks by the Spirit and knows that whatsoever is not of faith is sin.

Really? On this ground, if a professed believer parried a reprimand by saying the Spirit had moved him to the action in question, and that he had faith enough to believe it was right, what the proper answer would be, I am at a loss to imagine.[62]

Furthermore, if the Spirit has inwardly given believers everything necessary, why did the Spirit ensure that they have the external, written Scriptures? Are they a luxury, or an essential? Are they merely useful, or a necessity? Are they Christ's advice for the believer, or are they Christ's royal law of the believer's liberty (Jas. 1:25; 2:8)?

---

[62] In a further response, the writer explained: 'It depends on the definition of sin. I suggested that, for those under the law, sin is the transgression of that law. So if you can find a law that says: "Sexual immorality is a sin", then to those under that law it is a sin, and they have *ipso facto* broken that law. However for those not under law, but who are led by the Spirit, as Paul was, what the law says is irrelevant (in that immediate context)'. There then followed a nuanced discussion on 1 Cor. 6:12,18. For my part, in this I see a failure to distinguish things indifferent and commands. I repeat a note in the Introduction; namely, in another discussion, this same writer stated: 'The spirit has pre-eminence over the written word, or the letter'. Even if we replace 'spirit' with 'Spirit' it sounds little better! Do not miss the confusion in the unscriptural link (the virtual equivalence) between 'the written word' and 'the letter'.

I am convinced that both the written word and the inward Spirit are essential, and bound together. Nowhere is my position better exemplified than in 1 John 2:

> You have been anointed by the Holy One, and you all have knowledge. I write to you, not because you do not know the truth, but because you know it, and because no lie is of the truth... I write these things to you about those who are trying to deceive you. But the anointing that you received from him abides in you, and you have no need that anyone should teach you. But as his anointing teaches you about everything, and is true, and is no lie – just as it has taught you, abide in him (1 John 2:20-27).

A superficial reading of this text could lead to the view that the Spirit is all, and there is no need of any human or external teaching. And yet that cannot be! If that were the case, John would have no need to write and tell these believers what they already knew perfectly well by the inward work of the Spirit. John's words are not merely useful; they are vital. The apostles were blessed with direct revelation. We are not. We have revelation through the apostles as recorded in Scripture.

Getting back to Galatians, as Moo said:

> The interpretation of the phrase 'law of Christ' is central to my [Moo's and mine – DG] argument. Unfortunately, Paul provides little contextual information.[63] We have, however, already noticed that Paul uses similar language in 1 Corinthians 9:21, where, the context suggests [it makes it plain!] 'the law of Christ' is distinguished from the Mosaic law. Coupled with the claim that Christians are no longer 'under the (Mosaic) law', this makes it unlikely [this is far too weak] that the 'law of Christ' is

---

[63] Is it because the early believers knew full well what the apostle was talking about? Was it obvious to them? Would they not, quite naturally, think that what the apostle was writing was an integral part of Christ's law? Certainly, he had taken great pains to establish his apostolic credentials right at the start of the letter (Gal. 1:1 – 2:21). And this is general throughout the New Testament. Witness the number of times he goes out of his way to establish and maintain his apostolic authority, and speak of the apostolic foundation of the church (1 Cor. 3:10-11; Eph. 2:19-22; 3:5, and so on). Notice the way Peter later speaks in exalted, but proper, terms of Paul's writings (2 Pet. 3:15-16).

the Mosaic law interpreted and fulfilled by Christ. Rather, the phrase is more likely [to be] Paul's answer to those who might conclude that his law-free gospel provides no standards of guidance for believers. On the contrary, Paul says, *though no longer directly responsible to Moses' law, Christians are bound to Christ's law.*

I pause. This is the point: 'Though [they are] no longer directly responsible to Moses' law, Christians are bound to Christ's law'. In other words, they are under Christ's law. Exactly so.

Moo went on:

> In what does this 'law' consist? Since... Galatians 5:14..., the demand for love [must be] a central component of the 'law of Christ'. But it is unlikely that Paul confines the law to this demand alone [certainly not!], for, as we have seen, Paul also stresses in this context the fruit-bearing ministry of the Spirit. Coupled with the centrality of the Spirit in Paul's teaching about what it means to live as a Christian, this strongly suggests [it is stronger that that!] that the directing influence of the Spirit is an important part of this law of Christ... Jeremiah 31:31-34... Ezekiel 36:26-27. It is more difficult to determine whether the law of Christ includes specific teachings and principles... I think it highly probable [it is certain!] that Paul thought of the law of Christ as including within it teachings of Jesus and the apostolic witness, based on his life and teaching.

Moo, in part, quoting Richard N.Longenecker:

> The law of Christ 'stands in Paul's thought for those prescriptive principles stemming from the heart of the gospel (usually embodied in the example and teachings of Jesus), which are meant to be applied to specific situations by the direction and enablement of the Holy Spirit, being always motivated and conditioned by love'.
> Does the 'law of Christ' include Mosaic commandants? Of course. We may expect that everything within the Mosaic law that reflected God's 'eternal moral will' for his people is caught up into and repeated in the 'law of Christ'.[64]

---

[64] Douglas J.Moo: 'The Covenants and the Mosaic Law: The View from Galatians', Affinity Theological Study Conference: *The End of the Law?*, February, 2009, pp20-22, emphasis mine. On the whole, a fine statement, but, as so often, Moo could have been stronger at certain

As Adeyemi put it:

> The identity of *nomos* in Galatians 6:2 is shaped by the genitive qualifier, *tou Christou*. This may be a genitive of source, suggesting that this 'law' comes from Christ. In this sense *nomos* in Galatians 6:2 is 'the standard set by Christ' for believers to follow as a new standard or system of conduct... The... form of *nomos* and the genitive phrase *tou Christou* affirm the distinct nature of this 'law' as coming specifically from Christ.[65]

Braye, I submit, is wrong. Galatians 5 and 6 confirm that the believer really *is* under the law of Christ.

1 John 3:4

I quote the entire paragraph to give the context, highlighting the critical words:

> See what kind of love the Father has given to us, that we should be called children of God; and so we are. The reason why the world does not know us is that it did not know him. Beloved, we are God's children now, and what we will be has not yet appeared; but we know that when he appears we shall be like him, because we shall see him as he is. And everyone who thus hopes in him purifies himself as he is pure. *Everyone who makes a practice of sinning also practices lawlessness (anomian); sin is lawlessness (anomia).* You know that he appeared in order to take away sins, and in him there is no sin. No one who abides in him keeps on sinning; no one who keeps on sinning has either seen him or known him. Little children, let no one deceive you. Whoever practices righteousness is righteous, as he is righteous. Whoever makes a practice of sinning is of the devil, for the devil has been sinning from the beginning. The reason the Son of God appeared was to destroy the works of the devil. No one born of God makes a practice of sinning, for God's seed abides in him, and he cannot keep on sinning because he has been born of God. By this it is evident

---

points. As for Longenecker, the Mosaic commandments are frequently used by Christ and his apostles, but they are always nuanced, used as a paradigm, and never as straight rules. As before, see my 'The Law on the Believer's Heart'.

[65] Adeyemi pp440-441. See Wallace p113.

who are the children of God, and who are the children of the devil: whoever does not practice righteousness is not of God, nor is the one who does not love his brother (1 John 3:1-10).

The relevant Greek is *ho poiōn tēn hamartian, kai tēn **anomian** poiei; kai hē hamartia estin **anomia***; literally, 'practices sin also lawlessness practises; and sin is lawlessness'. Here we reach the crux of the text for our purposes. Now *anomia* can mean 'the condition of one without law – either because he is ignorant of it, or because he has a certain law and is violating it and showing contempt for it'.[66] The word bears these alternative meanings in Scripture. How can we decide? By the context, as always; always by the context.

In certain contexts, the words *anomia, anomos* and *anomōs* speak of being destitute of the law in question, whatever that law may be. Let me give three examples.[67]

Take Acts 2:23. Peter, preaching Christ, told the Jewish crowd on the day of Pentecost: 'You have taken [him] by lawless hands, have crucified [him], and put [him] to death' (NKJV; see also ESV). The Jews were responsible for crucifying Christ but, to do the dirty work, they used Roman hands, Gentile hands, 'lawless hands'. The NASB, translating the phrase, 'by the hands of godless men', has a marginal note: 'Lawless hands, or, men without the law; that is, heathen'. The NIV correctly notes: 'Of those not having the law (that is, Gentiles)'. Peter, steeped in Jewish thought, was using the phrase, 'lawless men', in the Jewish sense. The men he was talking about were 'men without the law'. That is to say, they were law-less, outside the law of God, the law of Moses; they were Gentiles. The Jews boasted that they had the law of Moses. They were the only people to have it (Deut. 4:7-8,32-34; Ps. 147:19-20; Rom. 2:14; 3:1-2; 9:4; 1 Cor. 9:20-21). All the rest were 'law-less'. So, as Peter said, Christ was crucified by the Jews (who had the law of Moses) making use of the Gentiles (who did not have the law of Moses, the without-the-law people) to do the work. See also Matthew 20:18-

---

[66] See Thayer.

[67] In these cases, it would be better to describe those involved as law-less and not lawless; that is (Moses') law-less.

19; and Galatians 2:15, where 'Jews by nature' are contrasted with 'sinners of the Gentiles' or 'Gentile sinners' (NIV). 'Sinners' and 'Gentiles', in such a context, means those who are law-less, outside the law of Moses, beyond the pale.

As Leonard Verduin put it: The 'lawless' men of Acts 2:23 were not:

> ...lawless in the sense of 'wicked', but 'lawless' in the Jewish sense – 'without the law'.[68] In other words, they were law-less... The Jews prided themselves on being law-havers, the only people to whom God had given his law; this put all the rest in the 'lawless' category... [Christ was crucified by the Jews who used] the Gentiles, the without-the-law people... [as] their tool.[69]

Now for the second text, 1 Corinthians 9:21. I have already looked at it. Here are the relevant words: 'To those outside the law (*anomois*) I became as one outside the law (*anomos*) (not being outside the law (*anomos*) of God but under the law of Christ'; literally, 'to those without law (*anomois*) as without law (*anomos*) (not being without law (*anomos*) to God...)...'. The Gentiles did not have the law of Moses; they were, in that sense, law-less. They were outside the Jewish pale.

And then Romans 2:12: 'For all who have sinned without the law (*anomōs*) will also perish without the law (*anomōs*)'. Clearly, the apostle is referring to the Gentiles who, though they were sinners, did not have the law of Moses. In that sense, they were law-less. They were outside the Jewish pale.

So much for the first meaning of the words in question: law-less. But, of course, in other contexts, the words *anomia, anomos* and *anomōs* speak of having a certain law, but showing contempt for it, and violating, breaking or transgressing it, whatever that law may be. Here are some examples:

> Then will I declare to them: 'I never knew you; depart from me, you workers of lawlessness (*anomian*)' (Matt. 7:23).

---

[68] Note Verduin's proper use of 'the' law.

[69] Leonard Verduin: *The Anatomy of a Hybrid: A Study in Church-State Relationships*, The Christian Harmony Publishers, Sarasota, 1992, p71.

The Son of Man will send his angels, and they will gather out of his kingdom all causes of sin and all law-breakers (*anomian*) (Matt. 13:41).
You are full of hypocrisy and lawlessness (*anomias*) (Matt. 23:28).
He was numbered with the transgressors (*anomōn*) (Luke 22:37).
Blessed are those whose lawless deeds (*anomiai*) are forgiven, and whose sins are covered (Rom. 4:7).
Just as you once presented your members as slaves to impurity and to lawlessness (*anomia*) leading to more lawlessness (*anomian*), so now present your members as slaves to righteousness leading to sanctification (Rom. 6:19).[70]
Do not be unequally yoked with unbelievers. For what partnership has righteousness with lawlessness (*anomia*)? Or what fellowship has light with darkness? What accord has Christ with Belial? Or what portion does a believer share with an unbeliever? What agreement has the temple of God with idols? (2 Cor. 6:14-16).
That day will not come, unless the rebellion comes first, and the man of lawlessness [some mss, *hamartias*, 'of sin'; others, *anomias*, 'of lawlessness'] is revealed, the son of destruction, who opposes and exalts himself against every so-called god or object of worship, so that he takes his seat in the temple of God, proclaiming himself to be God. Do you not remember that when I was still with you I told you these things? And you know what is restraining him now so that he may be revealed in his time. For the mystery of lawlessness (*anomias*) is already at work. Only he who now restrains it will do so until he is out of the way. And then the lawless one (*anomos*) will be revealed (2 Thess. 2:3-8).
The law is not laid down for the just but for the lawless (*anomois*) and disobedient, for the ungodly and sinners, for the unholy and profane, for those who strike their fathers and mothers, for murderers, the sexually immoral, men who practice homosexuality, enslavers, liars, perjurers, and whatever else is

---

[70] How can anybody be *more* without law than without it? *more* law-less than law-less? They can, of course, be *more* lawless; that is, *more* sinful, showing *more* contempt for, and violation of, the law they are under. Omitting the 'more' (literally not in the Greek, but obviously the apostle's meaning), does not alter the case. To be law-less is to be law-less. Take a line; it is either straight or it is not. It cannot be *more* straight.

contrary to sound doctrine, in accordance with the gospel of the glory of the blessed God with which I have been entrusted (1 Tim. 1:9-11).

Jesus Christ, who gave himself for us to redeem us from all lawlessness (*anomias*) and to purify for himself a people for his own possession who are zealous for good works (Tit. 2:13-14).[71]

You have loved righteousness and hated wickedness (*anomian*) (Heb. 1:9).[72]

I will be merciful toward their iniquities, and I will remember their sins [and their lawlessnesses (*anomiōn*)] no more (Heb. 8:12).

I will remember their sins and their lawless deeds [*anomiōn*] no more (Heb. 10:17).[73]

Righteous Lot, greatly distressed by the sensual conduct of the wicked (for as that righteous man lived among them day after day, he was tormenting his righteous soul over their lawless (*anomois*) deeds that he saw and heard)... (2 Pet. 2:7-8).

In all the above, the issue is not which law is being referred to in any particular passage. That, at this stage, is immaterial. Rather, the issue is that the words *anomia, anomos* and *anomōs*, in these passages, mean breaking the law which the people in question are under; any law. Law-breaking in this context is sin, and *vice-versa*. That is what the words *anomia, anomos* and *anomōs* are referring to: men violating, showing contempt for, the law that they are under.

Richard Chenevix Trench:

While *anomos* is once at least in the New Testament used negatively of a person without law, or to whom a law has not been given (1 Cor. 9:21)... [and] of the greatest enemy of all law, the Man of Sin, the lawless one (2 Thess. 2:8), [nevertheless] *anomia* is never... the condition of one living without law, but always the condition or deed of one who acts contrary to law... Thus the Gentiles, not having a law (Rom. 2:14) might be charged with sin, but they, sinning without law (Rom. 2:12;

---

[71] Christ did not need to die to redeem us from any lack of law. All he had to do was issue that law, give it to us! It was our law-breaking, our sin, that made redemption essential.

[72] If the word ought to be *adikian*, this verse plays no part in this debate.

[73] Note the same Greek word in Heb. 8:12 and 10:17, where it is translated 'sins' and 'lawless deeds', respectively.

3:21), could not be charged with *anomia*. It is true, indeed, that, behind that law of Moses which they never had, there is another law, the original law and revelation of the righteousness of God, written on the hearts of all (Rom. 2:14-15).[74]

William Edwy Vine:

> *anomos* 'without law', also denotes 'lawless' [see] Acts 2:23; 2 Thessalonians 2:4,8; [see] 2 Peter 2:8 where the thought is not simply that of doing what is unlawful, but of flagrant defiance of the known will of God.
>
> *anomia*, akin to *anomos* is most frequently translated 'iniquity' (2 Thess. 2:7)... In 1 John 3:4... the real meaning of the word [is] 'everyone that does sin (a practice, not the committal of an act) does also lawlessness; and sin is lawlessness'. This definition of sin sets forth its essential character as the rejection of the law, or will, of God and the substitution of the will of self.[75]

As I say, the context must determine which of the two meanings is correct in any particular passage.

So what about 1 John 3:4? The context could not be plainer; that is why I quoted it from verse 1 to verse 10. Here are the relevant words: 'Everyone who makes a practice of sinning also practices lawlessness; sin is lawlessness (*anomia*)... sins... sin... sinning... practices righteousness is righteous, as he is righteous... sinning... sinning... the works of the devil... sinning... sinning... practice righteousness'. John is not talking about mere *possession* of a law, or lack of it, but the *practice* of actual sinning and actual righteousness, the doing of works, obedience or disobedience to the law in question. These people are not law-less, but lawless; they are kicking over the traces, showing contempt for the law in question, the law which they are under. They have a law, they are under that law, they are obliged to obey it, but they break it, they do not keep it. We are talking about contempt of law, violation of law, transgression of law.

---

[74] Richard Chenevix Trench: *Synonyms Of The New Testament*, section 66.

[75] W.E.Vine: *Expository Dictionary Of New Testament Words*. Vine, 'an English biblical scholar, theologian, and writer... traces the words of the Bible... back to their ancient *koinē* Greek root words and to the meanings of the words for that day' (Wikipedia).

I say this not because all the major translations agree – but they do! – but because the context absolutely demands it. John is not concerned with possession of the law in question. He takes that for granted, as a given. All men are under one law or another.[76] Rather, he is concerned with a man's attitude to the law in question; in particular, his doing (or otherwise) of that law. Unrighteousness, sin, wickedness, in this connection is not a man's lack of law; it is failure to keep the law, whatever that law may be.

And as for the 'law' in question, just read the entire letter: it is full of commands and instructions and imperatives concerning Christ and his gospel. The very word 'commandment' comes seven times in the letter. It is impossible to miss the overtones of John 12:47-50; 13:1 – 16:33. John's words in 1 John 3:1-10 could almost be coming directly from the mouth of Christ himself. In the context, it is patent that John means the law of Christ – he can only mean the law of Christ. He never mentions the law of Moses once in his entire letter. And in the context of 1 John, it is clear that John is telling believers that they have to keep the law that they are under. He is urging them to obey that law, he is commanding them to keep it. I cannot read his words in any other way. As the apostle says elsewhere in his letter:

> By this we know that we have come to know him, if we keep his commandments. Whoever says, 'I know him', but does not keep his commandments is a liar, and the truth is not in him, but whoever keeps his word, in him truly the love of God is perfected. By this we may know that we are in him: whoever says he abides in him ought to walk in the same way in which he walked (1 John 2:3-6).
>
> Everyone who believes that Jesus is the Christ has been born of God, and everyone who loves the Father loves whoever has been born of him. By this we know that we love the children of God, when we love God and obey his commandments. For this is the love of God, that we keep his commandments. And his commandments are not burdensome (1 John 5:1-3).

He certainly raises his doctrine to the highest possible pitch:

---

[76] As before, see my 'All Men Under Law'.

The reason the Son of God appeared was to destroy the works of the devil. No one born of God makes a practice of sinning, for God's seed abides in him, and he cannot keep on sinning because he has been born of God. By this it is evident who are the children of God, and who are the children of the devil: whoever does not practice righteousness is not of God (1 John 3:8-10).

Now, although the phrase is not mentioned, this can only be the law of Christ. No other law will fit the bill. As I hinted, John had remembered Christ's discourse in John 12:47-50; 13:1 – 16:33 (brought in any case to his memory by the Holy Spirit in accordance with Christ's promises – John 14:26; 16:12-15). Christ's commands, his law, are synonymous in this context, and obedience to the law of Christ (the commands of Scripture) is proof positive of the inward work of the Spirit. To claim to be led by the Spirit and yet not obey Scripture is a contradiction in terms.

In short, although the believer is not under the law of Moses, he is not law-less; he is under the law of Christ. And he is obligated to keep it. The believer really is free – in particular, set free from sin (Rom. 6:22), and free from the law of Moses (Gal. 5:1). But liberty is not licence. There is a rule for believers to live by. They are 'under law towards Christ', that 'perfect law of liberty'. They are ruled by 'the law of Christ', following 'this rule', 'walk[ing] by the same rule', having taken Christ's 'easy yoke', being taught by the Spirit 'to observe all things' which Christ commanded (Matt. 11:28-30; 28:20; 1 Cor. 9:21; Gal. 6:2,16; Phil. 3:16; Jas. 1:25; 2:12). Obedience to that law is essential.

If we cite the entire context of 1 John 3:4, the position could not be more explicit:

> You have been anointed by the Holy One, and you all have knowledge. I write to you, not because you do not know the truth, but because you know it, and because no lie is of the truth... I write these things to you about those who are trying to deceive you. But the anointing that you received from him abides in you, and you have no need that anyone should teach you. But as his anointing teaches you about everything, and is true, and is no lie – just as it has taught you, abide in him... See

what kind of love the Father has given to us, that we should be called children of God; and so we are... Beloved, we are God's children now, and what we will be has not yet appeared; but we know that when he appears we shall be like him, because we shall see him as he is. And everyone who thus hopes in him purifies himself as he is pure. Everyone who makes a practice of sinning also practices lawlessness; sin is lawlessness (1 John 2:20-27; 3:1-4).[77]

The law of Christ, once again, virtually in a nutshell! In short, the believer *is* under the law of Christ, and this comprises the inward work of the Spirit *and* the external, written Scriptures.

And this passage is not unique. Consider Paul's letter to Titus. Note his opening emphasis upon his apostolic authority for issuing binding instruction, rule and command for Titus, in the first instance, then, through him, the believers in Crete, and then for all believers through this age:

> Paul, a servant of God and an apostle of Jesus Christ, for the sake of the faith of God's elect and their knowledge of the truth, which accords with godliness, in hope of eternal life, which God, who never lies, promised before the ages began and at the proper time manifested in his word through the preaching with which I have been entrusted by the command of God our Saviour (Tit. 1:1-3).

Having laid the foundation, the apostle proceeds to set out detailed instruction. Titus has to appoint elders in every church, every one of whom 'must hold firm to the trustworthy word as taught, so that he may be able to give instruction in sound doctrine and also to rebuke those who contradict it' (Tit. 1:10). Titus himself has to 'teach what accords with sound doctrine' (Tit. 2:1), he has to 'urge' (Tit. 2:6), to 'declare these things; exhort and rebuke with all authority. Let no one disregard you' (Tit. 2:15), 'remind them to be submissive to rulers and authorities, to be obedient...' (Tit. 3:1), 'to insist on these things, so that those who have believed in God may be careful to devote

---

[77] The theme continues in 2 and 3 John. Notice how many times John speaks of 'truth'. 'Truth' is inward (2 John 2), but clearly, by his use of 'command', 'walk in obedience to commands', 'teaching of Christ', it is also objective.

themselves to good works' (Tit. 3:8). 'Older women... are to teach what is good, and so train the young women' (Tit. 2:3-4). In short: 'Let our people learn to devote themselves to good works' (Tit. 3:14).

And yet, with all that, the apostle, in the same letter, can declare:

> The grace of God has appeared, bringing salvation for all people, training us to renounce ungodliness and worldly passions, and to live self-controlled, upright, and godly lives in the present age, waiting for our blessed hope, the appearing of the glory of our great God and Saviour Jesus Christ, who gave himself for us to redeem us from all lawlessness and to purify for himself a people for his own possession who are zealous for good works (Tit. 2:11-14).

Once again, we have the combination of the inward work of God's grace, this grace teaching believers from within, coupled with the outward apostolic command which has to be enforced by local elders in the *ekklēsia*, with believers mutually instructing and edifying one another, all the while taking responsibility for their own personal obedience, and all of it set out in the compass of the Scriptures.

Conclusion

Nothing that I have said in this article should be taken as casting any personal reflection on the integrity or practice of those who hold the view I have been trying to refute. I say this, not for the men in question – they know me too well to suspect any such thing – but for those who are observing this, as it were, from a distance. It is their exegesis, not the men themselves, that I have criticised. For the reasons I have given, I say their exegesis is faulty. Naturally, bad exegesis leads to a wrong conclusion. And a wrong conclusion inevitably leads to serious consequences. And, in this case, the consequences, I fear, are severe indeed. I have been conscience-driven to speak about what I see as the tendency, the appearance, the seeming-ness of their view, and where, if not checked, it might lead in the years to come. I wish I had not needed to write this article. Yet I have felt compelled to do it.

I am thinking of the rising generations – yes, plural – and about the effect, the likely effect, as I see it, of these views on them. It is not merely what is said (or, often more important, what is not said), but the big picture, the overall impression. How is this novel teaching likely to be heard and used by those not sufficiently sophisticated to grasp all its technical nuances? And I include myself in saying that; this new view is too subtle for me, I am afraid.[78] My main concern is that those who, in years to come, not grasping – or not bothering with – all the nuances, will eagerly latch onto the notion of 'no law', 'no rule', 'no commandment' in the law of Christ, and run with it. And run where?

Consequently, while we preach our liberty in Christ, while we stress the inward power of the Spirit, let us not forget to stress our obligation and responsibility to obey our Master, and our accountability to him for every thought, word and deed (Matt. 12:36-37; Rom. 2:16; 14:10; 2 Cor. 5:10, and so on). Let us make sure we give due weight to such warning passages as Hebrews 2:1-3; 6:4-12; 10:19-39. Let us not forget Christ's solemn words of warning (John 15:1-8) lying, as they do, right at the heart of his extended discourse in John 12:47-50; 13:1 – 16:33. Let us not forget that the majority (if not all) the warnings given by Christ, in his lifetime, were to professing believers. This is a vital part of the big picture of the New Testament. Unless we are crystal-clear in what we say on such issues, there is a real danger of unbridled talk of liberty degenerating into licence. Similarly, an excessive unbalanced emphasis on the inevitability of the Spirit's inward work in the believer might well lead to antinomianism or the

---

[78] As one example of the sort of thing I mean, take the very recent article, 'The Law of Christ' (christmycovenant.com), by John Dunn. He opens: 'Whatever may be said about the law of Christ, it must be acknowledged that it does not mean that the saints are now under the tutelage/enslavement of a new body of covenanted legal regulations sprinkled with blood, as was the old-covenant community, with blessings/cursing contingent upon their conditional obedience'.

notion of perfectionism.[79] These disgraceful aberrations have occurred, even in apostolic days. We should fear Jude 4 worse than the plague: 'For certain people have crept in unnoticed who long ago were designated for this condemnation, ungodly people, who pervert the grace of our God into sensuality and deny our only Master and Lord, Jesus Christ'.

Since the view I have been addressing has, to me at least, all the appearance of driving a wedge between the Spirit and the word in the law of Christ, I have spoken of the centrality and necessity of Scripture to the law of Christ. But just because I have stressed the written word, this must not be taken as an indication of any weakening of my commitment to the inward work of the Spirit. It is not the Spirit *or* the word; it is both at one and the same time. But in this article I have had to stress the place of Scripture.

Then again, the law of Christ, I am convinced, speaks of who Christ is, of what Christ approves. But how can we know what that is? By the Spirit directly, or by the Spirit through the written word? Surely we only know Christ, who he is, and what he approves, by what he has established through his apostles by the Spirit in the Scriptures. Consequently, we dare not suggest anything which might even hint at a divorce between Christ and the written word. On the contrary, we must jealously guard, at all costs, the indissoluble link between the two, right at the heart of the new-covenant law of Christ.

I also want to lay emphasis on the fact that the believer's obedience to the commands of Scripture takes the form of a duty, an obligation, a definite act of intention, will and obedience on the believer's part. True, this obedience is only possible by the power of the Spirit, but the believer does not live a life of obedience to Scripture as some sort of reflex or subconscious response to the Spirit. The believer's progressive sanctification is not monergistic.[80] This does not in any way imply walking in the

---

[79] Will it end up with the Orwellian '"Law" bad; "Spirit" good' and so encourage believers to adopt Situation Ethics?

[80] Monergistic sanctification states that the believer's progressive sanctification is the work of God through the Holy Spirit alone, as

power of the flesh. I am talking precisely in the terms which the apostle himself uses:

> Therefore, my beloved, as you have always obeyed, so now, not only as in my presence but much more in my absence, work out your own salvation with fear and trembling, for it is God who works in you, both to will and to work for his good pleasure (Phil. 2:12-13).

I know the advocates of the view I am criticising will protest that they do emphasise obedience to written Scripture. I fully acknowledge the fact. But this is so vital a matter, I must stress my concern yet again. It is the *tendency* of words which is so important here. We all know that it is not what people are told or read; it is what they think they are hearing or reading. True, in the end, the responsibility lies with the hearer and reader, but the publisher, the writer or the preacher has to do all he can to make sure his hearers and readers do not get the wrong end of the stick. I take my own medicine, I hasten to add.

But I go further; there is no smoke without fire. Whatever their protests, these writers do give the very definite impression, at least to me, that they are driving a wedge between the internal Spirit and the external word. Unless they are prepared to use words such as 'command' and 'law' and 'rule' when talking about the law of Christ, despite their protests to the contrary, they are giving the impression, to put it no stronger, that they regard such conformity as a tack on, an 'alongside', and not something absolutely integral to the law of Christ.[81]

---

opposed to synergistic sanctification, which argues that the human will cooperates with the Spirit.

[81] In correspondence with one who disagrees with me on this issue, this is what he wrote: 'All of Scripture serves to teach us and to provide guidance and instruction on what living as those who are united to Christ is supposed to look like because we are yet imperfect. This does not mean we must not obey what Christ commands us. But our drive to obey comes from within'. I agree – *except* – I would strengthen it by bringing in the sense of obedience under the law of Christ. After all, however occasional the phrase may be in Scripture, 'the law of Christ' is a scriptural phrase! So I would re-word my correspondent's statement: 'All of Scripture serves to teach us and to provide guidance and

I also think that they, while rightly emphasising the discontinuity of the covenants, are failing to stress sufficiently the continuity of Scripture. The contrast that is drawn in the New Testament between the letter and the Spirit is primarily eschatological. Whereas the law of Moses was written on stone, the law of Christ is written on the heart. Yes, but the Scriptures remain a constant throughout. How often Christ quoted them to the Jews who also would have seen no gap between them and the stone tablets. In the new covenant, we must not divorce the inward work of the Spirit from the external written Scriptures.

Yet again, I think I can hear the howls of disbelief and protest. Yes, I grant that they do speak of the necessity of obedience to Scripture, but, as I keep saying, I am thinking of the tendency down the line. And that, I am afraid, compels me to say that their doctrine is dangerous; dangerous because it flows from a wrong exegesis.

In what follows, I am not, I hasten to add, trying to taint anybody by association. Perish the thought! But there is nothing new under the sun. In writing this article, I have been reminded of the Anabaptist controversy between the mainstream and the Spiritualists, who stressed the inward Spirit to the detriment of the external word.

And not only the Anabaptists. I feel I have been engaging in something like a re-run of the antinomian controversy in the UK in the 1640s,[82] during which, in 1647, Thomas Collier published the second edition of his *The Exaltation of Christ in the Days of the Gospel*. He dealt with those who argued that since 'Christ has promised to write his laws in the hearts of his people, and that they shall be all taught of God, and that he would send his Spirit which would teach them all things, [then] for those thus taught of God, it is too legal for them to walk by Scripture'. Collier replied.

---

instruction (*and governance and rule as an integral part of Christ's law*) on what living as those who are united to Christ is supposed to look like because we are yet imperfect. This does not mean we must not obey what Christ commands us. But our drive to obey comes from within'. *This is no splitting of hairs!*

[82] I am speaking historically here when I talk about the antinomian controversy.

He agreed 'that God makes this promise good, [and] he writes his law in the heart where he once comes in a way of grace'. Yes, but it was his opponents' conclusion that he did not like. So he wrote against it: 'God... puts his Spirit in [his people], makes them fully willing to walk according to the rule of Scripture, for the Spirit and the word do answer [correspond with] each other'. Collier talked much of 'the rules of Christ... the rule of Scripture... this rule... the rules of Scripture... Those whom Christ teaches, he teaches to walk according to the rules that he prescribes [for] them'. Collier went on to say that such men as he was writing against can fail to 'rightly divide between law and gospel, between legal rules and gospel rules... the rules of Christ', and between the two covenants.[83] I fear I am reading something very like this today. And that is why I have written.

And then there is the old Keswick concept of sanctification: 'Let go, and let God'. Once again, while my opponents might well protest that, since they state that Scripture must be obeyed, there should be no danger of such an aberration, alas, I am not so sanguine.

In summary, then, as I have shown, the view that I have been contesting leans on translations which, on more than one occasion, and on key texts, go against the mainstream versions. Those who are minded to adopt this new view should, at the very least, be aware of the fact. If I adopted a minority translation, a translation adopted by no major version, I would be prepared to do so, prepared to take the full consequences of my action, *but I would give a very serious health warning to all who might follow me*. I also repeat that the view in question stems from faulty exegesis, and leads to a conclusion that is strikingly at variance with the overall impression given to us when we look at the big picture of Scripture.

I hope nobody thinks me too big for my boots when I say that I have written out of love for my brothers with whom I disagree. I have also written out of love for the watching, wondering and bewildered saints, both in the New Covenant Grace group and the

---

[83] Collier pp88,91-93. I am grateful to Chris Hanna for giving me a pdf of Collier's book, and drawing my attention to the relevant section.

wider public. Furthermore, I have written out of love for sinners, unbelievers. But above all, I have written out of love for Christ and his truth. I believe I can say all this with a sincere heart. Please forgive the inordinate length of this article. It is the seriousness of the matter that has moved me to make my position as clear as I can.

Finally, I close with David's words, nuanced, of course, by the new covenant:

> Oh how I love your law! It is my meditation all the day. Your commandment makes me wiser than my enemies, for it is ever with me. I have more understanding than all my teachers, for your testimonies are my meditation. I understand more than the aged, for I keep your precepts. I hold back my feet from every evil way, in order to keep your word. I do not turn aside from your rules, for you have taught me. How sweet are your words to my taste, sweeter than honey to my mouth! Through your precepts I get understanding; therefore I hate every false way (Ps. 119:97-104).[84]

Nothing would please me more than the thought that all of us who advance new-covenant theology could join our hands, our hearts and our voices, and echo David's words, and do it with as much vehemence as we extol our liberty in Christ by the inward working of his Spirit. I pray that my article may further this end. I have written for it. I have certainly *not* written to stoke the fire of controversy which is already burning too fiercely.

---

[84] See my *Psalm 119*.

One Command or Many in One?

Mainstream new-covenant theologians hold that believers are under the law of Christ, and that the Scriptures are an integral part of that law. Recently, however, some have begun to argue that this is not so. Believers are not under the law of Christ, they say. There are no external commands in that law since it is entirely inward, the work of the Spirit forming Christ within believers. Although believers must and will obey Scripture, they do so as a kind of reflex action, using Scripture as an invaluable source to inform their way of life, but to talk of believers being under the rule, the law, the commanding governance of Scripture, as an integral part of the law of Christ, means a return to the killing bondage of the old covenant under 'the letter'.

I have argued that this is wrong, depending as it does upon a faulty exegesis of certain key passages of Scripture. I have further argued that it ends up with something close to a mystical,[1] hyper-Calvinistic approach to progressive sanctification. Moreover, I am concerned that its long-term consequences will prove disastrous in other ways. While I do not accuse its advocates of it themselves, I do see the danger of antinomianism and perfectionism in those who, in years to come, adopt this new view without understanding *and applying* the complicated – I might say, tortuous – but necessary distinctions and qualifications it involves.[2]

Let me explain. As I have I read the numerous contributions to the discussion on this topic, I have been left with the very strong impression that a growing number are rejecting the very idea that believers should think and talk in terms of 'law', 'rule' or 'commandment' in connection with the Scriptures.[3] In my view,

---

[1] That is, the absorption of the human into the divine.

[2] For my arguments, see my 'Believers Under the Law of Christ' and 'The Obedience of Faith'. On 'the law of Christ' as the believer's rule, see my *Christ* pp211-278,481-527.

[3] It surely goes without saying that I am not arguing that the Scriptures are a mere list of rules. I will return to this.

they so emphasise the internal work of the Spirit that they are in danger of seriously weakening the role of the external Scriptures. I know they will be horrified by what I say, but I am afraid this is the distinct impression I have received. As such, I can only regard this new approach as a serious mistake.

With one important nuance, David White agrees with this new view, but not, I hasten to add, with my assessment of it. In his paper, 'The Law and the Mind of God',[4] he agrees that believers are indeed under the law of Christ, but only if we understand that law to consist of but one commandment; namely, Christ's 'new commandment' to love (John 13:34). There are no other commands in the law of Christ. Taking these words of Christ, 'A new commandment I give to you, that you love one another: just as I have loved you, you also are to love one another' (John 13:34), and linking them with Moses and the old covenant, he asserts:

> The 'new commandment' of Christ will stand in the same place in this new covenant as the ten commandments had in the old, Mosaic covenant.

He goes on to refer to John 13:34-35; 14:15-24; 15:9-17, saying: 'Here... is the sum of that which is termed 'the law of Christ'. In developing his case, White quotes Christ's words in Matthew 22:34-40, with our Lord's reference to Leviticus 19:18 and Deuteronomy 6:5. Having been asked to say which was the greatest commandment in the law, Jesus declared:

> You shall love the Lord your God with all your heart and with all your soul and with all your mind. This is the great and first commandment. And a second is like it: You shall love your neighbour as yourself. On these two commandments depend all the law and the prophets (Matt. 22:37-40).

White comments:

> At the heart of the whole Mosaic law, at its very core... are these two great pillars, which hold up the whole structure, the second being the extension of the first. Jesus has highlighted this fact in the very week he is to inaugurate his new covenant. Now, he

---

[4] I am engaging with the proof copy.

gives new meaning, new emphasis – fulfilment – to what the Mosaic law had always been about. He completes the picture to which that old law pointed. He provides substance, now, to the former shadows. At the heart of the new covenant will be this: love for God's Son, seen in identical love for God's people. And just as it was the adherence to the law of Moses which was to display to the nations around that Israel was the people of the living God, so it is here. 'By this', Jesus says, 'all men will know that you are my disciples'. The hallmark of the new covenant is the love of believer for believer. This is the 'covenant commandment'. And this, I strongly suggest, is what Paul refers to as 'the law of the Christ'... 'Carry each other's burdens, and in this way you will fulfil the law of Christ' (Gal. 6:2). Do you see how what Paul says restates what Jesus has instituted as the new commandment of the new covenant? Sacrificial love, which is prepared to shoulder the load for our brothers, our sisters, is precisely what brings to completion (fulfils, not 'keeps') the law of the Christ.

This 'monologue' is what is referred to also in other terms. It is 'God's law' for the believer. It has been elevated by Jesus, the King of Kings, as the 'prince of laws' from the old covenant – thus it is the 'royal law'. It is the 'law which brings freedom'. At the end of his life on this earth, John will also reflect on this single covenant commandment in his letters.

I believe that all this plays into the current debate over the law of Christ. Since I feel that White's paper might well be used by some to bolster them in the new concept of the law of Christ that I have spoken about, I want to respond, under three headings:

Christ and Moses compared

Christ's new-covenant commandment

Christ's use of Leviticus 19:18 and Deuteronomy 6:5

Christ and Moses compared

While there are similarities between the old and the new covenants, Scripture stresses the contrast between them.[5] Israel

---

[5] I quote from my 'Covenant Theology Tested': 'The two Testaments are strictly continuous (apart from the 400 year gap), but the two

was overwhelmingly an unregenerate nation, held under the law of Moses, which served as a child custodian over them as a people, as a temporary covenant for them alone, lasting until the coming of the Seed, Christ (Gal. 3:23-25; 4:1-7). Now that Christ has fulfilled the old covenant, and established the new, believers have died to the law of Moses[6] and are under the law of Christ, which law gives them motives for obedience, and instructions on how to calibrate it, what to aim for, including principles by which to work out the inward grace of the Spirit as they have to face ever-changing circumstances (Rom. 6:17; Phil. 2:12-13). The old covenant was a ministry of condemnation, even death; the new covenant is a spiritual, glorious ministry (2 Cor. 3.3-11,17-18). So, as White put it: 'The old covenant had said: "If you keep my commandments, you will live". The new covenant declares: "If you love me, you will keep my commandments".' And: 'The Christian is not "under" law at all in the same way that the old-

---

covenants are radically different, and have to be contrasted by us because they are contrasted in Scripture. The one, the Mosaic covenant, the old covenant, was the covenant of the flesh, outward, a shadow, ineffective, condemning, killing, a covenant of death, a temporary covenant which was fulfilled by Christ and abolished because it was weak and useless. The other covenant, the new covenant, is superior in that it is spiritual, of the Spirit, inward, the reality, effective, saving and permanent. While the Reformed want to talk in terms of the continuity of the two Testaments, this, in fact, is virtually irrelevant. What really matters is the fundamental disjoint of the two covenants. See John 1:17; Rom. 8:3; 10:4; 2 Cor. 3:6-9; Gal. 3:19; Heb. 7:18,22; 8:13. This is precisely what the Reformed will not face up to'.

[6] Elsewhere I have looked at the problem of how Gentiles believers who, never being under the law of Moses, could be said to have died to it: 'Paul was speaking either of his own personal experience as a Jew, or else he was speaking of the Jews and not Gentiles. And even when he was clearly addressing Gentiles, he was often rebuking them for seeking to go under the law, allowing themselves to be put under it by false teachers, Judaisers, or going back to the slavery of pagan principles – this last, having nothing to do with the law of Moses at all! Christ has redeemed his people from all bondage. Even so... there are some passages where such explanations still do not satisfy. Rom. 2:14-15 is the explanation of all such' (my *Christ* p37). I went on to tackle this important passage.

covenant member was'. I agree. I also agree that while we should use the old covenant to illustrate the new, we should never forget the superiority of the latter.

This, of course, is precisely what the writer to the Hebrews does throughout his letter. In particular, he compares and contrasts Christ and Moses, the heads of the two covenants:

> Jesus the apostle and high priest of our confession... was faithful to him who appointed him, just as Moses also was faithful in all God's house... Jesus has been counted worthy of more glory than Moses... Moses was faithful in all God's house as a servant, to testify to the things that were to be spoken later, but Christ is faithful over God's house as a son (Heb. 3:1-6).

We know that Moses, in the first covenant, received, and faithfully delivered, the whole law to Israel (Deut. 4:5). Likewise, Christ, in the new covenant, delivered his law to his people:

> The law was given through Moses; grace and truth came through Jesus Christ (John 1:17).
> Long ago, at many times and in many ways, God spoke to our fathers by the prophets, but in these last days he has spoken to us by his Son (Heb. 1:1-2).[7]

Moses, of course, had foretold this:

> The Lord your God will raise up for you a prophet like me from among you, from your brothers – it is to him you shall listen... The Lord said to me... 'I will raise up for them a prophet like you from among their brothers. And I will put my words in his mouth, and he shall speak to them all that I command him. And whoever will not listen to my words that he shall speak in my name, I myself will require it of him' (Deut. 18:15-19).

Now, I admit, we are not told explicitly that whereas Moses gave Israel 'his' law, Jesus has given his law to his new Israel, 'the Israel of God' (Gal. 6:16). But note the context linking 'the law of Christ' (Gal. 6:2) and 'the Israel of God'.[8] Moreover, when we

---

[7] As the prophets' words were written down as authoritative revelation, so were Christ' (and his apostles').

[8] By the context, I mean that these two verses come in the closing words of the letter to the Galatians, one of the major New Testament books

are told that God has spoken to us by Christ, it does not mean that Christ was a mere channel of information. The truth is, like Moses, Christ was a lawgiver, issuing his law repeatedly throughout his ministry, principally in his Sermon on the Mount (Matt. 5 – 7), his last great discourse (John 12:47-50; 13:1 – 16:33), and in his great commission before his ascension (Matt. 28:18-20). Even a cursory glance at the Gospels will confirm it.

John Reisinger, in his *In Defense of Jesus, the New Lawgiver*, answering Richard Barcellos' book *In Defense of the Decalogue: A Critique of New Covenant Theology*, asked:

> Whether Moses is the greatest lawgiver that ever lived, including the Lord Jesus Christ himself or whether Jesus replaced Moses as the new prophet and lawgiver in the very same sense as he replaced Aaron as the new high priest?

He went on:

> These two contrary principles underlie the two positions. New-covenant theology defends [I would say, proclaims] Jesus as the new, greater, full and final lawgiver who replaces Moses. We insist that the laws of Christ, given to the children of the kingdom of grace, make higher demands than those given by God to Israel at Sinai... We insist that Christ is the new lawgiver... To view Christ as only an exegete, even as the greatest exegete, is to reduce the Sermon on the Mount to nothing more than a true and spiritual understanding of the law given to Moses... New covenant theology prefers to view the Sermon on the Mount as a vital part of the new law of the kingdom of grace given by the new prophet and king of the church.[9]

---

dealing with the subject of law. The two topics, 'the law of Christ' and 'the Israel of God', therefore, cannot be mere throwaways. Indeed, it would be nearer the truth to call them the climax to the letter: 'Do not go back to the law of Moses or pagan law. You are no longer old Israel or pagans (Gal. 3:26-29). You are the Israel of God (1 Pet. 2:9-10; see also Eph. 2:19; Phil. 3:20), and you have your own new law: the law of Christ'. Furthermore, do not forget that Galatians is the earliest New Testament book: the apostle put down this vital marker right at the start of the history of the church.

[9] John G.Reisinger: *In Defense of Jesus, the New Lawgiver* pp12-16.

Christ, in his Sermon on the Mount, not only took some principles from the Mosaic law and made them more intense, he upheld others – in particular the love commandment (Lev. 19:18 – see Matt. 5:43-44) – and made others redundant. Clearly, Christ was not renewing the Mosaic covenant, but, right at the start of the new age, he was instituting his own law for the new covenant. He was setting out a new law, under a new covenant, in a new age, for new men.[10] And as Reisinger said: 'The laws of the kingdom of grace established by our Lord Jesus Christ are higher and more demanding than any laws God ever gave to Israel through Moses'.[11]

This is the point I wish to establish, and White agrees with me: as Moses was Israel's lawgiver, so Christ is the lawgiver for his people. Christ, of course, is far more than his people's lawgiver, but since 'the law of Christ' is the issue under debate, I concentrate on this fact. Christ is the lawgiver in the new covenant. It must be right, therefore, to call his commands 'the law of Christ'; they can be nothing else.

William Gadsby, writing on 'the law of liberty' (Jas. 1:25), having said 'that the Holy Ghost has been pleased to set forth this law by a diversity of terms', began by quoting Isaiah 2:3 and Micah 4:2: 'Out of Zion shall go the law' (see also Jer. 31:33; Ezek. 36:27). Stating that 'this law is called "the law of Christ"... (Gal. 6:2)', he went on:

> The law of works was given by Moses, but this law, which is grace and truth, came by Jesus Christ (John 1:17); for, we are not without law to God, but under the law of Christ (1 Cor. 9:21), for so the passage should be rendered.[12]

Referring to Isaiah 42:1, Gadsby quoted John Gill:

> The gospel, the product of divine wisdom [is] the gospel of God, whose judgment is according to truth, the rule of human judgment in things spiritual and saving, and by which Christ judges and rules in the hearts of his people. This he brought forth

---

[10] See my *Christ* especially pp236-241,493-500, and my 'The Law the Believer's Rule?'

[11] Reisinger p9. See my 'The Penetrating Law of Christ'.

[12] Gadsby went into details, stressing the 'of'.

out of his Father's bosom, out of his own heart, and published it in person to the Jews, and, by his apostles, to the Gentiles, who, being converted by it, became subject to his rule and government.

Gadsby went on, referring to Isaiah 42:4, the isles waiting for the law of the Messiah: 'Now... what law can this be?' Gadsby asked. 'Surely not the killing letter [2 Cor. 3:6-9]! No. It is the precious gospel by which he judges and rules in the hearts of his people – a law quite distinct from the law of Moses'. On 'a law shall proceed from me' (Isa. 51:4), Gadsby declared:

[It came] from Christ the Head of his church. [It was] not the Sinai law, but the gospel, the law of Christ. It is the very same law mentioned in Isaiah 2:3... This is Zion's law... delivered by Zion's King to the children of Zion, the church of the living God. And this law, gospel, doctrine, or word is by way of eminence called 'the word of the kingdom' (Matt. 13:19), 'the word of salvation' (Acts 13:26), 'the word of the gospel' (Col. 1:5), 'the word of God's grace' (Acts 20:32), 'the word of faith' (Rom. 10:8), 'the word of reconciliation' (2 Cor. 5:19), 'the word of life' (Phil. 2:16; 1 John 1:1), 'the word of Christ' (Col. 3:16), 'the faithful word' (Tit. 1:9), 'the word of the oath' (Heb. 7:28), 'the word of Christ's patience' (Rev. 3:10), and 'the word of the saint's testimony' (Rev. 12:11). This is the word of the Lord that went from Jerusalem, the vision of peace; and a precious word it is. It is the word or law of Christ, the Prince of Peace, the sceptre of his kingdom, which is a right sceptre (Ps. 45:6; Heb. 1:8) and rod of his strength by which he rules his people... There is no law so strong and forcible, so attracting and engaging, or that is so cheerfully obeyed, as this precious gospel, which is the law of the Spirit of life in Christ Jesus... This law is called 'the law of faith' (Rom. 3:27)... The gospel [is] the law of faith... It is the gospel that faith obeys and by which it walks... The... 'obedience to the faith' (Rom. 1:5)... By 'faith' here is not meant the grace of faith, but the doctrine of faith, which is the truth of the gospel of God... If the gospel be no rule of obedience... I am at a loss to know what the apostle meant when he tells us that 'the mystery, which was kept secret since the world began, but now is made manifest, and by the scriptures of the prophets, according to the commandment of the everlasting God, [is] made known to all nations for the obedience of faith' (Rom. 16:25-26)... How can this precious gospel be more clearly

88

revealed, and made known by the commandment of God, for the obedience of faith, if it be no rule of obedience?... The gospel is called the truth in direct opposition to the law (John 1:17).[13]

White recognised the obvious, self-evident link between commands and law – indeed, their virtual interchangeability: '"law" conveys its instructions by "commands" or "commandments"', he said. I agree! So, when we read 'law' we read 'commandment', and when we read 'commandment' we read 'law'. If we are talking about Moses, we are talking about the law of Moses; if we are talking about Christ, we are talking about the law of Christ. Whenever we read of Christ issuing a command, we are reading an element of his law. And it's not just in the literal use of 'commandment' or 'law', is it? Consider Jesus' final statement to his disciples:

> All authority in heaven and on earth has been given to me. Go therefore and make disciples of all nations, baptising them in the name of the Father and of the Son and of the Holy Spirit, teaching them to observe all that I have commanded you. And behold, I am with you always, to the end of the age (Matt. 28:18-20).

New converts have to be taught to observe everything Christ 'commanded'. Now what else can this be but Christ's law? But notice the opening of this commission. While the word 'command' is not used, what else do all the imperatives amount to but Christ's command to his people for all time: 'Go... make... baptise... teach'? As White agreed, when we meet 'law' we meet 'commandment', and when we meet 'commandment' we are in the realm of 'law' – whether or not we are talking about Moses or Christ. 'The law of Christ', as a phrase, is rare in the New Testament, but as a concept it pervades it.

Nor must 'the law of Christ' be limited to Christ's own words. As we shall see, in the very discourse where he was most clearly issuing his 'new commandment' to his disciples, Christ explicitly told them that he would give the Spirit in order to give them the

---

[13] William Gadsby: 'The Perfect Law of Liberty or the Glory of God revealed in the Gospel' in *Freedom From The Law*, CBO Publications, Ossett, 2015, pp48-78. See my 'The Obedience of Faith'.

full revelation of his word – that is, his law: the Spirit would lead the apostles into all truth and so, through that revelation, grant them foundational authority over all believers for all time (1 Cor. 3:10-11; Eph. 2:20; Rev. 21:14). Therefore it is no surprise to read the apostles insisting on this right to issue commands in the name of Christ; that is, the law of Christ.

Just one example must suffice:

> Paul, an apostle – not from men nor through man, but through Jesus Christ and God the Father, who raised him from the dead – and all the brothers who are with me: To the churches of Galatia... I am astonished that you are so quickly deserting him who called you in the grace of Christ and are turning to a different gospel – not that there is another one, but there are some who trouble you and want to distort the gospel of Christ. But even if we or an angel from heaven should preach to you a gospel contrary to the one we preached to you, let him be accursed. As we have said before, so now I say again: If anyone is preaching to you a gospel contrary to the one you received, let him be accursed. For am I now seeking the approval of man, or of God? Or am I trying to please man? If I were still trying to please man, I would not be a servant of Christ. For I would have you know, brothers, that the gospel that was preached by me is not man's gospel. For I did not receive it from any man, nor was I taught it, but I received it through a revelation of Jesus Christ (Gal. 1:1-11).

Notice that Paul thought it was essential to open his letter to the Galatians in this way, which letter, as I remarked before, is the earliest New Testament document. Combining this with the way he finished the letter, we can see how the apostle put down two vital markers right at the start of the history of the church: under the direct authority of Christ, he, and the other apostles, would, by the Spirit, set out the full revelation of the glories of the new covenant (Eph. 3:1-12), and, of course, in so doing, they would flesh out Christ's one great commandment, and all, by writing Scripture (2 Tim. 3:14-17; 2 Pet. 3:14-18).

To summarise thus far: Christ issued his law to his people both in his own lifetime and through his apostles by his Spirit after Pentecost. And all this revelation, of course, is found objectively only in the written Scriptures. For obvious reasons, the Spirit's writing of Christ's law on the heart cannot fulfil that role. Hence, the Scriptures must be right at the heart of the law of Christ.

Christ's new-covenant commandment

Here are the words:

> A new commandment I give to you, that you love one another: just as I have loved you, you also are to love one another (John 13:34).

How should we understand Christ's words? How did his immediate hearers understand them? As one literal command? Surely not. In giving his apostles this one command he was clearly giving them an envelope containing a whole body of commands and principles, exhortations and instructions in summary form. Or, putting it another way, he was giving them a covering umbrella, a synopsis, to encapsulate or embody his entire law. It was, as it were, Jesus' text for this vital sermon or discourse in which he issued his law. It was the overall précis, summary or digest of what he was going to say, delineating its overall end, purpose and scope. It is as Paul told the Romans when referring to the Mosaic law:

> The commandments, 'You shall not commit adultery, You shall not murder, You shall not steal, You shall not covet', and any other commandment, are summed up in this word: 'You shall love your neighbour as yourself' (Rom. 13:9).

We may justly accommodate the apostle's words: 'The law of Christ is summed up in this word: "A new commandment I give to you, that you love one another: just as I have loved you, you also are to love one another (John 13:34)"'.

M.R.Vincent on 'commandment':

> The word [is used] for a single commandment or injunction, but [is] used also for the whole body of the moral precepts of Christianity... This new commandment embodies the essential principle of the whole law.

Clearly this is right. Notice how Christ both preceded and followed his statement with a whole continuous stream of commandments. Moreover, note how, within this series of commands, he indicated that this discourse was designedly incomplete. Do not miss the fact that it was in this very discourse that he issued his promise of the Spirit to lead the apostles into the full and complete revelation of what he had wanted to say, both here and throughout his ministry. And he was not content to leave it at saying it once! All this prepares us for post-Pentecost Scriptures: the apostles would flesh out the encapsulating principle of 'the one new-covenant commandment'. This is why I am sure that the answer to my chosen question in the title of this article is that Christ's one commandment encapsulates the apostolic Scriptures as the law of Christ. We are talking about many commands in one. The closing book of Scripture makes it clear enough when it speaks of 'the endurance of the saints', 'those who keep the commandments of God and hold to the testimony of Jesus', 'those who keep the commandments of God and the faith of Jesus' (Rev. 12:17; 14:12). We are indeed, speaking of many commandments.

Let me quote the relevant scriptures in John 13 – 16. First, the one overall commandment:

> A new commandment I give to you, that you love one another: just as I have loved you, you also are to love one another (John 13:34).

Now for the series of commandments within Christ's discourse:

> You call me Teacher and Lord, and you are right, for so I am. If I then, your Lord and Teacher, have washed your feet, you also ought to wash one another's feet. For I have given you an example, that you also should do just as I have done to you... If you love me, you will keep my commandments... Whoever has my commandments and keeps them, he it is who loves me... Whoever does not love me does not keep my words. And the word that you hear is not mine but the Father's who sent me... Abide in me... If you keep my commandments, you will abide in my love, just as I have kept my Father's commandments and abide in his love. These things I have spoken to you, that my joy may be in you, and that your joy may be full. This is my commandment, that you love one another as I have loved you. Greater love has no one than this, that someone lay down his life for his friends. You are my friends if you do what I command

92

you... These things I command you, so that you will love one another (John 13:13-15; 14:15,21,24; 15:4,10-14,17).

And now, within this last great discourse, replete as it is with Christ's commandments gathered under the umbrella of his one 'new commandment', we meet the far-reaching promise of the gift and ministry of the Spirit to enable the apostles to complete the task of setting out Christ's law for all his people for all time, to the end of the age:

> These things I have spoken to you while I am still with you. But the Helper, the Holy Spirit, whom the Father will send in my name, he will teach you all things and bring to your remembrance all that I have said to you... When the Helper comes, whom I will send to you from the Father, the Spirit of truth, who proceeds from the Father, he will bear witness about me... I have said all these things to you to keep you from falling away... I have said these things to you that... you may remember that I told them to you... I still have many things to say to you, but you cannot bear them now. When the Spirit of truth comes, he will guide you into all the truth, for he will not speak on his own authority, but whatever he hears he will speak, and he will declare to you the things that are to come. He will glorify me, for he will take what is mine and declare it to you. All that the Father has is mine; therefore I said that he will take what is mine and declare it to you (John 14:25-26; 15:26; 16:1,4,12-15).

In light of this, as I said under the first heading, it is no surprise to read the apostles insisting on the right to issue commands in the name of Christ. And what else can this be but the 'the law of Christ'?

If we imagine ourselves back in the very early days of the church, just after Pentecost, discussing Christ's promise, what do you think might be going through our minds? Whether or not we would have foreseen, by the apostolic writings, issued in the name and authority of Christ, a mushrooming of myriad instructions, commandments and exhortations explaining, expanding, enlarging upon and enforcing his one great commandment, I cannot say. But, this is precisely what happened. Take Paul and John:

If anyone thinks that he is a prophet, or spiritual, he should acknowledge that the things I am writing to you are a command of the Lord (1 Cor. 14:37).

We have confidence in the Lord about you, that you are doing and will do the things that we command. May the Lord direct your hearts to the love of God and to the steadfastness of Christ. Now we command you, brothers, in the name of our Lord Jesus Christ, that you keep away from any brother who is walking in idleness and not in accord with the tradition that you received from us. For you yourselves know how you ought to imitate us... [We gave you] an example to imitate. For even when we were with you, we would give you this command... We command and encourage [you] in the Lord Jesus Christ... Brothers, do not grow weary in doing good. If anyone does not obey what we say in this letter, take note of that person, and have nothing to do with him, that he may be ashamed. Do not regard him as an enemy, but warn him as a brother (2 Thess. 3:4-15).

As I urged you when I was going to Macedonia, remain at Ephesus so that you may charge certain persons... The aim of our charge is love that issues from a pure heart and a good conscience and a sincere faith... I received mercy for this reason, that in me, as the foremost, Jesus Christ might display his perfect patience as an example[14] to those who were to believe in him for eternal life... This charge I entrust to you, Timothy, my child, in accordance with the prophecies previously made about you, that by them you may wage the good warfare... (1 Tim. 1:3,5,16,18).

Follow the pattern[15] of the sound words that you have heard from me, in the faith and love that are in Christ Jesus (2 Tim. 1:13).[16]

Beloved, I am writing you no new commandment, but an old commandment that you had from the beginning. The old commandment is the word that you have heard. At the same time, it is a new commandment that I am writing to you, which is true in him and in you... This is the message that you have

---

[14] 'Example', 'pattern', *hupotupōsis.*

[15] See previous note.

[16] Do not miss the role of the *commanding* army officer (2 Tim. 2:4, NIV) and, especially, the need to compete *lawfully, nomimōs,* according to the *rules* (2 Tim. 2:5), in the illustrations which Paul immediately set out in which he used the same word as in: 'The law [of Moses] is good, if one uses it *lawfully'* (1 Tim.1:8). Clearly, we are in the realm of new-covenant law.

heard from the beginning, that we should love one another... this is his commandment, that we believe in the name of his Son Jesus Christ and love one another, just as he has commanded us. Whoever keeps his commandments abides in God, and God in him... We are from God. Whoever knows God listens to us; whoever is not from God does not listen to us. By this we know the Spirit of truth and the spirit of error (1 John 2:7-8; 3:11,23-24; 4:6).[17]
I rejoiced greatly to find some of your children walking in the truth, just as we were commanded by the Father. And now I ask you, dear lady – not as though I were writing you a new commandment, but the one we have had from the beginning – that we love one another. And this is love, that we walk according to his commandments; this is the commandment, just as you have heard from the beginning, so that you should walk in it (2 John 4-6).

And this is only the merest sample of the apostles issuing a stream of commands, rules and principles, accompanied by spiritual motives, all with the authority of Christ and in his name; in other words, giving believers the law of Christ. Not wishing to extend this article, I limit myself to just one comment, by Gill, on 1 Corinthians 14:37:

Let him acknowledge that the things that I write unto you are the commandments of the Lord; if he is a true prophet, and really a spiritual man, he will clearly see, and therefore ought to own, that the rules here prescribed... are perfectly agreeable to the commands of Christ, and are to be esteemed as such, being delivered under the influence and direction of his Spirit; and which the prophet and spiritual man must discern and allow, if they have the Spirit of God; for whatever was commanded by the apostles under divine inspiration, was all one as if immediately commanded by Christ himself.

---

[17] Compare these words of Christ: 'Whoever is of God hears the words of God' (John 8:47). 'Everyone who is of the truth listens to my voice' (John 18:37). Gill on John 18:37: 'Hears [Christ's] voice, the voice of his gospel, and that not only externally, but internally, so as to approve of it, rejoice at it, and distinguish it – and the voice of his commands, so as cheerfully to obey them from a principle of love to him'.

And here is an example of Paul, taking Christ's commandment (using the decalogue), and expanding it for believers, and in precise detail:

> Owe no one anything, except to love each other, for the one who loves another has fulfilled the law. For the commandments, 'You shall not commit adultery, You shall not murder, You shall not steal, You shall not covet', and any other commandment, are summed up in this word: 'You shall love your neighbour as yourself'. Love does no wrong to a neighbour; therefore love is the fulfilling of the law. Besides this you know the time, that the hour has come for you to wake from sleep. For salvation is nearer to us now than when we first believed. The night is far gone; the day is at hand. So then let us cast off the works of darkness and put on the armour of light. Let us walk properly as in the daytime, not in orgies and drunkenness, not in sexual immorality and sensuality, not in quarrelling and jealousy. But put on the Lord Jesus Christ, and make no provision for the flesh, to gratify its desires (Rom. 13:8-14).

And so it goes on, right to the end of Romans.

From all this, we can see that Christ issued his law to his people both in his own lifetime and through his apostles by his Spirit after Pentecost. Was this just for the first disciples? Of course not! So where shall we, today, read the law of Christ, the apostolic pattern, rules and commandments, as issued directly by Christ and then by his Spirit though his apostles? Only in the written Scriptures! Hence, the Scriptures must be right at the heart of the law of Christ.[18]

The first believers had the original manuscripts (not all at once, of course). Surely they regarded those precious documents as the word or law of Christ to them directly. This, surely, was one of the main reasons which moved later believers to gather all these scattered documents, Scriptures (2 Pet. 3:14-18) and

---

[18] '[Moses] at Mount Sinai... received living oracles to give to us' (Acts 7:38). 'The Jews were entrusted with the oracles of God' (Rom. 3:2). 'Though by this time you ought to be teachers, you need someone to teach you again the basic principles of the oracles of God' (Heb. 5:12). 'Whoever speaks, [let him be] as one who speaks oracles of God' (1 Pet. 4:11).

preserve and publish them in one volume. They recognised their authority, their value and purpose. They knew that Paul's command to Timothy applied to them in their day, and they wanted succeeding generations of believers to have the same. This is our inheritance. Taking our Bible, reading it through its apostolic interpretation and application, we know we have Christ's law to us. In particular, we know that the apostolic command to Timothy applies to us, as it has to all the saints ever since the apostle issued it:

> Continue in what you have learned and have firmly believed... the sacred writings, which are able to make you wise for salvation through faith in Christ Jesus. All Scripture is breathed out by God and profitable for teaching, for reproof, for correction, and for training in righteousness, that the man of God may be complete, equipped for every good work (2 Tim. 3:14-17).

Christ's use of Leviticus 19:18 and Deuteronomy 6:5

Let me re-state what I said at the start. White, taking 'A new commandment I give to you, that you love one another: just as I have loved you, you also are to love one another' (John 13:34), and linking this with Moses and the old covenant, he asserts:

> The 'new commandment' of Christ will stand in the same place in this new covenant as the ten commandments had in the old, Mosaic covenant.

He goes on to refer to John 13:34-35; 14:15-24; 15:9-17, saying: 'Here... is the sum of that which is termed 'the law of Christ'.

This is highly significant. White here says that as the old-covenant law had its summary, so does the new. I agree. But I go on to maintain that just as the old-covenant summary did not do away with the full version of that law, with its detailed commandants, but, rather, complemented it, neither does the new-covenant equivalent of Christ's law do away with its full version. What is more, as with the old covenant, Israel had the law's summary written on stone tables, with the full version in the Book of the Law, so, in the new covenant, Christ's law is written on the heart of his people and in the external Scriptures.

We can go further. Deuteronomy 6:5 (the first table) with Leviticus 19:18 (the second table) is the biblical summary of the entire law. Jesus said so (Matt. 22:37-40). But just as this summary did not do away with the entire law of 613 commandments, neither does Christ's one commandment – which, as I have explained, represents a synopsis of his entire law – do away with the entire body of commandments and imperatives in the rest of the New Testament.[19] In other words, Jesus' use of Leviticus 19:18 and Deuteronomy 6:5 confirms the way we must regard the Scriptures as an integral part of the law of Christ.

This approach, in particular, to Leviticus 19:18 is important. It comes entirely and only from Christ. Before his use of the verse, followed by Paul writing his letters to the churches, there are no explicit references to the verse in Jewish writings.[20] In clear contrast, in the New Testament this verse is the most frequently quoted passage from the Pentateuch (Rom. 13:9; Gal. 5:14; Jas. 2:8). This can only mean that the apostolic emphasis on Leviticus 19:18 is particularly and especially a gospel emphasis, deriving from Christ himself, who first used it in this way (Matt. 5:43-44; 19:19; 22:39; Mark 12:31; Luke 10:27). Thus an undisputable link is established between Leviticus 19:18 and Christ's law. With the apostolic use of Leviticus 19:18, following on from Christ's use of it, we are firmly in the realm of Christ, not Moses, as lawgiver.

---

[19] For one thing, Christ's new-commandment has no reference to loving, serving and obeying God himself, but who can doubt that this belongs to Christ's law?

[20] 'Explicit references to Lev. 19:18 are lacking in Jewish literature before Paul... In contrast, Lev. 19:18 is the Pentateuchal passage most often cited in the New Testament... The stimulus to focus thus on Lev. 19:18 must therefore be peculiarly Christian and is best explained as deriving from Jesus himself'. (James D.G.Dunn: *The Epistle to the Galatians*, A & C Black, London, 1993, p291. Ben Witherington: *Grace in Galatia: A Commentary on... Paul's Letter to the Galatians*, T.&T.Clark, Edinburgh, 1998, p383 agreed, but noted a Qumran reference.

Using the fact that the ten commands and/or Leviticus 19:18 (with Deuteronomy 6:5) summarises the entire law, let me extend the thought a little. No Jew could work out for himself all the individual commandments by using the summary; he needed all the detailed commandments in addition.[21] What is more, God himself, having written the decalogue on the stone tablets, insisted that the full law had to be written in a book – and not only in the book of the law, but on the door posts, and elsewhere:

> And Moses wrote down all the words of the Lord... Then he took the Book of the Covenant and read it in the hearing of the people... 'Come up to me on the mountain and wait there, that I may give you the tablets of stone, with the law and the commandment, which I have written for their instruction' (Ex. 24:4,7,12).
> And the Lord said to Moses: 'Write these words, for in accordance with these words I have made a covenant with you and with Israel'... And he wrote on the tablets the words of the covenant, the ten commandments (Ex. 34:27-28).
> You shall bind them as a sign on your hand, and they shall be as frontlets between your eyes. You shall write them on the doorposts of your house and on your gates. (Deut. 6:8-9; see also 11:18-20).
> Take this Book of the Law and put it by the side of the ark of the covenant of the Lord your God, that it may be there for a witness against you (Deut. 31:26).

Hence the stone tablets, the book of the law, and the household and personal writing of the words of the law, were integral to the covenant.

All this plays into the new covenant. The new covenant is undeniably superior to the old in many respects – not least that God's law is now written on the heart. But this in no way mitigates against the written law of Christ in Scripture.

Let me take one example (as used by White also). James, having referred to what he called 'the royal law according to the Scripture' (Jas. 2:8), which is Leviticus 19:18 in the hands of

---

[21] Take Deut. 14:1-21 for instance.

Christ,[22] commanded his readers: 'So speak and so do as those who will be judged by the law of liberty' (Jas. 2:12). Making a contrast with the law of Moses, he speaks of another law, the 'royal law', the fulfilment of Leviticus 19:18 (Rom. 13:9; Gal. 5:14), which can be none other than 'the law of Christ' (Gal. 6:2), 'this rule' by which the Israel of God must walk (Gal. 6:16; Phil. 3:16), 'the law towards Christ' or 'Christ's law' (1 Cor. 9:21), 'the law of faith' (Rom. 3:27),[23] 'the law of the Spirit of life in Christ Jesus' (Rom. 8:2), the gospel. *This* is the law by which believers must live and by which they will be judged. *This* is the easy yoke and light burden which Christ enables his people to delight in, that law which encompasses the entire word of God, as interpreted and applied by Christ and the apostles in the new covenant. This is the law by which believers will be judged. All this raises an important question: How can believers be judged by a law if that law is not objective? This, it seems to me, makes it inevitable that the law of Christ must include the objective, written Scriptures. James had already said enough to make this point:

> Put away all filthiness and rampant wickedness and receive with meekness the implanted word, which is able to save your souls. But be doers of the word, and not hearers only, deceiving yourselves. For if anyone is a hearer of the word and not a doer, he is like a man who looks intently at his natural face in a mirror. For he looks at himself and goes away and at once forgets what he was like. But the one who looks into the perfect law, the law of liberty, and perseveres, being no hearer who forgets but a doer who acts, he will be blessed in his doing (Jas. 1:21-25).

Yes, 'the word' is 'implanted' in the believer, but, clearly, it is also external and objective. A believer has to 'hear the word',

---

[22] I see in the 'royal' a reference to the law of Christ the King. Moo thought 'royal' 'is probably an allusion to Jesus' own teaching' (Moo: 'The Law' p217).

[23] The word is *kanōn* in Gal. 6:16 and Phil. 3:16, 'any rule or standard, a principle or law' (see Joseph Henry Thayer: *A Greek-English Lexicon of the New Testament*, Baker Book House, Grand Rapids, Ninth Printing 1991). 'Law' in Rom. 3:27 could aptly be translated 'rule'. In other words, 'the rule of faith'.

'look into the word', 'look into the perfect law', not merely look into his heart, and listen to the inward voice. Above all he has to do it, and will be judged by it (Jas. 2:12). How is this possible unless that 'word', that 'perfect law' is objective? What else can it mean? James' words make sense only if he is talking about the Scriptures as a vital part of the law of Christ, that law which is over believers, that law which forms the objective standard by which they will be judged. Of course, James is referring primarily to the Old Testament, but 2 Timothy 3:14-17 and 2 Peter 3:14-18 warrant the extension of his words to the New Testament. They more than warrant it; they ensure it.

Thomas R.Schreiner:

> I have argued from both Galatians and 1 Corinthians that the law of Christ should be defined as the law of love. We see in 1 Corinthians 9 that Paul's flexibility and sacrifice on behalf of his hearers represents the same kind of sacrificial love that Christ displayed in going to the cross. The life of Christ, then, exemplifies the law of love. It would be a mistake to conclude that there are no moral norms in the law of Christ, for Romans 13:8–10 makes it clear, as do many other texts in Paul, that the life of love cannot be separated from moral norms.[24]

My question is: Where shall we find these 'moral norms' but in the Scriptures? Thus, accommodating Schreiner's words, Christ's commandment to love cannot be separated from the objective written Scriptures. Christ's one commandment does not remove the Scriptures from the law of Christ. Rather, it guarantees that the Scriptures are at the heart of his law. In a sermon on Romans 13:8-10, Schreiner declared:

> There are two mistakes that we may fall into when defining love. What is the first blunder in judgment? The first mistake is to say that since love fulfils the law we no longer have any need for commandments. Some understand these verses to say that the only moral guideline Christians need is love. After all, verse 8 says that the only thing we owe one another is love, and that the one who loves his neighbour has fulfilled the law. Furthermore, verse 9 says that the different commands of the [Mosaic] law are

---

[24] Thomas R.Schreiner: *40 Questions About Christians and Biblical Law*, Kregel, 2010, p103.

summed up in love. They argue, therefore, that we do not actually need commandments anymore. All we need to ask ourselves about any course of action is the question found in verse 10. Does our action actually hurt our neighbour? If it does not hurt our neighbour, if it does our neighbour good, then that action must be loving, and thus we fulfil the law, for Paul says in verse 10 that love is the fulfilment of the law. Those who believe this way bristle against imposing any commands upon believers. They think this is a form of legalism. They condemn as legalism any commands which say 'you should do this', or 'you should not do this'. They insist that believers are not under any 'commands', except the command to love one another.

Schreiner went on:

I want to put the spotlight on the massive error that is found in this view. When Paul says that love is the fulfilment of the law, he does not intend to say that we have no need for commandments. To say that love is the fulfilment of the law does not imply that we can dispense with all commandments. Instead, specific commandments are mentioned in verse 9 so that we will see how love looks in action. One cannot commit adultery, murder, steal, and covet and claim to be loving. Specific commandments are given so that we will see in a concrete and practical way how love manifests itself in everyday life.

He concluded:

We must let God's word in the Scriptures define for us what is loving. Otherwise, we will fall prey to the deception of the world. To sum up [this] point, certainly love involves more than the keeping of commandments, but it never involves anything less than keeping them. Love goes beyond the keeping of God's law, but it never goes around the keeping of God's law. Commandments guard us from inadequate definitions of love and provide us with an objective standard by which we can test our lives. If we claim to be walking in love but fail to keep God's commandments, then our profession is contradicted by our practice.[25]

---

[25] Sermon by Thomas R.Schreiner: 'Loving One Another Fulfils the Law: Romans 13:8-10'.

I ask again: Where will we find 'God's law, God's commandments'? Israel found the law of God for them – the Mosaic law – in the Scriptures as far as they had been completed in their day. Where can we, as believers, find the law of Christ? In all Scripture, of course. For a start, see 2 Timothy 3:14-17 and 2 Peter 3:14-18.

Stephen J.Wellum:

All Scripture is authoritative and thus provides the norm for Christian ethics. What is our standard for ethics? How do we establish moral norms? The simple answer: all of Scripture is our standard and it alone establishes moral norms. In this regard, 2 Timothy 3:15-17 is a crucial text. Paul describes Scripture, specifically the Old Testament, as God's breathed-out word and thus fully authoritative for Christians. In other words, the entire Old Testament, including the law-covenant, [along with, now, the New Testament] functions for us as the basis [better, authority] for our doctrine and ethics. Although Christians are not 'under the law' as a covenant, it still functions as Scripture and demands our complete obedience[26]... Christian ethics is not antinomian... Our triune God has not left us to ourselves; Scripture is our sufficient and authoritative moral standard... We determine what is morally binding upon us today by appealing to the entirety of Scripture viewed through the lens of Christ and the new covenant. Although Christians are not 'under the [Mosaic] law' as a covenant, it still functions for us as [part of] Scripture. As with any biblical text, however, before we directly apply it to our lives, we must first place it in its covenantal location and then, second, we must think through how that text points forward, anticipates, and is fulfilled in Christ. It is only by doing this that we correctly apply any biblical text to our lives as Christians... In answering the question – what is the moral law for Christians today? – we... first gladly confess that the entirety of Scripture is our standard. But we must simultaneously add that all of Scripture's moral teaching is only binding upon us in light of its fulfilment in Christ... Both the replacement and fulfilment of the old covenant by the new is taught in the New

---

[26] Wellum noted that on this point we should see Brian S.Rosner: *Paul and the Law: Keeping the Commandments of God*, Downers Grove, InterVarsity Press, 2013, p31.

Testament.[27] On the one hand, in the new covenant, the old is replaced by the law of Christ (1 Cor. 9:20-21). Instead of reliance upon the law [of Moses], we rely upon Christ (Gal. 2:19-20; Phil. 3:4-14), and we discern God's will in Christ and apostolic instruction (Gal. 6:2; 1 Cor. 7:19; 9:21). As Rosner contends: 'Christians are not under the law of Moses, but under the law of Christ, the law of faith and the law of the Spirit. We have died to the [Mosaic] law, Christ lives in us and we live by faith in the Son of God... We do not keep the [Mosaic] law, but fulfil the law [of Moses] in Christ and through love. We do not seek to walk according to the [Mosaic] law, but according to the truth of the gospel, in Christ, in newness of resurrection life, by faith, in the light and in step with the Spirit'[28]... In order for Christians, then, to determine what God's moral law is, we must apply all of Scripture in light of Christ.[29]

Fred G.Zaspel:

Even as redeemed men and women we struggle against remaining sin. God in grace through Christ has broken sin's previously over-powering grip (Rom. 6), but we are men and women caught between two worlds. We have been redeemed out of this present world and are citizens of heaven, enthroned with Christ himself. Yet we live in this present evil world and feel the downward tug of it. We are properly living in two worlds and are torn in two very [*sic*] opposing directions. We are sanctified in Christ Jesus and feel the overwhelming force of his powerful grace at work in us drawing us to ever higher levels of glory. But in our struggle with sin we are a walking civil war (Gal. 5:17).[30] This, in turn, is one of the great reasons why God has given us his law.[31] It provides for us an objective standard to correct the

---

[27] See Rosner pp111-134.

[28] Rosner p134.

[29] Stephen J.Wellum: 'Progressive Covenantalism and the Doing of Ethics'.

[30] While I agree that we are in such a war, I disagree with Zaspel's view of this verse. See my *Christ* p150.

[31] The law of God for the believer is the law of Christ. I quote from my *Christ*: 'When, in Scripture, we meet "the law of God", we must ask ourselves which covenant we are talking about. If it is the old covenant, then "the law of God" is the "the law of Moses". If it is the new covenant, then "the law of God" is "the law of Christ"' (my *Christ* pp218-219,483-487). Zaspel would agree. In his review of *New*

confused deceitfulness sin has brought to our hearts. The deceitfulness of sin is such that we seldom stop to consider sin's consequences. We do not adequately consider the evil of sin. There is a blind folly about sin, and we need God's law to inform our conscience to keep us from justifying what it condemns. What a depth of sin resides in our heart!
This is James' point [in James 1:13-18]. We are sinners. We sin because we want to. Our sin is our own fault. Our will is still tainted with a tendency to evil that has not yet been fully eradicated. And this is why our trials carry with them such occasions for sin.[32]

And it is also why we need an objective standard to be over us, to govern our aspirations, emotions, attitudes, wills and actions. And that objective standard is Scripture.

By way of illustration, take the following passage:

Finally, then, brothers, we ask and urge you in the Lord Jesus, that as you received from us how you ought to walk and to please God, just as you are doing, that you do so more and more. For you know what instructions we gave you through the Lord Jesus. For this is the will of God, your [progressive] sanctification [or holiness, footnote]: that you abstain from sexual immorality; that each one of you know how to control his own body in holiness and honour, not in the passion of lust like the Gentiles who do not know God; that no one transgress and wrong his brother in this matter, because the Lord is an avenger in all these things, as we told you beforehand and solemnly warned you. For God has not called us for impurity, but in holiness. Therefore whoever disregards this, disregards not man but God, who gives his Holy Spirit to you. Now concerning

---

Covenant Theology: Description, Definition, Defense, by Tom Wells and Fred Zaspel, Thomas R.Schreiner wrote: 'Wells and Zaspel emphasise that the Mosaic covenant has come to an end with the coming of Jesus Christ... The Sinai covenant has been set aside now that Christ has come. Indeed, the Mosaic covenant points to Christ and is fulfilled in Christ. They do not conclude from this that believers are no longer under moral norms. Rather, believers are subject to the law of Christ, and the law of Christ is discerned from the New Testament'.
[32] Fred G.Zaspel: 'Thoughts from James on Sovereignty, Sin and Grace' in *Ministry of Grace: Essays in Honour of John G.Reisinger*, New Covenant Media, Frederick, 2007, p178.

brotherly love you have no need for anyone to write to you, for you yourselves have been taught by God to love one another, for that indeed is what you are doing to all the brothers throughout Macedonia. But we urge you, brothers, to do this more and more, and to aspire to live quietly, and to mind your own affairs, and to work with your hands, as we instructed you, so that you may walk properly before outsiders and be dependent on no one (1 Thess. 4:1-10).

Notice how the apostle commands believers to be progressively sanctified, how he spells out his meaning in detail, and enforces the love commandment both by the inward work of the Spirit and his own commandment, and all within the compass of the external Scriptures. See also Matthew 5:43-44; Galatians 5:14; Ephesians 5:1-2; Hebrews 13:1; 1 Peter 1:22; 1 John 4:7-12, for instance. The inward teaching of the Spirit does not in the least way diminish the absolute need of the apostolic commands recorded in Scripture.

Conclusion

In light of this, I regard any weakening (however slight at first) of the sense of the binding authority of Scripture upon believers, and their response to it by determined obedience, in the power of the Spirit, to its rule and governance as the law of Christ, as a thoroughly retrograde step, and one to be resisted at all costs. I am convinced that the right exegesis of the relevant scripture passages firmly secures both the inward work of the Spirit in the believer's heart, and the written Scriptures, right at the heart of the law of Christ. I say it is essential for believers to maintain both. Putting it negatively, I assert that believers should stoutly resist any move which might threaten either, or, in the least respect, upset the scriptural balance between the two.

The Obedience of Faith

Synopsis

In this article I trace how those who argue that the believer is not under the law of Christ, and that the Scriptures are not part of the law of Christ, but who emphasise the inward work of the Spirit at the expense of the believer's deliberate obedience to the commands of Scripture, end up with a view of progressive sanctification that is very similar to the hyper-Calvinistic view of conversion.

Introduction

Paul could not have been more explicit in the opening remarks of the letter to the Romans:

> Paul, a servant of Christ Jesus, called to be an apostle, set apart for the gospel of God, which he promised beforehand through his prophets in the holy Scriptures, concerning his Son, who was descended from David according to the flesh and was declared to be the Son of God in power according to the Spirit of holiness by his resurrection from the dead, Jesus Christ our Lord, through whom we have received grace and apostleship to bring about the obedience of faith for the sake of his name among all the nations, including you who are called to belong to Jesus Christ (Rom. 1:1-6).

Paul's readers (hearers) could have been left in no doubt as to the apostle's purpose, both in life and this letter: he wanted to bring as many as possible to 'the obedience of faith'. And, in saying this, he was thinking not only of unbelievers. As he so plainly stated, God had commissioned him 'to bring about the obedience of faith for the sake of his name among all the nations, *including you who are called to belong to Jesus Christ*'. Clearly, he wanted believers, as well as unbelievers, to come to 'the obedience of faith', to produce 'the obedience of faith'. He knew that this was God's work for him, this was God's purpose for his ministry.

Whatever was he talking about? What was he consumed by? What is 'the obedience of faith'?

Speaking of unbelievers, can there be any doubt that the apostle wanted them to hear the gospel, yield to it, submit to Christ, obey the call, invitation and command to repent and believe and so be saved? Of course not. Obedience to the gospel command is a vital aspect of conversion (Acts 5:32; Rom. 2:8; 2 Thess. 1:8; Heb. 5:9; 12:25; 1 Pet. 1:2,22; 3:1; 4:17). It is precisely what we want today, is it not? We want to carry out our Lord's standing commission (Matt. 28:18-20; Mark 16:15-16; Luke 24:47), and preach the gospel to all in order to see as many sinners as possible converted to Christ, as many sinners as possible brought to 'the obedience of faith'. May we live to see 'the word of God continue to increase, and the number of the disciples multiply greatly... and a great many... become obedient to the faith' (see Acts 6:7). 'The weapons of our warfare are not of the flesh but have divine power to destroy strongholds. We destroy arguments and every lofty opinion raised against the knowledge of God, and take every thought captive to obey Christ' (2 Cor. 10:4-5).[1] As far as unbelievers go, this is 'the obedience of faith'.

---

[1] This note applies to this paragraph and the next. John Gill: The person thus affected 'clearly sees Christ to be the alone, able, willing, full, and suitable Saviour, and so becomes obedient to him, both as a Saviour and a King. Such an enlightened soul looks to him alone for life and salvation, ventures on him, and relies upon him, and is desirous and willing to be saved by him in his own way. He receives and embraces all his truths and doctrines with faith and love, and obeys them from the heart, and cheerfully and willingly submits to all his commands and ordinances. For though he is taken by the grace of God, and all his strongholds, reasonings, and high thoughts are demolished by the power of God in the gospel, and he himself is carried captive, yet [it is] not against but with his will [that he is made] to be a voluntary subject of Christ, and cheerfully to submit to the sceptre of his kingdom'. M.R.Vincent in his *Word Studies in the New Testament*: 'The obedience is the new stronghold into which the captives are led. This is indicated by the preposition *eis* "into" or "unto"'. Do not miss how all this follows hard upon 2 Cor. 9:13. See the following note.

But what about believers? Is it not clear that the apostle wanted them to live holy, Christ-like, sanctified lives by believing, submitting to, and obeying Scripture? Of course. Obedience to gospel commands is a vital aspect of progressive sanctification (2 Cor. 2:9; 9:13; 10:4-5; 7:15; 10:6; Gal. 5:7; 2 Thess. 3:14; Philem. 1:21; see faith and works linked in Heb. 11:1-40; Jas. 2:14-26).[2] This is what Paul was talking about. So he knew what he had to do. He had to set out the gospel to inform his readers' minds, yes. But, more than that, he wanted to inform their minds in order to stir their hearts and, in this way, move their wills to obedience to the gospel, to get them to work out its consequences in daily life, and to put it into practice. This is why he wrote his letter to the Romans. And this is what we find. Putting it simplistically, we may say that in the first eleven chapters of his letter the apostle sets out his doctrine, and in the last five chapters he issues his call, and gives his commands, to the believers for their obedience.[3] All this he makes clear right from the start. Could anything be more patent? As far as believers go, this is 'the obedience of faith'.

In light of what is to come, let me stress this. The apostolic way of producing 'the obedience of faith' was to preach the gospel and write Scripture. Naturally, as far as we are concerned, the latter was completed by the apostles, but the standing principle is as plain as a pikestaff: the Scriptures are right at the heart of 'the obedience of faith'. And our mission, as believers, is to do what we can to bring about this 'obedience of faith' – in the conversion of sinners, and the progressive sanctification of saints, beginning with ourselves.

Referring to Matthew 28:18-20, John Piper put it this way:

---

[2] As for 2 Cor. 9:13, see previous note. Paul describes their generosity thus: 'Your submission [obedience, NIV, NASB] that comes from your confession of the gospel of Christ' (2 Cor. 9:13). 'You yield yourselves in willing subjection to the gospel precepts, evinced in acts, as well as in profession' (Jamieson, Fausset and Brown).
[3] Compare the first three and the last three chapters of Ephesians.

The aim of Christian missions is to cause people to obey a new Commander. [Progressive] sanctification is happening where the words of Jesus are being obeyed.[4]

And those 'words of Jesus', and all they encompass, are found in Scripture – Matthew 28:18-20 in the first instance, but *in toto* from Genesis to Revelation as nuanced by the apostles.

Getting back to Romans: Paul clearly felt himself impelled by Christ's commission to bring all to 'the obedience of faith'. He was a driven man. Take Romans as a case in point. As he moves through the letter, although he does not repeatedly use the phrase, nevertheless he keeps returning to 'the obedience of faith', and that by sinners and saints. You can sense how intensely he felt the 'burden' (responsibility) of it, so vital a matter was it to him. Paul wrote Romans – the pinnacle of Scripture – with this as his stated purpose!

Take Romans 6. Having explained that believers are united to Christ, he immediately moves to the consequences of this massive truth, issuing commands and backing them up with an extended and powerful argument:

> Let not sin therefore reign in your mortal body, to make you obey its passions. Do not present your members to sin as instruments for unrighteousness, but present yourselves to God as those who have been brought from death to life, and your members to God as instruments for righteousness. For sin will have no dominion over you, since you are not under law but under grace. What then? Are we to sin because we are not under law but under grace? By no means! Do you not know that if you present yourselves to anyone as obedient slaves, you are slaves of the one whom you obey, either of sin, which leads to death, or of obedience, which leads to righteousness? But thanks be to God that you who were once slaves of sin have become obedient from the heart to the standard of teaching to which you were committed, and, having been set free from sin, have become slaves of righteousness. I am speaking in human terms, because of your natural limitations. For just as you once presented your members as slaves to impurity and to lawlessness leading to more lawlessness, so now present your members as slaves to righteousness leading to sanctification (Rom. 6:12-19).

---

[4] John Piper: 'How the Spirit Sanctifies', a sermon on Rom. 15:14-21.

And so on. It is all here: scriptural exposition to give light to the mind, to warm the heart and thus call for submission of will and obedience of life. In other words, 'the obedience of faith'.

Take Romans 8:12, where the apostle states that believers are 'debtors'; that is, they are obligated (see NIV, NASB). The word *opheiletai* is emphatic. Paul is speaking of those who are 'held by obligation' and the consequent 'duty of people who owe'.[5] Naturally, he includes himself. As he had explained right from the start of the letter, he too was a debtor, he had an obligation: 'I am under obligation (*opheiletēs*) both to Greeks and to barbarians, both to the wise and to the foolish. So I am eager to preach the gospel to you also who are in Rome' (Rom. 1:14-15). He knew that it was by the preaching of the gospel that he could bring sinners and saints to 'the obedience of faith',[6] and he was under 'obligation' to do all he could to bring it about.

Having made sure that he had placed that firmly on the record, on reaching Romans 8, Paul links himself with his readers to declare: 'So then, brothers, we are debtors (*opheiletai*), not to the flesh, to live according to the flesh' (Rom. 8:12). He is telling the Romans the same as the Galatians: 'If [since] we live by the Spirit, let us also keep in step with the Spirit' (Gal. 5:25), let us walk in the Spirit. Now, as I have explained elsewhere,[7] this 'walking in the Spirit' cannot be divorced from determined – though willing and joyful – submission to the Scriptures. The two go hand in hand. No man – sinner or saint – can obey Scripture but by the Spirit, and no man walking in the Spirit can do anything other than regard Scripture as his sovereign rule and guide. Thankfully, in the new covenant, not only is the law of Christ written on the believer's heart *and* in the Scriptures, but every believer has the Spirit. Thus, in Romans 8 and in Galatians 5 – 6, having set out the doctrine of the gospel in writing Scripture, the apostle is calling for obedience of life on the basis of what he has written. Calling for it? He is demanding it! He is

---

[5] See Thayer. *opheilō* is 'to must', to have to, to have a duty to.
[6] As I have explained times without number, preaching is more than 'pulpit work'.
[7] See my 'Believers Under the Law of Christ'.

commanding his readers to obey! Do not misread the 'let us' of Galatians 5:25; it is explained by the 'obligation' of Romans 8:12. He is calling for 'the obedience of faith'; he is writing expressly to get it. Scripture is at the heart of it.

Still he has not exhausted the theme. Take Romans 12. After setting out, in the first eleven chapters of the letter, the most glorious statement of the gospel in all Scripture, the apostle comes to this:

> I appeal to you therefore, brothers, by the mercies of God, to present your bodies as a living sacrifice, holy and acceptable to God, which is your spiritual worship. Do not be conformed to this world, but be transformed by the renewal of your mind, that by testing you may discern what is the will of God, what is good and acceptable and perfect (Rom. 12:1-2).

He appeals for obedience on the basis of his doctrine. But, once again, do not misread the apostle. He might 'appeal', but the apostolic appeal is nothing less than a command! 'In light of the gospel, live lives that reflect it'. This is what he is commanding. He wants 'the obedience of faith'. He is calling for it, demanding it.

And so it goes on, right to the end of the letter. Look how the apostle closes, not forgetting the way he had opened the letter:

> Now to him who is able to strengthen you according to my gospel and the preaching of Jesus Christ, according to the revelation of the mystery that was kept secret for long ages but has now been disclosed and through the prophetic writings has been made known to all nations, according to the command of the eternal God, to bring about the obedience of faith – to the only wise God be glory for evermore through Jesus Christ! Amen (Rom. 16:25-27).

'The obedience of faith'! There is no mistaking it: one of the chief ends of the gospel ministry is to bring both sinners and saints to 'the obedience of faith'. This end is the responsibility that Christ laid on the apostle, right from his conversion, and it explains the apostle's life-long 'obligation' (Rom. 1:14-15). As Christ had made clear to him:

I have appeared to you for this purpose, to appoint you as a servant and witness to the things in which you have seen me and to those in which I will appear to you, delivering you from your people and from the Gentiles – to whom I am sending you to open their eyes, so that they may turn from darkness to light and from the power of Satan to God, that they may receive forgiveness of sins and a place among those who are sanctified by faith in me.

Paul knew what this entailed. As he told Agrippa:

Therefore... I was not disobedient to the heavenly vision, but declared first to those in Damascus, then in Jerusalem and throughout all the region of Judea, and also to the Gentiles, that they should repent and turn to God, performing deeds in keeping with their repentance (Acts 20:16-20).

Do not miss the final clause. Paul did not want conversions in the sense of 'making a decision'. He wanted real conversion leading to life-long obedience to reflect the reality of the repentance. And he wrote and taught Scripture for it, issuing commands in the name of Christ to sinners for their conversion, and then to the converts for their progressive sanctification. It is just as the Lord himself had said at the close of his own earthly ministry:

All authority in heaven and on earth has been given to me. Go therefore and make disciples of all nations, baptising them in the name of the Father and of the Son and of the Holy Spirit, teaching them to observe all that I have commanded you. And behold, I am with you always, to the end of the age (Matt. 28:18-20).

As I have explained, the believer's obedience to the externally written Scriptures arises from the inward writing of the law of Christ in his heart, in the power of the Spirit. *Both the inward and the outward are vital.* The fact that Paul sets all this out so clearly in writing this letter to the Romans is a clear demonstration of it.

D.Martyn Lloyd-Jones on Romans 7:6 raised a very important question: 'What are the differences, in detail, between life lived "in the Spirit" and the old way of living "according to the writing" and "under the law" and "in the flesh"?' He answered it thus:

First, there is the difference between an external and an internal relationship to the law of God, in other words, to morality. This difference is well described in 2 Corinthians 3:3, where Paul says: 'Forasmuch as you are manifestly declared to be the epistle of Christ, ministered by us, written not with ink, but with the Spirit of the living God'. Before, it was, as it were, a writing 'with ink', but it is no longer that, it is now a writing with the Spirit. But, further, 'not in tables of stone' – that is something outside you. Well, where is the writing now? In 'fleshy tables of the heart'. The old law was outside a man, written on stones, written with ink, something you looked at with your physical eyes. That is no longer the position. It is now engraven and written and implanted in the fleshy tables of the heart, in the very centre of the personality, in the deepest recesses of our being. We are no longer looking at something outside ourselves, we are considering something that is already within us, and working within us. Hebrews 8 states it. The author is quoting what Jeremiah had said in the 31st chapter of his prophecy. God says that he is going to make a new covenant with the people – 'not the old covenant that I made with your fathers', but a 'new covenant'. What are the characteristics of the new covenant? 'I will put my laws into their minds, and write them in their hearts'. Before, he had put the laws on tables of stone which he handed to Moses, and Moses brought them down to the people. But in the new covenant he is going to 'put (his) laws into their minds, and (imprint) write them in their hearts'.

Here we meet with a fundamental distinction between the two covenants, the two ways of life. Before you become truly Christian you try to conform to a standard and a pattern outside yourself; but to be a Christian means that the standard is inside you. Of course, in one sense it is still outside, *but the important fact is that it is now inside as well.*[8] You read it in the Word, but it is also in your mind and in your heart. You are not only looking at something external, you are also aware of that which is within. You do not have to be persuaded to look at that which is outside you; there is now a power within you calling your attention to it, a principle operating in the centre of your personality. The same truth is stated in Philippians 2:13: 'Work out your own salvation with fear and trembling. For it is God that works in you (inside you) both to will and to do of his good pleasure'. The apostle rejoices that we have become dead to the

---

[8] My emphasis.

114

law, and that we are delivered from the law which formerly held us because we can now serve 'in newness of Spirit, not in the oldness of the writing'. It is within us, in our minds and in our hearts.

Lloyd-Jones, of course, was addressing a congregation already persuaded of the priority of the written word. Consequently, he rightly stressed the inward work of the Spirit writing the law of Christ on the believer's heart. But in light of what I am talking about here, the same doctrine needs to be stressed the other way round. Both the inward and outward are essential for 'the obedience of faith'.

'The obedience of faith'. Obedience to what? Obedience to Scripture under the impulse of the Spirit. It is this unbreakable link between faith and obedience to Scripture that I now want to develop.

Faith and obedience linked

While the following extract from Romans concerns unbelievers coming to Christ, the underlying principle is precisely the same for the believer.[9] Paul made the point I am trying to stress, thus:

> How then will they call on him in whom they have not believed? And how are they to believe in him of whom they have never heard? And how are they to hear without someone preaching? And how are they to preach unless they are sent?... But they have not all obeyed the gospel... So faith comes from hearing, and hearing through the word of Christ (Rom. 10:14-17).

Paul preached the gospel to bring sinners to faith; that is, to obey the gospel, submit to Christ, obey Christ, receive Christ as Saviour and Lord.[10] And we know what he meant by 'preaching the gospel':

---

[9] I have already made the link; or, rather, as I have shown, Paul did right at the start of Romans.

[10] 'The word of God continued to increase, and the number of the disciples multiplied greatly in Jerusalem, and a great many of the priests became obedient to the faith' (Acts 6:7).

I did not shrink from declaring to you anything that was profitable, and teaching you in public and from house to house, testifying both to Jews and to Greeks of repentance toward God and of faith in our Lord Jesus Christ... I do not account my life of any value nor as precious to myself, if only I may finish my course and the ministry that I received from the Lord Jesus, to testify to the gospel of the grace of God... I have gone about proclaiming the kingdom... I testify to you this day that I am innocent of the blood of all, for I did not shrink from declaring to you the whole counsel of God... For three years I did not cease night or day to admonish every one with tears. And now I commend you to God and to the word of his grace, which is able to build you up and to give you the inheritance among all those who are sanctified (Acts 20:20-32).

Notice that the apostle was talking about his approach to both sinners and saints. Furthermore, do not miss the way he concluded this parting address, commending the saints to God and Scripture – to both, please note – to bring about their continued edification. And he was not thinking of Scripture merely as a source of information for the children of God!

Clearly, faith and obedience to the gospel, obedience to Scripture, are intimately linked, and indissolubly so. It can be put in the negative. Unbelief is disobedience. The condemning sin for sinners is their refusal to obey the gospel and trust Christ as Saviour and Lord (John 3:18,36; 16:7-9). The reward-losing sin for believers is their refusal to obey the commands issued by Christ and the apostles using all Scripture.[11] Unbelief and disobedience – or, faith and obedience – are Siamese twins (Rom. 2:8 with 2 Thess. 2:12, both ESV). The apostle made the link more than once: 'Just as you [Gentiles] were at one time disobedient to God but now have received mercy because of their [Israel's] disobedience, so they too have now been disobedient in order that by the mercy shown to you they also may now receive mercy. For God has consigned all to disobedience, that he may have mercy on all' (Rom. 11:30-32). Again: God complained of

---

[11] While the believer will never be condemned for disobedience, he will lose his reward (1 Cor. 3:8,14-15; 4:5).

Israel that through their unbelief they were 'a disobedient and contrary people' (Rom. 10:21).

All this applies as much to the believer as to the unbeliever: believers have to produce 'the obedience of faith'; not to do it is 'disobedience'. The believer's 'obedience of faith' is his submission to all gospel commands, and the keeping of them. And this law of Christ is written both in the believer's heart and in Scripture.

Many might be asking themselves: Why make such a song and dance about something so obvious? I agree. Or rather, I did agree until very recently – when I discovered that some new-covenant theologians teach in a way that threatens these principles. They say that the believer is *not* under the law of Christ; rather, he has that law written within him by the Spirit, and while the Spirit moves the believer to obedience to Scripture, it is not as a command, imperative, law or rule. Indeed, Scripture is not an integral part of the law of Christ. Moreover, since the believer has the law of Christ written within his heart, and since the Spirit moves him to obedience, there must be no talk of command, duty or accountability when thinking of the believer's obedience to Scripture in his progressive sanctification. True, the believer will obey Scripture, must obey Scripture, but there must be no talk of 'law' in connection with this.[12] All such talk smacks of 'bondage'.

This is wrong. The believer *is* under the law of Christ, and Scripture *is* at the heart of that law. And although the Spirit does move the believer to obedience, even so the believer deliberately obeys Scripture, submitting himself to it as God's commandment and law. It all plays out in 'the obedience of faith'. When a man believes, who does the believing, who does the obeying of the gospel command? Is it God? Or is it the man himself? Is the man responsible? Or is it down to the Spirit? Is the man active or passive? Is his obedience deliberate, or is it some kind of reflex action under the prompting of the Spirit? Does the man consciously obey the commands of Scripture, or does he do it

---

[12] In my 'Believers Under the Law of Christ' I commented on the illogicality at the heart of this.

117

incidentally, indirectly? In all this, the doctrine I am writing against ends up with a passive view of progressive sanctification reminiscent of the old Keswick teaching of 'Let go, and let God'. In fact, it verges towards the hyper-Calvinistic denial of duty faith.

It is this that I wish to examine.

The link with hyper-Calvinism

Let me start at the beginning. As for unbelievers, hyper-Calvinists do not like duty faith. Sinners should not be commanded or invited to trust Christ, they say. Since they are dead in sin, it is not logical to invite or command them to repent and believe. I agree with that last. It isn't logical. But that's not the question. Is it biblical? That is the question! And as I have shown elsewhere, duty faith is biblical. Let me remind you of the definition I used in my *The Gospel Offer is Free*:

Duty faith is the duty, the obligation, the responsibility, of all sinners to trust Christ. The gospel preacher must command all sinners to believe.

I then spelled this out:

A command implies a duty. The gospel commands all sinners to repent; therefore it is their duty to repent. The gospel commands all sinners to believe; therefore it is their duty to believe.[13]

As far as the unbeliever goes, the hyper-Calvinist argues that since the sinner is dead then he has no responsibility to believe and thus obey the gospel. And that's the end of the story. The sinner has to wait patiently, passively attend preaching services and ordinances, waiting, hoping, that God might effectually work in him and grant him assurance that he is redeemed. The man

---

[13] See my *Offer* pp19-34. Please note, it is not the duty of an unconverted sinner to believe that Christ died for him in particular; his duty is to trust Christ. In any case, the sinner cannot know the former until he has done the latter; and even if he could, he would be exercising historical faith, accepting a fact, when what is required is saving faith, reliance upon Christ.

himself has no responsibility to believe, and is not accountable for his unbelief. This is utterly wrong on more than one count.[14]

But in this article I am not concerned with duty faith as it applies to the sinner, the unbeliever, but with the duty of *believers* to obey God's commands in Scripture. As I have shown, dealing with the former raises important principles for the latter. It is the believer's duty to obey the commands of Scripture. This obedience is an integral part of being under the law of Christ. In coming to faith in Christ, believers are united to Christ, delivered from the bondage of the Mosaic law, and brought under the easy yoke of their Redeemer. In other words, they are under his law. From the moment of their conversion, as Paul explains in Romans 6:15 – 7:6, they are slaves of Christ, and married to him, subject to his law (Eph. 5:22-24; Col. 3:18; Tit. 2:5; 1 Pet. 3:1). Christ's law is written both on the believer's heart by the indwelling Spirit *and* written in Scripture. The believer, moved by the Spirit, empowered by the Spirit, must and will obey his Redeemer and Lord as he has revealed his mind in Scripture.[15]

So as to leave no misunderstanding on this, the view that I am disputing says that since the believer has the law of Christ written within his heart, and since the Spirit moves him to obedience, there must be no talk of command, duty or accountability when thinking of the believer's obedience to Scripture in his progressive sanctification. True, the believer will obey Scripture, must obey Scripture, but there must be no talk of 'law' in connection with this. All such talk smacks of 'bondage'. In reply, I say that this teaching has all the makings of a hyper-Calvinistic view of progressive sanctification.

What do I mean by hyper-Calvinism in this regard? Consider this conversation between the Jews and Christ:

---

[14] As I say, I have dealt with it in my *Offer*. See also my *Septimus*; *Eternal*; *No Safety*.

[15] See above and my *Christ*; 'Believers Under the Law of Christ', and so on.

'What shall we do, that we may work the works of God?' Jesus answered and said to them: 'This is the work of God, that you believe in him whom he sent' (John 6:28-29).[16]

What did Jesus mean by 'the work of God'?

Either it is the work which God himself does, or else it is the work God requires men to do. If the former, then since the Jews asked Christ what they had to do (John 6:28), they must have been asking how they could do what only God can do, and Christ told them how to do it. A most remarkable suggestion! Did they want to create? Did they want to rule all nations? Or what? The notion is absurd. We can dismiss it. What is more, Christ's answer, to 'believe in him whom he sent', can hardly be described as God's own work. Sinners have to believe, not God![17]

But were the Jews thinking in a much more subtle way – were they thinking of saving faith as the work of God in his elect? In other words, were they asking how God would work in them, enabling them to believe? This too we can dismiss. The suggestion that they had reached this level of spiritual understanding, and reached it *before* believing,[18] and were sincerely asking how God would work faith in them, is too much to swallow. Saving faith came into the conversation only *after* the Jews had asked their question about the work of God, and it arose only because Christ raised it. It had not entered the minds of the Jews.

---

[16] For the next part of this article, I have lightly edited my *Offer* pp43-47.

[17] I acknowledge, of course, the obvious; 'the works of God' *can* mean God's own works. When Jesus told his disciples that the blind man had been born blind so 'that the works of God should be revealed in him' (John 9:3), this is precisely what he was talking about. God was going to display *his* works – his compassion, his power, and so on – in giving the man sight. Yes, of course. But Jesus made this very clear by saying the works of God were to be *revealed in* the man; God was about to demonstrate his compassion and his power. But this is very different to John 6:28-29.

[18] They were not spiritual men; the context offers abundant proof of their carnality.

Above all, the idea introduces a dreadful confusion. The Jews were asking about what *they* had to do, not what God would do. The confusion is this: When a sinner believes, who does the believing? Is it the sinner or God? It is the sinner. It can only be the sinner. While faith is the *gift* of God (Eph. 2:8), it is never called the *work* of God. Although God gives faith to the elect sinner, working in him, it is the sinner who believes (Eph. 2:8-10; Phil. 2:12-13). The Holy Spirit does not believe for the sinner; God does not do the believing.

John Gill had it right when he said: 'It is the convinced sinner, and not God or Christ, or the Spirit, who repents and believes'.[19] 'Faith... as a principle, is purely God's work; [but] as it is an act, or as it is exercised under the influence of divine grace, it is man's act'.[20] Yes, indeed, 'it is man's act'. The upshot is, even if the Jews were asking about saving faith – which they were not – they were asking about what God required of them, not what he would do in them.

Let me stress this. The fact is, the Jews were not talking about God's *own* work at all! They wanted to know what *they* had to do. They wanted to know how *they* could please God, what did he require of *them*, what was *their* duty. Indeed, they had asked their question only because Christ had spoken of what they ought to 'labour' for (John 6:27). This is what they wanted to know, and this is what Christ told them. The work under discussion was not the work which God *does*, but the work which *pleases* him, the work God *requires*. As Thomas Goodwin put it: 'By works of

---

[19] John Gill: *The Cause of God and Truth*, W.H.Collingridge, London, 1855, p112.
[20] *Gill's Commentary*, Baker Book House, Grand Rapids, 1980, Vol.5 p654. 'Faith, as it is our act, is our own; hence we read of *his* faith, and *my* faith, and *your* faith, in Scripture' (John Gill: *Sermons and Tracts*, Old Paths Gospel Press, Choteau, Vol.4 p185, emphasis his). 'Whilst faith is unquestionably God's gift, it must be your act' (Frank White: 'Should an anxious enquirer be exhorted "to pray"?'..., being an article in: *The Sword and the Trowel...*, edited by C.H.Spurgeon, Passmore and Alabaster, London, 1867, p39).

121

God they mean works acceptable to God'.[21] Lexicons tell us it is 'the works required and approved by God, the deeds that God desires'.[22] Joseph Henry Alford: '"The works of God" must not be taken to mean "the works which God works", but... "the works well pleasing to God"'.[23] As the NIV translates it: 'What must we do to do the works God requires?' And Jesus, by his answer, was telling them: 'This is your responsibility, this is what you must do to please God, this is what God requires of you, this is the work of God, this is your duty'. 'Do not labour for the food which perishes, but for the food which endures to everlasting life, which the Son of Man will give you,[24] because God the Father has set his seal on him... This is the work of God, that you believe in him whom he sent' (John 6:27,28). Alford again: 'The meaning is not that faith is wrought in us by God... but... working the work of God is to believe on him whom he has sent'.[25] Believing in Christ is that which pleases God, it is what God requires, it is what he demands, it is the sinner's duty.[26]

---

[21] Thomas Goodwin: *Of the Object and Acts of Justifying Faith* in *The Works of Thomas Goodwin*, Vol.8, The Banner of Truth Trust, Edinburgh, 1985, p584.

[22] Joseph Henry Thayer: *A Greek-English Lexicon of the New Testament*, Baker Book House, Grand Rapids, Ninth Printing 1991; William F. Arndt and F.Wilbur Gingrich: *A Greek-English Lexicon of the New Testament and Other Early Christian Literature*, The University of Chicago Press, Chicago... and The Syndics of the Cambridge University Press, London, 1957.

[23] Henry Alford: *The New Testament for English Readers...*, Vol.1 Part 2, Rivingtons, London, 1863, p518.

[24] Of course, salvation, and all the things which accompany it – repentance, faith, and so on – are gifts and graces which only God can give and produce. This is not at issue.

[25] Alford p518.

[26] 'The work of God is to believe. Faith includes all the works which God requires' (M.R.Vincent: *Word Studies in the New Testament*, Macdonald Publishing Company, Florida, Vol.1 p441). Compare 'the work of the LORD' (Jer. 48:10), the work God requires, 'which is said with respect to the Chaldeans, who were enjoined to destroy the Moabites, which is called the work of the Lord, because he had given them a commission to do it; and which was to be done by them... This is a general rule... every man has work to do for God' (Gill: *Commentary*

Consider Christ himself. He did 'the works of God'. What did this entail? Take the curing of the blind man. Yes, God was about to reveal his works in making the blind man see (John 9:3), but as Jesus immediately went on to say: 'I must work the works of [God] while it is day; the night is coming when no one can work' (John 9:4). Clearly, Christ was speaking of the work *he himself* would do. Yes, it was 'the work of God' in that it would be done by God's power (John 14:10), and would please God; yet, in making the blind man see, whilst it was God's work which Christ did, *it was Christ who did the work*. It was one of *his* works (John 15:24).

Christ's curing the blind man is not an isolated example of the way he pleased his Father by his works. Christ's entire life and death was a constant demonstration of it. Coming into the world, he set out his manifesto: 'I have come... to do your will, O God' (Heb. 10:5-7,9). Addressing his disciples, he elaborated the point: 'My food is to do the will of him who sent me, and to finish his work' (John 4:34). In other words, Christ was saying he delighted to obey God his Father, to carry out his commands, to complete the work, the duty, the Father had given him to do. In this way Christ was at work. 'My Father has been working until now, and I have been working' (John 5:17), he told the Jews. True, as he explained, 'I can of myself do nothing' (John 5:19,30), but even so his works were *his* own works; *he* did them. In all this, he could say, 'I do not seek my own will but the will of the Father who sent me' (John 5:30); in other words, I do my works in order to please the Father; indeed, 'I always do those things that please him' (John 8:29); 'the works which the Father has given me to finish – the very works that I do – bear witness of me' (John 5:36), 'for I have come down from heaven, not to do my own will, but the will of him who sent me' (John 6:38). Of 'the works that I do in my Father's name' (John 10:25), one – which he called 'the will of the Father' – was not to lose any who had been

Vol.4 p209). Compare also '[Christ's] works' (Rev. 2:26): 'By his works are meant [here], not the works which were done by him... but the works which are commanded, and required by Christ to be done by his people... [such] as the work of faith... and every act of obedience' (Gill: *Commentary* Vol.6 p949).

given him by the Father (John 6:39); this work he did (John 17:12). Further, we hear him praying in the garden: 'O my Father, if it is possible, let this cup pass from me; nevertheless, not as I will, but as you will' (Matt. 26:39). It was just as he had said: 'I have come... to do your will, O God' (Heb. 10:5-7,9). And he completely fulfilled and accomplished all the work the Father had given him to do: 'I have glorified you on the earth. I have finished the work which you have given me to do' (John 17:4), 'I have accomplished it'. We hear it loud and clear in his triumphant cry on the cross, 'It is finished' (John 19:30), 'it is accomplished'.

In short, Christ did the works of God; that is, he did those works (John 14:31; 15:10) and said those words (John 12:49; 14:10,24) which God commanded him, which God required of him, and which pleased the Father (John 10:37). But it was Christ himself who did the works. While they were 'the works of God', they were *Christ's own* works. Christ promised his disciples: 'He who believes in me, the works that I do he will do also; and greater works than these he will do' (John 14:12).

In John 6:28-29, therefore, the Jews were asking, as William Gurnall put it, about 'that part of his will which above all he desires should be done – called therefore with emphasis "the work of God" (John 6:29)'.[27] And this is what Christ meant when he told them to believe. God requires you to believe, he told them. In short, Christ preached duty faith.

The principle is established: God requires sinners to believe; it is their duty; it is what pleases him. Not, it goes without saying, that sinners can believe by their own power: 'No one can come to me unless the Father who sent me draws him' (John 6:44), Christ declared. Even so, sinners are accountable for their unbelief:

> Whoever believes in [Christ] is not condemned, but whoever does not believe is condemned already, because he has not believed in the name of the only Son of God (John 3:18).

---

[27] William Gurnall: *Christian in Complete Armour*, The Banner of Truth Trust, Vol.2 pp49-50. The Jews said 'works' (*ta erga*). Jesus replied 'work' (*to ergon*).

Whoever believes in the Son has eternal life; whoever does not obey the Son shall not see life, but the wrath of God remains on him (John 3:36).

I [Jesus] will send [the Spirit] to you. And when he comes, he will convict the world concerning sin... concerning sin, because they do not believe in me (John 16:7-9).

All this is part and parcel of 'the obedience of faith'.

So what?

What does all this have to do with the believer and his progressive sanctification? I suggest there is a very close parallel. In fact, the principle comes over directly from the one to the other. God commands all men everywhere to repent and believe, to look to him for salvation (Isa. 45:22; Acts 17:30). Repentant faith, therefore, is every sinner's duty. 'Ah, but that's for salvation, whereas we are talking about progressive sanctification'. So we are! We are talking about 'the obedience of faith'. As I have shown, all men are obliged to give God 'the obedience of faith'. The point is here, God's commanding men does not cease when the sinner trusts Christ. God commands believers as well as unbelievers! Take just one example: 'Grow in the grace and knowledge of our Lord and Saviour Jesus Christ' (2 Pet. 3:18). Is that not a command? Is it not a command in Scripture? Is this not a part of the law of Christ? Is it not an aspect of 'the obedience of faith'?

Conscious of what will be said by way of reply, let me stress yet again that just as the sinner cannot repent and believe without the operation of the Spirit (John 6:44), neither can the believer yield willing submission to Christ under his law except by the inward power and grace of the Spirit. As I have said, he can only live to God by walking in the Spirit (Gal. 5:25). None of this is at issue. Nevertheless, the point still stands. God does not stop commanding once a man is converted. I have already quoted the apostle's statement to Agrippa:

I... declared first to those in Damascus, then in Jerusalem and throughout all the region of Judea, and also to the Gentiles, that they should repent and turn to God, performing deeds in keeping with their repentance (Acts 26:19-20).

But this obedience is only possible by the Spirit. As the apostle put it:

Work out your own salvation with fear and trembling, for it is God who works in you, both to will and to work for his good pleasure (Phil. 2:12-13).[28]

The letter to the Hebrews is the book of all books setting out the glories of the new covenant. In approaching his conclusion, its writer left his readers with a clear exposition of the principle:

Now may the God of peace who brought again from the dead our Lord Jesus, the great shepherd of the sheep, by the blood of the eternal covenant, equip you with everything good that you may do his will, working in us that which is pleasing in his sight, through Jesus Christ, to whom be glory forever and ever. Amen (Heb. 13:20-21).

It is as the prophet had foretold:

I will give them one heart, and a new spirit I will put within them. I will remove the heart of stone from their flesh and give them a heart of flesh, that they may walk in my statutes and keep my rules and obey them. And they shall be my people, and I will be their God (Ezek. 11:19-20).[29]

---

[28] The point is beautifully illustrated in this: 'By the grace of God I am what I am, and his grace toward me was not in vain. On the contrary, I worked harder than any of them, though it was not I, but the grace of God that is with me. Whether then it was I or they, so we preach and so you believed' (1 Cor. 15:10-11). Paul worked. He worked hard. He preached with saving result. But it wasn't he – it was God. It wasn't flesh – it was grace. But, even so, he worked, and worked hard. See Rom. 12:3; 1 Cor. 12:6.

[29] Calvin commented: 'God does not wish us to be like stones. Let us strive therefore and stretch all our nerves, and do our utmost towards acting uprightly. But Paul advises that to be done with fear and trembling; that is, by casting away all confidence in one's own strength... Paul gives the reason, because, says he, it is God who works both to will and to accomplish (Phil. 2:13)'.

I will sprinkle clean water on you, and you shall be clean from all your uncleannesses, and from all your idols I will cleanse you. And I will give you a new heart, and a new spirit I will put within you. And I will remove the heart of stone from your flesh and give you a heart of flesh. And I will put my Spirit within you, and cause you to walk in my statutes and be careful to obey my rules (Ezek. 36:25-27).

Just as the sinner is obligated to repent and believe, so the believer is obligated to obey scriptural commands and live worthy of his calling. The believer's duty to obey God is no less a duty and obligation than the unbeliever's. If he fails, he sins.[30] As Matthew 5 – 7 and John 12:47-50; 13:1 – 16:33 make clear, Christ is his people's lawgiver. And as for post-Pentecost Scriptures, are they not full of apostolic commands calling for the believer's obedience? And not only direct commands. The apostles set out a host of principles which believers are duty-bound to apply in their daily lives. And do not forget Christ's addresses to the churches (Revelation 1 – 3). Look how that book begins:

The revelation of Jesus Christ, which God gave him to show to his servants the things that must soon take place. He made it known by sending his angel to his servant John, who bore witness to the word of God and to the testimony of Jesus Christ, even to all that he saw. Blessed is the one who reads aloud the words of this prophecy, and blessed are those who hear, and who keep what is written in it (Rev. 1:1-3)

Too many treat prophecy as mere advance information, when the fact is Christ issues his word, all his word, for us to apply to our lives as principles and commands which we have to obey. And there is nothing passive about it. As Christ still commands all his disciples:

You call me teacher and Lord, and you say well, for so I am... I... your Lord and teacher... have given you an example, that you

---

[30] As I have already noted, there is a difference between the unbeliever and the believer. Unbelief (that is, not obeying the gospel) for the sinner is condemning (John 3:18,36; 16:7-9); for the saint it is reward-losing (1 Cor. 3:8,14-15; 4:5).

should do as I have done to you... If you know these things, blessed are you if you do them (John 13:13-17). A new commandment I give to you, that you love one another; as I have loved you, that you also love one another (John 13:34). Believe... in me... believe me (John 14:1,11). If you love me, keep my commandments (John 14:15). He who has my commandments and keeps them, it is he who loves me (John 14:21). He who does not love me does not keep my words; and the word which you hear is not mine but the Father's who sent me (John 14:24). Abide in me (John 15:4). This is my commandment, that you love one another as I have loved you (John 15:12). You are my friends if you do whatever I command you (John 15:14). These things I command you, that you love one another (John 15:17).

Nor is it just isolated verses. The overall picture of the believer's progressive sanctification throughout the New Testament is as far removed from the passive as it is possible to get. Thus, believers – who are God's 'workmanship' – produce 'good works, which God prepared beforehand'. But, I emphasise, it is the believers themselves who do the good works. God doesn't. 'We are his workmanship, created in Christ Jesus for good works, which God prepared beforehand that *we* should walk in them' (Eph. 2:10). Of course, believers can only do those works by God's grace, by the Spirit's power, but the point stands; believers do the works, believer have to do the works, it is their duty, they are obliged to obey God's commands, and they are accountable to Christ if they do not. And they discover God's commands in Scripture.[31]

---

[31] Compare this Facebook post from an advocate of the system I am contesting: 'We are not dependent upon law prescriptions to produce in us what only the Spirit can effect through his word. We don't learn to love others (the chief fulfilment of the law [of Moses] and fruit of the Spirit) by reading/obeying written detailed "how to" prescriptions (laws). We learn what love looks like and acts like by reading of Christ, the incarnate fulfilment, his tenderness toward sinners, his tireless ministry of mercy and good works, his love for the Father, and the grand display of their triune love for the world through the cross. In this way, we see that love is shaped like a person. It is the gospel of Jesus-Christ-shaped, grace-empowered, self-sacrificing, redeeming, merciful, sin-cancelling, and cross-centric. This love is informed in [to?] our minds as we saturate ourselves in him through the written word. But it is not

In short, the idea that the believer is not under the law of Christ, and that the Scriptures are not an integral part of that law, and that the believer is anything less than fully active in determined obedience to the revealed will of God written in Scripture, is wide of the mark.

Yes, the believer has a renewed will, having been regenerated by the Spirit, and, yes, the Spirit moves him to obedience. But this obedience is not passive, some kind of reflex reaction to the Spirit. As the sinner has to obey the gospel, so does the saint. The Spirit does not obey gospel commands for the believer any more than he repents and believes for the sinner, although he is the ultimate cause of all gospel obedience. While the Spirit is the prime mover of all faith and obedience, nevertheless both the sinner and the saint must deliberately obey God's commands. It is their duty to obey. And they are answerable to God if they do not. Accommodating the words of the apostle (Rom. 3:27), we would not go far wrong to call this 'the law of the gospel'. Sticking to Scripture, it is 'the obedience of faith'.

---

empowered in our volition [will, decision, deliberate choice, resolve] by prescriptive law(s) that binds us "to do" upon pain of death. Rather, God's love is empowered in us by the Spirit, in conformance with the gospel pattern of Christ. He gives us a living will/volition and ability to love with Christ's own love'. While there is much to applaud in this (without the Spirit, no amount of Scripture will produce godliness, and so on), notice the lack of emphasis on the believer's deliberate obedience to the law of Christ as found in apostolic commands in Scripture; indeed, notice the stress the other way!

129

Hans Denck:
The Inner and the Outer Word

Hans Denck was born in Bavaria in 1495 and died of the bubonic plague in Basel in 1527. Although he himself was not happy to be known as an Anabaptist, it is almost certainly right to call him such. But it is equally certain that he was far from being a typical Anabaptist – if ever such a person existed. The truth is, if John Calvin was on the right of the Reformation, to the right of Martin Luther, with the Anabaptists on the left of Luther, then Denck found himself well and truly on their left wing. He was what we might call a Spiritual or Mystic Anabaptist. Indeed, it has been claimed that he was a proto-Quaker. No wonder, then, that he met with criticism – and worse!

Denck, himself, was a gentle man, averse to controversy, non-fanatical, friendly, courteous, modest, very intelligent and passionate. Having graduated from Ingolstadt university in 1519, fluent in Latin, Greek, and Hebrew, his first job was to edit a three-volume Greek dictionary. In September 1523, he became headmaster of a school in Nuremburg, married, and he and his wife soon had a child. About this time he was greatly influenced by a mystical book, the *Theologia Germanica*.

After leaving Nuremberg, Denck joined the Anabaptists, being baptised as a believer by Balthasar Hubmaier in May 1526. Within a short while he had published three small works: *Whether God is the Cause of Evil*, *The Law of God*, and *Paradoxa: He Who Truly Loves the Truth*.

W.R.Estep:

[Denck] had a deep appreciation for the Old Testament and, therefore, he and Ludwig Haetzer made the first translation of the Hebrew prophets into German at Worms in the summer of 1527... The original edition was reprinted ten times and was used by both Zwingli (1529) and Luther (1532).

Denck was not in sympathy with Luther over the law of Moses. Estep again:

131

[Denck's] knowledge of the *torah* and the Hebrew text of the Old Testament, coupled with his understanding of Christianity as primarily discipleship led him to address what he considered a Lutheran misconception of the law in the only major Anabaptist work on the subject. In response to Luther's *Bondage Of The Will*, Denck wrote his *On the Law of God: How the Law is Made Void and Yet Must be Brought to Fulfilment.*

He was further disturbed by what he considered to be the antinomianism – or, at least, the lack of progressive sanctification – in Luther's followers.[1] As Estep explained:

Doubtless Denck's own experience with the Lutheran establishment in Nuremberg and his observations regarding the failure of the Lutheran movement to produce a transformation of life in its followers, motivated him to deal with the subject in the light of his own understanding of the [Mosaic] law, discipleship, and spirituality. Denck says in *Concerning the Law of God* that he has been compelled to write this treatise because of 'half-truths' that some had been led to accept for one reason or another. He charges that the whole world confesses Christ with their lips but deny him with their lives. This, he claims, is based upon the notion that Christ has fulfilled the law [of Moses] and therefore the Christian is delivered from it. However, he quotes Matthew 5:17 to support his position that even though Christ has fulfilled the law, this does not mean that Christians are under no obligation to live exemplary lives just as Christ himself lived.

Denck thought this all stemmed from Luther's misunderstanding of the gospel at this vital point:

The antinomianism that Denck saw in Luther's teachings and in what he considered the unreformed lives of Luther's followers, he declared was a perversion of the gospel due to a misunderstanding of Christ's fulfilment of the requirements of the [Mosaic] law.

To over-simplify a complicated conversation, Denck had an idiosyncratic position on the believer's relationship to the Mosaic law – a sort of halfway house between covenant theology and new-covenant theology. Estep:

---

[1] Luther himself had serious misgivings about the same. It has not gone away. See my *Battle* pp52-57,168-174.

Denck claims that this rather paradoxical idea of the Christian [being] still under the law [of Moses] while Christ has satisfied its requirements and, therefore, fulfilled the law, is explained by the work of the Holy Spirit in the Christian's life.

Denck warned of legalism based, as he saw it, on 'the dead letter'.[2] He wrote:

Whoever has received the new covenant of God, that is, in whose heart the law [of Moses] was written through the Holy Spirit,[3] is truly righteous. Whoever supposes he will accomplish keeping the law through the book, ascribes to the dead letter what belongs to living Spirit.[4]

Again:

Whoever does not have the Spirit and presumes to find it in the Scripture, seeks light and finds darkness.[5]

Nevertheless, even though Denck could write in such a denigrating way about Scripture, he stood firm on the necessity of holiness of life:

Whoever is born of God will bear witness to the truth. Whoever rejects it will also be rejected by God. Cursed be the one who does not truly love God and does not keep his commandments.

Estep quoted Clarence Bauman:

Denck holds that the letter of the [Mosaic] law is transcended in that its intention is internalised and becomes the rule of Christ within through the power of the Spirit.[6]

---

[2] Denck was mistaken. The 'dead letter' or 'killing letter' (Rom. 7:6; 2 Cor. 3:6-11) does not refer to the believer under the law of Christ in Scripture, but to the believer going back under the Mosaic law.

[3] Denck was mistaken. The law written on the believer's heart is not the law of Moses but the law of Christ. See my *Christ* pp211-321,481-555.

[4] See previous note.

[5] See Ruth Anne Abraham: 'Reclaim the Wisdom of Hans Denck'. Abraham is a contemporary Mennonite advocate of Denck's teaching.

[6] Clarence Bauman: *The Spiritual Legacy of Hans Denck: Interpretation and Translation of Key Texts*, Brill, Leiden, p16. W.R.Estep: 'Law and Gospel in the Anabaptist/Baptist Tradition', *Grace Theological Journal* 12.2, 1991, pp189-214.

As for the comparison between inner and outer truth, Denck was adamant:

> He who truly possesses truth can determine it without Scripture. The scribes [that is, Lutheran theologians] could never attain to this because they did not receive their truth from the truth. From those, on the other hand, who have it in their hearts... the written law was abolished. Not that they may discard it; rather, even though they do not always understand its full testimony, they have truth and righteousness in their hearts by which they are not misled.[7]

There is no doubt that Denck thought that the inner word is the ultimate truth. Scripture is necessary, but only in a secondary sense. Denck valued Scripture, he said, above all earthly treasure, but whereas the Scriptures are temporary – written on paper – it is the inner word that is eternal:

> Holy Scripture I hold above all human treasure but not as high as the word of God that is living, powerful and eternal – unattached and free of all elements of this world; for, since it is God himself, it is Spirit and not letter, written without pen and paper so that it can never be eradicated. Therefore, salvation is not bound to Scripture, however useful and good it might be in furthering it... But a devout heart, containing a true spark of divine zeal, is improved through all things.[8]

Moreover, according to Denck the believer's holiness of life arises, not out of an active obedience to Scripture, but by a passive outworking of the inner light. As Mika Ojakangas expressed it:

> [For] Hans Denck... not the Bible but the inner truth spoken and written by Christ 'from the beginning until the end of the world in the hearts of men' has supreme authority on earth: 'Wherever it directs me, I will go; and where it prevents me, I will flee'... It

---

[7] Malcolm B.Yarnell III (editor): *The Anabaptists and Contemporary Baptists: Restoring New Testament Christianity*, B&H Publishing Group, Nashville, 2013, pp13-14.

[8] Abraham. See also Amy Hollywood and Patricia Z.Beckman (editors): *The Cambridge Companion to Christian Mysticism*, Cambridge University Press, Cambridge, 2013, p129.

drives me 'without my willing and doing', or, better still, it drives me only when my willing and doing cease, when I hold still and lose myself in the standstill... of the soul.

Ojakangas summarised it thus:

> To put it bluntly, these radicals and mystics were Catholics without the Church, and Protestant without the word. Like Catholics, they believed in the spark of God's light operating in every man, but like good Lutherans, they refused to subject this spark to the authority of the Church. Like Luther, moreover, they admitted that the Bible is important, but they believed that Scripture bears witness to God's truth only mediately, whilst the experience of the inner word is its immediate expression. Through this experience the believer becomes free and autonomous.[9]

Wilson Varkey put it this way:

> The significance of [Denck's] pneumatology is that he recognised the distinction between the outer and the inner word; that is to say, the word written in the Bible and that which is written in the heart, respectively. He writes: 'I esteem Holy Scripture above all earthly treasures, but not so highly as the word of God which is living, powerful, eternal, free and independent all elements of this world: for as it is God himself, so it is the Spirit and not the letter, and written without pen and paper, so it that can never more be blotted out'. [This] does not mean that Denck rejected the Scripture totally... He asserted that Scripture and law in themselves are holy and good. However, without the help of the Spirit no human being is able to use them correctly... The true believer becomes capable to listen to the whole testimony of the Scripture and to discern everything only by the anointing of the Spirit. The discernment of the law through the letter of the Old and New Testaments can never be achieved without God's Spirit.

This last, of course, is right. No man can grasp or apply Scripture without the Spirit. But it is what Denck went on to deduce that

---

[9] Mika Ojakangas: *The Voice of Conscience: A Political Genealogy of Western Ethical Experience*, Bloomsbury Publishing, New York, 2013, p77.

led him so badly astray. He elevated the inner light above the external Scriptures:

> [This] proves... that Denck regarded Scripture as an external testimony to an internal truth... He writes: 'All commands, morals, laws, insofar as they are comprehended in the Old and New Testaments, are superseded for the true scholar in Christ, for he has a word written in the heart by which he loves God alone, and according to this he is able to judge what to do and what to leave alone even though he has nothing in writing... It is expounded to him through the anointing of the Holy Ghost'. Denck believed, in opposition to Luther and Calvin, that the Spirit works in the inner being of a person without the pre-condition of external means... It is the new covenant which is written in the hearts of people by the Spirit... So for him, Scripture is not univocally the word of God, but a 'witness' authenticated by the inner word. On this account... Denck... subordinates the Scripture to the Spirit.[10]

Denck thought that there is only one command for the believer; namely, Christ's command to love. Thomas N.Finger spelled out where this led Denck when coupled with his emphasis on the inner word at the expense of the outer:

> Denck... reduced the law to loving God alone; when the Spirit wrote this law on hearts, people need not worry about its prescriptions and satisfactions. The inner word revealed God more directly for Hans Denck than outer, biblical words... This elevation of the inner salvation process over its outward, historical mediation, eventually led Denck to Spiritualism.[11]

Estep on this command to love:

> [Denck] puts much emphasis upon the dynamics of the new birth, for, [he] points out, the new man in Christ Jesus is under the compulsion of love to live the Christian life.

Denck himself:

---

[10] Wilson Varkey: *Role of the Holy Spirit in Protestant Systematic Theology...*

[11] Thomas N.Finger: *A Contemporary Anabaptist Theology: Biblical, Historical, Constructive*, InterVarsity Press, Downers Grove, 2004, pp120,261; see also p50.

Christ not only proclaimed or wrote the law of God externally for his followers, as did Moses. Rather, he speaks and writes it to them in their hearts from the beginning of the world to the end (Heb. 8:10; Jer. 31:33). Whoever has the law in his heart lacks neither path nor feet, neither light nor eyes, nor anything that is necessary to fulfil the will of God... Those who are true pupils of Christ keep the whole Mosaic law, even if they have never read it... Whoever has received the new covenant of God – that is, whoever has the law written in his heart by the Holy Spirit – is truly just (Romans 5 [but *passim*]). Whoever thinks he can bring this about by reading the Bible, and by keeping the law, ascribes to the dead letter what belongs to the living Spirit.[12]

Let Rufus M.Jones sum it all up:

During the first period of his life in Nuremberg, [Denck] was closely identified with the Lutheran movement, but he soon shifted his sympathies, and aligned himself with the radical tendencies which at this period were championed in Nuremberg by Thomas Muenzer... Muenzer read Tauler's[13] sermons from

---

[12] Denck had 'spirit'. Hans Denck: *On the Law of God* in *The Radical Reformation*, edited by Michael G.Baylor, Cambridge University Press, 1991, pp136,142.

[13] Johannes Tauler (c1300-1361) was a German mystic, a Catholic preacher and theologian. Here is a sample of Tauler's teaching: 'Many men go astray, running after external works and discipline'. 'How very often we may be blinded, to our own hurt, by unnecessary and external works of love, which prevent our perceiving the divine inspiration and our own infirmities. Although such works may have been done in love, both great and godlike, and may not be really evil in themselves, still they are not that which is best and most perfect'. 'For God is a lover of hearts, and communes not with anything that is external. He desires an inner, living, love, which is ever ready to turn to all things that are divine and virtuous, where and in whomsoever they may be found; for there is more truth in such a one than in a man who prays as much as all the rest of the world, and sings so lustily that his song reaches to heaven; or in anything that he can do by fasting, watching, or anything else externally'. 'God himself has set [believers] free... Paul says, that those who are driven or led by the Spirit are under no law'. 'The right foundation of a perfect Christian life does not consist only of external works, though they are a help, but much more of good work in the heart, by which sin is avoided and virtue brought forth' (Johannes Tauler: *The Inner Way*, Methuen & Co., London, 1901, pp60,71,103,105). Arthur

his youth up; in his own copy of these sermons, preserved in the library at Gera, a marginal note says that he read them almost continually, and that here he learned of a divine interior teaching.

Muenzer passed his mystical views on to Denck:

> It was Muenzer's teaching of the living voice of God in the soul, his testimony to the reality of the inner heavenly word, which God himself speaks in the deeps of man's heart, that won [Denck]... to the new and perilous cause.

Denck's course, alas, was now firmly set towards the mystical, the inward, away from things outward, and he was encouraged in his thinking by another friend:

> [Denck] also formed a close friendship with Ludwig Hetzer, who, like Muenzer, taught that the saving word of God must be inward, and that the Scriptures can be understood only by those who belong to the school of Christ.

The fact is:

> Already in this Nuremberg period, Denck became fully convinced that Luther's doctrine of sin and justification was an artificial construction, and that his conception of Scripture... was destined to clamp the new-found faith in iron bonds, tie it to outworn tradition, and make it incapable of a progressive and vital unfolding.

Denck did not hide his 'light' under a bushel, and, naturally, he soon found himself in hot water for making his views known:

> As a result of this change of attitude, [he] was banished from the city of Nuremberg, January 21, 1525, and from this time until his early death he was homeless and a wanderer. He spent some months – between September 1525 and October 1526 – in Augsburg endeavouring to... give the chaotic movement of

---

Wollaston (editor): 'His mystical doctrine of the inner and outer, of the letter and the spirit, tended irresistibly towards the overthrow of Catholicism, so far as in his day is consisted in mere formalism and obedience to external rule' (Tauler p12). Yes, no doubt this is true, but it is also impossible to miss how this emphasis on the inward at the expense of the outward could lead to trouble for more than Catholics.

Anabaptism a definite direction, with the main emphasis on the mystical aspect of religion. He hoped to call a halt to the vague socialistic dreams and the fanatical tendencies that put the movement in constant jeopardy and peril,[14] and he was striving to call his brotherhood to an inner religion, grounded on the inherent nature of the soul, and guided by the inner word rather than on 'a new law' set forth in the written word.

Here we reach the crunch point. Denck found himself so stressing the inward that he inevitably played down the external – the Scriptures. Why was he so strong against the believer consciously obeying the law of Christ written in Scripture? Because he thought that those who stress the necessity of obedience to Scripture, obedience to the law of Christ as written in the word, were promoting legalism:

> [Denck] was, consistently with his fundamental ideas, profoundly opposed to every tendency to make Christianity a legal religion. His friends, the Anabaptists, were inclined to turn the gospel of Christ into 'a new law', and to make religion consist largely in scrupulous obedience to this perfect law of life. To all this he was radically alien, for it was, he thought, only another road back to a religion of the letter, while Christ came to call us to a religion of the spirit. 'He who has not the Spirit', he wrote, 'and who fails to find him in the Scriptures, seeks life and finds death; seeks light and finds darkness, whether it be in the Old or in the New Testament'. 'He who thinks that he can be made truly righteous by means of a book is ascribing to the dead letter what belongs to the Spirit'.

It surely goes without saying that nobody can be made righteous simply by the word. A sinner has to be regenerated, brought to repentance and faith in Christ, by the Spirit, and so be united to Christ. But, as the New Testament makes abundantly plain, God uses his written word in all this.[15] And the same applies to the

---

[14] Which would, within a few years, lead to the debacle at Munster. In 1534 some Anabaptists took over the town of Munster, announced the end time had come, and committed horrible sins in the name of Christ. This was an appalling disaster for the Anabaptists as a whole, doing their cause – indeed the cause of God – much harm for many years.

[15] I quote from my *Baptist Sacramentalism: A Warning to Baptists* p255: '"I have begotten you through the gospel", Paul declared (1 Cor. 4:15).

believer. Only the Spirit can enable the believer to live to the glory of God, but, yet again, as the New Testament makes clear, in this work the Spirit uses Scripture. Denck faced up to the question in light of his view: 'So why did God give us the Scriptures?' His answer is illuminating. Jones:

> [Denck] does not belittle or undervalue the Scriptures – he knew them almost by heart and took the precious time out of his brief life to help to translate the prophets into German – but he wants to make the fact forever plain that men are saved or lost as they say 'yes' or 'no' to a light and word within themselves. 'The holy Scriptures', he writes in his dying testimony, 'I consider above every human treasure, but not so high as the word of God which is living, powerful, and eternal, for it is God himself, Spirit and no letter, written without pen or paper so that it can never be destroyed. For that reason, salvation is not bound up with the Scriptures, however necessary and good they may be for their purpose, because it is impossible for the Scriptures to make good a bad heart, even though it may be a learned one. A good heart, however... is improved by everything, and to such the Scriptures will bring blessedness and goodness'.

There is truth in this, of course – the Scriptures can never, without the Spirit, make men righteous. Nevertheless, the believer must obey God in his word, and so live a holy life before men. Yes, that obedience must be from the heart, by the Spirit,

---

How does God bring this about? "Of his own will he brought us forth by the word of truth" (Jas. 1:18). "The word of truth" certainly means the Scriptures, the gospel (2 Cor. 6:7; Eph. 1:13; Col. 1:5; 2 Tim. 2:15; see also 1 Pet. 1:23 with Heb. 4:12). "Faith comes by hearing, and hearing by the word of God" (Rom. 10:17). But I think there is something more. "Of his own will... the word of truth" also includes God's decree, his authoritative command – as his effective word at creation: "God who commanded light to shine out of darkness... has shone in our hearts to give [us] the light of the knowledge of the glory of God in the face of Jesus Christ" (2 Cor. 4:6). In short, God uses the preaching of the gospel to regenerate and convert his elect – and he does it in some mysterious, but effective, way like in his fiat at creation: "Let there be light" – "and there was light" (Gen. 1:3). "The law of the LORD [which, in new-covenant terms, is the entire Scripture] is perfect, converting the soul" (Ps. 19:7)'.

and it can only be by the Spirit, working in those who have come to Christ, but, even so, this obedience is conformity to the objective Scriptures, and not 'merely' to the inner word.

Despite his mystical view, despite his emphasis on the inward at the expense of the outward, Denck continued to press believers to godliness:

> The Scriptures – the external word – as he many times, in fact somewhat tediously, declares, are witnesses and pointers to the real and momentous thing, the word which is very near to all souls and is written in the heart, and which increases in clearness and power as the will swings into parallelism with the will of God, and as the life grows in likeness to the divine image revealed in Christ. This inward life and spiritual appreciation do not give any ground for relaxing the moral obligations of life. No fulfilling of the [Mosaic] law by Christ, no vanishing of the outward and temporal, furnish any excuse to us for slacking a jot or tittle of anything which belongs to the inherent nature of moral goodness. 'Christ', he says, 'fulfilled the [Mosaic] law, not to relieve us of it, but to show us how to keep it in truth. The member must partake of what the Head partakes'. To love God alone and to hate everything that hinders love is a principle which, Denck believes, will fulfil all law, ancient or modern.[16]

Yes, but that one command is worked out in Scripture in a host of commands and principles which believers are duty-bound to apply to their lives, and to do so in a deliberate, resolved, way, and all by the power of the Spirit.[17]

Conclusion

The positive
Among the positive lessons we can draw from the life of Hans Denck, I choose three. We need to learn from Denck in these areas, and emulate him in our practice:

---

[16] Rufus M.Jones: 'Hans Denck and the Inward Word' in: *Spiritual Reformers in the 16th and 17th Centuries*, Macmillan and Co., Limited, London, 1928, pp17-45.

[17] For my arguments supporting all I say in this article, see my 'Believers Under the Law of Christ'; 'The Obedience of Faith'; 'One Command or Many in One?'

1. The believer must live a life of holiness. Those who are justified and positionally sanctified must show it by their progressive sanctification. Indeed, those who are Christ's, those who have the Spirit, will be motivated by the Spirit to live a godly life to the glory of God.

2. We must beware of a cold, dry – merely legal – view of justification. Notice my use of 'merely'. Justification by faith is forensic, but not only so. We must cultivate a 'felt Christ' and a 'felt justification'.[18] As Joseph Hart put it:

> *Let us ask the important question,*
> *(Brethren, be not too secure),*
> *What it is to be a Christian,*
> *How we may our hearts assure.*
> *Vain is all our best devotion,*
> *If on false foundations built;*
> ***True religion's more than notion,***
> ***Something must be known and felt.***

Again:

> *The faith that unites to the Lamb*
> *And brings such salvation as this,*
> ***Is more than mere notion or name,***
> *The work of God's Spirit it is:*
> *A principle, active and young,*
> *That lives under pressure and load;*
> *That makes out of weakness more strong,*
> *And draws the soul upward to God.*

3. We must never minimise the inward work of the Spirit. It is one of the glories of the new covenant. The Reformed too often stress the word at the expense of the Spirit. We who advocate new-covenant theology must never cease to stress that it is both the Spirit and the word, working perfectly in tandem.[19]

The negative

There are four warnings I draw from the life of Hans Denck:

---

[18] See my *Four 'Antinomians'*; *Assurance*.
[19] See my '"The Law" in "The Law of Christ"'.

1. Denck did not understand that the believer, in his union with Christ, has died to the law of Moses (and pagan law). And this guarantees his progressive sanctification (Rom. 7:4-6; Gal. 2:19-20; 3:1-5,25; 4:1-7; 5:1,13-16,18,25; 6:2). It is only because the Spirit has set him free from the law of sin and death (Rom. 8:1-4), the killing ministry (Rom. 7:6; 2 Cor. 3:6-11), that he can live to glorify God. This we must constantly maintain.

2. Denck went badly astray on the role of the Scriptures. The inward work of the Spirit is vital, writing Christ's law on the believer's heart, yes, but the external Scriptures, inspired by the Spirit, are no less vital. The believer is under the law of Christ, and by the Spirit is enabled to rejoice in the obedience of faith to the Scriptures. As I have noted, the 'dead letter' (Rom. 7:6; 2 Cor. 3:6-11) does not refer to the believer living under the law of Christ in Scripture, obeying it by the Spirit, but to the believer trying to live a spiritual life under the Mosaic law. There is nothing 'dead' or legalistic about the believer obeying the law of Christ written in Scripture by the inward work of the Spirit. In so doing, he is *not* returning to the old covenant.

3. The believer is not passive in his progressive sanctification, but decidedly active. Denck was wrong on this. Neither Christ nor the Spirit does our obeying for us. We, ourselves, have to obey Scripture, and, by God's grace, we are moved and empowered to love and obey God in his word. The believer is free from the law of Moses (Gal. 4:21 – 5:1), yes, but he has to walk in the Spirit (Gal. 5:25), and he will, by the Spirit's power, do so; that is, he has to live by the power of the Spirit in obedience to Christ as revealed both within him and in the external Scriptures. In so doing, he fulfils the law of Christ (Gal. 6:2).

4. Denck rightly deplored worldliness in believers, and properly stressed the necessity of progressive sanctification – godliness of life – but, alas, he prescribed the wrong regime to bring it about. As such, he speaks to us in our day. We, too, have to struggle with this issue. We must not repeat his mistake. And this is especially relevant to those of us who advocate new-covenant theology. While we must stress the believer's liberty, and the

inward work of the Spirit, let us, at the same time, and with equal vehemence, stress the believer's responsibility under the word of God. It is not the Spirit or the word; it is both. It is not the inner or the outer; it is both. It is not: 'Let go, and let God!' It is:

> Therefore, my beloved, as you have always obeyed, so now... work out your own salvation with fear and trembling, for it is God who works in you, both to will and to work for his good pleasure (Phil. 2:12-13).

> Now may the God of peace who brought again from the dead our Lord Jesus, the great shepherd of the sheep, by the blood of the eternal covenant, equip you with everything good that you may do his will, working in us that which is pleasing in his sight, through Jesus Christ, to whom be glory forever and ever. Amen (Heb. 13:20-21).

> Therefore, beloved, since you are waiting for [new heavens and a new earth], be diligent to be found by him without spot or blemish, and at peace. And count the patience of our Lord as salvation, just as our beloved brother Paul also wrote to you according to the wisdom given him, as he does in all his letters when he speaks in them of these matters. There are some things in them that are hard to understand, which the ignorant and unstable twist to their own destruction, as they do the other Scriptures. You therefore, beloved, knowing this beforehand, take care that you are not carried away with the error of lawless people and lose your own stability. But grow in the grace and knowledge of our Lord and Saviour Jesus Christ. To him be the glory both now and to the day of eternity. Amen (2 Pet. 3:14-18).

Antinomianism
Reformed and Mystical

Yes, I know the title is bizarre, but all will, I hope, become clear.

Reformed antinomianism

A Reformed antinomian? As odd an oxymoron as you can get, you might think. But no! The Reformed are deeply concerned about antinomianism within their ranks.

In the second decade of the 21st century, antinomianism is one of the buzz words in evangelical circles. The Reformed are up in arms about it – at least, up in arms about what they see as antinomianism among the advocates of new-covenant theology. But, truth to tell, they are also wrestling with it much closer to home. They have a home-grown antinomianism, an antinomianism flourishing in their own backyard. Naturally, they do not like it, not one little bit!

Mark Jones, a Reformed writer, has gone into print about it, and the title of his book says it all: *Reformed Theology's Unwelcome Guest.*[1] He states:

> As someone with some scholarly acquaintance with post-Reformation Reformed theology, particularly in the area of Puritanism, I have been dismayed at some of the theology that passes as Reformed, when in fact it has corollaries to [has counterparts in?] seventeenth-century antinomianism.[2]

David B.Garner sets out what he sees as the Reformed-antinomian mantra:

> Don't you know? You are free. The gospel is free. Do you feel obligated, responsible, duty-bound? That's not grace. Don't you know any sense of obligation, desire for reward, or fear of

---

[1] Mark Jones: *Reformed Theology's Unwelcome Guest*, P&R Publishing, Phillipsburg, 2013.
[2] Jones xvi.

disappointing God is evidence that legalism still holds you captive? Let go and let God. Celebrate your justification and reject the compulsion![3]

So, how do the Reformed propose to deal with this home-grown antinomianism? Judging by Jones' book, and the range of endorsements it has received from Reformed scholars,[4] their perceived antidote is a repeat prescription of what was tried before; namely, to fall back to the 'cure' attempted in the 1640s in England. And what was that? The Westminster Assembly, called in order to sort out the rampant antinomianism of the time, turned to John Calvin's threefold use of the law of Moses, and, more particularly, to its refinement and extension at the hands of covenant theologians.[5] Mainstream Reformed teachers today are convinced that the Puritan preventative of antinomianism (and, they hope, its cure) remains the best on offer. They would say it is scriptural. And Jones' book is his attempt to spell it out by making extensive use of Reformed writers and the Westminster standards. As he himself said:

I make no apologies for depending on Reformed authors. We will see how various Reformed luminaries... have addressed such topics as the law [of Moses], the gospel and good works... My commitment to the Westminster standards is resolute, and so this work unashamedly fits in the Westminster (Puritan) tradition.[6]

It is not, of course, my place to offer advice to the Reformed, but even so I will. Before you try to fend off what you perceive as antinomianism, make sure you really understand what it is! That's the first thing. Much of what you dismiss as

---

[3] David B.Garner: 'You Just Might Be An Antinomian', a favourable review of Jones' book. Garner is being ironic.

[4] At the opening of Jones' book there are endorsements by Gert van den Brink, Michael A.G.Haykin, Steven J.Lawson, Derek Thomas, Carl R.Trueman, Cornelis P.Venema and Guy Prentiss Waters. J.I.Packer wrote the Foreword.

[5] See my 'The Law and the Confessions', 'Preparationism in New England', 'John Eaton: Antinomian?'

[6] Jones xvi.

antinomianism is, in fact, apostolic teaching. Instead of falling back on the Westminster standards (and the host of writers who have gone into print on the basis of those standards), why not put those standards to one side for once, and actually read Scripture unfiltered? Specifically, I suggest you weigh Romans 6 – 8, 2 Corinthians (especially chapter 3), Galatians, Ephesians 2, Philippians 3 and Hebrews – and that's just for starters. Once you come to terms with the un-glossed teaching in these passages, then you will be in a position to recognise real antinomianism and deal with it. After all, a man is not an antinomian simply because he disagrees with Calvin, or because he is not a covenant theologian (which Calvin himself was not) or a 'Westminster man'! Acts 17:11, *sola Scriptura*, in your terms, still rules the roost, I hope. It is worse than useless trying to fight a disease that you have misunderstood in a patient you have misdiagnosed, and then giving him the wrong medicine.

I have a vested interest in making this plea. For I am what is known as a new-covenant theologian, and I have set out my views, and the arguments behind them, in scores of books, articles, videos and discourses. And, for my pains, I have been charged with antinomianism. But just because a man emphasises the believer's liberty in Christ, and does so based on the exegesis of the passages cited in the previous paragraph, it does not make him an antinomian. If it does, then it puts Paul and the writer of the letter to the Hebrews in the dock!

Having said that, I readily admit that there is such a thing as real antinomianism, and that some contemporary teachers are getting pretty close to it. And it needs stopping! I am not for a minute defending real antinomianism – if I need to say such a thing. After all, I have written and spoke often enough against the accursed error. Even so, I state it categorically once again.

However, as I have said, it is not really my place to offer advice to the Reformed on how to deal with their own problems, and that's not my reason for writing this article. My real purpose in raising this internecine fight in the Reformed camp is somewhat different. The truth is, I was struck by some comments by J.I.Packer in his Foreword to Jones' book, and I thought them worth pursuing a little further.

Packer pinpoints the problem. The issue is progressive sanctification.[7] Quite right! And, having nailed the issue, Packer goes back to history to trace the source of the trouble:

> With regard to [progressive] sanctification, there have been mystical antinomians who have affirmed that the indwelling Christ is the personal subject who obeys the law in our identity once we invoke his help in obedience situations, and there have been pneumatic antinomians who have affirmed that the Holy Spirit within us directly prompts us to discern and do the will of God, without our needing to look to the law to either prescribe or monitor our performance. The common ground is that those who live in Christ are wholly separated from every aspect of the pedagogy of the law.

I pause. As you can see, Packer rightly divides antinomians into two – mystical and spiritual (or pneumatological). The mystical antinomians say it is Christ, himself, who actually lives the holy life in, through and for the believer. The pneumatological antinomians attribute this godliness of life to the Spirit using the law written on the believer's heart. The link between the two, the common bond between them, is that the believer is not accountable under an external law, and that he is passive in his progressive sanctification. So far so good with Packer.

But when he speaks of 'the law', because of his Reformed position, Packer is, of course, referring to the law of Moses. And in the case of Reformed antinomians (whether mystical or spiritual), he is right to do so. The Reformed are convinced that the law the believer has to deal with is the law of Moses. Since Reformed antinomians teach that the believer is not under the law of Moses, Packer's concerns apply strictly only to them. For the

---

[7] The sinner, on coming to faith, is united to Christ and is justified and positionally sanctified. Thus, in God's sight, in Christ he is accounted or made righteous, free of sin and condemnation, and perfectly separated unto God. See, for instance, 1 Cor. 1:2,30; 6:11; Eph. 5:25-27; Heb. 10:10-18; 13:12. In his Christian life, he has to work out his perfection in Christ, and he will be moved to do so by the Spirit under the direction of Scripture; this is his progressive sanctification or holiness of life. But this, alas, is imperfect. The believer will only be absolutely sanctified in the eternal state. See my *Fivefold*.

Reformed, following Calvin, the Mosaic law (or rather, as they define it, 'the moral law', or the ten commandments) is the believer's perfect rule and the whip to drive the believer to attain to it in his progressive sanctification. Packer deplores that some Reformed teachers are leading their followers away from submission to the law of Moses.

But this is not the real issue. Christ has fulfilled the law of Moses, and thus rendered it obsolete (Matt. 5:17-20; Rom. 8:1-4; 10:4; Heb. 7:11-19; 8:6-13). What is more, the believer has died to the law of Moses in order to be married to Christ. Above all, it is only because he has died to the law of Moses and is united to Christ that there is any possibility of him living a sanctified life, bearing fruit to God (Rom. 6:14; 7:4-6).[8] And this means that the Reformed antinomianism Packer deplores simply reflects his failure to grasp apostolic teaching.

Nevertheless – nevertheless – Packer does make a valid point. Indeed, he makes a *vital* point. Although the believer is free from the law of Moses (Gal. 5:1), this does not mean that he is free from all law. Antinomianism (of whatever variety) rears its head when believers think themselves free of all law all together, when their mis-exegesis of Scripture leads them to maintain this so-called freedom. Mis-exegesis? Yes. Take, for example, Paul's words to the Romans: 'Sin will have no dominion over you, since you are not under law but under grace' (Rom. 6:14). If men grab this verse out of context – as some do – they can so easily run away with the idea that believers are free of all law altogether.[9] But this is utterly wrong. The context makes it clear. The believer no longer lives in the old age, the age of the old covenant. He is free from the law of Moses since it has been fulfilled by Christ and rendered obsolete. Yes, it still acts as a paradigm for the believer, but, even so, he has died to that law. And that is why sin will no longer rule over him. But the apostle is not for a moment suggesting that the believer is free of law altogether! The context,

---

[8] For my arguments behind all this, see my works, especially my *Christ*.

[9] The 'consistent' Reformed get round this by glossing the text to read 'the curse or condemnation of the law', or by calling on one of the other various 'escape routes' they are so fond of. See my *Christ* pp99-110,392-408. Do not skip the extracts!

as I say, puts it beyond doubt. For Paul immediately goes on (Rom. 6:15 – 7:6) to teach that the believer is under law to Christ. Although the apostle does not use the phrase in the context, nevertheless by his two illustrations he makes this very point: the believer is under the rule, the governance, the law of Christ. Christ is both his slave master and his husband. He is under the law of Christ. As the apostle declares:

> Though I am free from all, I have made myself a servant to all, that I might win more of them. To the Jews I became as a Jew, in order to win Jews. To those under the law I became as one under the law (though not being myself under the law) that I might win those under the law. To those outside the law I became as one outside the law (not being outside the law of God but under the law of Christ) that I might win those outside the law. To the weak I became weak, that I might win the weak. I have become all things to all people, that by all means I might save some. I do it all for the sake of the gospel, that I may share with them in its blessings (1 Cor. 9:19-23).[10]

Paul is clear: he is not under the law of Moses, but he is under the law of Christ; the law of Christ is the law of God for him. Packer's words, therefore, need correcting here. Although he talks of the law of Moses, the real law is the law of Christ. Steven J.Lawson (in his endorsement of Jones' book) supplied the necessary adjustment to Packer:

> Sad to say, portions of the Reformed community have given shelter to this new antinomianism, claiming that personal obedience to the law of Christ is merely optional.

So, properly nuancing Packer's words, antinomianism does arise when men say that believers are free from the law of Christ. This is doctrinal antinomianism. And we must not be surprised if the very suggestion today that believers are not under the binding law of Christ leads to practical antinomianism tomorrow.

With that vital adjustment to his words, let Packer go on with his description of the antinomianism he wants to correct. This is how antinomians (as he defines them) talk:

---

[10] See my 'Believers Under the Law of Christ'.

The freedom with which Christ has set us free, and the entire source of our ongoing peace and assurance, are based upon our knowledge that what Christ, as we say, enables us to do he actually does in us for himself. So now we live, not by being forgiven our constant shortcomings, but by being out of the law's bailiwick altogether; not by imitating Christ, the archetypal practitioner of holy obedience to God's law, but by burrowing ever deeper into the joy of our free justification, and of our knowledge that Christ himself actually does in us all that his and our Father wants us to do. Thus the correlating of conscience with the Father's coded commands and Christ's own casuistry of compassion need not and indeed should not enter into the living of the Christian life, as antinomians understand it.

Let me unpack this. It is a proper mixed bag, I'm afraid. Packer wants believers under the law of Moses, whereas the New Testament teaches that believers have died to the law of Moses, and are under the law of Christ. So in reading the above from Packer, 'law' has to be understood in two ways: the law of Moses and the law of Christ. As I have explained, for the Reformed, antinomianism, as they see it, arises when believers do not submit themselves to Calvin's view of the law of Moses as their perfect rule and whip to produce progressive sanctification. For new-covenant theologians, however, antinomianism arises when believers do not submit to the law of Christ. That's the first correction which must be made to Packer's words.

Secondly, within Packer's garbled account, we come across some biblical gems, which, alas, he dismisses. Contrary to Puritan teaching, the believer's assurance does not come from the evidence of his progressive sanctification, but from the inner witness of the Spirit taking him to Christ, and to his sinless standing before God in Christ.[11] And, contrary to Packer's dismissal of it, the believer *is* moved to progressive sanctification by setting his mind and heart on Christ (Col. 3:1-17, for instance), not by concentrating on rules and regulations. On the other hand, Packer is right to stress the authority of the Scriptures in the believer's life. But, there again, it is not the Scriptures alone. It is both the Scriptures and the inward work of the Spirit. But the

---

[11] See my *Assurance*.

point that Packer wants to make – and I agree with him in this – is that antinomianism looms when men weaken the role of Scripture in the law of Christ.

To put it another way, we are talking about the objective and subjective. The Reformed are heavy on the objective – the Scriptures, the word (actually, they mostly talk of the ten commandments in this connection). Antinomians are heavy on the subjective – the inward Christ, the inward Spirit, the inward law on the believer's heart. But the scriptural position is that it is both, with the objective Scriptures instructing, monitoring and calibrating the subjective.

Packer comes to his conclusion thus:

> The bottom line of all this? The conclusion of the matter? Here, as elsewhere, the reaction of man does not lead to the righteousness of God, but rather obstructs holiness. In God's family, as in human families, an antinomian attitude to parental law makes for pride and immaturity, misbehaviour and folly. Our true model of wise godliness, as well as our true mediator of God's grace, is Jesus Christ, our law-keeping Lord. Mark Jones's monograph is the work of a Puritan-minded scholar and theologian who understands these things well, has researched historic antinomianism with thoroughness, and has many illuminating things to say about it. His book is a pioneering overview that I commend most warmly, particularly to pastors. Why to them? Start reading it, and you will soon see.[12]

Certain things stand out in all this. 'Mystical antinomians... and... pneumatic antinomians... have affirmed that the Holy Spirit within us directly prompts us to discern and do the will of God, without our needing to look to the law [nuanced, as I have explained] to either prescribe or monitor our performance'. 'The Father's coded commands... need not and indeed should not enter into the living of the Christian life, as antinomians understand it'. And then we have Garner's: 'Don't you know any sense of obligation, desire for reward, or fear of disappointing God is evidence that legalism still holds you captive? Let go and let God. Celebrate your justification and reject the compulsion!'

---

[12] J.I.Packer's Foreword to Jones x-xi.

These antinomian mantras are serious errors. So, while Packer is confused and confusing, he does put his finger on some vital points. What is the role of the Scriptures in the law of Christ? Are believers under that law? Are believers passive in their progressive sanctification? Or are they decidedly active? Is it all a question of love? Or is there a measurable, verifiable standard of obedience?

Mystical antinomianism

Unfortunately, with few exceptions, Jones deliberately did not name those he had in mind,[13] so I have drawn examples of mystical antinomianism from the writings of John Crowder[14] and Steve McVey.[15] Not all the following is bad, let me say at once, but there are clear indications of which way the wind is blowing. And as always, don't forget it is what people think they read, what they take away, that is all important. And on that score, I am categorical. If these principles gain ground, antinomianism will run rampant.

In what follows from Crowder, note his emphasis against the believer's personal effort and obedience to Scripture, his teaching that the believer is assimilated into Christ, and that progressive sanctification is not to be thought of in terms of the believer's obedience to Scripture by the Spirit, but by his subjective thinking of Christ.[16]

---

[13] Jones xvi.

[14] In what follows from Crowder, unless otherwise stated, I have quoted from his *Mystical Union: Stuff they never told you about the finished work of the cross*, Sons of Thunder Ministries & Publications, Kindle Version, 2010.

[15] Steve McVey: *52 Lies Heard in Church Every Sunday: and why the truth is so much better*, Harvest House, 2011.

[16] The new-covenant motive and standard for the believer's obedience is, of course, Christ (Rom. 12:1-2; 2 Cor. 6:14 – 7:1; Eph. 4:32 – 5:2; Col. 3:1-2; Tit. 2:11-15; 3:3-8, and so on), but all this is to be calibrated by Scripture, and is brought about by the believer's personal obedience to Scripture, in the power of the Spirit.

Mystical antinomianism – a working description
Crowder:

> There is a growing interest in authentic, mystical Christianity: a mysticism rooted in a person (him knowing us and us knowing him), not in human attempt at spiritual disciplines or mental ascent... As a new creation, you have been liberated from the struggle of self-improvement. Absolutely flawless, our old, fearful, sinful, blemished, selves have been eradicated once and for all. Perfected once and for all by [Christ's] sacrifice, we can drink daily from the fountain of our union with him, no longer expecting defeat. As our mind changes regarding the truth of our identity, our outward lives bear corresponding fruit. No longer believing the false humility... that we are 'still sinners'... We are sons and daughters – our true identity shines from the inside out chock-full of inheritance. Right here. Right now.

> So many see Jesus as the one we must 'imitate'... rather than the our substitute who accomplished all things pertaining to salvation on our behalf.

> Mystical union... we are talking about our union with Christ. We are in him, and he is in us. Mysticism is the experience of this union with God.

> The Reformers did not go far enough... They missed it on the topic of indwelling sin in the believer. This is where the Puritan derailed and took the ship into a downward spiral... The Reformers were not reformed enough... The cross united us to Christ, not just positionally, but effectively. It doesn't just cover our sins, but eradicates sinfulness itself from us.

Passive progressive sanctification
Crowder again:

> The centrality of the new birth and new creation is found in the saving act of Christ – not in our feeble attempts at mustering faith. Our faith-response to that saving act – however important – relies for its validity of the act itself. Our response is merely a recognition and experience of facts.

> The church is obsessed with her own transformation, evidenced by a mountain of self-help books. The contemplative journey is not a path of becoming. It is a path of realising what we've already become in him. We are awaking to a transformation that

has already taken place. Our journey is a discovery of the true self. And this is but the by-product of something much greater – the discovery of Christ in us... Beyond simple – the gospel is an absolutely effortless unveiling of the truth of the Godhead in you. We are not arriving into him, but realising he arrived into us.

It's high time the church gets delivered from God pleasing... Does happy, effortless Christianity sound scandalous to you? Does a daily walk of joyful, sinless existence seem like an impossibility? If the answer is 'yes' then allow me to introduce you to the gospel. At least, the gospel as you may have never heard it before. The original version is so easy and pleasurable that it's offensive... It is a gloriously happy message of effortless union with God.

This is a book [Crowder's] designed to challenge the believer... You will be challenged to stop striving to get closer to God.

God didn't save you so you could do good. He saved you so you could be dead and he could work through you. He doesn't want you trying to please him. He is only pleased with Christ... God doesn't help you. God does things for you.[17]

Scripture
Crowder again:

The Bible is not the word of God. Yes, the Bible is fully inspired and it's the means by which we see Jesus. But Jesus Christ – not the Bible itself – is the word... Christ is the ultimate text... In the Scriptures, I can no longer see regulations and legalisms that seem to come 'in addition' to him... Grace must be the lens through which I see all else. I begin to see him – the fulfilment of the law – jumping off every page.

Summing it up
Crowder confused positional and progressive sanctification:

Sanctification is not a process. It is a *Person*. The Bible tells me so! *And because of him you are in* Christ Jesus, who became *to us wisdom from God, righteousness and* sanctification *and*

---

[17] Crowder: *Mystical* pp54,88, quoted by Kelly M.Kapic (editor): *Sanctification: Explorations in Theology and Practice*, InterVarsity Press, Downers Grove, 2014, p245.

redemption (1 Cor. 1:30, ESV). *He is your sanctification.* Any system that tries to draw your attention away from the person of Christ and onto your own efforts is antichrist in nature. Your union with God is not an incomplete relationship that comes progressively. Time is not the magic formula that makes you holy. Jesus' sacrifice made you holy. Christ's work was enough to purify you, spirit, soul and body... Christ has replaced you![18]

And, finally, Steve McVey. I allow that his statements are provocatively simplistic – and, no doubt, deliberately so – but, once again, I repeat my warning: it is not only what we say or write, but what people think we say or write, that counts – and the latter more than the former in many respects. What will men gather when they are told that the following are lies?

> When we do wrong we are out of fellowship with God
> You should live by the teachings of the Bible
> God only speaks today through the Bible
> Your sins can disqualify you from being used by God
> We need to seek spiritual power
> We should live by Christian morals
> You grow in holiness
> You should pray to love Christ more
> We are positionally righteous
> Christ empowers us to keep God's law
> If you don't forgive others, God won't forgive you
> It's better to burn out for Christ than to rust out
> The truth will set you free

Conclusion

The antinomians I write against teach in a way that may be summarised thus: The Holy Spirit, Christ formed in the believer, releases the believer from all law. The believer has no duty to obey the law of Christ. The way to be holy is to do nothing, but rest in God's action. To demand obedience to Scripture in order to produce a life of holiness is to fall back into legalism. We should stop talking about 'law', 'command', 'rule' and 'duty';

---

[18] John Crowder: 'Sanctification is Not a Process', being an article drawn from his *Mystical*. See my *Fivefold*.

rather, we should stress the inner Christ, the inward work of the Spirit, and the law written on the heart.

Although there are elements of truth in some of this, the overall effect is disastrous, and represents a tragic misunderstanding of the new covenant. The scriptural position is that the believer is free from the law of Moses (Gal. 4:21 – 5:1), but by walking in the Spirit (Gal. 5:25) – that is, living by the power of the Spirit in obedience to Christ as revealed both within him and in the external Scriptures – he fulfils the law of Christ (Gal. 6:2).

Listen to the apostle (and this is only one of scores of such passages) as he calls believers to holiness of life:

Let not sin therefore reign in your mortal body, to make you obey its passions. Do not present your members to sin as instruments for unrighteousness, but present yourselves to God as those who have been brought from death to life, and your members to God as instruments for righteousness. For sin will have no dominion over you, since you are not under law [that is, the law of Moses] but under grace. What then? Are we to sin because we are not under law but under grace? By no means! Do you not know that if you present yourselves to anyone as obedient slaves, you are slaves of the one whom you obey, either of sin, which leads to death, or of obedience, which leads to righteousness? But thanks be to God, that you who were once slaves of sin have become obedient from the heart to the standard of teaching to which you were committed, and, having been set free from sin, have become slaves of righteousness. I am speaking in human terms, because of your natural limitations. For just as you once presented your members as slaves to impurity and to lawlessness leading to more lawlessness, so now present your members as slaves to righteousness leading to sanctification. For when you were slaves of sin, you were free in regard to righteousness. But what fruit were you getting at that time from the things of which you are now ashamed? For the end of those things is death. But now that you have been set free from sin and have become slaves of God, the fruit you get leads to sanctification and its end, eternal life. For the wages of sin is death, but the free gift of God is eternal life in Christ Jesus our Lord... My brothers, you... have died to the law [of Moses] through the body of Christ, so that you may belong to another, to him who has been raised from the dead, in order that we may bear fruit for God. For while we were living in the flesh, our sinful passions, aroused by the law [of Moses], were at work in our members to bear fruit for death. But now we are released from the law [of Moses], having died to that which held us captive, so that we serve in the new way of the Spirit and not in the old way of the written code (Rom. 6:14 – 7:6).[19]

---

[19] The 'written code' (literally, 'the letter'), of course, refers to the Mosaic law, not to the external Scriptures.

Christ the Covenant?

Consider this prophecy from Isaiah:

> Behold my servant, whom I uphold, my chosen, in whom my
> soul delights; I have put my Spirit upon him; he will bring forth
> justice to the nations. He will not cry aloud or lift up his voice,
> or make it heard in the street; a bruised reed he will not break,
> and a faintly burning wick he will not quench; he will faithfully
> bring forth justice. He will not grow faint or be discouraged till
> he has established justice in the earth; and the coastlands wait for
> his law. Thus says God, the Lord, who created the heavens and
> stretched them out, who spread out the earth and what comes
> from it, who gives breath to the people on it and spirit to those
> who walk in it: 'I am the Lord; I have called you in
> righteousness; I will take you by the hand and keep you; I will
> give you as a covenant for the people, a light for the nations, to
> open the eyes that are blind, to bring out the prisoners from the
> dungeon, from the prison those who sit in darkness. I am the
> Lord; that is my name; my glory I give to no other, nor my
> praise to carved idols. Behold, the former things have come to
> pass, and new things I now declare; before they spring forth I tell
> you of them' (Isa. 42:1-9).

The relevant words are these: 'I will give you as a covenant for
the people, a light for the nations'. To whom was God speaking?
We need be in no doubt. In the New Testament, Isaiah 42 is
quoted of Christ:

> Behold, my servant whom I have chosen, my beloved with
> whom my soul is well pleased. I will put my Spirit upon him,
> and he will proclaim justice to the Gentiles. He will not quarrel
> or cry aloud, nor will anyone hear his voice in the streets; a
> bruised reed he will not break, and a smouldering wick he will
> not quench, until he brings justice to victory; and in his name the
> Gentiles will hope (Matt. 12:18-21).[1]

---

[1] See also Matt. 3:17; 17:5; Mark 1:11; Luke 4:18-21; 9:35; John 3:34.

Christ is the covenant. As Isaiah said again in his prophecy: 'I will keep you and give you as a covenant to the people' (Isa. 49:8).[2]

Christ is the covenant; that is, Christ is the new covenant. In this brief article I want to ask how we should understand this. And there is need, since some new-covenant theologians interpret this prophecy in a way which leads to far-reaching consequences, radical consequences, unbiblical consequences. For reasons which will become apparent, I will call their interpretation 'the mystical view'.[3] Before we adopt this view, we must make sure that its interpretation of the prophet is right. In this, as in all things, we need the Berean spirit (Acts 17:11), searching the Scriptures to verify every claim. And that is what I want to do here.[4]

Let Chad R.Bresson make the mystical case. Speaking of the believer, Bresson declared:

> All behavioural norms, including those detailed in the decalogue, are ultimately defined by and expressed in the person and work of Jesus Christ.[5]

Very good. As far as it goes. However, although I would not fault a man for a word, notice what Bresson did *not* say. While he spoke of the person and work of Christ, he failed to mention the words, the teaching, the commands of Christ. And this was a very serious omission. Christ was a preacher, a teacher, a prophet. Indeed, Moses made this very point (Deut. 18:15-18). Bresson's omission (if an omission can do such a thing) cast a long shadow. I take note of his 'ultimately': yes, the believer's standard is

---

[2] All those I engage with in this article agree with me that this is Christ, not Israel.

[3] I could call it 'the personified view' or 'the enfleshment view'. By 'mystical', I do not mean 'mystery'. Of course, the union of the believer with Christ is a mystery, but the mystical here is the real danger of thinking in terms of absorption of the human into the divine.

[4] Not that I give the full arguments behind what I say. For that, see my works, especially *Christ*; 'Believers Under the Law'.

[5] Chad Richard Bresson: 'Christ, Our Covenant: A Brief Survey'.

'ultimately' Christ, but Christ and his commands are inseparable, and both he and they are spelled out in Scripture, and only in Scripture; especially, in accordance with Christ's promise (John 16:12-15), the post-Pentecost writings, where 'the person and work [and words] of Jesus Christ' are fully explained and expounded. *Christ, his person, his work, his words **and** the Scriptures are inseparable.* The fact that Bresson failed to mention this, let alone stress it, was, as I say, a very serious omission.

To move on: Bresson argued that the ideas of 'covenant' and 'law' cannot be separated.[6] Consequently, when speaking of the new covenant, he concluded that to say that 'Christ is the covenant' is the same as saying that 'Christ is the law' of that covenant. And since we know that in the new covenant God writes his law on the heart (Jer. 31:33), this means that Christ himself is written on the believer's heart. So, for the believer, according to Bresson, Christ is written on the heart, Christ is the law, Christ is the covenant. Or, rather, the Holy Spirit, the indwelling law of Christ, is the law of Christ. Thus the law of Christ is a person – the Holy Spirit:

> The Holy Spirit is the indwelling law of Christ, causing new-covenant members to obey Christ the law in conformity to his image... The Holy Spirit... dwells in believers to guide their steps and conform them to Christ. Just as the old-covenant community was structured by written revelation which centered in Moses, so the new-covenant community is ordered by the 'law of Christ' as personified and incarnated in the person of Jesus Christ, applied by the Holy Spirit, and given in the writing of the apostles and prophets (Eph. 2:20). The indwelling Holy Spirit, the law written on the heart, is the norm for Christian living.

I pause. This paragraph is confusing. On the one hand, the law of Christ (that is, the person of Christ) is 'given in the writing of the apostles and prophets', and yet, on the other hand, these writings

---

[6] Bresson: 'Christ, Our Covenant: A Brief Survey'. See Zachary S.Maxcey: 'Picture-Fulfilment New Covenant Theology: A Positive Theological Development?' I understand that those who formerly used 'picture-fulfilment' to describe their position no longer like this terminology.

are not the believer's norm; that vital role belongs solely to 'the indwelling Holy Spirit, the law written on the heart'. Not only that, Christ himself is the law. So, which of the three is it? According to Bresson, the written revelation has given way to the inward Spirit and Christ, and this, not Scripture, is the believer's norm. We learn of Christ in the Scriptures, yes, but while those Scriptures tell us about Christ (and his law – the two being the same), while they inform us, they are not part of the law of Christ itself; rather, 'the Holy Spirit is the indwelling law of Christ'.

This is a radical statement. Is it right? At the very least, Bresson has switched attention away from the Scriptures, fixing it almost exclusively on the inward work of the Spirit, on the person of the Spirit. While, during the time of the old covenant, the norm for Israel was the written law, for Bresson, now, in the new covenant, the norm for the believer is the inward Spirit. Thus the believer's standard, the norm of Christian living, is subjective, not objective.

'The Holy Spirit is the indwelling law of Christ'. Is this right? True, the Spirit indwells the believer (John 14:17; Rom. 8:11), but where, in Scripture, are we told that the Spirit is the law of Christ? We read of 'the law of the Spirit of life' in contrast with 'the law of sin and death' (Rom. 8:2), certainly, but I know of no place which states (or even hints) that the Spirit himself is the law of Christ, or is the believer's norm. The Spirit regenerates sinners, gives them a new heart, and rules, governs and motivates them to obey Scripture, yes. Believers, no longer being under Mosaic or pagan law,[7] are under the Spirit's regime, under the law of liberty, the law of Christ, yes, but this does not mean that the Spirit, himself, is the law of Christ.

Then again, while Bresson was right to say that believers are 'ordered by the law of Christ' – I would say '*under* the law of Christ' (1 Cor. 9:20-21)[8] – where do we read that the Holy Spirit is the law, 'is the norm', for believers? Scriptural obedience producing Christ-likeness (Rom. 8:29), not the Spirit, is the

---

[7] Of course it is a part of Christ 's law that the believer is subject to the State's law (Rom. 13:1-7). But we are talking of the spiritual realm.
[8] See my 'Believers Under Law'.

believer's norm. If Bresson had been right, the apostles would never have written Scripture in the form they did – with countless commands, spelling out what is required of believers. The Spirit would be doing the job, working in each believer's heart. The apostles would never have needed to write the way they did.

Again: Did the old-covenant revelation 'centre in Moses'? Moses was the mediator, the agent (Gal. 3:19) who *delivered* the law to Israel, yes, but was the law 'centred' in Moses? Not that I have ever read in Scripture. Is this a big point? Well, in saying this Bresson was effectively preparing the ground for what was to come.

Bresson: 'The law of Christ [is] personified and incarnated in the person of Jesus Christ'. Yes, Christ is the law for the believer – that is, he is the believer's standard, and his work for them is their motive for attaining that standard – but Bresson was going much further than this when he argued that Christ himself is the law, and is so actually, in that he is the law personified. The truth is, Bresson, speaking of the law of Christ, was yet again moving the focus away from Scripture. Indeed, it wasn't long before he was explicit:

> Because Christ has obeyed the law on behalf of his people and has become a law for his people, unlike the external Mosaic law, the law of Christ as the Spirit applied to the redeemed is able to effect and enable the obedience and love that is in accord with Christ's obedience and love. For the new-covenant church, the law of God is no longer an external standard that demands compliance with the will of God. The law of Christ as the indwelling Spirit is now an internal person who causes and inclines us to obey God from the heart... Christ is now the objective standard by which all holiness in the Christian life is measured. The progression of history to a final new covenant guarantees the 'law of Christ', as personified and incarnated by Jesus Christ, and applied by the Spirit who is written on the heart, to be sufficient for the church.[9]

---

[9] Chad Richard Bresson: 'What Is New Covenant Theology?' Do not miss the gloss. The Spirit is not written on the heart; the law of Christ is (Jer. 31:33).

163

Let me deal first with Bresson's use of 'objective'. When he said that 'Christ is... the objective standard by which all holiness in the Christian life is measured', he did not mean that the law of Christ is objective, since he had already stressed that this law is internal, not external. If Bresson *had* argued that the law of Christ is objective, and had worked out that principle, I would not be engaging with him in this article.

Now for the thrust of the extract above: Bresson argued that Christ is the law, and the law of Christ, applied by the Spirit, 'effects' and 'enables' the believer's obedience. And this led on to the crunch: 'For the new-covenant church, the law of God is no longer an external standard that demands compliance with the will of God. The law of Christ... as personified and incarnated by Jesus Christ, and applied by the Spirit who is written on the heart, [is] sufficient for the church'. In other words, the law of Christ is Christ himself, and this law is entirely inward, and it is this inward law, not Scripture, that is the believer's standard.

These are far-reaching claims which carry large consequences. I agree with Bresson – the law of Moses is not the believer's rule, while the law of Christ certainly is – but, contrary to Bresson, the law of Christ, the law of God for the believer, is found in Scripture as well as being written on the believer's heart. The objective nature of the law of Christ must be maintained.

We must be clear about where we have reached. There can be no doubt that Bresson's mystical approach seriously threatens the authority of Scripture by removing it from the law of Christ, having made the law of Christ entirely inward and subjective. Do not miss 'the law of God is no longer an external standard that demands compliance with the will of God. The law of Christ as the indwelling Spirit is now an internal person who causes and inclines us to obey God from the heart'. As we saw earlier, according to Bresson, 'the Holy Spirit is the indwelling law of Christ, causing new-covenant members to obey Christ the law in conformity to his image... The Holy Spirit... dwells in believers to guide their steps and conform them to Christ'. Little wonder, then, if this teaching gains ground, believers will no longer regard themselves as being under any obligation to obey Scripture, no longer having to make any effort to obey Scripture; rather, they will reason that the inward Christ and his Spirit is all they need, and all they are accountable to – if, indeed, 'accountable' is still on the agenda.[10] They will look upon Scripture as a source of information, certainly, but Scripture will not be the objective authority which reveals the required norm or standard for their obedience.

Moreover, it is important not to miss Bresson's passive emphasis in all this. The inward law 'effects' and 'enables', 'causes' and 'inclines' the believer's obedience. As Bresson went on to say:

> Christ is 'the LAW we need to obey' since he (and no longer the decalogue), in and of himself, is the standard by which all holiness is measured. The stone tablets have been exchanged for a person, a person who has fulfilled and now incarnates the tablets. Not only has he imputed that work to those who could never obey the law and were under its condemnation, in that imputation he has placed a new law on the heart, the Spirit, to conform us to the incarnation of the tablets.

I thoroughly endorse Bresson's point that the law of Christ is not the decalogue. But, bearing in mind what I have already set out from his works, when I read Bresson saying that the Spirit is the law of Christ, and the Spirit, written on the heart, conforms the believer to Christ, I, at least, am left with the unmistakable impression that the believer's submission to Scripture as part of the law of Christ has gone. Let me underline the passivity here. While I unreservedly agree that the Spirit 'causes and inclines' believers 'to obey' and 'conform' them to Christ, Bresson's lack of emphasis on the believer's responsibility to obey Scripture, coupled with his (to put it mildly) lack of emphasis on the believer's accountability to God for failure to obey, is highly charged, to say the least.

Bresson proceeded to drive home his point:

> The transfiguration... cannot be understated[11] in consideration of Christ as the law incarnate. We do not simply obey Christ

---

[10] See below.

[11] Bresson surely meant 'overstated'.

because he is the lawgiver, though he is surely that.[12] When that voice that shakes the foundations of the heavenly temple booms out: 'This is my beloved Son, listen to him', it's not merely in the context of Moses. The gloriously transfigured Messiah descends that mount not merely as the new Moses, the ultimate lawgiver, but as the new law... Unlike Deuteronomy 33, the new Moses descends the Sinai of transfiguration empty handed. Why? Because the former code has been incarnated in a person... He also descends empty handed because there is no new code to deliver. The entire paradigm for obedience has been flipped on its head.

I pause again. Of course, Christ came down from the mount of transfiguration 'empty handed'. Unlike Moses, Christ did not ascend the mountain to receive the law, the revelation from God. He had come from heaven bringing that revelation. Indeed, he himself is the revelation, the word (John 1:1-2,14). Do not miss Christ's repeated references to 'my commandments', 'my words', 'my teaching' and the like (John 12:47; 13:34; 14:15,21,23, for instance). Whereas Moses was the messenger, and only the messenger of his covenant, Christ is the message as well as the messenger of the new covenant (John 1:17; see also Heb. 3:1-6).

But, according to Bresson, the believer is under no external 'code': 'The former code has been incarnated in a person [that is, Christ]' who has 'no new code to deliver'. Indeed, 'the entire paradigm for obedience has been flipped on its head', which means, I suppose, that unlike Israel in the old covenant, believers have no written law to obey. But this is wrong. Christ delivered no new code to his disciples? What about Matthew 5 – 7 and John 12:47-50; 13:1 – 16:33, for a start? I have just mentioned Christ's repeated 'my commandments'. Now where do we discover these discourses, these commandments, this revelation? In our hearts? Or in Scripture? Are we ruled by the subjective or the objective? by feelings or revealed facts?

As for the mountain comparison, we read of Jesus going up 'on the mountain' – not the mount of transfiguration – where 'he opened his mouth and taught' (Matt. 5:1-2); he taught his law, he

---

[12] This is right. Christ is the lawgiver. But Bresson was not conceding that the Scriptures are integral to Christ's law.

did not receive it. And on the mountain of transfiguration, God, from the cloud, declared: 'This is my beloved Son, with whom I am well pleased; listen to him' (Matt. 17:5), saying it in the presence of Elijah and Moses (representing the prophets and the law). No wonder then that after the cloud had melted away, 'they saw no one but Jesus only' (Matt. 17:8). On both occasions, on both mountains, Jesus the lawgiver is manifest. And since believers have to listen to Christ, obey Christ, where can they hear his word today?

Moreover, Bresson displayed a fundamental misunderstanding over this matter of 'the code'. Paul is explicit: The believer does not serve 'in the old way of the written code [or the letter]'. He writes:

> My brothers, you... have died to the law through the body of Christ, so that you may belong to another, to him who has been raised from the dead, in order that we may bear fruit for God. For while we were living in the flesh, our sinful passions, aroused by the law, were at work in our members to bear fruit for death. But now we are released from the law, having died to that which held us captive, so that we serve in the new way of the Spirit and not in the old way of the written code [or the letter] (Rom. 7:4-6).
>
> God... has made us sufficient to be ministers of a new covenant, not of the letter but of the Spirit. For the letter kills, but the Spirit gives life. Now if the ministry of death, carved in letters on stone, came with such glory that the Israelites could not gaze at Moses' face because of its glory, which was being brought to an end, will not the ministry of the Spirit have even more glory? For if there was glory in the ministry of condemnation, the ministry of righteousness must far exceed it in glory. Indeed, in this case, what once had glory has come to have no glory at all, because of the glory that surpasses it. For if what was being brought to an end came with glory, much more will what is permanent have glory (2 Cor. 3:5-11).

Now what does the apostle mean when he speaks of 'the code'? From the *context* of these passages (Romans 6:1 – 7:6; 2 Corinthians 3:5 – 4:6), it is clear that when Paul talks of 'the code' or 'letter' he is referring to the age of the old covenant, the time when unregenerate Israel was under an external law, written

167

in stone and in the book of the law. The believer does not belong to that old age. Just as Paul, speaking of himself and all believers, could say that God 'has delivered us from the domain of darkness and transferred us to the kingdom of his beloved Son' (Col. 1:13), so it is true that God has transferred believers from the old age to the new. And as stark and real as the contrast is between darkness and light, so is the tremendous contrast between the two ages.

We must be clear about this contrast. It is vital. In the old covenant, the law of that covenant was entirely external, written on stone and in the book of the law; in the new covenant, the law of that covenant is internal, written on the heart (Jer. 31:33), as well as written in Scripture. This is one contrast. But there is a further, though intimately connected, contrast. The old covenant was with unregenerate Israel, whereas in the new covenant, every believer, is of necessity, regenerate; that is, every believer has a new heart, a new mind, a new spirit, a new will (Ezek. 36:25-27). And it is this newness of the heart, the inward aspect of the law of Christ, which constitutes the great contrast between the new and old covenants. And it is at this point that great care is needed. While the overwhelming issue is one of contrast, there is a measure of continuity between the covenants, and one aspect of the continuity lies in the external nature of the law in both ages. But whereas in the old covenant the law was entirely external, in the new covenant the law is written both internally and externally; that is, in the believer's heart and in Scripture.

And when we read that in the new covenant the law is written on the heart, we are, of course, not to think in literal terms. Believers have not undergone some form of heart surgery with a physical inscription of the law on the physical heart. Rather, speaking spiritually, the Spirit gives the sinner a new heart, and by means of that new heart, the child of God is given a love for Christ's law, a delight in it, a desire to treasure and keep it. God, by his Spirit, moves him thus:

> I will sprinkle clean water on you, and you shall be clean from all your uncleannesses, and from all your idols I will cleanse you. And I will give you a new heart, and a new spirit I will put within you. And I will remove the heart of stone from your flesh and give you a heart of flesh. And I will put my Spirit within

you, and cause you to walk in my statutes and be careful to obey my rules (Ezek. 36:25-27).

The believer, therefore, gladly takes the words of David who, being in the new covenant by anticipation, expressed it in this way: 'Oh how I love your law! It is my meditation all the day' (Ps. 119:97).[13] The believer says this of Scripture because Scripture, as nuanced by apostolic teaching, is the law of Christ, and God has given him a heart to love that law.

As a result – and this is the pertinent point – believers, obeying Scripture from the heart, by the Spirit from a renewed heart, in union with Christ, can, by no stretch of the imagination, be likened to unregenerate Israel trying to keep a purely external law, in the power of the flesh. I cannot stress this too strongly. This is the contrast.

In Romans 7:4-6 and 2 Corinthians 3:5-11, the apostle was not for a moment suggesting that the believer is not under written Scripture – especially post-Pentecost Scripture. After all, Paul was writing such at the very time he was setting out his doctrine![14] What he was saying is that the believer is no longer in the old age, no longer attempting to obey the relevant law with an unregenerate heart, in the power of the flesh. This is the point. This is the contrast. This is what Paul was talking about when he said that believers do not serve 'in the old way of the written code' (Rom. 7:6).

Bresson took his doctrine further: Christ is the law, and this law, being entirely internal, 'causes' and 'effects' the believer's conformity to Christ. I have already drawn attention to this. Bresson re-stated the claim, yet again effectively removing the necessity of the believer's submission to Scripture, removing the sense of obligation and responsibility for scriptural obedience, and accountability for failure:

As this incarnate law [Christ] descends the Sinai of transfiguration, he descends to finish his work in his own person of breaking the tyranny of the law... and in doing so, descends as

---

[13] See also Ps. 119:47-48,113,127,163,165. For the way to understand these statements, see my *Psalm 119*.

[14] See also 1 John 2:20-21,27 for the same point.

169

a law that will cause his people to conform to his standard, his image... The law written on hearts of flesh comes to dwell among his people, even as the lawgiver, law, and judge begins his rule from the heavens. This isn't simply an exchange of code for code. The new law written on hearts of flesh causes conformity to the image of the Son. This 'law' is alive, doing what the old code could never do... effecting transformation in those who are 'under' it.

This is so important, I must highlight the relevant words: the law of Christ 'causes' and 'effects' the believer's obedience. I do not deny – indeed, I glory in the fact – that the Spirit motivates and enables the believer to obey, but Bresson, by stressing God's activity and arguing against the *rule* of Scripture, has ended up in an unscriptural position: the believer is passive.

Notice, further, Bresson's use of quotation marks for 'law' and 'under'. Why? Those who advocate the mystical view are anxious to avoid all talk of the believer being 'under the law of Christ', especially when Scripture is put at the heart of that law (along with the work of the Spirit). But, as I have shown,[15] Christ's law is a real law, a more penetrating law than the Mosaic law, and the believer *is* under it! Bresson, however, by his use of quotation marks, was yet again chipping away at these vital principles.

He continued:

And what of the imperatives that are so dominant in the old-covenant schema? The imperatives of the new covenant don't 'replace' the old code. Christ himself replaces the code and then implants himself in his people via the Spirit on hearts of flesh. The imperatives are the means by which Christ through his Spirit is conforming us to the image of God in his Son. Yes, even the smattering of old-covenant code which appear in the New Testament, even those moral principles in the backdrop of the decalogue, no longer have the same function as they did in the old covenant. They cannot simply be listed in the same way as code (Christ himself is the code, applied to the heart by the Spirit).

---

[15] See my 'Believers Under Law'; 'The Penetrating Law of Christ'.

True it is that the law of Christ is not a mere 'list', but this does not mean that it is not objectively written in Scripture. Nobody could accuse any apostle of writing a mere list! Nevertheless, the apostles spelled out hundreds of commands and principles which the believer has to work out and apply in particular and ever-changing circumstances – work out, apply *and obey*. Even though Bresson recognised that there are 'imperatives of the new covenant', and although he agreed that the believer has a 'code', he maintained that this 'code' is entirely inward, and thus, as before, left no place for the Scriptures in that 'code' or law. Moreover, if Bresson is right, the believer is no longer actively submitting to Scripture, but is passively living out the inward work of the Spirit – or, more precisely, the Spirit is working it out through him. Christ, by his Spirit, is responsible, not the believer: 'The imperatives are the means by which Christ through his Spirit is conforming us to the image of God in his Son'. As I have explained elsewhere,[16] this is getting close to hyper-Calvinism, or the Keswick teaching of 'Let go, and let God'.[17] Indeed, it is not far removed from quietism.[18]

Bresson went on:

> The imperatives... are no longer external, but internal, being worked out of us in the transformation of the Spirit. We work out the imperatives of the new covenant, we do the imperatives because conformity through them to the image of Christ is who we are. To suggest that the imperatives are new code replacing old code is pulling an old paradigm into the new, when in fact, the very nature of commands and imperatives in the new covenant has been changed.

Yes, as Bresson did agree, believers 'work out' commands, they 'do the imperatives', but the truth is, he claimed, these commands

---

[16] 'The Obedience of Faith'.

[17] 'Obedience isn't acquiescence to an external demand, but the manifestation of an inward reality' (Chad Richard Bresson: 'The Incarnation of the Abstract: New Covenant Theology and the Enfleshment of the Law'). 'Manifestation' by whom? Does the Spirit manifest it? Or does the believer manifest it by his active obedience to Scripture, moved by the Spirit?

[18] 'Abandonment of the will as a form of religious mysticism'.

or imperatives are really 'worked out of [them by] the Spirit'. As I say, according to this – when coupled with Bresson's relegation of Scripture (at best) to the sidelines – the believer's conformity to Christ really amounts to little more than a passive experience of the Spirit working within him. The believer becomes a virtual spectator watching the Spirit (and/or Christ) produce Christ-likeness in and through him:

> Thus, Christ's descent from Sinai transfiguration and his ascent to his throne must change everything we ever thought about law, law-keeping and imperative-obeying. Christ the King is Christ the law. The very fingers that carved out the words in the tablets have now taken on flesh and have become the word imprinted by the Spirit on the heart... The one who became a new covenant for his people now creates covenant-keepers through his Spirit who produces covenant-keeping. The new *torah*, who is both the original lawgiver and perfect lawkeeper, produces obedience in those who are indwelt by the Spirit, the law written on the heart... This is the new covenant. Things are not the same.[19]

And yet, as we know, God's promise in the new covenant is explicit: 'I will put my Spirit within you, and cause you to walk in my statutes and be careful to obey my rules' (Ezek. 36:27). Who needs these 'statutes' and 'rules' – the believer or the Spirit? Who needs to be 'careful'? And who has to walk in obedience to God's statutes and rules? Yes, the Spirit causes the believer to obey Scripture, but it is the believer himself who knows he must be careful to obey and who, by God's grace, does obey.

In what follows, note Bresson's use of Isaiah 42:6. His case depends on his mystical interpretation of the prophet.[20] Do not miss the opening 'because':

> Because Christ has become a covenant for his people and the Spirit has descended to indwell Christ's people as the law written on the heart, there is an altogether new dynamic inherent to the question of new-covenant ethics. No longer do imperatives find their impetus from without as was true of the Mosaic code... but from within. The nature of the command itself is no longer external, but internal. Obedience isn't

---

[19] Chad Richard Bresson: 'Christ, the New Torah'.
[20] Why did he not quote an apostle making the case?

acquiescence to an external demand, but the manifestation of an inward reality.

I agree that the believer's 'impetus' is internal, and not external, but this inward 'impetus' directs the believer to obey Scripture, and thus to conform him to Christ. Not for Bresson, however:

> [Since] the law is a person [that is, Christ] [it] means [that] the law of the new covenant is not encoded in external imperatives or principles.[21]

Finally, we come to the ultimate in this mystical interpretation of Isaiah 42:6. According to Steve Fuchs:

> When we understand Christ to be the law, we are really saying the Spirit of Christ... Christ becomes law, a law which causes righteousness to be manifest in his people, by indwelling them as Holy Spirit. He and the Spirit are one, and in the same way we are made one in nature with them by their indwelling us.[22]

What? Are we, as believers, 'made one in nature with [Christ and his Spirit] by their indwelling us'? This is nothing less than downright mysticism, not to say deification. I do not find this in Scripture. Believers 'share in Christ' and 'the Holy Spirit' (Heb. 3:14; 6:4), yes, and they are made 'partakers of the divine nature' (2 Pet. 1:4), yes, but this does not mean they are one in nature with Christ and the Spirit, deified.[23] This mystical teaching, however, gets close to the Finnish school:

> Christ himself is life, righteousness and blessing, because God is all this in nature and substance. Therefore justifying faith means participation in God's essence in Christ.[24]

---

[21] Quoted by Maxcey.

[22] See previous note.

[23] As once we were 'in Adam', so now we are 'in Christ' (Rom. 5:12-19; 1 Cor. 15:22,48-49). C.H.Spurgeon: 'We become partakers of the divine nature... in any sense anything short of our being absolutely divine' (sermon number 551).

[24] Tuomo Mannermaa, quoted by J.Todd Billings: 'The Contemporary Reception of Luther and Calvin's Doctrine of Union with Christ: Mapping a Biblical, Catholic and Reformational Motif' in R.Ward

There is another possibility:

> Docetism... produces distorted thinking about the subject of holiness or sanctification. The human element in our Christian life is played down in favour of the life of Christ (his purely divine life) being lived in and through us. In popular jargon, 'Let go, and let God' sometimes means that human effort has no place in holy living. The believer in effect is not only being divinized, but is actually being absorbed into the being of God. The real distinction between God and man which was established in creation is blurred. So, to quote another popular cliché, the believer is only a suit of clothes that Jesus wears![25]

A summary of the points at issue

According to the mystical view, believers should understand that:

'Christ is the covenant' (Isa. 42:6 and 49:8), and he is so literally.

Christ (and/or his Spirit) constitutes the law of Christ, and he does so personally and really.

The law of Christ is entirely inward.

The written Scriptures are not part of the law of Christ.

Union with Christ means that they and Christ have one nature. In other words, they are deified.

They are passive in their obedience. Their obedience is entirely by Christ or his Spirit. They observe Christ working through and in them by his Spirit. This is the way of conformity to Christ.

These far-reaching conclusions are clearly contrary to the countless apostolic appeals, exhortations, commands, arguments and instructions which we find in the post-Pentecost Scriptures, urging, demanding and calling believers to be proactive, as responsible men and women under God, in their progressive

---

Holder (editor) *Calvin and Luther: The Continuing Relationship*, Vandenhoeck & Ruprecht, Gottingen, 2013, pp166-167.
[25] Graeme Goldsworthy: 'The Gospel and Wisdom' in *The Goldsworthy Trilogy*, Paternoster, Milton Keynes, reprinted 2014, p373.

sanctification. Let me take one verse to make the point. There is no possibility of passivity about this command:

> Strive... for the holiness without which no one will see the Lord (Heb. 12:14, ESV).
> Make every effort... to be holy; without holiness no one will see the Lord (NIV).

I hasten to add that in saying this I do not for a moment deny that this obedience is only possible by the work of God within the believer:

> Now may the God of peace who brought again from the dead our Lord Jesus, the great shepherd of the sheep, by the blood of the eternal covenant, equip you with everything good that you may do his will, working in us that which is pleasing in his sight, through Jesus Christ, to whom be glory forever and ever. Amen (Heb. 13:20-21).

But it is not either/or. It is both:

> Therefore, my beloved, as you have always obeyed, so now, not only as in my presence but much more in my absence, work out your own salvation with fear and trembling, for it is God who works in you, both to will and to work for his good pleasure (Phil. 2:12-13).

As Jameson-Fausset-Brown explained:

> 'Salvation' is 'worked in' (Phil. 2:13; Eph. 1:11) believers by the Spirit, who enables them through faith to be justified once for all; but it needs, as a progressive work, to be 'worked out' by obedience, through the help of the same Spirit, unto perfection (2 Pet. 1:5-8). The sound Christian neither, like the formalist, rests in the means, without looking to the end, and to the Holy Spirit who alone can make the means effectual; nor, like the fanatic, hopes to attain the end without the means... God makes a new heart, and [yet] we are commanded to make us a new heart; not merely because we must use the means in order to the effect, but the effect itself is our act and our duty (Ezek. 11:19; 18:31; 36:26).[26]

---

[26] See also the extracts from Graeme Goldsworthy: 'The Gospel in Revelation' in *The Goldsworthy Trilogy*, Paternoster, Milton Keynes, reprinted 2014, pp238-239,281-282 and Wayne Grudem: *Systematic*

As I say, the conclusions which come from the mystical interpretation of Isaiah 42:6 (and Isaiah 49:8) contradict the overwhelming weight of Scripture. So much so, it is staggering to think that they depend on two texts (in truth, one text) which no New Testament writer ever interprets in this mystical way. Indeed, they depend on two texts which no New Testament writer ever uses to expound the glories of the new covenant and the law of Christ. Above all, they depend on two texts ('Christ the covenant') which no New Testament writer even quotes![27]

So what of Isaiah 42:6 and 49:8?

Edward J.Young pointed out that 'covenant' and 'light' are closely connected: 'Those who receive the covenant at the same time receive light, and those to whom the light comes have thereby participated in the covenant'. As Christ is the covenant, therefore, so he is the light. Now just as Christ is not a literal light, just as the prophet's description of Christ as 'a light' is figurative, so with 'a covenant'. Moreover, the prophet did not actually predict that Christ would be the covenant. Do not miss the 'as' in 'I will give you as a covenant for the people, [as] a light for the nations': Christ was given as a covenant, as a light: 'I have come into the world as a light' (John 12:46, NIV). In other words, once again, we should be thinking in figurative terms. Of course, it is perfectly correct to say that Christ is the new covenant as long as we understand it figuratively or symbolically, and not literally. This, however, is not to imply that the prophecy lacks any fullness. As Young put it:

> The language is striking, for the servant is actually identified as a covenant... That the servant is identified with the covenant of course involves the idea of his being the one through whom the covenant is mediated, but the expression implies more. In form it is similar to our Lord's: 'I am the resurrection and the life' (John

Theology..., Inter-Varsity Press, Leicester, 1994, pdf link pp655-657, in 'Believers Under the Law of Christ'.
[27] The New Testament quotes Isa. 42, as I have noted, but it never uses either text to argue Christ as 'the covenant'. Indeed, when Paul and Barnabas quote Isa. 49:6 (Acts 13:46-49), they leave out the reference.

11:25], or the phrase in Isaiah 49:6: 'To be my salvation'. To say that the servant is the covenant is to say that all the blessings of the covenant are embodied in, have their root and origin in, and are dispersed by him. At the same time, he is himself at the centre of all blessings, and to receive them is to receive him, for without him there can be no blessings... Moses was a mediator of the [old] covenant, but the servant *is* the [new] covenant.[28] In New Testament terms, this means that they to whom God sovereignly bestows the grace of salvation receive the servant himself. Parallel to the expression 'covenant of the people' is the phrase 'light of the Gentiles'. Not merely does the servant bring light or lead into light, but he is himself the light. Light is a figurative description of salvation (Isa. 49:6).[29]

Let me repeat the vital words: 'To say that the servant is the covenant is to say that all the blessings of the covenant are embodied in,[30] have their root and origin in, and are dispersed by him. At the same time, he is himself at the centre of all blessings, and to receive them is to receive him, for without him there can be no blessings'. In other words, as the apostle put it: 'Christ is all, and in all' (Col. 3:11). Thus, in accordance with Luke 24:27,32 and 1 Peter 1:10-12, Isaiah's prediction of Christ in the new covenant, Christ as the sum and substance of the new covenant, led to Colossians 3:11 as the apostolic summary of his prophecy. When writing to the Ephesians, Paul spelled it out in more detail:

> Blessed be the God and Father of our Lord Jesus Christ, who has blessed us in Christ with every spiritual blessing in the heavenly

---

[28] Compare: ' Consider Jesus... who was faithful to him who appointed him, just as Moses also was faithful in all God's house. For Jesus has been counted worthy of more glory than Moses – as much more glory as the builder of a house has more honour than the house itself... Now Moses was faithful in all God's house as a servant, to testify to the things that were to be spoken later, but Christ is faithful over God's house as a son' (Heb. 3:1-6).

[29] Edward J.Young: *The Book Of Isaiah*, Wm. B.Eerdmans, 1972, Vol.3 pp119-121, emphasis his. Young (p278) referred the reader to the above for his comments on Isa. 49:8.

[30] By 'embody', Young surely meant something like 'unite, gather together, be the sum of', not 'give it a bodily form'.

places, even as he chose us in him before the foundation of the world, that we should be holy and blameless before him. In love he predestined us for adoption as sons through Jesus Christ, according to the purpose of his will, to the praise of his glorious grace, with which he has blessed us in the Beloved. In him we have redemption through his blood, the forgiveness of our trespasses, according to the riches of his grace, which he lavished upon us, in all wisdom and insight making known to us the mystery of his will, according to his purpose, which he set forth in Christ as a plan for the fullness of time, to unite all things in him, things in heaven and things on earth. In him we have obtained an inheritance, having been predestined according to the purpose of him who works all things according to the counsel of his will, so that we who were the first to hope in Christ might be to the praise of his glory. In him you also, when you heard the word of truth, the gospel of your salvation, and believed in him, were sealed with the promised Holy Spirit, who is the guarantee of our inheritance until we acquire possession of it, to the praise of his glory (Eph. 1:3-14).

But this is a far cry from the mystical view. I stress again that the prophet's language is figurative, poetic. As Young said: 'Light is a figurative description of salvation (Isa. 49:6)'.

The *Pulpit Commentary*:

The covenant between God and his people being in Christ, it is quite consistent with Hebrew usage to transfer the term to Christ himself, in whom the covenant was, as it were, embodied.[31] So Christ is called 'our salvation' and 'our peace', and again, 'our redemption' and 'our life'. This is the ordinary tone of Hebrew poetry, which rejoices in personification and embodiment. A prose writer would have said that the servant of the Lord would be given as the mediator of a covenant between Jehovah and his people.

In other words, 'Christ is the covenant' means that Christ is the mediator of the covenant. The prophet was expressing himself figuratively, poetically.

John Gill enlarged on this:

---

[31] See previous note.

Christ is... the representative of his people in [the covenant], the surety, mediator, messenger, and ratifier of it, the great blessing in it, the sum and substance of it. All the blessings and promises of it are in him, and as such he is 'given'.

Once again, in the apostle's words: 'Christ is all' (Col. 3:11).

C.H.Spurgeon, preaching on Isaiah 49:8, opened by speaking of Christ as the mediator and surety of the covenant. He went on:

And I doubt not, we have also rejoiced in the thought that Christ is the sum and substance of the covenant; we believe that if we would sum up all spiritual blessings, we must say: 'Christ is all'. He is the matter, he is the substance of it; and although much might be said concerning the glories of the covenant, yet nothing could be said which is not to be found in that one word: 'Christ'.[32]

It is at this point that the mystical teaching leaves the rails. Its mistake becomes patent the moment we think of transubstantiation. I am sure we can all hear echoes of Martin Luther insisting on the literal reading of the text: 'This *is* my body' (Matt. 26:26). For the papist, this means that the priest holds the very flesh of Christ in his hands. For Luther it meant consubstantiation, the very flesh of Christ in the bread. Both have got it wrong. The same goes for the mystical view of Isaiah 42:6.

As soon as we apply the mystical interpretation to parallel statements such as Christ is the branch, the stem of Jesse, the root of David (Isa 4:2; 11:1,10; Jer. 23:5; 33:15; Zech. 3:8, 6:12; Rev. 5:5), the lamb (John 1:29,36), a horn (Luke 1:69),[33] the bread (John 6:33-35,48,51,58), the vine (John 15:1,4-5), the light (Matt. 4:16; Luke 2:32; John 8:12, 9:5; 12:35-36,46), the lion (Rev 5:5), the door or sheep gate (John 10:7-9), the shepherd (John 10:11,14), its wrongness becomes as clear as noonday.

How can we literally eat the flesh and drink the blood of Christ (John 6:48-56)? The Jews took this deliberately (John 6:52), and most of the disciples found it 'hard' (John 6:60,66). Christ, of course, was speaking spiritually, figuratively, not

---

[32] Sermon number 103.
[33] '"Horn" symbolises strength' (NIV footnote).

literally (John 6:63).[34] In the very early days of the church, do not forget, pagans chose to interpret all this literally, and so could claim that the believers were cannibals. It seems to me that in these days some new-covenant theologians are adopting an interpretation that these critics would have eagerly latched onto. Bresson, speaking for those of like-mind with himself, is sensitive to criticism from other new-covenant theologians:

> While this [mystical] group has nowhere denied the necessity of obedience in the Christian experience of the new-covenant member, the existence of obligation between kingdom-citizen and the King [Christ], or the command and demand nature of the New Testament imperatives, there has been a persistent drumbeat of criticism from others in the new-covenant theology movement that the incarnational and objective approach to new-covenant ethics is... inherently antinomian... As awareness of the views expressed by this... [mystical] group have increased... so too has the volume of rhetoric aimed at cementing [classic] new-covenant theology's affirmation of command, demand, and obedience.[35]

I am securely in this critical group, and I remain unrepentantly critical of the mystic view. Let it be understood that I am not accusing Bresson and his friends of antinomianism. Do not miss the 'inherently'. I am concerned with long term consequences. We surely realise that it is not only what we say, but what people think we say, what people hear, that counts. What people bring to our words, and then take away with them, carries more weight than what we intend to say. We need to keep this in mind at all times, and do what we can to prevent our hearers and readers getting the wrong impression, and drawing the wrong conclusions. Hence the 'inherently'.

But, as I have made clear in this article, I have further criticisms of the mystical view in addition to that of inherent antinomianism. So much so, I am fully committed to do all in my power to maintain classic 'new-covenant theology's affirmation

---

[34] How often men go wrong here. Take John 2:19-22; 3:3-15; 4:13-15; 6:34,52.
[35] Chad Richard Bresson: 'The Incarnation of the Abstract: New Covenant Theology and the Enfleshment of the Law'.

of command, demand, and obedience'. The believer is under the law of Christ, and that law is objectively revealed in Scripture. Moreover, the believer is responsible for obedience and is accountable for any disobedience. In saying this, I do not in the least draw back from what I have declared concerning the perfection and freedom from condemnation that the believer has in Christ,[36] nor do I retract what I have said about the absolute necessity of the Spirit's motivating power and grace; the believer can only obey, will only obey, Scripture because he has a new heart and the Spirit motivates him to Christ-likeness. And I have written this article as part of my contribution to the upholding of this scriptural balance.

Conclusion

Believers are under Christ as slave-master (Rom. 6:11-23), are united to him in marriage, in order to bear children for his praise (Rom. 7:1-6), are joined to Christ as branches to the vine (John 15:1-8), 'share in Christ' and 'the Holy Spirit' (Heb. 3:14; 6:4), and are made 'partakers of the divine nature' (2 Pet. 1:4), but none of this is literal.

Those who, with Bresson, advocate the literal reading of 'Christ is the covenant', run the risk (to put it no higher) of making Christ the believer's actual law, making that law to be entirely inward, and thus removing the Scriptures from the law of Christ, and, in so doing, at the very least play down the demand for the believer's accountable submission to the objective law of Christ in Scripture. This can only lead to a passive view of the believer's conformity to Christ. I have certainly met evidence of it.

But we know that the Spirit gives the elect a new heart in regeneration (writing Christ's law on the heart), unites them to Christ by faith, and moves them to obey Scripture (Phil. 2:13) to grow in likeness to Christ. There is nothing passive about progressive sanctification. As Christ still commands all his disciples:

---

[36] See, for instance, my *Fivefold*; *Four 'Antinomians'*.

You call me teacher and Lord, and you say well, for so I am...
I... your Lord and teacher... have given you an example, that you
should do as I have done to you... If you know these things,
blessed are you if you do them (John 13:13-17). A new
commandment I give to you, that you love one another; as I have
loved you, that you also love one another (John 13:34).
Believe... in me... believe me (John 14:1,11). If you love me,
keep my commandments (John 14:15). He who has my
commandments and keeps them, it is he who loves me (John
14:21). He who does not love me does not keep my words; and
the word which you hear is not mine but the Father's who sent
me (John 14:24). Abide in me (John 15:4). This is my
commandment, that you love one another as I have loved you
(John 15:12). You are my friends if you do whatever I command
you (John 15:14). These things I command you, that you love
one another (John 15:17).

And Christ continues to rule his people by Scripture. As Isaac
Watts put it:

> *Praise to the goodness of the Lord,*
> *Who rules his people by his word.*

In conclusion, while I reject the mystical view, 'Christ is the
covenant' does indeed convey a glorious truth, one which needs
trumpeting abroad: Christ is the sum and substance of the new
covenant. 'Christ is all' (Col. 3:11).

The Law of Moses

In this section, the 'law' to which I refer is almost always the law of Moses. The context will make it clear if another law is meant.

I show that 'law' is a highly-nuanced word in Scripture. Many people go wrong at this point because they simply collate or coalesce references to 'law', paying scant attention to the context, or none at all, especially the *newness* of the new covenant. Having set out what Scripture means by 'the law', I then go on to show that all men are under law in one form or another. Adam was, all men ever since have been, Israel was under the law of Moses, Christ came under the law of Moses, and believers are under the law of Christ. I then close this opening section with two chapters challenging unbelievers as to which law they are under.

What Is the Law?

There is an enormous amount of confusion, not to say misinformation, in much that is said and written about 'the law'.[1] Let me explain.

Most evangelicals think of 'the law' as a moral system encapsulated in the ten commandments.[2] This is a bad, bad mistake, and the source of much misunderstanding and trouble. True, 'the ten commandments' *is* a biblical phrase, but its use in Scripture is very rare, and the law is never defined in this way, never! The phrase 'ten commandments' occurs only three times in the entire Bible (Ex. 34:28; Deut. 4:13; 10:4), never once in the New Testament. Of course, the 'tablets of stone', and 'the ministry... written and engraved on stones' are mentioned in the New Testament (2 Cor. 3:3,7), but whether these are references exclusively to the ten commandments or to the entire Sinai covenant is debatable.

So where did the idea – that 'the law' means 'the ten commandments' – come from? It originated with Thomas Aquinas in the 13th century, was developed by the Reformers, and reached its zenith in the following hundred years under the Puritans. It is still with us. And it confuses – and worse than confuses – the debate over the law right at the start.

How does the Bible speak of 'the law'?

The two main words are *torah* (instruction)[3] in the Old Testament, and *nomos* in the New. Sometimes 'the law' refers to

---

[1] Reader, you are advised to read this article before the next.

[2] For this article, I have lightly edited my *Christ* pp25-26; see also pp214-218,336,481-483.

[3] The meaning of *torah* is 'teaching', 'doctrine', or 'instruction'; the commonly accepted 'law' gives a wrong impression. We should, perhaps, think in terms of 'custom, theory, guidance or system' (see Wikipedia).

the entire Scriptures;[4] sometimes the Old Testament;[5] sometimes the Pentateuch,[6] or Moses' teaching;[7] sometimes the ten commandments (but whether just the ten commandments is open to question);[8] sometimes a system or universal principle;[9] sometimes the Mosaic covenant;[10] sometimes several of these concepts coalesce.[11]

Take Romans 3:19 as a particular example: 'Now we know that whatever the law says, it says to those who are under the law, that every mouth may be stopped, and all the world may become guilty before God'. The context tells us what 'the law' is here. It must refer to more than the ten commandments, and more than the Pentateuch. After all, in Romans 3:10-18, Paul quotes extensively from the Psalms, and from Ecclesiastes and Isaiah, all the while talking about 'the law'. Some, however, limit 'the law' of Romans 3:19 to what they call 'the moral law', the ten commandments. This is wrong. 'The law' here refers to the entire Old Testament, especially the Mosaic law.

To summarise: In Scripture, the word 'law' is capable of several meanings. It certainly is not always(!) the ten commandments. In fact, it overwhelmingly refers to *all* the Mosaic legislation. Let me give some evidence for what I say.

---

[4] Ps. 19:7, for instance.

[5] John 10:34 quoting Ps. 82:6; John 12:34 alluding to Dan. 7:14; John 15:25 quoting Ps. 35:19 and 69:4; 1 Cor. 14:21 quoting Isa. 28:11-12, for instance.

[6] John 1:45; Luke 16:16; 24:44; Gal. 4:21, for instance.

[7] Josh. 1:7-8; 2 Kings 14:6; John 5:46; 1 Cor. 9:9, for instance. 1 Cor. 9:9 is the only place where Paul used the phrase, 'the law of Moses', probably meaning the five books of Moses.

[8] Rom. 7:7,14, for instance.

[9] Rom. 7:21,23; 8:2a, for instance. 'The law of faith' (Rom. 3:27) clearly means the *principle* of faith. See my *Christ* pp214-218,481-483.

[10] Deut. 5:1-3,5-22; 6:1; 9:9,11,15; 10:4-5,8, for instance. (I admit 'the law' does not appear in these verses – as a phrase – but they are clearly talking about it).

[11] Matt. 11:13; 12:5; John 1:17; 12:34, for instance.

Moses spoke 'every *precept* [*commandment*, NASB and NIV]...
according to the *law*... saying: "This is the blood of the *covenant*
which God has *commanded* you"... According to the *law* almost
all things are purified with blood' (Heb. 9:19-22). 'Moses came
and told the people all the *words* of the LORD and all the
judgments... And Moses wrote all the *words* of the LORD... He
took the book of the *covenant* and read [it]... And Moses took the
blood, sprinkled it on the people, and said: "This is the blood of
the *covenant* which the LORD has made with you according to
all these *words*"' (Ex. 24:3-8). What were these *words*, these
judgments, this *covenant*, this *law*? Everything which God made
known to the Hebrews leaving Egypt (Ex. 12 – 13), in the
wilderness of Sinai (Ex. 15 – 16; 19:1 – 24:8, and far beyond),
the covenant (Ex. 19:5), the words the LORD commanded (Ex.
19:7), the ten commandments (Ex. 20), the judgments (Ex. 21 –
23). Clearly, law, commandments, precepts, statutes, words of the
LORD, judgments and covenant are all encompassed in the one
word 'law'. Indeed, 'law' includes virtually everything from
Exodus 12 to the end of Deuteronomy (the renewal of the law in
Moab), including Leviticus and Numbers.

In particular, when Paul spoke of 'the law', he almost always
meant the Jewish law, the law of God given to Israel through
Moses as recorded in the first five books of the Bible.

There is another point: Paul frequently used the word 'law'
without the definite article – a fact which many readers of the
English New Testament may not be aware of, since the
translators have often introduced the definite article to make the
text read 'the law', instead of what Paul actually wrote; that is,
'law'. But the lack of the article, contrary to how it might seem, is
Paul's way of stressing his concept of law, not the opposite.

In short, 'the law' in Scripture really amounts to the revelation of
God to Israel, principally through Moses on Sinai, including (but
far from being restricted to) the ten commandments engraved on

the two stone tablets. And this is the overriding meaning we should attach to 'the law'.[12]

---

[12] In saying this, I except biblical prophecies of the new covenant. The law of the new covenant, the law of Christ, contrary to covenant theologians, most definitely is *not* the law of Moses. Jer. 31:32 (Heb. 8:9) expressly states that the new covenant is not like the old covenant. Consequently, but this is not the only reason, the new law in the new covenant is not like the old law of the old covenant. It is, in fact, very different! As for which 'law' it is that fulfils such prophecies, see my *Christ* pp299-321,543-555; 'The Prophets and the New Covenant'.

To Whom Did God Give the Law?

With regard to the law of Moses, Paul divides the human race into two.[1] All are sinners, but some have sinned 'without law'; the rest have sinned 'in the law' (Rom. 2:12). This is the biblical divide – those 'under the law', and those 'without law' (1 Cor. 9:20-21). Those 'in the law' have the law of God; those 'without law' do not. Clearly, therefore, the law could not have been given to all men. If it had, Paul's division would have been utterly meaningless; indeed, nonsensical.

Those 'in' or 'under' the law are the Jews, God having made known his entire law to Israel (Rom. 3:1-2; 9:4); those 'without law' are, therefore, non-Jews, Gentiles. We are specifically and repeatedly told that God did not reveal his law to any other nation but Israel.[2] He did not deal in this way with any other people

---

[1] For this article, I have lightly edited my *Christ* pp27-37; see also pp337-341. Reader, you should read the previous article before this.
[2] Israel became a nation in Egypt (Gen. 46:3; Deut. 26:5), particularly at the exodus leading to Sinai (Gen. 12:1-2; 17:2-14; 46:3,26-27; Ex. 1:5,7; 2:24-25; 3:6-8,10,15-18; 4:5,22-23; 6:2-8; 7:4,16; 8:1; 9:1; 12:2,17; 13:3-10; 15:11-18,26; 16:22-30; 18:1; 19:3-6; 31:13-17; 32:11-14; 33:13; Deut. 4:20,34; 16:1; 27:9; 28:9; Ps. 114:1-2; Ezek. 20:5-12,20; Acts 7:14,17), and confirmed at the giving of the covenant just before entering Canaan (Deut. 26:18; 27:9). This is when God distinguished them from all other nations by starting their calendar, giving them the feasts and the sabbath as an integral part of his law. 'What great nation is there that has such statutes and righteous judgements as are in all this law which I set before you this day?' (Deut. 4:8). Deut. 4:7 shows the same in his nearness to Israel and his willingness to hear their prayers. In short, Deut. 4:32-38. Israel's position was *unique*, not merely *special*. Now these things are clearly contrasted to the creation-gift of beasts, birds, fish, planets and the like 'which the LORD your God has given to all the peoples under the whole heaven as a heritage' (Deut. 4:17-19). The contrast is enforced further: 'But the LORD has taken you and brought you out of the iron furnace, out of Egypt, to be his people, an inheritance' (Deut. 4:20). And, as I say, one of the greatest distinctions God made between Israel and all other nations was to give his law to

(Deut. 4:6-45; 5:26; 7:6-11; Ps. 147:19-20; Rom. 9:4). The principle underlies Romans 9:30-32. We are told expressly that the Gentiles do not have the law (Rom. 2:12-14), but that it was given to the Jews, being 'the statutes and judgements and laws which the LORD made between himself and *the children of Israel* on Mount Sinai by the hand of Moses' (Lev. 26:46), God immediately reiterating the point with the closing verse of Leviticus: 'These are the commandments which the LORD commanded Moses *for the children of Israel* on Mount Sinai' (Lev. 27:34).[3] Right from the start, while the people were camped in the wilderness of Sinai, even as Moses was called up to the mountain to receive the law, God prefaced it all: 'Thus you shall say to *the house of Jacob*, and tell *the children of Israel...*' (Ex. 19:3-6). God opened the ten commandments thus: 'I am the LORD your God, who brought *you* out of the land of Egypt...' (Ex. 20:2). And after the re-giving of the law, God could declare to Moses: 'According to the tenor of these words I have made a covenant with you and with *Israel*' (Ex. 34:27). (See also 2 Kings 17:13; 2 Chron. 5:10; 6:11; Neh. 9:1,13-14; *etc.*).

Nor was it the last time Israel was reminded of the fact. Solomon called Israel to 'take care to fulfil the statutes and judgements with which the LORD charged Moses *concerning Israel*' (1 Chron. 22:13). When Israel was removed from the land and taken into captivity, the king of Assyria replaced the children of Israel in Samaria with foreigners. These foreigners, it is recorded, brought their own gods, and their own 'rituals'. Rejecting the law of the Hebrews, they did not 'follow *their*

Israel – and to no others. The law divided, separated, Israel from all other people. See Ps. 103:7.

[3] This is not to be confined to the so-called 'ceremonial law' – see my *Christ* pp99-110,392-408. For now, notice how this blanket description in the closing verse of Leviticus includes at least the second, third, fourth, fifth, seventh, eighth and ninth commands (Lev. 19:3,4,11-13,16,30; 20:9,10; 23:3; 24:10-23; 26:1,2) of the so-called 'moral law'. As for the rest, the first commandment is implied throughout Leviticus – see in particular Lev. 26:1, the sixth in Lev. 19:16-18, and transgression of the tenth is pervasive – Paul found it so (Rom. 7:7), since the Jews thought it summed up the law, and to break it to be the root of all sins.

statutes or *their* ordinances, or the law and commandment which the LORD had commanded *the children of Jacob*, whom he named *Israel'* (2 Kings 17:34). Addressing Israel, God could speak of 'the statutes, the ordinances, the law, and the commandment which he wrote for *you'* (2 Kings 17:37), promising Israel they would not 'wander any more from the land which I gave *their* fathers – [but] only if *they* are careful to do according to all that I have commanded *them*, and according to all the law that my servant Moses commanded *them'* (2 Kings 21:8). As with the land, so with the law – both had been given to Israel, and no others. When God revealed his law to Israel, he expressly commanded them not to do as the pagans did, but to 'observe my judgements and keep my ordinances... [to] keep my statutes and my judgements' (Lev. 18:1-5,26-30). Centuries after Sinai, God had to complain that Israel had not done this: 'You have not walked in my statutes nor executed my judgements, but have done according to the customs of the Gentiles which are all around you' (Ezek. 11:12), they had 'conformed to the standards of the nations around' them (NIV), breaking God's law (Deut. 12:29-32).[4] This makes sense if, and only if, God's (and Israel's) laws were different to the laws, principles, statutes, norms, judgements and standards of the pagans.

Asaph reminded Israel that the LORD 'established a testimony in *Jacob*, and appointed a law in *Israel*, which he commanded *our* fathers' (Ps. 78:5). Daniel, when praying for the children of Israel, could speak of God's 'laws, which he set before *us* by his servants the prophets' (Dan. 9:10-13). God reminded Hosea, concerning Israel: 'I have written *for him* the great things of my law' (Hos. 8:12). And 'God, the one of Sinai... God, the God of *Israel'* (Ps. 68:8, NIV), commanded Israel to 'remember the law of Moses, my servant, which I commanded him in Horeb *for all Israel*, with the statutes and judgements' (Mal. 4:4). In Numbers 15, God said the law applied to the Jews, and those who would be reckoned Jews – proselytes and sojourners.

---

[4] If Ezek. 5:5-7 translation is right – but see footnote (NKJV, NIV) – Israel was worse than the pagans (Ezek. 16:47).

To say that the law applies to the entire human race, is to render these statements and demands utterly superfluous and meaningless. What is more – and a glance at the passages quoted above will confirm it – we are talking about the law, the law of God, the law of Moses, the whole law, the law in its entirety. The law was given to Israel, for Israel, to distinguish Israel from all others.

Nor was this a mere quirk of history. As I have noted, God treated the Jews as special, showing special regard for them in giving them his law. This was his *purpose*. He gave his law to the Jews *in order to* distinguish them from all others. Division was God's intention in giving the law to the Jews. Division! Separation! Distinction was God's great concern for Israel (Lev. 20:24,26).[5] And it was the law that especially marked the Jews out from the Gentiles, serving as a dividing wall, a partition, a demarcation between them and the pagans (Gal. 3:23-25 – note the 'we' and 'our'; Eph. 2:11-16). The law regulated their national and personal life in every respect. Finally, it was a temporary measure confining Israel until the coming of Christ (Gal. 3:19-24).

Moses, when repeating God's law in Moab, made it plain to whom it was given, declaring: 'Hear, O *Israel*... The LORD our God made a covenant with *us* in Horeb... He said: "I am the LORD your God who brought you out of the land of Egypt, out of the house of bondage"' (Deut. 5:1-2,5-6). God said 'Israel', and he meant Israel, and only Israel. It was only Israel whom he had delivered from Egypt.[6] But not only was the preface to the ten commandments peculiar to Israel. The fourth commandment concerned the sabbath which was a special sign for Israel (Ex. 31:13,16-17; Ezek. 20:12,20),[7] and the fifth commandment referred to the land promised to Israel. In addition, the overwhelming bulk of the hundreds of other commandments

---

[5] God's presence also distinguished them from all other people (Ex. 33:16).
[6] The exodus from Egypt continued to preface references to the law. See 2 Kings 17:36, for instance.
[7] See my *Sabbath Questions*.

contained in the law were spelled out in terms which belonged only to Israel. In short, Gentiles were not brought out of Egypt – in fact many of them (that is, the Egyptians) perished in Egypt or the Red Sea.[8] Gentiles were not given the sabbath as a special sign that they were the people of God. Gentiles were not given the pillar of cloud and fire. Gentiles were not given the manna. Gentiles were not given the promised land – the truth is, they had to be removed from it. Gentiles were not given the ordinances of the tabernacle. And so on. As just one example of how these things are linked, take Nehemiah 9:5-15.

Sadly, all this has too often been forgotten, and the law which was given uniquely to Israel, and applied only to them, has been mistakenly applied to Gentiles in the gospel age, to the confusion of both law and gospel.[9]

What is more, not only did God at Sinai give his law to Israel, and only to Israel, but prior to Sinai, nobody had the law – not even the patriarchs (Deut. 5:3; Rom. 5:13).[10] Notice how explicit Moses was at the repetition of the law in Moab, when reminding the Israelites of the first giving (and its re-giving) of the law at Horeb (Sinai): God did not make the covenant 'with our fathers, but with us' (Deut. 5:3). Who were these 'fathers'? and who were the 'us'? The 'fathers' were the patriarchs and their descendants who had died before the giving of the law at Sinai; God did not give his law to them. The 'us' were the Israelites – the people (with their children) who, having been delivered from Egypt, were gathered as the nation of Israel at Sinai – it was to them that God originally gave the law, and it was to their children that he was now renewing it in Moab. That generation of Hebrews at Sinai, therefore, was the first to receive the law. The patriarchs – the 'fathers' – who lived before the children of Jacob even entered Egypt, let alone left it – did not have the law. The song of Moses, when he 'blessed the children of Israel before his death',

---

[8] Some pagans had joined the Israelites as proselytes (Ex. 12:38,48-49; see Neh. 10:28; Est. 8:17; Isa. 56:3).

[9] See my *Christ* pp99-110,392-408.

[10] As I have said, Israel *as a nation* did not exist before the exodus and the giving of the law. The giving of the law was a vital aspect of *making* them into a nation.

is plain: 'The LORD came from Sinai, and dawned on them from Seir... from his right hand came a fiery law for them... Moses commanded a law for us, a heritage of the congregation of Jacob... Levi... shall teach Jacob your judgements, and Israel your law' (Deut. 33:1-4,8,10).[11] (See also Deut. 11:1-7; 29:9-15).[12]

That nobody had the law before Sinai is clear – since Paul expressly pointed out that the law came – 'was added' – 430 years after God's covenant with Abraham (Gal. 3:16-17,19). It was *revealed* at Sinai; it was not *renewed*. How can it be claimed that God gave the law to Adam at creation, or to the patriarchs? Yet many do say it! No! As Christ said, when replying to the Pharisees' question over the divorce-certificate regulation introduced by Moses (Deut. 24:1-4): 'From the beginning [Adam] it was not so' (Matt. 19:7-8). The law was given to Moses 430 years *after* the promise to Abraham, not given to Adam hundreds of years *before* Abraham. In stressing this, I am not straining out arithmetical or historical gnats. To say that Adam was given the Mosaic law is to miss a point of major consequence, contradicting Paul's argument in Romans 5 and Galatians 3.[13] The law was given to Moses long after God had revealed his saving purpose in and to Abraham.

This is a point of such importance, I must take a few moments to explain what I am talking about.

---

[11] Not only did the law have a beginning on Sinai; it had an end-point also, and that by God's intention. Paul said the law 'entered' the Jewish world at the time of the exodus (Rom. 5:20; Gal. 3:17,19), as a temporary system for the Jews, to last only until Christ came (Gal. 3:19), when he fulfilled it, thus bringing it to the end God had designed for it (Matt. 5:17-18; Rom. 10:4; 2 Cor. 3:7,11; Heb. 7:18; 8:13; 9:8-9). Right from the start, it was 'fading away' (2 Cor. 3:11,13, NIV). See my 'Three Verses Misunderstood'.

[12] The words, 'him who is not here with us today' (Deut. 29:14-15), refer to the descendants of the Israelites, not to all the rest of the human race.

[13] See my *Christ* pp116-177,412-468. Adam, of course, was given his own commandment which he broke (Rom. 5:14).

The eschatological importance of the epoch of the law

This point – the place of the law in salvation history, the eschatological importance of the epoch of the law – cannot be over-stressed. This word 'eschatological' will come again and again in these pages. Let me explain how I am using it. I am thinking of the way in which God, in time, works out his eternal decree to save his elect, and thus exalt his Son in their final glorification. I have in mind the way God arranges everything to bring about his purpose, the place every last thing has in that great plan. 'Salvation history' is one of the great themes (the *greatest* theme?) of the Bible. It permeates Romans 3 – 11 and Galatians 3 – 4, for example. So what is this 'salvation history' that I am talking about? The 'salvation' aspect is God's redemption of his elect, culminating in their eternal glorification in the image of Christ. But what of the 'history'? This needs nuancing. God decreed the redemption of his elect – the purpose, means and ends of their redemption – in eternity, but he is accomplishing it in time, as a part of history. Adam, the promise to Abraham, the law at Sinai, the coming, life, death, resurrection and ascension of Christ, Pentecost, the return of Christ, and so on, are 'milestones' in this historical process which is divided into two great ages, two great eras, two great dispensations or epochs – before Christ and after Christ.[14] Everything centres on Christ and his work. He (in his death, burial and resurrection) is the watershed of the two ages, the climax of all history, including and especially salvation history.

The two ages in question are very different. Adam is the head, the founder, of one age; Christ, of the other (Rom. 5:12-19). Adam's age is characterised by flesh, sin, law and death.[15] Christ's age is characterised by the Spirit, righteousness, grace and life. All humanity is by birth united to Adam, and comes

---

[14] I am leaving aside the eternal age following the second coming of Christ – which lies outside history – to concentrate on 'this present time' (Rom. 8:18) in contrast to the age preceding it.

[15] I am not contradicting myself; law characterised Adam's age even though he was not given the law of Moses. See my 'All Men Under Law'.

under the regime of the first age through Adam's sin. All the elect are united to Christ (from eternity, by God's decree; in experience, through faith in Christ), and come under the regime of the new age in, by and through Christ's death, burial and resurrection.

It is at this point that the time element of the word 'history' needs nuancing. The truth is, the two ages are running alongside each other, and have done so since the beginning of salvation history. It is not that Adam's age lasted until Christ's resurrection; Adam's age is still with us. That is why I am using the present tense: Adam's age *is* characterised by flesh, sin and law. All humanity *is* by birth united to Adam and *comes* under the regime of the first age through Adam's sin – *is* not *was*. So when I speak about salvation history, I am thinking of two ages, yes, but not merely in the sense of time. Rather, I am thinking more particularly in terms of their characteristics. I am thinking of two realms, two regimes. The old, Adamic, age or realm is the age or realm of the flesh, sin, law and death. The new, Christian, age or realm is the age or realm of the Spirit, righteousness, grace and life. The work of Christ took place in time, in history, and was the historical break-point or watershed for these two ages or realms, certainly, but for any particular individual the transformation comes at the point of saving faith. Conversion brings a change of regime, a change of age, a change of covenant. 'If anyone is in Christ, he is a new creation; old things have passed away; behold, all things have become new' (2 Cor. 5:17). Speaking to believers, Paul could declare: 'The Father... has delivered us from the power of darkness and conveyed [transferred] us into the kingdom of the Son of his love' (Col. 1:12-13). Peter: 'You are a chosen generation, a royal priesthood, a holy nation, his own special people, that you may proclaim the praises of him who called you out of darkness into his marvellous light; who once were not a people but are now the people of God, who had not obtained mercy but now have obtained mercy' (1 Pet. 2:9-10).

And when and what will be the culmination of salvation history? That, too, centres on Christ. The culmination will be when Christ 'delivers the kingdom to God the Father... that God may be all in all' (1 Cor. 15:24-28).

So when I talk of the 'eschatological significance of the epoch of the law in salvation history', I mean the status of the law in this scheme of salvation, how it fits into God's accomplishment of salvation – that is, its place both in time and characteristics. The law was given at a particular time and lasted for a limited time and for a specified purpose. What was its role? What is its role today? In other words, I am speaking about the law in two senses – historical and experiential – historical, for humanity; experiential, for the individual.

Having explained what I mean by the place of the law in salvation history, let me take up my main theme once again. The law, the whole law, was given to the Jews, for the Jews, at Sinai. How fitting, therefore, for Paul to call it 'our fathers' law', 'the law of the Jews' (Acts 22:3; 25:8).[16] When addressing Felix, Paul could easily link his 'worship [of] the God of my fathers' with 'the law and... the prophets' (Acts 24:14). How apt, therefore, was his reminder to the Jews – as distinct from the Gentiles – that they had the law (Rom. 2:27). How pointless if all men had it!

Think of the way in which Paul preached to the Gentiles.[17] Think of his experience at Lystra (Acts 14:11-18). The Gentiles were about to worship him and Barnabas. How did the brothers stop the pagans? What arguments did they use? Did they cite the first and second commandments? They did not! Instead, from nature they challenged pagan folly in trying to worship them. In effect, they asked: 'Does not nature teach you?'[18] If the Gentiles had been given the law, why did Paul not quote it against them? The fact is, since the Gentiles did not have the law, Paul could not use it in his approach to them, and he made no attempt to do so. The same goes for his preaching to the Athenians in the

---

[16] Peter called it 'our law' (that is, of the Jews, as opposed to belonging to you) when speaking to a Gentile (Acts 10:28, NIV).

[17] See my *Christ* pp51-63,116-157,348-368,412-447, where I more fully question and probe the Reformed claim that the preaching of the law must precede the preaching of the gospel to Gentile sinners.

[18] Compare 1 Cor. 11:14.

Areopagus (Acts 17:18-34). Paul used what the pagans were familiar with.[19]

Compare this approach with Christ addressing the rich young Jew (Matt. 19:16-22).[20] Think of Peter preaching to 'Jews and proselytes' (Acts 2:10); he was able to quote freely from the Old Testament (Acts 2:16-21,25-31,34-35). Again, when preaching to the Jews in the temple (Acts 3:11-26), he referred to Moses and 'all the prophets, from Samuel and those who follow, as many as have spoken'. In particular, he pointed them to 'the covenant which God made with our fathers' (Acts 3:18,22-26), and later quoted the Psalms (Acts 4:11). Think of Stephen's approach when he was preaching to the Jews: 'You... who have received the law', he said (Acts 7:52-53). Likewise, Paul used the law when preaching to the Jews (Acts 13:39; 22:3,12; 23:3,5; 28:23, for instance) – as in his defence against the Jews (Acts 24:14; 25:7-8), speaking of 'our people' and 'the customs of our fathers' (Acts 28:17). *But never once did he use the law when addressing Gentile unbelievers.* Why not? Because he only used the law when he could say: 'I speak to those who know the law' (Rom. 7:1).

None of this was an accident. The preachers of the New Testament knew where their unconverted hearers were coming from. They knew that the Jews had the law, and therefore the

---

[19] I do not say there are no Old Testament echoes whatsoever in these addresses. After all, Paul, a converted Jew, was steeped in those Scriptures, including the law. Naturally, he thought and spoke in such terms. Compare, for instance, Acts 14:15 with Ex. 20:11. But although he *thought* like this, never once in these addresses did Paul explicitly quote the Old Testament – which the pagans did not know – yet he quoted a Greek poet (Acts 17:28) – which they did know. See also Tit. 1:12. Paul's *arguments*, of course, were Christian, not pagan. Here is the lesson. A preacher must use terms which his hearers can understand – or else explain them. He has to adjust his language to suit his hearers, not the other way around. On preparationism, see my *Christ* pp51-63,116-157,348-368,412-447, and throughout my works.

[20] Incidentally, the Reformed like to think preaching what they like to call 'the moral law' (the ten commandments) prepares sinners for Christ. But when addressing the rich young Jew, Christ used all the law, not just sixteen verses of it! Note his use of Lev. 19:18.

gospel preachers were able to use it. The Gentiles did not have the law, so they did not refer them to it. In this, they were following Amos who, addressing the nations, Damascus, Gaza, Tyre, Edom, Ammon, Moab, Judah and Israel, reproved them for their sins (Amos 1:1 – 2:16).[21] Not once did the prophet mention the law when speaking to pagans, but on turning to Judah he immediately complained that 'they have despised the law of the LORD, and have not kept his commandments' (Amos 2:4).[22]

The overtones of James' statement in Acts 15 are unmistakable: 'Moses has had throughout many generations those who preach him in every city, being read in the synagogues every sabbath', he declared (Acts 15:21). 'Synagogues' and 'sabbath' are not Gentiles terms![23] Years later, when Paul arrived at Jerusalem, James told him about the believing Jews in Jerusalem who 'have been informed about you that you teach all the Jews who are among the Gentiles to forsake Moses' (Acts 21:21-25). Paul did not deny it.[24] The implication is clear. The Jews were

---

[21] See also Ezek. 25 – 30, for instance.

[22] I admit Amos did not explicitly refer to the law when addressing Israel at this time, although he alluded to it. The point is, however, the prophets often reproved Israel, but never pagan nations, for breaking the law. When Isaiah spoke to the 'rulers of Sodom' and told them to 'give ear to the law of our God', and to the 'people of Gomorrah' concerning sacrifices (Isa. 1:10-11), he was being ironical. He was in fact addressing Judah, calling Judah a virtual Sodom and Gomorrah – as the context makes plain. 'They declare their sin *as* Sodom' (Isa. 3:9). As God, through Jeremiah, said of Jerusalem: 'All of them are *like* Sodom to me, and her inhabitants *like* Gomorrah' (Jer. 23:14). See Deut. 29:23; Amos 9:7; Rev. 11:8. Returning to Amos, while it is true the prophet did not reprove Israel specifically for breaking the law, he did speak of them as distinct from the nations in having the prophets (Amos 2:11; 3:7-8), being chosen (Amos 3:2); having the feasts (Amos 5:21-22,25), being the chief nation (Amos 6:1).

[23] See Acts 22:12,19; 26:11; *etc*.

[24] A week later, catching sight of Paul in the temple, the (unbelieving) Jews from Asia stirred up the crowd, vociferously complaining that 'this is the man who teaches all men everywhere against the people, the law, and this place' (Acts 21:28).

under Moses; the Gentiles were not.[25] Note further the contrast between Paul's actions (as a Jew) and the requirements laid upon Gentiles, as recorded in Acts 21:21-25. As the apostle explained: 'To the Jews I became as a Jew... to those who are under the law, as under the law... to those who are without law, as without law'. Why? In order to 'win the more... I do [this] for the gospel's sake' (1 Cor. 9:19-23).

Acts 2:23 is very interesting in this connection. Peter, preaching Christ, told the Jewish crowd on the day of Pentecost: 'You have taken [him] by lawless hands, have crucified [him], and put [him] to death'. The Jews were responsible for crucifying Christ but, to do the dirty work, they used Roman hands, Gentile hands, 'lawless hands'. The NASB, translating the phrase, 'by the hands of godless men', has a marginal note: 'Lawless hands, or, men without the law; that is, heathen'. The NIV correctly notes: 'Of those not having the law (that is, Gentiles)'. Christ had already foretold this is what would happen: 'The Son of Man... will be delivered to the Gentiles and will be mocked and insulted and spit upon. They will scourge him and kill him' (Luke 18:31-33). Peter, steeped in Jewish thought, was using the phrase, 'lawless men', in the Jewish sense. The men he was talking about were 'men without the law'. That is to say, they were law-less, outside the law of God, Gentiles. The Jews boasted of their having the law. They were the only people to have it. All the rest were 'law-less'. So, as Peter said, Christ was crucified by the Jews (who had the law) making use of the Gentiles (who did not have the law, the without-the-law people) to do the work. See also Matthew 20:18-19; and Galatians 2:15, where 'Jews by nature' are contrasted with 'sinners of the Gentiles' or 'Gentile sinners' (NIV). 'Sinners' and 'Gentiles', in such a context, means those who are law-less, lawless, outside the law, beyond the pale.

When the Jews wanted Christ put to death, they could tell Pilate: '*We* have a law, and according to *our* law he ought to die'

---

[25] To develop this: Would Paul tell Jews to forsake Moses, and yet – allowing for sake of argument that they were under Moses – tell Gentiles to stay under his law? Even worse: would Paul tell believing Jews to leave Moses, yet make believing Gentiles come under Moses? This is the nub of the question I address in my *Christ*.

(John 19:7; see Lev. 24:16), but the Roman governor had already told them: '*You* take him and judge him according to *your* law' (John 18:31). When the Jews of Corinth brought Paul to court before Gallio, accusing him of persuading 'men to worship God contrary to the law' (Acts 18:11-16),[26] Gallio refused to entertain the case, on the grounds that it was none of his business. He roundly told them he would not get involved in 'a question of words and names and your own law'; '*your own* law', I emphasise. With a dismissive, 'Look to it yourselves; for I do not want to be a judge of such matters', he cleared the court. Claudius Lysias spoke in a similar way when writing to Felix, calling the accusation laid against Paul by the Jews, 'questions of *their* law' (Acts 23:29), no concern of his, something outside his jurisdiction, comprehension and competence. The Jews confirmed this by telling Felix they had 'wanted to judge [Paul] according to *our* law' (Acts 24:6). Festus was in the same quandary as Felix. While he was familiar with 'the custom of the Romans', he was 'uncertain of such questions' as he was now being asked, 'questions... about *their own* religion' (Acts 25:16,19-20). Paul, standing before Agrippa, was happy to think his judge was an 'expert in all customs and questions which have to do with the Jews', including the words of the prophets. '*Our* religion', he called it (Acts 26:1-5,26-27) – with the clear implication that Gentiles generally speaking had at best only a limited knowledge of God's revelation to the Jews, and their customs, religion and *law*. All this is strange, to put it mildly, *if these Gentiles had been as much under the law as the Jews*. I realise these Gentiles were politicians as well as magistrates, soldiers or kings, and I would not treat their words as the final authority on biblical principles, but they do nothing to contradict the claim that the law was given only to the Jews.[27]

And what of Hebrews 7:11? We are told that 'under [the levitical priesthood] the people received the law'. While it is not

---

[26] The law of Moses, they meant, not the law of Corinth.

[27] In my *Christ* pp99-110,392-408, I deal with the objection that such passages are concerned with the ceremonial or judicial law. They are not! As I keep saying, we are talking about the whole law.

easy to determine precisely what the writer meant, at the very least we may speak of a link between the levitical priesthood, the Israelites and the law. In fact, it is much stronger than this. It was *under* the levitical priesthood that Israel received the law. The NIV and the NASB use the word *basis*; Israel received the law *on the basis* of the levitical priesthood. Now who received the levitical priesthood? The Jews. The Jews and no others. No Gentiles had the levitical priesthood. Consequently, only the Jews could have received the law, since no people could have the law without the levitical priesthood, and *vice-versa*. The two were inextricably linked (Heb. 7:11-12,14,18-19,22,28). The two stood or fell together: 'The priesthood being changed, of necessity there is also a change of the law' (Heb. 7:12). Under this system – unique to the Jews – the law required Levi to collect the tithe from his brothers – not all men (Heb. 7:5). And so on.

Therefore, of all nations, Israel alone received the law.

But what about Romans 3:19?

What about Romans 3:19?

The verse reads: 'Now we know that whatever the law says, it says to those who are under the law, that every mouth may be stopped, and all the world may become guilty before God'. Surely this teaches that all men – Jews and Gentiles – are under the law? But, no, it does not, even though at first glance it seems like it.

As I have shown, the context proves that 'the law' here includes at least the ten commandments, but more; it is the Old Testament as a whole. It is the law, the law in its entirety. Furthermore, note how Paul said that the law speaks to those who are under it. This ought to give pause for thought. If all men are under the law, then Paul wrote what amounts to a truism. The fact that he made such an observation at all – the law speaks to those who are under it – indicates there is something to be taken notice of. To whom was he referring? Who were those who were 'under the law', those to whom the law speaks? The context from Romans 2:1 and on is conclusive. He was clearly referring to the Jews. *They* were under it. It was given to *them*. The law certainly stopped their mouths. They had the law, they were under it, but since they failed to keep it, it condemned them. It took away all their excuse. Pharisees might think that *knowing* the law, *having* the law, was all that counted (John 5:39,45; 7:49; 9:28; Rom. 2:17-29), but, far from being justified by possession of the law, they would 'be judged by the law', 'for', as the apostle explained, 'not the hearers of the law are just in the sight of God, but the doers of the law will be justified' (Rom. 2:12-13).

But what of the Gentiles in Romans 3:19? The words, 'to those who are under the law', imply there are others who are *not* under the law. The Gentiles, Paul explained, did not have the Jews' advantage – they were not given the law, they were not under it (Rom. 2:12-15). Even so, some of them, at least, were living up to the light they had – and 'by nature do the things in the law... who show the work of the law written in their hearts' – and in this respect did better than the Jews.[28] This does not mean that some Gentiles by their works were free of sin and so avoided God's wrath. No! The point is, God is impartial. The Jews who had the law will be judged, and the Gentiles who did not have the law will also be judged, and both will be judged fairly by God (Rom. 1:18 – 3:20). What is more, if the Gentiles, who never had the advantage of receiving the law, were unable to voice any excuse for their sin, how much more guilty were the Jews – who had the law, and boasted about it (Rom. 2:17-24)! The Jews had the light of God's word (Ps. 119:130). The Gentiles did not. But even so, all sinned and were 'guilty before God' (Rom. 3:19,23); the Jews against the law, and the Gentiles against some sort[29] of moral consciousness. And both were responsible. The principle is clear: more light, more responsibility!

This is Paul's argument. Whether or not men had the law, Paul had already 'charged both Jews and Greeks that they are all under sin' (Rom. 3:9). As he said, quoting and citing the Old Testament (the law): 'There is none righteous, no, not one... none... none... none... For there is no difference; for all have sinned and fall

---

[28] See the next article for a thorough examination of Rom. 2:14-15.
[29] I admit my expression is (deliberately) vague. I will go into it further in the next article.

short of the glory of God' (Rom. 3:9-23). And as with sin, so with salvation, there is no difference between Jew and Gentile (Rom. 3:28-31; 10:12-13). God is impartial between them. In short: 'Now we know that whatsoever the law says, it says to those who are under the law, that every mouth may be stopped, and all the world may become guilty before God' (Rom. 3:19). The Jews – who had the law – were silenced by it. The Gentiles – who did not have the law – had no excuse in any case. Hence, all the world is guilty before God. 'God has bound all men over to disobedience' (Rom. 11:32, NIV). 'The Scripture has confined all under sin' (Gal. 3:22) – all men, 'all things' (Gal. 3:22, NASB margin), 'the creation... the creation... the creation... the whole creation' (Rom. 8:19-22). In short: 'Both Jews and Greeks... are all under sin... For all have sinned and fall short of the glory of God' (Rom. 3:9,23).

In other words, Romans 3:19 supports the claim that the law was given to the Jews, and not to the Gentiles.

Many Reformed teachers will have none of it. The law was given to all men in Adam, they say; it was reinstated to all men through Moses; and all men are under the law today. Some go further. Men will be under it in eternity.[30]

These statements are wrong on several counts. Although it is claimed that men know the law of God by nature, and have done so from Adam, it is significant that such teachers never include

---

[30] A staggering – not to say, ridiculous – claim. The law is 'made', 'not... for a righteous person, but for the lawless and insubordinate' (1 Tim. 1:9-12). Will the eternal glory be populated by men and women who need a law against murder, sodomy and 'any other thing that is contrary to sound doctrine', and glory in it? Reformed writers refer to 'the permanence and glory of the moral law'. My *Christ* is my attempt to write on the permanence and the glory of the *gospel*. The glory of the law was fading and passing away even as it was given (2 Cor. 3:7-18). As the New Testament expressly states, it was a temporary measure, 'added' until the Christ's fulfilment of his Father's will in his first coming, and has no glory now in comparison to the gospel since Christ fulfilled and thus abolished it (Gal. 3:19; Eph. 2:15; Heb. 7:18; 8:7-13; 9:5-10).

the sabbath in trying to justify their claim. Let us think about this for a minute. Are we really to believe that pagans know they must rest from Friday sunset to Saturday sunset? Can anybody tell us of a pagan people, completely without Scripture, which keeps the sabbath? or feels guilty for not keeping it? Can anyone point to any man – including the patriarchs –- before Exodus 16, who kept the sabbath?

Furthermore, the notion that the moral law was *reinstituted* or *reinstated* or *restated* on Sinai because it had fallen into obscurity, is without a shred of evidence. Romans 5:20 disproves it: the law – the whole law – *entered* at Sinai; it was not *restated* because it had fallen into obscurity! It entered the world at that time. More of this anon. Much more!

But the simple point I wish to make in this article is that the law was given to the Jews at Sinai. It was not given to the Gentiles, either at Sinai or at creation. It was not given to the Gentiles, full stop.

But what of those places in the New Testament where Paul addresses believers as those no longer under the law? Since he must have been including Gentiles in at least some of the passages, does this not mean that the Gentiles *were* under the law, after all? The answer is, No! As I come to the passages, I will deal with the question in detail, but for now I simply state that on several occasions, Paul was speaking either of his own personal experience as a Jew, or else he was speaking of the Jews and not Gentiles. And even when he was clearly addressing Gentiles, he was often rebuking them for seeking to go under the law, allowing themselves to be put under it by false teachers, Judaisers, or going back to the slavery of pagan principles – this last, having nothing to do with the law of Moses at all! Christ has redeemed his people from all bondage.

Even so, reader, there are some passages where such explanations still do not satisfy. Romans 2:14-15 is the explanation of all such. I now turn to these very important verses.

Romans 2:14-15

Let me quote the verses:

> For when Gentiles, who do not have the law, by nature do the things in the law, these, although not having the law, are a law to themselves, who show the work of the law written in their hearts, their conscience also bearing witness, and between themselves their thoughts accusing or else excusing them.

I wish to deal with two main views of the passage. First things first, however.[1]

What is the context?

As always, this is vital. The context always holds the key to the interpretation. The passage opens (verse 12) with 'for', linking it with what has gone before, arguing from what has gone before. As I explained in the previous article, Paul is here showing the impartiality of God's judgement of all sinners, whether Jew or Gentile; 'there is no partiality with God' (Rom. 2:11). Judgement is the context, and the context is judgement. Paul is not trying to praise Gentiles in Romans 2:14-15. In fact, he is not speaking to Gentiles at all. Rather, he is reminding Jews that God is fair in his judgement. In particular, he says, although the Jews have received the law (given to them by God) and the Gentiles have not, the truth is, some Gentiles (though without the law) live to a standard which puts the Jews (who have the law) to shame. *And God notes the fact!* Jews might think they get special treatment because they received the law, but they are mistaken. God looks at the heart revealed in the life, the actions and the works of a man, *not his advantages.* God looks at what a man does with his opportunities and advantages. He does not accept the man just because he gave him those opportunities and advantages. Romans 2 teaches it plainly. As for the Jews bragging about having the

---

[1] For this article, I have lightly edited my *Christ* pp38-48; see also pp342-347.

law, the boot is on the other foot; more light brings more responsibility (John 9:39-41; 15:22,24). This is the context.

Now for Romans 2:14-15. The word 'law' appears several times in the two verses. With the exception of the clause, 'are a law to themselves', the law in question is the law of Moses. And when Paul spoke of 'Gentiles, who do not have the law', he did not mean that some Gentiles have the law and others do not. The comma is very important.[2] Gentiles, Gentiles as Gentiles, Gentiles as a whole, do not have the law. Although there is no article before Gentiles – it is Gentiles, not *the* Gentiles – it makes no difference. As I have pointed out,[3] the frequent lack of the definite article before 'law' only serves to strengthen the notion of 'the law'. 'The Gentiles' or 'Gentiles' – it is all the same. Gentiles do not have the law. This is part and parcel of being a Gentile! As I showed in the previous article, the law was given to the Jews and not to the Gentiles. In Romans 2:14-15, Paul takes this point for granted, and builds on it. Contrasting Jew and Gentile (Rom. 2:9-10), the apostle speaks, on the one hand, of those who 'have sinned without law' – Gentiles – and on the other, of those who 'sinned in the law' – Jews (Rom. 2:12). Only the Jews were given the revelation of God's 'knowledge and truth in the law' (Rom. 2:20). The Gentiles were not. They were 'in darkness' (Rom. 2:19). They did not have the law.

So far, so good. The Gentiles do not have the law. We have seen this much before. But, even so, Reformed writers, as I have explained, do not always accept this obvious point, so clearly revealed in Scripture. They often claim that the ten commandments were given to all men, and that they were written on the hearts of the pagans. Romans 2:14-15 says nothing of the sort. Quite the reverse! It expressly says that Gentiles did not have the law! If this fact is ignored or explained away, Paul's point is lost.

---

[2] There is no punctuation in the original. This always has to be supplied. Over this first comma, there is no debate, and it is, as I say, of the utmost importance to take full account of it.

[3] See my 'What Is the Law?'

What about the punctuation of Romans 2:14-15?

This, as I have noted, has to be supplied. No manuscript gives us the definitive punctuation. This is simply a fact. Whatever version we use, the translators have supplied the punctuation. Now then, should the second comma come just after 'by nature', or just before? In other words, there are two possibilities:

1: 'When Gentiles, **who do not have the law by nature,** do the things in the law'
2: 'When Gentiles, who do not have the law, **by nature do the things in the law**'

Which is it? The overwhelming majority of scholars and translators opt for the second.

The placing of the comma is no quibble. If the comma is placed as in the first possibility, 'by nature' qualifies the 'having' of the law: Gentiles do not have the law, and it is by nature that they do not have it. If the comma is placed as in the second possibility, 'by nature' qualifies the 'doing' of the law: Gentiles do not have the law, but some of them by nature do the things in the law.

Let me take the first; that is, 'by nature' qualifies the fact that the Gentiles do not have the law. Is this right? Was Paul saying that Gentiles do not have the law by nature? Now *phusei* (by nature), it is true, can mean 'by birth, by physical origin', and such a use would be in keeping with other scriptures (Rom. 2:27; Gal. 2:15, for instance).[4] Consequently, if, in Romans 2:14-15, the comma comes after 'by nature', the passage reads: 'When Gentiles, *who do not have the law by reason of birth*, do the things in the law'.

As I say, this makes excellent sense. But it may not be the right position for the comma!

---

[4] Rom. 2:27 also confirms the earlier point; namely, Jews have the law whereas Gentiles do not. The original is 'you who with letter'. The NKJV supplied the word 'your' in 'you... with *your* [letter or] written code'. The NASB put it as 'you who though having the letter of the law'. In other words, Paul is contrasting Gentiles, who do not have the law, with Jews, who do.

The alternative – and the most common – version, which puts the comma before 'by nature', simply says that Gentiles do not have the law; whether by reason of birth, or otherwise, is not specified.

To sum up thus far: Jews had the law; Gentiles did not. But whether or not this is by reason of birth depends on the comma coming before or after 'by nature'. Whichever it is, it makes no difference to the overall argument concerning the possession of the law. Gentiles do not have the law. Whether or not they do not have it 'by nature' does not alter the fact that they do not have it in the first place.[5]

But this, of course, leads to a second point – one with far-reaching consequences. Granted that Gentiles do not have the law, when it says they 'do the things in the law', how do they do these things? Do they do them 'by nature' or what? Once again, it depends on the comma.

There are two main possibilities

1. If the comma comes *after* 'by nature', in what I will call the minority version, Romans 2:14-15 reads: 'When Gentiles, who do not have the law by nature, do the things in the law, these, although not having the law, are a law to themselves, who show the work of the law written in their hearts, their conscience also bearing witness, and between themselves their thoughts accusing or else excusing them'. This means, *some* say, that even though Gentiles by virtue of birth do not have the law, in some cases they keep it. And, although it is not specified here, since no sinner can keep the law by his own power, this must mean they keep the law by grace. In other words, the verses are speaking about Gentiles who are in the new covenant;[6] that is, they are Gentile believers.

---

[5] Of course, the Jews after Sinai had the law by virtue of birth. But Rom. 2:14-15 is concerned with Gentiles, not Jews.

[6] See my *Christ* pp299-321,543-555 for the new covenant, and, especially, what 'the law' is in that covenant. It is one of the major issues in the debate over the law.

2. If the comma comes *before* 'by nature', in what I will call the majority version, Romans 2:14-15 reads: 'When Gentiles, who do not have the law, by nature do the things in the law, these, although not having the law, are a law to themselves, who show the work of the law written in their hearts, their conscience also bearing witness, and between themselves their thoughts accusing or else excusing them'. According to the majority version, this means that even though Gentiles do not have the law, by nature some of them have a measure of the law ('the work of the law') written on their hearts, and this, coupled with an active conscience, enables them to live out – to a certain degree – the things the law demands ('the things in the law') even though they do not have the law as such. That is to say, all Gentiles, even though they do not have the law, have a rudimentary knowledge of it written in their hearts, and some of them live up fairly well to the light they have.

These are the two possibilities I wish to consider.[7] I will give my reasons for rejecting the first, and accepting the second, the majority view. In short, Romans 2:14-15 is speaking of unbelieving Gentiles who do not have the law – whereas the Jews do – yet in some cases Gentiles more nearly keep the law than do the Jews. But let me consider the two possibilities before I show why I plump for the second.

---

[7] We can dismiss the Pelagian view that some Gentiles keep the law by their own natural ability. Original sin and human depravity rule it out (Job 14:4; Ps. 51:5; Rom. 1:18-32; 3:9-20,23; 8:7; 1 Cor. 2:14; Gal. 3:22; Eph. 2:1-3; 4:17-19). Far from being within the power of *nature*, it takes the *supernatural* work of the Spirit to make a dead sinner live, and give him heart-delight in God and his law (John 3:1-8; Jer. 31:33-34; Heb. 8:6-13). See also Matt. 23:37; John 5:40; 6:44-45; 12:37-40; Acts 26:18; Rom. 5:10; 1 Cor. 1:21; Gal. 4:8; Eph. 5:8; Col. 1:21. Which law is the law in the new covenant is a major issue in the debate over the law.

Possibility 1. *The minority view: Does Romans 2:14-15 teach that some Gentiles are believers, and therefore keep the law by the provisions of the new covenant?*

As I have said, if the comma comes after 'by nature', as in the minority version, Romans 2:14-15 states that even though Gentiles by reason of birth do not have the law, some of them keep it. Although it is not here specified, these Gentiles keep the law because they are in the new covenant. In other words, they are Gentile believers who keep the law by grace (with an implied contrast, perhaps, with 'by nature'). In short, although Paul does not say so, the passage refers to believing Gentiles in the new covenant (Jer. 31:33; Heb. 8:10; 10:16). Romans 2:6-11 is cited in support.[8]

But this claim simply does not fit the overall context of Romans 1:18 – 3:20; namely, man's sin, and the consequent wrath of God on all mankind. The context is king, remember! And, as we have seen, judgement is the context. Above all, Paul is here considering God's justice, his judgement, his fairness in executing wrath on all the human race, both Jew and Gentile. Consequently, to introduce at Romans 2:14-15 the thought that some Gentiles are converted and possess the blessings of the new covenant (the law written on the heart) without so much as a whisper of an explanation, seems forced. Very much so. Something jars. By this stage in the letter, Paul has not sufficiently set out the gospel to be able to introduce the concept of the new covenant and its provisions. Yet, we are asked to believe, Paul did it, and did it without any reference to Jeremiah (or Ezekiel or any other prophet), and with no comparison to the old covenant. He did it, apparently, as an aside.[9] Contrast the way

---

[8] It is almost always taken for granted that the law written in the heart in the new covenant is the law of Moses. But this is to beg the question – a big question, at that! Perhaps the biggest question of them all. See my *Christ* pp299-321,543-555. As I have already said, it is one of the major issues in this debate.

[9] Moreover, he did it as an aside within an aside; Rom. 2:13-15 is in brackets, which have to be supplied, of course. The argument runs from Rom. 2:12 directly to Rom. 2:16, missing out the verses in between: 'For

the writer to the Hebrews brought in the new covenant (Heb. 8:1-13; 10:15-18), having built his case solidly over several chapters, and the way Paul himself spoke of it in 2 Corinthians 3. Are we to think Paul could mention such a momentous matter *in passing* in Romans 2? Surely not! Paul was not speaking of the new covenant in Romans 2:15. The context is judgement!

But what of Romans 2:7,10? Here Paul does speak of believers who by their attitude and works show their inward experience of grace; at least, this is how I understand the verses.[10] If this is so, does Romans 2:7,10 not support the view that Romans 2:14-15 speaks of Gentiles in the new covenant? I think not. The two passages, Romans 2:4-11 and 2:12-24, deal with different things. Up to the end of Romans 2:3, Paul has been setting out a massive indictment of the human race, and God's impartial judgement of sinners on the basis of their works, and he has yet more to say about it. But he does not develop his argument in the verses which immediately follow. It is in Romans 2:12-24 where he does that. What is his argument? Just this: God's impartial judgement of sinners is according to their works;

---

as many as have sinned without law will also perish without law, and as many as have sinned in the law will be judged by the law... in the day when God will judge the secrets of men by Jesus Christ, according to my gospel'.

[10] Some think Paul is speaking of the hypothetical case – if a man could keep the law perfectly, he would be justified. While I think this is a truth (see below, and my *Christ* pp75-98,158-177,369-391,448-468, I do not think it is what Paul is saying in Rom. 2:7,10. In brief, this is because the contrast in Rom. 2:6-11 is not between those who keep the law *perfectly* – and are justified – and those who keep *90% of it* (well, the ten commandments – see Jas. 2:10-11) – and are condemned – but between those who seek after God and godliness, and those who do not; the latter are 'self-seeking'. The law does not come into it. Paul does not even mention it. But what of Rom. 2:13? In this verse, Paul *does* state the hypothetical case – perfect obedience to the law would bring justification. Yes. But the difference lies in the fact that Paul has now introduced the idea of law. Even so, in Rom. 2:13 Paul is not merely stating a hypothetical case. He is driving home the point that *having* the law is not enough – it is *doing* the law which counts. God's judgement is according to works.

having the law of Moses makes no difference. Jew (or Gentile, for that matter) may condemn others, but 'do you think this, O man, you who judge those practicing such things, and doing the same, that you will escape the judgement of God?' (Rom. 2:3). The fact is, 'there is no partiality with God. For as many as have sinned without law will also perish without law, and as many as have sinned in the law will be judged by the law' (Rom. 2:11-12). As far as Paul's argument goes, it is verses 11-12, not 4-11, which follow on from Romans 2:3. 'Do you think this, O man, you who judge those practicing such things, and doing the same, that you will escape the judgement of God?... For there is no partiality with God. For as many as have sinned without law will also perish without law, and as many as have sinned in the law will be judged by the law'.

What I am saying is, Romans 2:4-11 is *not* a development of Paul's main argument; *rather, it is an aside – a passionate aside at that.* As I read it, Paul the preacher cannot help himself. Overwhelmed by what he has just written – about the wrath for God – in the verses leading up to Romans 2:3, he is moved with compassion for sinners, and he shows it.[11] The harrowing thought of the terrible consequences of God's wrath, in the judgement and condemnation of hardened and impenitent sinners, which the apostle has just set out in Romans 1:18 – 2:3, moves him – compels him – to interrupt his argument for a moment. He must get his passionate thoughts down 'on paper'! Running ahead of himself, almost breaking out into the positive aspect of the gospel, his feelings compel him to address ignorant sinners, those who 'despise the riches of [God's] goodness, forbearance, and longsuffering, not knowing that the goodness of God leads [them] to repentance', and who in consequence 'are treasuring up... wrath' for themselves (Rom. 2:4-5). He has to let his main argument go by the board for a moment. He must inject a note of hope into the thunderous cataract of warning and doom. This is why he declaims on the two sorts of men – the godly and the ungodly – the two classes being shown for what they are by their works. Wanting no sinner – Jew or Gentile – to come to

---

[11] Compare Rom. 9:1-5; 10:1.

'indignation and wrath, tribulation and anguish' (Rom. 2:8-9), Paul, by means of a searching question (Rom. 2:4), tries to bring sinners to repentance.

But this white-hot discussion is a digression from his main theme, which he left at the end of Romans 2:3; namely, God's impartial judgement based on works. It is, as I say, as he moves from Romans 2:10 to 2:11, and especially as he opens verse 12, that Paul lets go of his impassioned plea to sinners,[12] and gets back on course – God's impartial judgement – *but now he develops his case by introducing the notion of 'law'*. I stress this. Paul has not mentioned 'law' up to this point. This is why I say Romans 2:7,10 and 2:14,15 are not dealing with the same issues.[13] Whereas there is no mention of 'law' in Romans 1:1 – 2:11, 'law' is the dominant note of Romans 2:12-24.[14] Romans 2:4-11 and 2:12-16, therefore, deal with different things. Consequently Romans 2:7,10 and 2:14-15 do not describe the same people, or speak about the same issues.

Nor do I think Paul's later statement in Romans 2:28-29 militates against what I am saying. In Romans 2:25-29, Paul is moving on to yet another aspect of God's impartial judgement based on works; namely, it does not matter if a man is circumcised in the flesh or not. What matters is his heart, and the consequent effect on his life. Once again, this is not the issue in Romans 2:14-15.[15]

---

[12] As I have indicated, the 'for' in Rom. 2:12 builds on the fact that 'there is no partiality with God' (Rom. 2:11), not on the impassioned aside of Rom. 2:4-11.

[13] As above, Rom. 2:13-15 is in brackets. The main argument goes from Rom. 2:3 directly to Rom. 2:11, and from Rom. 2:12 directly to Rom. 2:16, missing out the verses in between. 'Do you think... that you will escape the judgement of God?... As many as have sinned in the law will be judged by the law... in the day when God will judge the secrets of men by Jesus Christ'.

[14] In Rom. 1:1 – 2:11 'law' is not mentioned; in Rom. 2:12-24 it comes 16 times; in Rom. 2:25-29, it comes another 5 times – plus 'written code' and 'letter'. I do not say 'law' always means the Mosaic law here, but overwhelmingly it does.

[15] See below for a note on Rom. 2:25-27. See also Rom. 4 where Paul deals with the way the two issues impinge, not on condemnation, but on

And what about the verses themselves (Rom. 2:14-15)? They cannot be speaking of the fulfilment of the promise of the new covenant. Romans 2:14-15 does not say that Gentiles have *the law* written on their hearts. Rather, they have *the work of the law* written on their hearts. Nor does Romans 2:14-15 say that Gentiles keep the law; it says 'when' they 'do the things in the law'. What is more, the words in Romans 2:14-15, 'who do not have the law', cannot apply to the regenerate since, according to God's promise in Jeremiah 31:33, the regenerate *do* have the law – written on their hearts: 'I will put my law in their minds, and write it on their hearts'. In addition, those spoken of in Romans 2:14 have only a *knowledge* of the law, whereas those in the new covenant *delight* in it. What is more, how can the regenerate be said to be 'a law to themselves'? They are under the law to Christ (1 Cor. 9:21; Gal. 6:2). Finally, it is significant that there is no mention whatsoever of the Holy Spirit in Romans 2:14-15 or its context.[16] For all these reasons, Romans 2:14-15 cannot be referring to regenerate Gentiles in the new covenant.[17]

None of this is quibbling. 'The work of the law'[18] is equivalent to 'a life which in some measure corresponds to the

---

justification. There he does it in the opposite order; circumcision (Rom. 4:9-12), then law (Rom. 4:13-16).

[16] When Paul raised the new covenant in 2 Cor. 3, he mentioned 'the Spirit' 6 times.

[17] Furthermore, if Rom. 2:14-15 does describe regenerate Gentiles, and if 'the work of the law' must be understood as 'the law', then it means that the law which is written on the heart in the new covenant must be the law of Moses (the law Paul was mainly speaking of in Rom. 2). And this needs proof. As I have said, I return to 'the law' in the new covenant in my *Christ* pp299-321,543-555. It is, as I keep pointing out, one of the major issues in the debate over the law and the believer.

[18] It is not the same as 'the works of the law' (Rom. 9:32; Gal. 3:10). Rom. 2:15 is concerned with Gentiles. The other verses are to do with the Jews – who had the law – and who were trying to keep it for justification. In Rom. 9:30-32, the contrast is drawn between Gentiles – 'who did not pursue righteousness' – and Israel – who did pursue 'the law of righteousness', but failed 'because they did not seek it by faith, but as it were, by the works of the law'. 'The works of the law' means the carrying out of *all* that the law requires. But this is not what Paul was

law', a long way short of saying that Romans 2:14-15 is concerned with Gentiles in the new covenant.

So much for the minority view of the passage. I do not think it holds up. If however the minority version *is* right, and the passage does refer to the new covenant, then it could be properly quoted as a verification of what I will have to say on that subject throughout my book. But it does not ring true, at least for me.[19] As a result, I am left with the second possibility.

Possibility 2. The majority view: Does Romans 2:14-15 teach that some unbelieving Gentiles live a life which shows a rudimentary knowledge of the law?

If the comma comes before 'by nature', Romans 2:14-15 states that even though Gentiles do not have the law, some of them, by the light of nature, coupled with an active conscience, live out to a certain degree the things the law demands – 'the things in the law' – thus showing some measure of the law – 'the work of the law' – written in their hearts. In other words, Gentiles, even though they do not have *the* law, have *a* law, a vague, rudimentary knowledge of law written in their hearts; they have a conscience, some sense of right and wrong. And some of them instinctively live up fairly well to the light they have.[20]

---

saying in Rom. 2:14-15. Here we are told, not that the law is written in Gentile hearts, and that they keep it, but: 'Gentiles... do *the things in the law*... who show the *work of the law* written in their hearts'. Nothing here, I suggest, about earning justification by keeping the Mosaic law. The Gentiles do not even have the law.

[19] Paul wrote 'Gentiles'. The context does not favour – to put it mildly – the notion of *believing* Gentiles. It is not convincing to say that Paul deliberately left 'the Gentiles' unspecific at this stage so that he could slowly build up his case! And it runs completely contrary to the idea that he introduced the new covenant here, since – if he did – he did so in a most abrupt manner, and dropped it just as abruptly – and all without any mention of 'the Spirit'.

[20] Generally this was the view of the Puritans, and many others. I understand Rom. 2:25-27 in this light also. The man with the 'written code and circumcision' (Rom. 2:27) is a Jew, whereas an 'uncircumcised man' (Rom. 2:26) is a Gentile. Paul proposes the case of

In addition, Romans 1:19-20,32 speaks of precisely the same thing as Romans 2:14-15.[21] Compare: 'Gentiles... show the work of the law written in their hearts' (Rom. 2:14-15), with the reference to all men in Romans 1:19-20: 'What may be known of God is manifest in them, for God has shown it to them. For since the creation of the world his invisible attributes are clearly seen, being understood by the things that are made, even his eternal power and Godhead, so that they are without excuse', 'that which is known about God is evident within them; for God made it evident to them' (NASB), 'what may be known about God is plain to them, because God has made it plain to them' (NIV). And according to Romans 1:32, all men know 'the righteous judgement of God', 'the ordinance of God' (NASB), 'God's righteous decree' (NIV). Surely this lies behind Peter's words in Acts 10:35: 'In every nation whoever fears him and works righteousness', 'does what is right' (NASB). While Cornelius was not a converted man at the time, he had a measure of light and he lived up to it. All this comes under Genesis 1:26-27: 'God created man in his own image'. God created man a moral creature, a rational creature. Man was given a conscience, he could weigh his actions and thoughts, he had been given a sense of right (and wrong, after sin entered the world). God 'has put eternity in their hearts' (Eccl. 3:11). This marks man out from the animal, and this is the meaning of Romans 2:14-15.

To sum up: the comma should come as in all the leading English versions;[22] that is: 'When Gentiles, who do not have the law, by nature do the things in the law'. In other words, Romans 2:14-15 speaks of unbelieving Gentiles[23] who, though they do not have the law, show by their lives that they have a rudimentary knowledge of right and wrong, and by an active conscience they

---

a Gentile who, though not having the law or circumcision, to a measure 'keeps the righteous requirements of the law' (Rom. 2:26).

[21] Note the *phusikēn* (natural) and *phusin* (nature) in Rom. 1:26-27, and *phusei* (by nature) in Rom. 2:14.

[22] But see NASB.

[23] If the correct punctuation is 'by nature do the things', it means that the Gentiles in question cannot be regenerate. Do the regenerate *by nature* keep the law? They do it *by grace*, do they not?

live up to that standard according to the light they have. The NIV footnote of John 1:9 is relevant: Christ 'gives light to every man who comes into the world'; or 'enlightens every man coming into the world' (NASB, margin). Every man has a conscience enlightened by a rudimentary knowledge of right and wrong.

We have a test-bed to hand. 'The law was given through Moses' (John 1:17), yes, but the people who lived before Moses were judged for their wickedness. Why? Because all are sinners (Rom. 3:9,23), whether before or after Moses, whether under the law or not, and because the sinners in question knew they were doing wrong. How did they know that? God explains: he does not judge sinners for breaking a law they were never under, but for suppressing the truth that is *in them* (Rom. 1:18-19).

Let me explore this a little. God gave his law to Israel on Mount Sinai through Moses. Also, 'by the law is the knowledge of sin' (Rom. 3:20), 'sin is lawlessness' (1 John 3:4), 'where there is no law there is no transgression' (Rom. 4:15), and 'sin is not imputed when there is no law' (Rom. 5:13). Yet even before Sinai 'death spread to all men, because all sinned... Death reigned from Adam to Moses, even over those who had not sinned according to the likeness of the transgression of Adam'. This was because through Adam 'sin entered the world, and death through sin, and thus death spread to all men, because all sinned' (Rom. 5:12-14). They sinned in Adam, and they sinned in their own right. They had no excuse. By creation they had known 'the truth', but, as a consequence of the fall, they had stifled this knowledge, and given God up. Therefore God gave them up to a life of sin and misery, including sexual perversion, envy, murder, the breakdown of family life, and the glorying in wickedness (Rom. 1:18-32). All this dates from Adam's fall, is with us yet, and will be with us until Christ shall come again. Not that things are as bad as they might be. This is earth, after all, and not hell! There is still a rudimentary knowledge of right and wrong in men. Conscience has not been entirely seared, let alone obliterated. This is the point of Romans 2:12-14. Nevertheless, 'the whole world lies under the sway of the wicked one' (1 John 5:19).

What evidence is there for it? Evidence in abundance. For the present day, the calling of witnesses would be superfluous.

Virtually every news bulletin and newspaper is full of violence and wretchedness. As for the start of the misery, and its development among men, the Bible tells us plainly about that. Even though the law had not been given, the variety of sins men committed, as recorded in the book of Genesis and the early chapters of Exodus, is legion. Murder, anger, hatred, war, plunder, idolatry, ill-treatment, slavery, adultery, drunkenness, lying, sexual abuse and depravity of almost every hue – including homosexuality, prostitution and rape, polygamy and incest – jealousy and envy, deceit, cheating, blasphemy, hypocrisy, and so on, all defiled humanity. And yet the law had not been given! After God's covenant with Noah (Gen. 9:1-7), men knew by direct revelation that murder was wrong, but, of course, they had instinctively known that long before Noah's time. I have already referred to: 'Does not nature teach you?'[24] In short, with the exception of the sabbath,[25] all the other commands of the ten were broken *before the ten commandments had been given.*[26]

But, and of far greater significance, notice that whatever sin was committed as recorded in the book of Genesis, God never once referred to any of the ten commandments. Of course not! They were not yet given to Israel. Israel, as a nation, did not yet exist. Yet the concept of wickedness and sin on the one hand, and righteousness on the other, is written plainly in the book (Gen. 6:5,9,11-12; 8:21; 13:13; 15:16; 17:23; 18:20,23-32; 20:4,6; 31:36; 34:7; 38:26; 39:9; 44:5; 50:17), as is the concept of obedience to commands (Gen. 6:14,22; 7:1-5,16; 8:15-18; 26:5). On occasion, God gave men direct revelation concerning sin (Gen. 9:1-7; 17:23; 20:3-7; 31:7-13,24,29), but generally not. Though there was some sense of God, some fear of God, in the human race (Gen. 20:11; 21:22-23), yet in this regard Jacob and

---

[24] Compare 1 Cor. 11:14.

[25] In Ezek. 20:18,21,24, God complained of sabbath-breaking by the Jews in the wilderness but not in Egypt, yet they sinned by idolatry before that (Ezek. 20:7-9). It is, of course, dangerous to argue from silence, but in Ps. 106:7, although the Jews in Egypt forgot God's many mercies, no mention is made of neglect of the sabbath.

[26] The sabbath was a special case. God gave it to the Jews in the wilderness, as recorded in Ex. 16. They immediately broke it!

his family stood out from pagans (Gen. 34:7; 39:9). Furthermore, changes in morality occurred as time passed. In truth, some things which had been commanded by God, and practiced by men *before* Sinai, were regarded as sins *after* Sinai; altar building, for instance (Gen. 26:25; 35:1). The theme continues when we come to the early chapters of Exodus; God commands or instructs men (Ex. 7:6; 12:50; 15:26; 16:4,16,23,28,32,34; 17:1; 18:16,20,23); his ordinances are set up (Ex. 15:25; 17:15, plus several before that); and men go on sinning (Ex. 9:27,34; 10:16-17), disobeying (Ex. 16:17-20). Yet the first appearances in the Bible of the word 'law' (apart from 'in-laws') come at Genesis 26:5; 47:26 (and this not *torah*); 49:10; Exodus 12:49; 13:9; 16:4,28 and 18:16,20, and how rare they are at that stage![27]

What is the explanation of all this? As I have said, Reformed teachers nearly always claim it was because the law of Sinai had been given to all men in Adam. There is no biblical warrant for it. In fact, it flies in the face of Scripture. The only explanation lies in Romans 2:14-15. A rudimentary knowledge of the work of the law is inscribed on all men's hearts since Adam's fall. This is what Romans 2:14-15 teaches. This is what the record of the days before Sinai declares. Men sinned in those days. Some had some commands from God, which some obeyed and others did not. But the sense of right and wrong, even though somewhat hazy, existed in men, and did so *before the Jews received a written law from God.* Indeed, even before the giving of the law to Israel, some pagans had a more finely-tuned sense of right and wrong than some of the godly. Take the episode of Abraham (and Sarah) lying to Abimelech king of Gerar, the latter's reaction, and his reproof of the father of the faithful (Gen. 20). Abimelech certainly showed a greater sense of morality than Abraham. The same can be said for Abimelech king of the Philistines and Isaac (and Rebekah) (Gen. 26). Hamor the Hivite, though he certainly had his faults, showed more integrity than Jacob's sons (Gen. 34).

---

[27] And they do not all refer to a law from God.

Where did pagans get their sense of right and wrong, their sense of injustice? Romans 2:14-15 is the clear biblical explanation.[28]

A notorious child-murderer is given what most people consider to be a lenient sentence, and there is a public outcry: 'It's not right! It's not fair! It's unjust! Something ought to be done about it!' I agree – but where did it come from, this sense of rightness and wrongness, fairness and unfairness? Two men are overheard having a quarrel: 'I helped you when you were in trouble, and now you won't do the same for me! It's not fair! You won't catch me twice!' Again, I ask, where does this talk of right and wrong, fair and unfair come from? Why do we speak to ourselves – sometimes to rebuke ourselves for an action or a word, but more often than not to excuse ourselves? Two children are playing on the mat: 'No! You went first last time. It's my turn now'. How do children know *instinctively* (whether or not the parents have taught them) that they should take turns? 'If there's a God, why does he allow war or famine or pestilence or earthquakes or whatever? Why do the innocent have to suffer as well as the guilty? If he's God, can't he stop it?' Where does this sense of good and bad, innocence and guilt, come from? How do we know that pain, misery and death are bad? Where does kindness come from? How do we know that kindness is good, and cruelty bad? I ask again: Where does all this 'morality' come from? Why is it universal in the human race? The explanation is Romans 2:14-15.

This is a point of far greater significance than at first appears, as I will now explain.

What bearing does this have on the rest of Scripture?

Just this: as I explained at the close of the previous article, since the Gentiles do not have the law of Moses, care must be taken in the exegesis of those New Testament passages which speak of sinners who were once under the law, but have by Christ been delivered from it. Those passages which were written to

---

[28] Interestingly, Moses, in recording these things, never tries to read the law back into the history.

converted Jews or proselytes present no problem. But what of those passages which were written to converted Gentiles? One explanation is that those believing Gentiles needed to be taught the Old Testament background to their faith, especially with regard to the law. Why? Because often they were being attacked by Judaisers who wanted them to submit to the law. Paul wrote to teach believers some basic facts about the law, in order to highlight the stupidity, the wrongness, of converted Gentiles going under the old, fulfilled and abolished Jewish system. And since they, as Gentiles, before conversion, were never under the law, why on earth would they think to put themselves under the very law from which Christ, by his death, released believing Jews? Paul would have none of it!

Having said that, there are a few remaining passages where it does appear that believing Gentiles had also in some sense been under the law in their unregenerate days, and were now delivered from it in Christ. The question is, how can these passages be explained? How were these Gentiles under the law before conversion? The answer is Romans 2:14-15.

Let me give but one illustration. Take Romans 7:4. Assuming that the recipients of the letter were *not* converted Jews or proselytes – and is that certain?[29] – then we have to face the fact that Paul told rank-Gentile believers that they have 'become dead to the law', they had 'died to the law' (NIV).[30] How can this be – since they were never under the law?

I make the following suggestion: Israel, having the law from Sinai, served as a model – a paradigm – to show how God deals with people under law. The Gentiles, while not under the law of Moses, are nevertheless under some sort of law (Rom. 2:14-15). While Romans 7:4, then, is strictly applicable only to Jewish believers, the principle applies equally to Gentile converts and 'their' law.

This has large consequences. Anticipating further developments, as we shall see, the history of the Jews shows the

---

[29] My best 'guess' is that the church in Rome contained a mixture of Jews, proselytes and Gentiles, all converted to Christ.
[30] The apostle declared: 'I... died to the law' (Gal. 2:19).

utter uselessness of sinners attempting justification by works. Since the Jews could not find salvation through the law, even the law given them by God, then no system of works will enable sinners to earn salvation. This leaves the human race in total, helpless bondage – a bondage from which only Christ can deliver.

This very important corollary comes directly from this look at Romans 2:14-15. Paul's teaching here is of far greater significance than it seems at first glance. From time to time throughout my *Christ Is All*, therefore, I refer back to this passage, and the explanation of it which I have put forward in this article.

All Men Under Law

Every man who has ever lived, without exception, has been under law. Every man now living is under law. Every man to be born will be born under law. Let me prove it.

Adam before he fell, was under law

God placed Adam under law:

> The Lord God took the man and put him in the garden of Eden to work it and keep it. And the Lord God commanded the man, saying: 'You may surely eat of every tree of the garden, but of the tree of the knowledge of good and evil you shall not eat, for in the day that you eat of it you shall surely die' (Gen. 2:15-17).

Eve, in her first response to the serpent, admitted:

> The woman said to the serpent: 'We may eat of the fruit of the trees in the garden, but God said: "You shall not eat of the fruit of the tree that is in the midst of the garden, neither shall you touch it, lest you die"' (Gen. 3:2-3).

And God, in addressing Adam in his judgement, was clear:

> Because you have listened to the voice of your wife and have eaten of the tree of which I commanded you: 'You shall not eat of it', cursed is the ground because of you; in pain you shall eat of it all the days of your life; thorns and thistles it shall bring forth for you; and you shall eat the plants of the field. By the sweat of your face you shall eat bread, till you return to the ground, for out of it you were taken; for you are dust, and to dust you shall return (Gen. 3:17-19).

Paul, writing to the Romans, declared:

> Death reigned from Adam to Moses, even over those whose sinning was not like the transgression of Adam (Rom. 5:14).
> Death reigned from the time of Adam to the time of Moses, even over those who did not sin by breaking a command, as did Adam (NIV).

The apostle used the word *parabasis*, 'transgression', 'the breach of a definite, promulgated, ratified law', used elsewhere of the breach of the law of Moses (Rom. 4:15; Heb. 2:2; 9:15). It is clear, therefore, that Adam, before he fell, was under law. It was not a written law, but it was a law.

All men, since the fall, have been under law

In addition to the evidence of nature, which he has given to every man, and for which he holds every man accountable (Ps. 19:1-6; 50:6; Acts 14:17; 17:24-29; Rom. 1:18-20,28,32; 10:18), God has expressly written a law within every man:

> Gentiles, who do not have the law [of Moses], by nature do what the law requires, they are a law to themselves, even though they do not have the law [of Moses]. They show that the work of the law is written on their hearts, while their conscience also bears witness, and their conflicting thoughts accuse or even excuse them on that day when, according to my gospel, God judges the secrets of men by Christ Jesus (Rom. 2:14-16).

This law, like the first, is not written in an outward sense. Nevertheless, it is a real law, and all men are held accountable to God for breaking it (Rom. 1:18-32; 2:14-16). All men 'know God's righteous decree that those who practice such things deserve to die' (Rom. 1:32). 'Sin indeed was in the world before the law [of Moses] was given, but sin is not counted where there is no law' (Rom. 5:13), for: 'Where there is no law there is no transgression' (Rom. 4:15). As Paul stated, literally: 'Through law [is] knowledge of sin' (Rom. 3:20).[1] So there must have been a 'law' before the Mosaic law, a law under which all men were

---

[1] What is said of the killing law in Rom. 3:20; 4:15; 5:13; 7:21-25; 8:2, of course, was especially true for Israel under the Mosaic law. But it also applies as a general principle for all men. All men are sinners both in Adam and in actual practice. All men are under law! Similarly, Rom. 7:7 literally reads: 'Sin I knew not unless by law'. Yes, Paul was referring to the Mosaic law, the tenth commandment, but, as before, the principle is general.

accountable and died as sinners, breakers of that law (see also Rom. 7:21-25; 8:2).[2]

Israel was given the law of Moses

Israel and Israel only, was given the law of God through Moses at Sinai:

> And now, O Israel, listen to the statutes and the rules that I am teaching you, and do them, that you may live, and go in and take possession of the land that the Lord, the God of your fathers, is giving you. You shall not add to the word that I command you, nor take from it, that you may keep the commandments of the Lord your God that I command you... See, I have taught you statutes and rules, as the Lord my God commanded me, that you should do them in the land that you are entering to take possession of it. Keep them and do them, for that will be your wisdom and your understanding in the sight of the peoples, who, when they hear all these statutes, will say: 'Surely this great nation is a wise and understanding people'. For what great nation is there that has a god so near to it as the Lord our God is to us, whenever we call upon him? And what great nation is there, that has statutes and rules so righteous as all this law that I set before you today?... The Lord spoke to you out of the midst of the fire. You heard the sound of words, but saw no form; there was only a voice. And he declared to you his covenant, which he commanded you to perform, that is, the ten commandments, and he wrote them on two tablets of stone. And the Lord commanded me at that time to teach you statutes and rules, that you might do them in the land that you are going over to possess (Deut. 4:1-2,5-8,12-14).
>
> Moses commanded [Israel] a law, as a possession for the assembly of Jacob (Deut. 33:4).

---

[2] 'Even though Gentiles did not technically live under the Mosaic law, they are still considered to be in the realm of the law, for they have [a rudimentary – Schreiner had 'the'] law written on their hearts and know what God expects of them. Such a view seems to be reflected in Galatians, where the desire of the Gentiles to submit to the law is described as a return to paganism. Such an indictment makes sense if Paul sees the Gentiles in a sense to be under the law' (Thomas R.Schreiner: *40 Questions About Christians and Biblical Law*, Kregel, 2010, p80).

[God] declares his word to Jacob, his statutes and rules to Israel. He has not dealt thus with any other nation; they do not know his rules (Ps. 147:19-20).

What advantage has the Jew? Or what is the value of circumcision? Much in every way. To begin with, the Jews were entrusted with the oracles of God (Rom. 3:1-2).

Israelites... to them belong the adoption, the glory, the covenants, the giving of the law, the worship, and the promises (Rom. 9:4).

Clearly, Israel had a law, the law of God through Moses, this law being written on stone (Ex. 24:12; 31:18; 32:15-16; 2 Cor. 3:3,7 and in the book of the law (Deut. 17:18; 28:58,61; 29:21; 30:10; 31:24-26; Josh. 1:8; 8:31; 23:6; 23:6; 24:26; *etc.*).

Christ was under law

We have the apostle's general statement:

When the fullness of time had come, God sent forth his Son, born of woman, born under the law, to redeem those who were under the law (Gal. 4:4-5).

Specifically:

At the end of eight days, when he was circumcised, he was called Jesus, the name given by the angel before he was conceived in the womb. And when the time came for their purification according to the law of Moses, they brought him up to Jerusalem to present him to the Lord (as it is written in the law of the Lord...) and to offer a sacrifice according to what is said in the law of the Lord... Now there was a man in Jerusalem, whose name was Simeon... and he came in the Spirit into the temple, and when the parents brought in the child Jesus, to do for him according to the custom of the law (Luke 2:21-27).

Jesus could say:

This charge [commandment] I have received from my Father (John 10:18).
I do as the Father has commanded me (John 14:31).
I have kept my Father's commandments (John 15:10).

The inspired writer gave us a commentary on all this:

When Christ came into the world, he said: 'Sacrifices and offerings you have not desired, but a body have you prepared for me; in burnt offerings and sin offerings you have taken no pleasure. Then I said: "Behold, I have come to do your will, O God, as it is written of me in the scroll of the book"... "Behold, I have come to do your will"... And by that will we have been sanctified through the offering of the body of Jesus Christ once for all (Heb. 10:5-10).

And we read of Jesus' obedience:

Being found in human form, [Jesus] humbled himself by becoming obedient to the point of death, even death on a cross (Phil. 2:8).
Although he was a son, he learned obedience through what he suffered (Heb. 5:8).

'Obedience' speaks of 'law'. Christ was under law.

The law to all men in the gospel offer

The gospel offer contains a law, a command, to be given to all men. Christ has commanded his disciples:

All authority in heaven and on earth has been given to me. Go therefore and make disciples of all nations, baptising them in the name of the Father and of the Son and of the Holy Spirit, teaching them to observe all that I have commanded you. And behold, I am with you always, to the end of the age (Matt. 28:18-20).
Go into all the world and proclaim the gospel to the whole creation. Whoever believes and is baptised will be saved, but whoever does not believe will be condemned (Mark 16:15-16).
Forgiveness of sins should be proclaimed in [Christ's] name to all nations, beginning from Jerusalem. You are witnesses of these things (Luke 24:47-48).
You will receive power when the Holy Spirit has come upon you, and you will be my witnesses in Jerusalem and in all Judea and Samaria, and to the end of the earth (Acts 1:8).

And in that gospel offer, there is a command to all men:

God... now... commands all people everywhere to repent, because he has fixed a day on which he will judge the world in righteousness by a man whom he has appointed (Acts 17:30-31).

The apostles showed the way:

> Repent and be baptised every one of you in the name of Jesus Christ for the forgiveness of your sins, and you will receive the gift of the Holy Spirit (Acts 2:38).
> Repent therefore, and turn back, that your sins may be blotted out (Acts 3:19).
> Your heart is not right before God. Repent, therefore, of this wickedness of yours, and pray to the Lord that, if possible, the intent of your heart may be forgiven you. For I see that you are in the gall of bitterness and in the bond of iniquity (Acts 8:21-23).
> 'Sirs, what must I do to be saved?' And they said: 'Believe in the Lord Jesus, and you will be saved, you and your household' (Acts 16:30-31).
> I did not shrink from declaring to you anything that was profitable, and teaching you in public and from house to house, testifying both to Jews and to Greeks of repentance toward God and of faith in our Lord Jesus Christ (Acts 20:20-21).
> I was not disobedient to the heavenly vision, but declared first to those in Damascus, then in Jerusalem and throughout all the region of Judea, and also to the Gentiles, that they should repent and turn to God, performing deeds in keeping with their repentance (Acts 26:19-20).

The believer is under law

The believer, though he has died to the law (the rudimentary law in his conscience and/or the Mosaic law) (Rom. 6:14-15; 7:4-6; 1 Cor. 9:20; Gal. 2:19), is under the law of Christ:

> A new commandment I give to you, that you love one another: just as I have loved you, you also are to love one another. By this all people will know that you are my disciples, if you have love for one another (John 13:34-35).
> If you love me, you will keep my commandments... Whoever has my commandments and keeps them, he it is who loves me. And he who loves me will be loved by my Father, and I will love him and manifest myself to him... If anyone loves me, he will keep my word, and my Father will love him, and we will come to him and make our home with him. Whoever does not love me does not keep my words. And the word that you hear is not mine but the Father's who sent me (John 14:15,21-24).

If you abide in me, and my words abide in you... If you keep my commandments, you will abide in my love, just as I have kept my Father's commandments and abide in his love... This is my commandment, that you love one another as I have loved you... These things I command you, so that you will love one another (John 15:7,10,12,17).

So the apostles are clear; the believer has been set free from the law of sin and death:

There is therefore now no condemnation for those who are in Christ Jesus. For the law of the Spirit of life has set you free in Christ Jesus from the law of sin and death. For God has done what the law, weakened by the flesh, could not do. By sending his own Son in the likeness of sinful flesh and for sin, he condemned sin in the flesh, in order that the righteous requirement of the law might be fulfilled in us, who walk not according to the flesh but according to the Spirit (Rom. 8:1-4).

But he is under law to Christ:

Though I am free from all, I have made myself a servant to all, that I might win more of them. To the Jews I became as a Jew, in order to win Jews. To those under the law I became as one under the law (though not being myself under the law) that I might win those under the law. To those outside the law I became as one outside the law (not being outside the law of God but under the law of Christ) that I might win those outside the law. To the weak I became weak, that I might win the weak. I have become all things to all people, that by all means I might save some. I do it all for the sake of the gospel, that I may share with them in its blessings (1 Cor. 9:19-23).

Bear one another's burdens, and so fulfil the law of Christ (Gal. 6:2).

The one who looks into the perfect law, the law of liberty, and perseveres, being no hearer who forgets but a doer who acts, he will be blessed in his doing... So speak and so act as those who are to be judged under the law of liberty (Jas. 1:25; 2:12).

And while this law of Christ is not a written code like the Mosaic law (Rom. 7:4-6; 2 Cor. 3:6-11; 1 Tim. 1:8-11), but is the inward working of the Spirit (Rom. 8:1-4) calibrated by the entire word of God (John 17:17; Rom. 15:4; 2 Tim. 3:16), nevertheless it is a real, objective, law (1 Tim. 1:5).

Thus all men have been, and all men will be, under law. All men are under the law of death to condemnation or under the law to Christ by his Spirit and thus to everlasting salvation.

Which law are you under?

Who's Your Husband?

Everybody has a husband. In fact, everybody is born into this world married to a husband. Moreover, some of us have died to our first husband, the one we were born married to, and we have been married to another husband.

Whatever am I talking about? Where do I get such ideas?

I am talking, of course in spiritual terms, and I get what I say from Scripture.[1] Where? In Romans 7:1-6. Listen to Paul:

> Do you not know, brothers – for I am speaking to those who know the law – that the law is binding on a person only as long as he lives? For a married woman is bound by law to her husband while he lives, but if her husband dies she is released from the law of marriage. Accordingly, she will be called an adulteress if she lives with another man while her husband is alive. But if her husband dies, she is free from that law, and if she marries another man she is not an adulteress. Likewise, my brothers, you also have died to the law through the body of Christ, so that you may belong to another, to him who has been raised from the dead, in order that we may bear fruit for God. For while we were living in the flesh, our sinful passions, aroused by the law, were at work in our members to bear fruit for death. But now we are released from the law, having died to that which held us captive, so that we serve in the new way of the Spirit and not in the old way of the written code.

The apostle, writing to believers,[2] tells them that they have died to their first husband – the law – in order to be married to a second husband, a new husband, the Lord Jesus Christ.

---

[1] For this article, I have lightly edited my *Christ* pp166-171,453-460. See also 'Romans 7:4-6' and 'The Believer's Marriage' in my series 'New-Covenant Theology Made Simple'.

[2] He calls his readers 'brothers', having already described them as those who are 'called to belong to Jesus Christ... loved by God and called to be saints' (Rom. 1:6-7). See also Rom. 3:21 – 6:23, noting the apostle's repeated references to his readers' personal experience of Christ.

From this we learn that all men are born married to 'the law', and many stay married to this husband until the end of their lives. Others, however – in their regeneration, in their coming to trust the Lord Jesus Christ – die to their first husband, and marry Christ. The subject, of course, is conversion.

So when I ask: 'Who's your husband?', I am asking if you are still married to the law, or if you have died to the law and so been married to Christ. I am, in fact, asking whether or not you have been converted. Converted? Have you been born again, regenerated by God's Spirit, the Spirit who has convicted you of your sin, and brought you to repentance and trust in Christ? If so, you have, in your conversion, died to your first husband – the law – and been united in marriage to Christ. So says the apostle.

He is not alone in saying such things. The prophets spoke of the believer's marriage to Christ. Take for instance, the wedding song of Psalm 45, which psalm, not least, is a prophecy of the Messiah, Christ. Addressing Christ's bride-to-be, the psalmist urges her:

> Hear, O daughter, and consider, and incline your ear: forget your people and your father's house, and the king will desire your beauty. Since he is your lord, bow to him... All glorious is the princess in her chamber, with robes interwoven with gold. In many-coloured robes she is led to the king, with her virgin companions following behind her. With joy and gladness they are led along as they enter the palace of the king (Ps. 45:10-15).[3]

As Isaiah declared: 'Your Maker is your husband' (Isa. 54:5).[4] And God, through Hosea, announced:

---

[3] See 'Christ the Best Husband: Or an Earnest Invitation to Young Women to Come and See Christ' (ccel.org), George Whitefield's sermon on Ps. 45:10-11.

[4] See 'Christ the Believer's Husband' (biblebb.com), an otherwise excellent sermon by Whitefield, sadly marred, however, by his unscriptural talk of the unbeliever being married to the law as a covenant of works, and the believer having died to the law as a covenant of works but being alive to the law as a rule of life. See below for more in this. On the covenant of works, see my 'The Covenant that Never Was'.

I will betroth you to me forever. I will betroth you to me in righteousness and in justice, in steadfast love and in mercy. I will betroth you to me in faithfulness. And you shall know the LORD. 'And in that day I will answer', declares the LORD, 'I will answer the heavens, and they shall answer the earth, and the earth shall answer the grain, the wine, and the oil, and they shall answer Jezreel, and I will sow her for myself in the land. And I will have mercy on No Mercy, and I will say to Not My People: "You are my people", and he shall say: "You are my God"' (Hos. 2:19-23).[5]

The apostle, himself, never tired of the theme. Writing to believers at Corinth and Ephesus, he said:

I feel a divine jealousy for you, since I betrothed you to one husband, to present you as a pure virgin to Christ. But I am afraid that as the serpent deceived Eve by his cunning, your thoughts will be led astray from a sincere and pure devotion to Christ (2 Cor. 11:2-3).[6]
Christ loved the church and gave himself up for her, that he might sanctify her, having cleansed her by the washing of water with the word, so that he might present the church to himself in splendour, without spot or wrinkle or any such thing, that she might be holy and without blemish (Eph. 5:25-27).

---

[5] See Rom. 9:22-33.

[6] Remember context here. It could not be more relevant to the question in hand. Paul is getting to grips with the law men. Calvin: 'That [Paul's] zeal... was to join [his readers] to Christ in marriage, and retain them in connection with him... All ministers [all believers – DG] are the friends of the Bridegroom... (John 3:29). Hence all ought to be concerned that the fidelity of this sacred marriage remain unimpaired and inviolable. This they cannot do, unless they are actuated [moved] by the dispositions [character, outlook, aims] of the Bridegroom, so that every one of them may be as much concerned for the purity of the church, as a husband is for the chastity of his wife. Away then with coldness and indolence in this matter... Let them, however... take care not to pursue their own interest rather than that of Christ, that they may not intrude themselves into his place, lest while they give themselves out as his friends, they turn out to be in reality adulterers, by alluring the bride to love themselves... We are married to Christ on no other condition than that we bring virginity as our dowry, and preserve it entire, so as to be free from all corruption'.

In short, the believer has died to the law and has been united in marriage to Christ (Rom. 7:4-6).

Nor does this exhaust the relevant New Testament use of marriage and weddings when referring to believers. It was at a wedding in Cana in Galilee that Christ performed his first miracle; that is, he showed his first sign of who he was, and what he was about to accomplish in fulfilling the old covenant and establishing the new (John 2:1-11).[7] Then we have Christ's repeated use of the picture (Matt. 9:15; 22:1-14; 25:1-13; Luke 12:35-36; 14:8). John the Baptist spoke in such terms (John 3:27-30). Finally, we have the references in the book of Revelation (Rev. 19:6-9; 21:2,9; 22:17).

What should we make of this? Clearly this dying, this release from our first marriage in order to enter into a second marriage, a new marriage with the Lord Jesus, in order to bear spiritual fruit, is of fundamental importance. It is vital that both the unbeliever and the believer should be clear on it.

What do covenant theologians make of Romans 7:4-6?

Well, this is not altogether easy to say. Covenant theologians offer a range of alternative explanations of how they understand the principles of Romans 7:1-6, and, as so often with covenant theologians, things soon get complicated. But let me do my best to summarise the Reformed interpretation of this important passage.

Although I am not sure that they often, let alone always, use the biblical terminology of 'marriage', even so, covenant theologians say that Adam had the moral law written within him, and that all men ever since have been born married to the moral law. By 'the moral law', the Reformed mean the ten commandments. This division of the law, it goes without saying, is patently unscriptural. Moreover, the claim that Adam had the ten commandments before he fell is, to say the least of it, very odd. Whatever did Adam make of commandments against sin

---

[7] Do not miss the link with the parable of the wineskins (Matt. 9:16-17), with its proximity to 'the bridegroom' (Matt. 9:15).

(such as adultery and theft) before he fell, before he had any concept of 'sin', before there was any woman with whom he could commit adultery, and before there was anybody to steal anything from? And what, I wonder, did he make of a commandment about his father and mother, when he wouldn't have had a clue who such people were? And, if it is true that all men are married to 'the moral law', why is it no tribe by nature has ever kept the sabbath, especially bearing in mind its *essential* observance of rest from Friday sunset to Saturday sunset? And why do we never read of any biblical preacher appealing to 'the moral law' when addressing unconverted pagans? Strange, is it not, if all men really are married to it? But there it is, according to covenant theologians, all men are, by nature, married to the moral law.

Now when sinners come to faith, they die to the law, and marry another husband. Indeed, they have to die to the first husband in order that they might marry the second. So said the apostle (Rom. 7:4-6). What do covenant theologians make of this? They say a mixture of things. You pays your money and you takes your choice, I suppose. They say that believers have died to the law as a covenant; or that they have died to the condemnation of the law; or that they have died to the ceremonial law; or... what? But in any case, whatever it is to which they have died, after their conversion, believers continue to be married (or are re-married) to the moral law as their perfect rule. So say covenant theologians. Once again, I am not sure they often, let alone always, use the apostle's language and talk of 'marriage', but there it is.

What should we make of this rigmarole? Not only is it riddled with unbiblical gloss after unbiblical gloss, but, yet again, I find it very odd. Were pagans ever married to the ceremonial law? If not, how could they die to it? Is the believer guilty of spiritual bigamy – being married to the moral law (after all, this is precisely what being 'under the moral law as the perfect rule' means) and, at the same time, being married to Christ? And which scripture tells us we can distinguish between the law as a covenant and the law as a rule? And doesn't the biblical concept of marriage have 'covenant' at its heart (Mal. 2:10-16)?

So much for covenant theology and Romans 7:4-6.

What do new-covenant theologians make of Romans 7:4-6?

Well, I can speak only for myself, of course. But I am convinced that all men are, by nature, married to the law, in that all men, by nature, have a rudimentary sense of right and wrong written in their conscience (Rom. 2:12-15). They also have the evidence of creation, which evidence they do not fail to notice (Ps. 19:1-6; Rom. 1:18-20), even though they suppress it (Rom. 1:21-32). In addition – and what an addition! – the Jews were singled out by God by being given a far greater revelation: through Moses on Mount Sinai, God gave his law to Israel, and for Israel, alone (Deut. 4:7-8,32-34; Ps. 147:19-20; Rom. 2:14; 3:1-2; 9:4; 1 Cor. 9:20-21). Hence, all men are under the law, married to the law: pagans to the law of nature and conscience, and Jews to the law of nature and conscience, and the Mosaic law. Paul gathers these threads to describe all men as being 'under the law', married to the law, by nature.[8] The sinner, coming to Christ, being converted, dies to the law – to the law full stop, to the law in its entirety – so that he may be united in marriage to Christ, and so come under Christ's rule and governance, and be endowed with Christ's Spirit in order to bear fruit within his new marriage, bear fruit as a result of his new marriage, bear fruit to the glory of his new husband.

Do not miss **the** *telling point in all this,* **the** *point of high significance.* The believer has not died to one law so that he can marry another law. Far from it! He has died to the law in order to be married to Christ – married to Christ, not to any law, not even the law of God! No law, no code, no regulation system could ever

---

[8] He does much the same in Gal. 3:21-25; 4:7. See my *Christ* pp38-48,347. I quote: 'Israel, having the law from Sinai, served as a model – a paradigm – to show how God deals with people under law. The Gentiles, while not under the law of Moses, are nevertheless under some sort of law (Rom. 2:14-15). While Romans 7:4, then, is strictly applicable only to Jewish believers, the principle applies equally to Gentile converts and "their" law' (*Christ* p48).

produce the fruit God requires. Not even the law of God. Paul expressly states this fact:

> Likewise, my brothers, you also have died to the law through the body of Christ, so that you may belong to another, to him who has been raised from the dead, *in order that we may bear fruit for God* (Rom. 7:4).

Only the Spirit of Christ, indwelling the child of God by reason of his union with Christ himself, can produce such fruit. Christ is all, Christ is the believer's husband, Christ is the covenant (Isa. 42:6; 49:8).[9]

And how vital this is. No law, not even God's law to Israel through Moses, can accomplish this glorious end. Only Christ, by his Spirit, because of the Father's sovereign decree, can do it. *Indeed, he has done it.* Paul, in gathering his argument together

---

[9] We must not make this mystical, of course. By 'mystical', I do not mean 'mystery'. Of course, the union of the believer with Christ is a mystery, but the mystical here is the real danger of thinking in terms of absorption of the human into the divine. If the Hebraism is pushed, serious consequences follow. With that in mind, I quote: 'The covenant between God and his people being in Christ, it is quite consistent with Hebrew usage to transfer the term to Christ himself, in whom the covenant was, as it were, embodied. So Christ is called "our salvation" and "our peace", and again, "our redemption" and "our life". This is the ordinary tone of Hebrew poetry, which rejoices in personification and embodiment. A prose writer would have said that the Servant of the Lord would be given as the mediator of a covenant between Jehovah and his people' (*Pulpit Commentary* on Isa. 42:6). John Gill: 'Christ is... the representative of his people in [the covenant], the surety, mediator, messenger, and ratifier of it, the great blessing in it, the sum and substance of it. All the blessings and promises of it are in him, and as such he is "given"' (*Commentary* on Isa. 42:6). C.H.Spurgeon when preaching on Isaiah 49:8 (sermon number 103), having opened by speaking of Christ as the mediator and the surety of the covenant, went on: 'And I doubt not, we have also rejoiced in the thought that Christ is the sum and substance of the covenant; we believe that if we would sum up all spiritual blessings, we must say: "Christ is all". He is the matter, he is the substance of it; and although much might be said concerning the glories of the covenant, yet nothing could be said which is not to be found in that one word: "Christ"'.

and pressing it home in Romans 8, makes this point right at the start:

For *God has done what the law, weakened by the flesh, could not do*. By sending his own Son in the likeness of sinful flesh and for sin, he condemned sin in the flesh, *in order that* the righteous requirement of the law might be fulfilled in us, who walk not according to the flesh but according to the Spirit (Rom. 8:3-4).

The argument behind all this is that death ends the legal obligations of marriage (Rom. 7:1-3). Indeed, it ends the marriage state itself. Likewise, the relationship between the sinner and the law ends when the sinner comes to faith in Christ, since by faith the believer is united to Christ in his death and resurrection, having died in and with him (Rom. 6:3-5). Do not miss the 'likewise' or 'so' at the start of Romans 7:4. It is all one continuous argument, with no chapter – let alone verse – division.

The believer, therefore, is no longer married to the law. He is married to Christ. And this means that whereas the unbeliever under the law must submit to the law – as a wife to her husband – the law has no rule, governance or jurisdiction over the believer. He is no longer under it! Indeed, he is dead to it.[10] 'We have been delivered from the law', said Paul (Rom. 7:6). 'Delivered'? The apostle uses a strong word – 'discharged', 'set at liberty', 'set free'. The believers is totally discharged or set free from the law. It has no authority over him any longer, it rules him no more. Just as a man, when he dies, is discharged from all obligations to the law,[11] so it is with the believer. He has complete freedom from all obligations to the Mosaic law as a rule of life. He is no longer in covenant with the law. He is at liberty, free from the law, released from the law, free to be married to Christ, and under his rule, under his law, in covenant with him. Indeed, he is not only free to be married to Christ: his marriage to Christ is an inevitable consequence and privilege of his being in the new-covenant. The

---

[10] Many confuse the illustration and say the law has died. It has not. The believer has.

[11] Once again, it is the merest quibble to point out that an executor has to discharge the debts of the deceased. Paul is not dealing with the law of probate, but with the ongoing life of the believer.

believer, therefore, is free of the law, is married to Christ, and, as a result, is under his sole governance.

Let me take this a little further

And there is need. We cannot be too much taken up with this glorious theme. To be 'under the law' means far more than 'the law defining something'. But this is claimed. Jonathan Bayes, for instance, grievously watered-down the apostle's teaching: 'Paul's main point has been that in the sphere of the flesh the law has a sin-defining function'.[12] This is worse than nonsense! Paul's *main* point? The apostle was saying a lot more than that! Marriage speaks of far more than 'defining' something. Bayes has degraded Paul's majestic doctrine to the level of the banal. Is this all marriage is: a definition of some sort of condition? Paul was talking about a regime, a jurisdiction, a state, a covenant, a union – a marriage, after all. And this is how we must talk. To be married to the law is to be under the rule of the law, under the rule, the headship or jurisdiction of Moses, in the Mosaic covenant.

And when it comes to the second marriage, in marrying Christ, is the believer to think of this as merely 'defining holiness' for him? To be married to Christ is to be under his rule and headship, in covenant with him, united to him, one with him, to have died with him, to have been raised with him, to have ascended with and to be seated with him in glory. This is how Paul speaks of it (Rom. 6:3-11; 7:4-6; Eph. 2:6,13; 5:22-33), and this is how we, as believers, must think and speak of our new position in Christ.

The illustration must not be glossed away. Its full import must be allowed to stand. Indeed, it must dominate all discussion on the believer and the law. When a man dies and his wife remarries, is she under the authority of her new husband or her old? Certainly not the old! The fact is, her former husband is no longer her husband at all. His death ended that marriage. It would be

---

[12] Jonathan F.Bayes: *The Weakness of the Law: God's Law and the Christian in New Testament Perspective*, Paternoster Press, Cumbria, 2000, p117.

unthinkable, even ridiculous, if a woman, being remarried after her first husband's death, deferred to the authority of her former (dead) husband. The fact is, that authority does not even exist![13] 'No one can serve two masters' (Matt. 6:24); that is, no servant (Luke 16:13) can serve two masters. In all this, we are in the realm of headship, rule, governance, union, covenant. The application is clear. No wife can obey two husbands, one dead and the other alive. No woman can serve two husbands. The fact is, she can have only one husband! She cannot be in covenant with two husbands!

The picture is plain. The unregenerate sinner is married to the law, but when the Spirit regenerates and converts him, he dies to the law, and is united to Christ by faith. From now on, he is no longer under the law, but under Christ; no longer under *its* rule, but under *his* rule. Instead of being in his first, unfruitful marriage – to the law – the believer is now in a marriage – to Christ – in which he produces fruit to God through his union with the Redeemer (Rom. 6:22; 7:4). He is in the new covenant, married to the Lord Christ himself.

And this is the climax of the passage. 'Fruit to God' can be produced only by those who have died to the law. Those who have not died to the law can produce nothing but 'fruit to death': 'For while we were living in the flesh, our sinful passions, aroused by the law, were at work in our members to bear fruit for death' (Rom. 7:5; see also Rom. 8:5-8). So, as long as we are married to the law, we cannot be married to Christ, and thus there is no possibility of being sanctified. For that, our bondage to the law has to cease. Then, and only then, can we start to live a new life in relationship to Christ. The old relationship must end, and this can only happen by death. It is only as we are married to Christ, free from the law, that we can begin to live a life of holiness.

---

[13] Again, it is the merest quibble to talk of the respect the woman has for her former husband, now dead. As with all biblical illustrations, we must grasp the main point.

Let me reinforce a vital point. In these verses, we are *not* talking about justification or positional sanctification.[14] We are talking about *the fruits and effects* of justification and positional sanctification; namely, progressive sanctification. Far from teaching that a believer is under the law for progressive sanctification (as covenant theologians), Paul asserts the very opposite. Unless a man is dead to the law, and married to Christ, he will never produce fruit to God; he will never be sanctified. In his first marriage – to the law – he produced sin and death. In his second marriage – to Christ – he produces righteousness. Paul especially underlines the fact that it is the believer's very freedom from the law which enables him to be sanctified. Staying under the law would make it impossible. The truth is, the opposite would occur. Sin would be aroused or excited by the law, and sin being stimulated, death would be the inevitable result. The law, therefore, cannot be the perfect rule for sanctification. It is an utter impossibility! As in Galatians 2:19 and 5:13-18, far from the law being the means of progressive sanctification, holiness of life is only possible to one who is free from the law. It is not merely that the law is *not* the means of sanctification. *Freedom from the law is the only means of sanctification.* Christ has set his people free from the law in order that they might be sanctified.

Phew! Let us pause for breath, and take stock! Read over once again the first six verses of Romans 7 – in more than one version – read them aloud – and just let the apostle's words sink in. Indeed, read over Romans 6:11 – 7:6. If the above is *not* what he is saying – then what *is* he saying? And whatever answer you come up with, go on to verse 7 and ask yourself whether or not your explanation would promote the apostle's question. I will come back to this.

Although this doctrine sounds startling, frightening, shocking to those who hold Calvin's third use of the law – that the law is

---

[14] In Romans, Paul speaks only of justification. For positional sanctification, see, for instance, 1 Cor. 1:2,30; 6:11; 2 Thess. 2:13; Heb. 2:11; 10:10,14,29; 13:12; 1 Pet. 1:2; Jude 1. The two, of course, are different ways of looking at the same glorious truth; namely, the believer's perfection in Christ in the sight of God, free of condemnation and accusation (Rom. 8:1,31-34; Eph. 5:25-27).

the believer's perfect rule, a whip to drive him to sanctification – this *is* the plain teaching of the apostle. And the law we are talking about is, I remind you, the Mosaic law, including the ten commandments. As so often, some try to say that Paul is here speaking about justification, about the penalty, demands and curse of the law, or about the law as a works covenant, claiming that, although the believer has died to the law as a curse, and so on, the law still stands as his rule of life. Paul is saying nothing of the sort! *He says the very opposite!* The believer has died to the law. It is simply not possible to divide or tinker this 'having died' into having died to the *curse* of the law but being alive to its *rule*.

In any case, Romans 7:1-6 is not concerned with justification. Romans 7:4 is saying the same as Romans 6:14, using a different illustration. Neither passage is limited to justification. Paul is not saying that believers are dead to the law as a way of justification. Paul is speaking about the two realms, the two ages – law and grace – in both historical and personal terms. The full force of the eschatological 'but now' (Rom. 7:6) must be grasped. The believer is living in a totally different and new age. He was a slave; he is free. His first marriage has ended; he is re-married. The two states – the former and the present – are totally incompatible. They cannot be cobbled together. The believer is not partly slave (and partly free), partly married to the law (and partly married to Christ). 'But now', thunders Paul (Rom. 7:6), with his sights set on the huge contrast between the new and old age for the believer, 'we have been delivered from the law, having died to what we were held by'.

Nor is Paul talking about a *misunderstanding* or *misuse* of the law, and contrasting *that* with the Spirit. He is contrasting the old covenant and the new, the old age and the new. The believer is in the new covenant, free from bondage to the law, and thus he will serve God by the Spirit, being in a totally new condition of life (2 Cor. 3:6), and he will bear fruit to God's praise (Rom. 6:22-23). Note the continuing – dominating – role for 'but now' in Paul's argument. Discontinuity and contrast are the words! See Romans 3:21; 5:9,11; 6:22; 7:6; 8:1; 11:30; 11:31 (second 'now' in NIV, NASB); 16:26. The two covenants, in the apostle's argument, could not be more strongly contrasted.

That this is the teaching of Romans 7 is easily proved. As so often with the apostle, in order to drive his point home, Paul asks a question, a question which naturally would be raised by an objector – or doubter – who has understood what Paul is teaching, *but can hardly credit it*. The objector asks his question to make sure he has heard Paul aright. I said I would come back to this. Consider the objector's immediate outburst in this case: 'Is the law sin?' (Rom. 7:7). 'Is the law sin?' What a question! But the fact that such a question can be asked – that such a question ought to be asked – and that very question Paul actually *did* ask – proves that Paul *is* equating the reign of sin and the reign of law. Of course the answer to the question is a resounding, No! 'Certainly not! On the contrary... the law is holy, and the commandment holy and just and good'; it is 'spiritual', declares the apostle (Rom. 7:7,12,13-14,16). But notice what Paul does not say: 'Oh, you have misunderstood me. Of course the law is not sin! How can it be? The believer is still under it as a perfect rule of life!' He says nothing of the sort. In fact, *he says the very opposite*. The believer has died to the law; he had to die to the law in order to be sanctified. Even so, the objector's question needs to be asked, and will be asked of those who teach scripturally on the law. Reformed teaching would never – could never – provoke such a question. If Paul had taught that the believer is married to the law, under the law – whether the moral law or whatever – nobody would have dreamt of asking: 'Is the law sin?' *But he did ask it!* The law is certainly not sin. No, it is not. But neither is the believer under the law.

The position is clear: the saint is no longer under the law (Rom. 6:14; Gal. 3:24-25; 5:18); he is delivered, freed or released from it (Rom. 7:6; 8:2). In fact, he has died to it (Rom. 7:4; Gal. 2:19). Think of that! *Died* to the law. The believer died to the law when he died with Christ (Rom. 6:1-8; Gal. 2:19-20; 1 Pet. 4:1-2). As for Christ himself, after he had died, he was no longer under the law *in any respect*. He died to sin and law (Rom. 6:7-10; 2 Cor. 4:10; 2 Tim. 2:11; 1 Pet. 4:1). 'It is finished' (John 19:30), he cried, speaking of many things, I realise, but not excluding his relationship to the law. He had fully satisfied it, and all its claims were met. He had fulfilled it (Matt. 5:17-18). Christ *fulfilled* the law, I say again. He did not arbitrarily destroy it, demolish it, invalidate it, violate it, explain it away, dismantle it, or repeal it. He fulfilled it, and therefore completed it.[15] Christ is now not under it. He was once. But, having been born under the law (Gal. 4:4), having lived under it, been cursed and died under it (Gal. 3:13), and then having risen again, he is freed from it (Acts 2:24; Rev. 1:18). Similarly, the believer died with Christ to the law, was freed from it so that he might produce holiness and righteousness (Rom. 7:4), *in order that* he might produce holiness and righteousness. No wonder the apostle declares: 'Christ is the end of the law for righteousness to everyone who believes' (Rom. 10:4).[16]

Any serious work on the law will – must – take full account of Romans 6:14 – 7:6. And Romans 7:4-6, the believer's marriage to Christ, marks the climax of the apostle's majestic argument. I freely admit that this doctrine is amazing. But it is the apostle's doctrine, and it is true of every believer. The believer, in Christ,

---

[15] See 'The Law the Believer's Rule?'

[16] One 'explanation' of Rom. 7:2-6 is to say a believer has two natures, his old nature has died, leaving his new nature married to the law! This is bizarre. The believer is not a spiritual schizophrenic! He does not have two natures. He is human! Christ alone has two natures. As for the believer, *he* has died – *he*, not his 'old nature' – and *he* – *he*, not his 'new nature' – is married to Christ. Another 'explanation' is to claim that, in Rom. 7:6, Paul was saying believers have been delivered, not from the law of God, the law of Moses, but from another law altogether; namely, the law of sin, which is defined as the law of God taken over by sin. But Paul was speaking about the law, not the law 'taken over' by anything! Another 'explanation' is to say Paul was speaking about the law 'as a script, a mere piece of writing' – the letter (Rom. 2:29) – that is, this writing divorced from the Spirit, and this is what is old, obsolete, and valueless. But when Paul said: 'We have been delivered from the law, having died to what we were held by, so that we should serve in the newness of the Spirit and not in the oldness of the letter' (Rom. 7:6), he meant believers are delivered from *the law*, not a piece of writing read without the Spirit. Paul distinguished between the Spirit and the law, not between the Spirit and the letter, or between two opposing approaches to the law. The believer's spiritual life is maintained and ruled by the Holy Spirit *in contrast to* the rule of the law. See my *Christ* pp200-207,478-480 for a closer examination of 'the letter'.

has died to the law so that he can be sanctified. This is what Paul teaches. Calvin, however, in his third use of the law, effectively says that in order to be sanctified, the believer must be re-married to the law – though on easier terms! Calvin was wrong! And so are all who follow him on the law.

Conclusion

So, reader, who is your husband? You have one! Who is it? If you have never died to the law, then you are still married to it. You can never be married to Christ until you die to the law. And if you are never married to Christ, not only will you never live a holy life to the glory of God: you will perish. You must die to the law and be married to Christ. And the only way that can happen is that you repent of your sin and cry out to Christ to save you – to wash you from your sin in his precious blood, and to clothe you in his righteousness. Do this, and you will be united to Christ in marriage, united to Christ in a covenant that will never end.

Extracts with comments

First, let the Reformed have their say.

The wrong view of the marriage
John Calvin in his *Commentary*:

> We must remember that Paul refers here only to that office of the law which was peculiar to the dispensation of Moses; for as far as God has in the ten commandments taught what is just and right, and given directions for guiding our life, no abrogation of the law is to be dreamt of; for the will of God must stand the same forever. We ought carefully to remember that this is not a release from the righteousness which is taught in the law, but from its rigid requirements, and from the curse which thence follows. The law, then, as a rule of life, is not abrogated; but what belongs to it as opposed to the liberty obtained through Christ, that is, as it requires absolute perfection: for as we render not this perfection, it binds us under the sentence of eternal death... The law is so far abrogated with regard to us, that we are not pressed down by its intolerable burden, and that its inexorable rigour does not overwhelm us with a curse.

I will let Douglas J.Moo respond to Calvin's view – 'delivered from the law insofar as it has power to condemn' which has become 'virtually the "orthodox" view in Reformed theology'. Moo drew attention to Romans 5 – 8 where: 'Paul focuses not so much on the condemnation that comes when the law is disobeyed... as [overwhelmingly! – DG] on the failure of the law to deal with the problem of sin. [Linking] the inability of the law' (Rom. 8:3), the stimulation the law gives 'sin in the person who is "bound" to it' (Rom. 7:4-6), the law's production of sin (Rom. 7:5,8), and its making the sin-problem worse (Rom. 7:9-11,13), Moo went on:

> This suggests [too weak – DG] that, as in Rom. 6:14, Paul in Rom. 7:4 is viewing the law as a 'power' of the 'old age' to which the person apart from Christ is bound. The underlying conception is again salvation-historical, as is suggested by the 'letter'/'Spirit' contrast in Rom. 7:6. Just as, then, the believer 'dies to sin' in order to 'live for God' (Rom. 6), so he or she is 'put to death to the law' in order to be joined to Christ. Both images depict the transfer of the believer from the old realm to the new. As long as sin 'reigns', God and righteousness cannot; and neither, as long as law 'reigns', can Christ and the Spirit... In being released from the law... the believer is, naturally, freed from the condemning power of the law. But we introduce categories that are foreign to Paul – at least at this point – by distinguishing between the law in its condemning power and the law as a 'rule of life'.

Moo issued a necessary warning: From this verse we cannot conclude 'that the law can play no role at all in the life of the believer'.[17] Quite. I, myself, have never said it. Rather, in all my works I keep saying the opposite! What is more, let us stop worrying about what the apostle *did not* say, and concentrate on what he *did* say. The believer has died to the law! *Died* to it! The law no longer rules him. What does *this* say about Calvin's third use of the law?

---

[17] Douglas J.Moo: *The Epistle to the Romans*, William B.Eerdmans Publishing Company, Grand Rapids, 1996, pp414-416.

The Puritan, Samuel Bolton, was at best hesitant on Romans 7:1-3, which verses, he could only grudgingly admit, 'seem to speak' – seem to speak? They do speak! But let Bolton give his own account. These verses, he alleges:

> Seem to speak of the abrogation of the law... That the apostle here speaks of the moral law is evident from the seventh verse [of Rom. 7]; and that believers are freed from it, see the sixth verse and others [Rom. 6:14; 8:2; 10:4, Gal. 3:19; 4:4-5; 5:18; 1 Tim. 1:8-10]. There seems, therefore, to be a great deal of strength in the Scripture to prove the abrogation of the law, that we are dead to the law, freed from the law, no more under the law.[18]

How weak, how grudging an admission is this! But grudging or not, it destroys Calvin's third use of the law – which Bolton wanted so much to defend.

John Bunyan took an inadequate view of the matter, an idiosyncratic view:

> Once [these husbands][19] are become dead to you,[20] as they then most certainly will when you close with the Lord Jesus Christ, then I say, your former husbands have no more to meddle with you, you are freed from their law... The sum then of what has been said is this, the Christian now has nothing more to do with the law, as it thunders and burns on Sinai, or as it binds the conscience to wrath and displeasure of God for sin; for from its thus appearing, it is freed by faith in Christ. Yet it is to have regard thereto, and is to count it holy, just and good.[21]

Why not let Paul tell us what he told us – and leave it at that?

---

[18] Samuel Bolton: *The True Bounds of Christian Freedom*, The Banner of Truth Trust, London, 1964, pp52-53.

[19] For some reason Bunyan introduced the plural to allow him to take his idiosyncratic view: the believer has died to his former husbands, namely, 'sin and... righteousness which is of the law'.

[20] Why not stick with the biblical expression? The believer has died to the law!

[21] John Bunyan: *Of The Law and A Christian*, in *The Entire Works of John Bunyan*, edited by Henry Stebbing, John Hirst, London, 1862, p536.

Thomas Boston:

> If you have a saving interest in Christ's death, you are dead with
> him to the law also... (Gal. 2:19-20)... Our Lord Jesus took on
> our nature to satisfy the law therein; the whole course of his life
> was a course of obedience to it, for life and salvation to us; and
> he suffered, to satisfy it in what of that kind it had to demand,
> for that effect. In a word, he was born to the law, he lived to the
> law, and he died to the law; namely, for to clear accounts with it,
> to satisfy it fully and get life and salvation for us with its good
> leave. He was 'made under the law, to redeem them that were
> under the law' (Gal. 4:4-5). And when once it fell upon him, it
> never left exacting of him, till it had got the utmost farthing,[22]
> and he was quite free with it, as dead to it (Rom. 7:4). In token
> whereof, he got up the bond, blotted it out, yes, rent it in pieces,
> nailing it to his cross (Col. 2:14). Now, Christ became dead to it,
> dying to it in his death on the cross: so that the holiness and
> righteousness of the man Christ did thereafter no more run in the
> channel in which it had run before, namely, from the womb to
> his grave – that is to say, it was no more, and shall be no more
> for ever, obedience performed to the law for life and salvation[23]
> – these having been completely gained and secured, by the
> obedience he gave it from the womb to the grave.

Christ died to the law, and the believer died to the law, says the
Scriptures; the believer died with Christ to the law 'as a covenant
of works', said Boston, but not as the rule of sanctification. In
other words, in effect the believer has *not* died to it! Even so,
Boston went on to argue, perfectly soundly: 'Your obedience will
run in another channel than it did before your union with Christ,
even in the channel of the gospel. You serve in newness of spirit,
in faith and love'. Excellent. How strange then to read this from
Boston: 'The frowns of a merciful Father will be a terror to you,

---

[22] At the time, the smallest British coin. In the US, the equivalent would
be the mill, 0.001 of a dollar.
[23] Note the gloss. If one is dead to the law, one is dead to it – not dead to
it merely in certain respects and for certain purposes. Because of his
theological system, Boston was limiting his otherwise excellent
statement to justification – when, clearly, the scripture he quoted (Rom.
7:4) comes from a passage dealing with progressive sanctification.

to fright you from sin'. Boston offered no verse in support. Then he contradicted himself:

> Love and gratitude will prompt you to obedience... You will not continue to serve in the oldness of the letter, as before; at what [which?] time the law was the spring of all the obedience you performed... you being alive to the law, and dead to Christ (Rom. 7:6)... If by faith you wholly rely on Christ's righteousness, the holiness of his nature, the righteousness of his life, and his satisfaction for sin, how is it possible but [that] you must be dead to the law? for the law is not of faith (Gal. 3:12).[24]

So which is it? Is the believer under the law or the gospel for sanctification? Is he moved to sanctification out of terror, or out of love and gratitude? Is he married to Christ or the law? He cannot be married to both!

The biblical view of the marriage
Colin G.Kruse:

> This analogy [Rom. 7:1-6] and its application constitute one of the clearest expressions of Paul's [doctrine] that Christians (Jews as well as Gentiles) are completely freed from all obligations to the Mosaic law as a regulatory norm. Like a person who has died they have been discharged from all obligations to the law... Underlying this notion of freedom from the law is the

---

[24] Thomas Boston: *The Beauties of Thomas Boston: A Selection of his Writings*, edited by Samuel M'Millan, Christian Focus Publications, Inverness, 1979, pp524-526.

assumption[25] that the period of the law has been brought to an end with the coming of Christ.[26]

Moo:

> Paul argues that a person's bondage to the law *must* be severed in order that he or she may be put into a new relationship with Christ... Death severs relationship to the law... but... not only... does Paul... illustrate the general principle that 'a death frees one from the law'... he also sets up the theological application... in which severance from the law enables one to enter a new relationship.[27]

F.F.Bruce:

> Death breaks the marriage bond – and death breaks a man's relation to the law. When Paul applies the analogy, we are conscious of a reversal of the situation; the believer in Christ is compared to the wife, and the law is compared to the husband, but whereas in the illustration it was the husband who died, in the application it is not the law that has died, but the believer; the believer has died with Christ – and yet it is still the believer who, no longer bound to the law, is free to be united with Christ. If, however, we put the matter in simpler terms, we can express Paul's meaning easily enough: as death breaks the bond between a husband and wife, so death – the believer's death-with-Christ – breaks the bond which formerly yoked him to the law, and now he is free to enter into union with Christ. His former association with the law did not help him produce the fruits of righteousness, but these fruits are produced in abundance now

---

[25] It is more than an 'assumption'. Paul has asserted it: 'But now the righteousness of God has been manifested apart from the law, although the law and the prophets bear witness to it – the righteousness of God through faith in Jesus Christ for all who believe' (Rom. 3:21-22), for instance. See the vital 'but now', or, in the context, 'now', throughout the New Testament, in such passages as Rom. 3:21; 5:9,11; 6:22; 7:6; 8:1; 11:30; 11:31 (second 'now' in NIV, NASB); 16:26; see also John 15:22,24; Acts 17:30; 1 Cor. 15:20; Gal. 4:9; Eph. 2:12-13; 5:8; Col. 1:26; Heb. 8:6; 9:26; 12:26; 1 Pet. 2:10. This eschatological point is vital.

[26] Colin G.Kruse: *Paul, The Law and Justification*, Hendrickson Publishers, Peabody, Massachusetts, 1997, pp207-208.

[27] Moo pp409,413-414, emphasis mine.

that he is united with Christ. Sin and death were the result of his association with the law; righteousness and life are the product of his new association; for (as Paul puts it elsewhere), 'the letter kills, but the Spirit gives life' (2 Cor. 3:6)... Such an attitude to the law must have seemed preposterous to many of [Paul's] readers then [adding, somewhat dryly], it has seemed preposterous to many of his readers since.[28]

Edgar H.Andrews:

Paul's metaphor [of death] is uncompromising. The believer has not died partially to the law, for death is total. He has not died temporally to the law, for death is final. His relationship to the law has not undergone some subtle change; it has been terminated. The believer's subjection to the law, his obligation to perform its requirements, has been swept away, 'through the body of Christ'. What does this mean? It means two things. First, the believer is freed from the law through the perfect obedience that Christ yielded to the law during his earthly life. Secondly, he is delivered from the punishment for his law-breaking through the death of Christ on his behalf. Thus the law can no longer make any demands upon the believer, either in respect of obedience, or in respect of punishment for transgression. Those demands have been fully and finally met by the man Christ Jesus. Is the believer, then, without law? Not at all. We are not 'without law towards God, but under law towards Christ' (1 Cor. 9:21). The context in which Paul makes this statement makes [it]... clear... that the 'law towards Christ', to which Paul did submit, was something other than the law of Moses.

Andrews went on to quote James Denney:

When the apostle tells us that through the law he has died to the law (Gal. 2:19), or that we have died to the law through the body of Christ (Rom. 7:4), or that we are not under law but under grace (Rom. 6:14)... he means that nothing in the Christian life is explained by anything statutory, and that everything in it is

---

[28] F.F.Bruce: *The Epistle of Paul to the Romans...*, The Tyndale Press, London, 1963, pp144-145.

explained by the inspiring power of that death in which Christ made all our responsibilities to the law his own.[29]

John Murray:

> What is this law?... The law... is surely the written law of the Old Testament, particularly the Mosaic law. Paul uses 'law' in this sense (Rom. 3:19; 5:13; 1 Cor. 9:8-9; 14:21; Gal. 3:10,19) and there is no need to look for any other denotation [such as the 'ceremonial' law – DG] here... The law binds a man as long as he lives, and the implication [better, Paul's teaching – DG] is that when he dies that dominion is dissolved... The writing [in Rom. 7:6] may refer to the two tables of stone on which the ten commandments were written or to the fact of the law as contained in Scripture.[30],

J.C.Philpot:

> The first husband is the law, and the second husband is Christ... Which is to be the rule of the wife's conduct when [she is] re-married; the regulations of the first or of the second husband?... When he [the first husband] is dead, have not all his rules and regulations [over her] died with him? And is his wife not entirely liberated from his control? If he is dead to her, she is equally dead to him. All his authority over her has ceased. And what should we think... of a wife who, instead of seeking to please her present husband, was always referring to the rules and regulations of her former partner...?

Philpot graphically contrasted the two husbands – the law and Christ. The first was:

> ...extremely harsh, [having] ruled [the woman] as with a rod of iron, always keeping her in bondage and terror... a cruel tyrant... Her second husband [is] a most affectionate and loving spouse... Is not the rule of love, as the rule of the second marriage, in every respect superior to the rule of command, which was the rule of the first?... The apostle has so clearly and beautifully opened up the subject... in Romans 7:1-4... [that] I wish that you might read this portion... in the light of the Spirit, and then you

[29] Edgar H.Andrews *Free in Christ: The Message of Galatians*, Evangelical Press, Darlington, 1996, pp89,114.
[30] John Murray: *The Epistle to the Romans...*, Two Volumes in One, Marshall Morgan and Scott, London, 1974, Vol.1 pp240,246.

would see how thoroughly dead the believer is to the law, both as a covenant and a rule, by virtue of his union to [Christ].[31]

William Gadsby:

> If any poor sinner, who has felt the authority of the law in his conscience and has been condemned by it, and who knows by experience that the letter kills, that the law works wrath, who has been led by the Spirit to the fountain open for sin and uncleanness, and has had the blood of sprinkling applied to his guilty conscience, and thereby has been brought to rejoice in Christ Jesus, knows that his sins are forgiven, and his iniquities blotted out; who has entered into Christ as his rest, and has been enabled by the Spirit to drink of the water of life, and has felt the precious bond of love, which has united Christ as his head and him together, cast out fear, and helped him to say with the inspired apostle: 'I, through the law, am dead to the law, that I might live unto God: I am crucified with Christ, nevertheless I live; yet not I, but Christ lives in me' (Gal. 2:19-20); and again: 'But now we are delivered from the law, that being dead wherein we were held, that we should serve in newness of spirit, and not in the oldness of the letter' (Rom. 7:6); I say, should any of this class venture to prove that the believer is dead to Moses, his first husband, and married to Christ; that he is ruled by the precious laws [*sic*] of Christ, his second husband, and thereby vindicate the honour of his dear head, who has redeemed him, and saved him, and made him free; the best character that [legal critics]... can give such a man, is a 'pulpit libertine'...
> I am inclined to think that if any woman who has married a second husband were to be told that she must be under her first husband's laws, both she and her husband would treat such an assertion with contempt.[32]

Striking the right note on Romans 7:4-6, Gordon D.Fee:

---

[31] J.C.Philpot: Three letters to 'a minister in Scotland' under Romans 7:4, *The Gospel Standard*, February 1, March 1 and May 1, 1861, pp92-93; republished as: *Dead to the Law: A Series of Letters on the Believer's relationship to the Law*, The Huntingtonian Press, Southampton, March 2000, pp22-23.
[32] William Gadsby: *The Works of the Late Mr William Gadsby, Manchester, in Two Volumes*, Vol.1, London, 1851, the 1870 edition, p6-7,19.

In keeping with the argument of Gal. 5:13-24, both the law and the flesh belong to the past, on the pre-Christ, pre-Spirit side of eschatological realities. The death of Christ and the gift of the Spirit have ended *torah* observance. [To say] that 'the law' to which believers have died is merely 'the law's condemnation'... is to miss the eschatological and covenantal character of much of this language as well as to read into the text something neither Paul says nor implies.[33]

D.Martyn Lloyd-Jones on Romans 7:6: '"We have been delivered from the law". This is a very strong word... Some translate it as "discharged", "set at liberty", "set free". We are no longer under the law; we have had a complete discharge from it'. Speaking of every believer, Lloyd-Jones continued, the law 'has no authority over him any longer; he has finished with' it. The question is, of course, 'in what sense has the Christian been delivered from the law?' First of all, 'the law which held us could not justify us, as we were told back in [Rom. 3:20]. We are freed from that'. So far, so good; all are agreed. Then, and of the utmost significance, he took up the issue over which the Reformed clash with Scripture:

> But the point about which the apostle is most concerned here is that we are delivered from the inability of the law to sanctify us. While we were under the law we could never be sanctified. The law can no more sanctify us than it can justify us. While we were held there we could not be joined to the one who can sanctify us as well as justify us. We had no freedom; but now we have been delivered. Now there is the possibility of sanctification. If I can get out of the clutches, as it were, of that first husband, and be joined to another, there is hope for me. There was no hope while I was under the law; but now I am set free. I am delivered from my inability to experience sanctification. This what the apostle is particularly concerned to emphasise.

I break off. Lloyd Jones then had a most intriguing passage: 'But [Paul was] concerned also to emphasise something further...

---

[33] Gordon D.Fee: *God's Empowering Presence: The Holy Spirit in the Letters of Paul*, Hendrickson Publishers, Peabody, Massachusetts, 1994, p504. Just so! Did he have anybody in mind, do you think?

namely, the work of the law in aggravating and inflaming our sins'. 'The law of God always leads to death... the law of God leads to sin; it aggravates it, it inflames [it]... it always produces death'. But, as he said earlier: 'We have been set free from this tendency of the law to aggravate our problem... we have now been delivered from the law'.[34]

Moo:

> The antithesis is not between the *misunderstanding* or *misuse* of the law and the Spirit, nor even, at least basically, between the outer demand and the inner disposition to obey, but between the old covenant and the new, the old age and the new... The believer, released from bondage to the law, can [better, will] serve in the new condition created by God's Spirit, a condition that brings life (2 Cor. 3:6) and fruit pleasing to God (Rom. 6:22-23).[35]

Lloyd-Jones:

> Let me put it plainly and clearly. The apostle teaches here that it was essential we should be married to [Christ]; because until we are married to him we shall never bear this fruit. We were married to the law, but the law was impotent; it could not bring

---

[34] D.Martyn Lloyd-Jones: *Romans: An Exposition of Chapters 7:1 – 8:4. The Law: Its Function and Limits*, The Banner of Truth Trust, Edinburgh, 1973, pp85-87,287-294. Note Lloyd-Jones' use of 'our' – 'the work of the law in aggravating and inflaming our sins'. Was he being a little lax here – or was he being precise? Rom. 7:5,7-11 does not refer to the regenerate. Paul, there, was speaking of his pre-regenerate days. The law did not produce sin in him; no, it is good and spiritual (Rom. 7:13-16). But sin used the law to arouse sinful desire in him. It was sin – not the law – which was the cause of the trouble. See Kruse p212. But did Lloyd-Jones deliberately use 'our' – speaking of believers? If so, then in one stroke he has obliterated Calvin's third use of the law. The law produces holiness in the believer (Calvin). The law arouses sin in the believer (Lloyd-Jones)! In any case, let us not forget what Lloyd-Jones said in the previous paragraph: 'We are delivered from the inability of the law to sanctify us. While we were under the law we could never be sanctified'. If that does not sound the death knell for the Reformer's third use of the law, what does?

[35] Moo pp421-422, emphasis mine.

forth children (fruit) out of us. But we are now married to one who has the strength and the virility and the potency to produce children even out of us. It is his strength that matters... Here is the real purpose of the marriage; we need one whose seed is so powerful, who can so impregnate us with his own holy nature that he will produce holiness even in us. That is why we are married to him, in order that 'we should bring forth fruit unto God'. His strength is so great, his might is so potent, that even out of us he can bear this progeny of holiness... This therefore is the apostle's argument. He says in effect: You had to be delivered from your marriage to the law before you could produce this fruit. You had to die to that law, that old marriage had to be dissolved, in order that you might be married to this mighty one who can produce the fruit in you. And he says it has happened. The central object of salvation is holiness. I would not hesitate to assert that it is sinful to say that you can stop at justification even temporarily, or say that a man can be justified and not sanctified. It is impossible... You cannot stop at justification... The whole object, the whole movement of salvation is to make us holy. So from the moment we are joined to him the process begins. From the moment of the marriage and the union... his power begins to work... and... we are already bringing forth something of this fruit, which is 'holiness unto God'.[36]

---

[36] Lloyd-Jones pp66-67.

Three Questions in One

Just the other day, someone posted a comment on one of my 'New-Covenant Made Simple' videos on YouTube, and this showed me that in my sermons, articles and videos I had inadvertently produced a little series of pertinent questions on the new covenant. I further thought it might be useful if I simply gathered these questions into a short article, with appropriate references to particular works. And here is the result. I am very grateful to the person who posted the original comment.

The three questions are:

1. Which mountain are you living on?

2. Who's your mother?

3. Who's your husband?

1.Which mountain are you living on?

This question is raised by Hebrews 12:18-24:

> For you have not come to what may be touched, a blazing fire and darkness and gloom and a tempest and the sound of a trumpet and a voice whose words made the hearers beg that no further messages be spoken to them. For they could not endure the order that was given: 'If even a beast touches the mountain, it shall be stoned'. Indeed, so terrifying was the sight that Moses said: 'I tremble with fear'. But you have come to Mount Zion and to the city of the living God, the heavenly Jerusalem, and to innumerable angels in festal gathering, and to the assembly of the firstborn who are enrolled in heaven, and to God, the judge of all, and to the spirits of the righteous made perfect, and to Jesus, the mediator of a new covenant, and to the sprinkled blood that speaks a better word than the blood of Abel.[1]

---

[1] See my 'The Two Mountains'; 'On Which Mountain Are You Living?'; 'Hebrews 12:18-24'.

So, which mountain are *you* living on? Sinai or Zion? Law or grace?

2. Who's your mother?

The question is raised in Galatians 4:21 – 5:1:

> Tell me, you who desire to be under the law, do you not listen to the law? For it is written that Abraham had two sons, one by a slave woman and one by a free woman. But the son of the slave was born according to the flesh, while the son of the free woman was born through promise. Now this may be interpreted allegorically: these women are two covenants. One is from Mount Sinai, bearing children for slavery; she is Hagar. Now Hagar is Mount Sinai in Arabia; she corresponds to the present Jerusalem, for she is in slavery with her children. But the Jerusalem above is free, and she is our mother. For it is written: 'Rejoice, O barren one who does not bear; break forth and cry aloud, you who are not in labour! For the children of the desolate one will be more than those of the one who has a husband'. Now you, brothers, like Isaac, are children of promise. But just as at that time he who was born according to the flesh persecuted him who was born according to the Spirit, so also it is now. But what does the Scripture say? 'Cast out the slave woman and her son, for the son of the slave woman shall not inherit with the son of the free woman'. So, brothers, we are not children of the slave but of the free woman. For freedom Christ has set us free; stand firm therefore, and do not submit again to a yoke of slavery.[2]

So, who is *your* mother? Hagar or Sarah? Law or grace?

3. Who's your husband?

The question is raised in Romans 7:4-6:

> Likewise, my brothers, you also have died to the law through the body of Christ, so that you may belong to another, to him who has been raised from the dead, in order that we may bear fruit for God. For while we were living in the flesh, our sinful passions, aroused by the law, were at work in our members to bear fruit

---

[2] 'Slavery Or Freedom'; 'Galatians 4:21 – 5:1'; 'Liberty or Bondage: Sarah or Hagar?'

for death. But now we are released from the law, having died to that which held us captive, so that we serve in the new way of the Spirit and not in the old way of the written code.[3]

So, who is *your* husband? Moses or Christ?

These three questions, of course, boil down into one: Which covenant or ministry do you belong to? The old, in stone, of death or the new, in the Spirit, of life? (2 Cor. 3:6-11).[4]

---

[3] 'Illustration: Marriage'; 'Romans 7:4'; 'The Believer's Marriage'; 'Who's Your Husband?'

[4] Many of my sermons, articles, videos and books. Of the latter, see, in particular, my *Glorious*.

The Law of Christ

Having set out the exegesis of key texts to show that the believer is under the law of Christ, I now want to explore what we should understand by that phrase. As I have said many times in my works, as many others also have found, the law of Christ is not easy to tie down. But as I have also said, this is not something to be alarmed about. It is just one more illustration of the newness of the new covenant. For a start, the old covenant could be set out in 613 commandments, ten of them carved in stone. The new covenant takes and applies the whole Bible, properly nuanced by the apostles. Admitting the difficulty in defining the law of Christ, however, does not mean that nothing specific can be said about it.

'The Law' in 'the Law of Christ'

We know what 'law' is in 'the law of Moses',[1] but what about 'law' in 'the law of Christ' (Gal. 6:2)?[2]

'The law of Moses' and 'the law of Christ' are (in the common parlance) very different beasts; that is, they are very different 'entities', 'systems', 'regimes'. And they are poles apart, not only in content, but in their whole basis, approach, ethos, outlook, attitude and mindset. It is all to do with 'Moses' and 'Christ' (John 1:17). The two laws belong to two distinct, contrasting ages, and are very different 'laws'. The law of Moses is a list of specific rules – the decalogue is *ten* commandments, after all. The law of Christ, however, is far wider, far bigger. And I am not thinking of a hundred commandments instead of ten! (Or, rather, a thousand commandments instead of the more-than six hundred in the Mosaic law!) The law of Christ is not a list at all. This is the point I am striving for. The law of Christ is a principle, an all-embracing principle. Anything more different to a list of rules, especially a list of 'do nots', would be hard to imagine. Christ's law is inflexible, but there is certain flexibility within it. Within limits, differences of judgment are allowed under Christ (see Rom. 14:1 – 15:7; Phil. 3:15-16, for instance). This is a remarkable aspect of the law of Christ. In general, law allows no room for conscience. In particular, the Mosaic law allows none. Summarising the essential difference between the two 'laws', the law of Moses and the law of Christ, we are talking about the difference between precept and principle.

The word 'law' takes different meanings in Scripture, according to the context.[3] In the New Testament, 'law' often carries all the overtones of Jewish law, the *torah*, but not always. Sometimes it means 'principle' or something similar. Take 'the law of faith'

---

[1] See the previous article.
[2] For this article, I have lightly edited my *Christ* pp214-218; see also pp336,481-483, adding a little more from other pages in that volume.
[3] See note 1.

(Rom. 3:27). I have already noted that Paul was not speaking about the 'law' of faith, in the sense of substituting faith in Christ for obedience to Mosaic commandments – in effect, one set of rules replaced by another. Rather, the idea is 'principle', the principle of faith. 'The law of the Spirit of life in Christ Jesus' (Rom. 8:2), is another example. Many teachers have rightly called on other words in trying to get to grips with this concept – 'principle', 'ordinance', 'norm', 'system', 'doctrine', 'teaching', 'order', 'method', 'demand', 'arrangement', 'force' or 'reign'.[4] Paul spoke of 'a pattern' (Phil. 3:17). Boasting is excluded, said Paul. 'By what law?' On what basis? By what principle? Not by substituting faith in Christ for works under Moses. No! Boasting is excluded by the fact that the concept of works, obedience to law, has gone, and has been replaced by a totally new principle or system or arrangement (Rom. 3:27-28). Indeed, it is a new age, 'the time of the new order' (Heb. 9:10, NIV). Law has been replaced by gospel.[5]

So why did Paul use 'law' in Romans 3:27, and speak of 'the *law* of faith'? Why did he not use something like 'principle'? Above all, why did he not coin a word? This is a most interesting question. It seems a contradiction in terms. 'The law of faith', I ask you! Obviously, the apostle had good reason for his choice.[6]

Could it be because of the high regard the Jews had for the law? Or because the apostle wanted to avoid the charge of novelty? Was it a Hebraism? Could it amount to nothing more than 'the doctrine or prescript of faith'? Could Paul have been using 'law' the way Greek-speaking Jews of the first century used it – in a general sense – just as we do today, when speaking of

---

[4] See my *Christ* pp279-298,481-527.

[5] See my *Christ* pp75-98,158-177,369-391,448-468; my 'Covenant Theology Tested'.

[6] See my *Christ* pp314-320,552-555 for the close parallel with Paul's deliberate use of the term 'Israel' in 'the Israel of God' (Gal. 6:16). This describes the people of the new covenant. The law of Moses was for Israel after the flesh. The law of Christ is for spiritual Israel, the Israel of God. Paul showed that both 'law' and 'Israel' have been taken over and *transformed* in the new covenant. And do not forget Paul's love of word play. I will say more on this.

'the [so-called] law of averages', 'the laws of music', 'the law of unintended consequences', 'the law of diminishing returns', and the like. As I say, it is a fascinating question: Why did Paul use the word 'law' in 'the law of Christ'?

Almost certainly Paul was drawing upon the Septuagint, the translation of the Old Testament into Greek for Jews with no Hebrew, completed just over a hundred years before Christ, the version most often quoted in the New Testament. After all, this was the way the Greek-speaking Jews – who could not understand Hebrew – read or heard the Greek word for 'law'. Did this matter? A great deal! They read it and *understood* it as a Greek word (*nomos*), not reading into it all the ideas and associations of the Hebrew word (*torah*) which it translated. Most of the scattered Jews of the time would have never read the law of Moses – they didn't have a copy of the Hebrew Scriptures, and, at best, would have only heard it read. In any case, as I have explained, most of them couldn't understand Hebrew. All this is highly relevant to Paul's use of the word – and even more relevant to the way his non-Hebrew readers would have understood him.

And, of course, the same goes for us today. When Paul uses *nomos* in connection with the law of Moses, we should think in Jewish terms, but when used in connection with the law of Christ, we should think in this Greek way. In addition, the *torah* was more than rules and regulations.[7] And in the new covenant, Christ is the *torah* in that his teaching is his *nomos*, and he himself *in toto* reveals God and what he requires of his people.

Then again, we must remember, Paul loved word play. He used it with 'law' in Romans 3:27: 'Where is boasting then? It is excluded. By what *law*? [The *law*] of works? No, but by the *law* of faith'. He used it in Romans 8:2-4: 'For the *law* of the Spirit of life in Christ Jesus has made me free from the *law* of sin and death. For what the *law* could not do in that it was weak through

---

[7] The meaning of *torah* is 'teaching', 'doctrine', or 'instruction'; the commonly accepted 'law' gives a wrong impression. We should, perhaps, think in terms of 'custom, theory, guidance or system' (see Wikipedia).

the flesh, God did by sending his own Son in the likeness of sinful flesh, on account of sin: he condemned sin in the flesh, that the righteous requirement of the *law* might be fulfilled in us who do not walk according to the flesh but according to the Spirit'. He used it in 1 Corinthians 9:19-23, when he explained the way in which he approached sinners with the gospel, how he accommodated himself to his hearers, so that 'I might win the more'. In particular, he said: 'To those who are without *law*, [I became] as without *law* (not being without *law* towards God, but under *law* towards Christ), that I might win those who are without *law*'.[8] It is very likely, therefore, that when he spoke of being 'under law towards Christ', 'under Christ's law', Paul deliberately chose to use 'law', precisely because of the association his word play entails. In particular, the apostle engaged in word play in 'the law of Christ' (Gal. 6:2). For 'law', we could also speak of the standard, the norm, the principle of Christ. (See earlier on 'the law of faith').

The law of Christ! What a staggering choice of phrase! As I have said, 'the law of Christ' is a seeming contradiction in terms. And look where the apostle coined it – at the end of Galatians! Galatians, of all places! After all he has said in the letter, it seems as though Paul must have blundered, forgotten himself and written an absurdity. It has been rightly called 'a breathtaking paradox'; 'the law of Christ', indeed! But of course the apostle hadn't blundered! He knew what he was doing! By using such provocative language, latching on to the word 'law' and attaching it to 'Christ', Paul was deliberately drawing attention to what he was saying. He was a teacher! He wanted the Galatians to understand and remember! And what was he saying? Bearing in mind Paul's entire argument throughout the first five chapters of the letter, 'the law of Christ' must be, at the very least, different to the law of Moses. I go further. It must be in stark contrast to the law of Moses.

---

[8] Rom. 9:6; Gal. 6:2,16; Phil. 3:3; 2 Thess. 3:11 (NIV); Philem. 10-11 are further examples of word play. God himself does it; see Mic. 1:8-16. Christ did it – see below. See my *Christ* pp172-176,460-464 for comments on Rom. 8:1-4.

Word play. Christ himself engaged in it: 'Take my yoke upon you... For my yoke is easy and my burden is light', he said (Matt. 11:29-30).[9] The concept of a 'yoke' was current in such phrases as 'yoke of the *torah*' and 'yoke of the commandments'. Clearly, however, Christ was speaking of a new yoke, an altogether different kind of yoke – 'my yoke' – not the old yoke of Moses, nor the Mosaic law as expounded by Christ. Christ, I repeat, was speaking of his *own* law, not the Mosaic law reinterpreted. There is a clear contrast between Christ's yoke and the yoke of the law. The Jews would have recognised at once Christ's word play, and would have readily grasped the substitution he was claiming, the substitution of himself and his law in the place of Moses and his law. The contrast is clear. The *Didache*, probably dating from about 80-140, called Christ's commandments 'the Lord's yoke'. What a contrast there is between the two yokes. Christ's is easy (Matt. 11:30),[10] the opposite of Moses' (Acts 15:10,28; Gal. 5:1). An easy *yoke*? What is this? Yet another contradiction in terms.

And this raises the very point – the vital point – I am trying to make. Christ has his law, his yoke for his people, but this is not a new list of laws replacing the old list (although, of course, there are specific commands for believers to obey in the gospel; witness the abundance of such in the letters of the New Testament). In speaking of the law of Christ, Paul was not referring to a new set of ten commandments, using 'law' in the old sense. We are talking about the *new* covenant. The old law has been replaced by the new. And the phrase makes its appearance, remember, at the end of Galatians. The apostle, having resolutely stood up to the Judaisers, having endured personal stress in publicly rebuking Peter, and having taught the Galatians so thoroughly – all of which he had done in order to rescue believers from the bondage of the Mosaic law – would not, as he closed his letter, bind believers with an even tighter and heavier yoke. It would have be unthinkable! He was not setting out a new legalism with the commands of Moses replaced by the

---

[9] See Christ's play on 'rock' in Matt. 16:18.

[10] Is there another word play here (in the Greek) between *chrētos* (easy) and *christos* (anointed, Christ)?

commands of Christ. For progressive sanctification,[11] what is wanted is not mere conformity to a set of rules, especially negative, but consecration, dedication and likeness to Christ.[12]

In short, while the law of Christ is a real law, it is a *new* law, a law very unlike the law of Moses. Consequently, when we speak of Christ's *yoke*, 'the believers' *rule*', 'the *law* of Christ', we should not think in Jewish terms, of the *torah*. Rather, we should think in terms of the broader, fuller, first-century meaning of the Greek word *nomos*. This is the way to understand 'the law of Christ', since this was the way the non-Hebrew-speaking believers of the first century (the overwhelming majority) would have understood Paul's words, written in Greek. We must put the same overtones on 'the *law* of Christ' as they did, and not impose Jewish nuances on the phrase.

Paul saw Christ as the new Moses in a new covenant, teaching his own law, a new *torah*, with the idea of *torah* qualified as above. So it would be better to think of the law of Christ, not as a set of rules, commandments and prohibitions, but rather as a life-principle within the believer empowered by the Spirit of Christ. It is Christ's teaching, life, death, and resurrection, and the coming of his Spirit upon and in his people, and the deposit of all truth from Christ into which he led the apostles (John 14:26; 16:12-15), which is the believer's new *torah*, the law of Christ. The law

---

[11] By 'progressive sanctification', I mean the believer's imperfect (in this life) outworking of the perfect positional-sanctification he has in Christ by virtue of his union with Christ at his conversion. The sinner, on coming to faith, is united to Christ and is justified and positionally sanctified. Thus, in God's sight, in Christ he is accounted or made righteous, free of sin and condemnation, and perfectly separated unto God. (See, for instance, 1 Cor. 1:2,30; 6:11; Eph. 5:25-27; Heb. 10:10-18; 13:12). In his Christian life, he has to work out his perfection in Christ, and he will be moved to do so by the Spirit under the direction of Scripture; this is his progressive sanctification or holiness of life. But this, alas, is imperfect. The believer will only be absolutely sanctified in the eternal state. See my *Fivefold*.

[12] 'Loving obedience is not to be equated with legalism' (David J.Gilliland: 'New Covenant Theology: Is There Still a Role for the Imperatives?', being a paper at the Providence Theological Seminary Doctrinal Conference, 2011, p12).

of Christ is not a list. It is power! 'The kingdom of God is not a matter of talk but of power' (1 Cor. 4:20, NIV).

A vital principle

In saying this, I would not be misunderstood. There are commands in the new covenant: a host of them! And we must maintain the union between the Spirit and the word. It is not a question of the Spirit or the Scriptures; it is not the Spirit above the Scriptures; it is the Spirit and the Scriptures! Indeed, in Christ there is more: in the new covenant, God not only gives his people the Scriptures, and also gives them his Spirit, but he writes his law – the gospel, Christ – on their hearts. The believer, therefore, is under all three, moved by all three, guided by all three: the Scriptures, the Spirit, and the law written in his heart, all three mutually calibrating each other,[13] and all three stirring the believer to assurance and progressive sanctification.

Douglas J.Moo:

Indeed, while not being 'under the law', [Paul] recognises a continuing obligation to 'God's law', in the form of 'Christ's law' (the Greek is *ennomos Christou*). The conceptualisation of this text provides as neat a summary of my view [Moo's, and mine – DG] of the law as the New Testament affords. It suggests that 'God's law' comes to his people in two forms: to Israel in the form of 'law', *torah*, and to Christians in the form of 'Christ's law'. Here we find the 'new-covenant theology' emphasis on two contrasting covenants worked out in terms of two different 'laws'. But the key question remains: How different are they?

'To answer this question', Moo said, 'we return to Galatians'; in particular, to Galatians 5:13 – 6:2. Moo went on:

To recapitulate: ...The teaching of the New Testament on the matter of the law of God is neatly summarised in the distinctions that Paul draws in 1 Cor. 9:20-21: the law of Moses, the *torah* ('law' simply), was given to the people of Israel to govern them until the coming of the Messiah; since his coming, the people of

---

[13] As just one example, link Rom. 8:1-4,9 with Gal. 6:2 and 2 Tim. 3:15-16. See my *Christ* pp154,231-232,256-257, for instance.

God are governed by the 'law of Christ'. Biblical law, in other words, is firmly attached to the temporal two-covenant structure that is the hallmark of 'new-covenant theology'.[14]

Moo again, now answering the question: 'What will guide and empower' believers – seeing they are not under the law? The answer, as he said, contains two components – the Spirit and, 'surprisingly, perhaps', the law.[15] Ah! But which law? Moo:

> The other reference to 'law' in this concluding section of Galatians comes in Gal. 6:2... The interpretation of the phrase 'law of Christ' is central to my [Moo's and mine – DG] argument. Unfortunately, Paul provides little contextual information.[16] We have, however, already noticed that Paul uses similar language in 1 Cor. 9:21, where, the context suggests [it makes it plain!] 'the law of Christ' is distinguished from the Mosaic law. Coupled with the claim that Christians are no longer 'under the (Mosaic) law', this makes it unlikely [it rules out the possibility!] that the 'law of Christ' is the Mosaic law interpreted and fulfilled by Christ. Rather, the phrase is more likely [it makes it certain!] [to be] Paul's answer to those who might conclude that his law-free gospel provides no standards of guidance for believers.[17] On the contrary, Paul says, though no longer directly responsible to Moses' law, Christians are bound to Christ's law. In what does this 'law' consist? Since... Gal. 5:14..., the demand for love [must be] a central component of the 'law of Christ'. But it is unlikely that Paul confines the law to this demand alone, for, as we have seen, Paul also stresses in this context the fruit-bearing ministry of the Spirit. Coupled with the centrality of the Spirit in Paul's teaching about what it means to live as a Christian, this strongly suggests that the directing influence of the Spirit is an important part of this law of Christ... Jer. 31:31-34... Ezek. 36:26-27. It is more difficult to determine whether the law of Christ includes specific teachings and

---

[14] Douglas J.Moo: 'The Covenants and the Mosaic Law: The View from Galatians', Affinity Theological Study Conference: *The End of the Law?*, February, 2009, pp20,27.

[15] See above for the staggering nature of this phrase: 'the law of Christ'.

[16] Is it because the early believers knew full-well what the apostle was talking about?

[17] A routine – but false – accusation levelled against all who advocate new-covenant theology.

principles... I think it highly probable [it is certain!] that Paul thought of the law of Christ as including within it teachings of Jesus and the apostolic witness, based on his life and teaching.

Moo, in part, quoting Richard N.Longenecker:

> The law of Christ 'stands in Paul's thought for those prescriptive principles stemming from the heart of the gospel (usually embodied in the example and teachings of Jesus), which are meant to be applied to specific situations by the direction and enablement of the Holy Spirit, being always motivated and conditioned by love'. Does the 'law of Christ' include Mosaic commandants? Of course.[18]

On the whole, a fine statement, but, as so often, Moo could have been stronger at certain points. The biblical evidence is overwhelming – 'the law of Christ' cannot be confined to the ten commandments. It certainly cannot be encapsulated in any list. And while the believer is under the entirety of God's word – all of it, including the Mosaic law (all of it, not just the ten commandments!) as nuanced by the new covenant – he has God's Spirit moving him and enabling him to fulfil that word. Alas, this fulfilment will never be perfect in this life. Nevertheless, 'the righteous requirement[19] of the law' *is* fulfilled in believers by the Spirit (Rom. 8:4). The child of God is fully, perfectly, justified and positionally sanctified, he is assured by the witness of the Spirit, and he is being progressively sanctified by God's grace in the power of that self-same Holy Spirit, the Spirit of holiness. Furthermore, he is being transformed into Christ's likeness with ever-increasing glory now (2 Cor. 3:18, NIV), and will, at Christ's return, be absolutely glorified by being made into his Saviour's likeness (John 17:24; Rom. 8:29-30; 1 John 3:2-3).

This is what we must understand by 'the law' in 'the law of Christ'. To distort the law of Christ by mixing it with the law of Moses, thereby forging a hybrid, a mongrel sort of 'Mosaic law of Christ', is tragic. Sadly, it is commonly done, leading multitudes of believers into a gloomy valley, where a weary, relentless struggle leads to a sense of increasing failure. How

---

[18] Moo pp21-22.

[19] The singular 'requirement' is what Paul wrote.

very different is this to the spirit of the new covenant, with its sense of ever-increasing glory and inexpressible joy in a life of growing Christ-likeness (2 Cor. 3:18; 1 Pet. 1:8-9).

The Law the Believer's Rule?

How should believers read, quote and use the law? Are they obliged to obey it as a command, as a rule? If so, are they obliged to obey all the commandments? Or what?

Different schools of thought come up with different answers.

At one extreme, there is the Reconstructionist: *Believers have to obey the law, all of it. This includes stoning for witches, adulterers, sabbath breakers, and so on. Believers must do all they can to bring about a Christian State which will enforce the Mosaic law on all its citizens.*

At the other extreme, there is the Antinomian: *Believers are utterly free of the law. Disobedience brings more grace and more liberty. This is what the 'no condemnation in Christ' means.*[1]

In this article, I have only one thing to say about these two: both are completely unscriptural.

Somewhere in the middle, we have the Reformed: *Believers are under the law for sanctification; the law is their perfect rule of life.*[2] *But when the Reformed say 'law', what they really mean is 'the ten commandments' (which they call 'the moral law'), but not the law's 600 plus other commandments.*[3] *They justify this severe narrowing*[4] *of the law by use of a non-scriptural (not to say, unscriptural) construct. They say that the law is divided into*

---

[1] If any reader thinks this is a caricature, he should see the evidence set out in my *Four* pp19-24.

[2] The third of Calvin's three uses of the law.

[3] In fact, because most of them think that the fourth commandment is partly moral and partly ceremonial, they really think believers are under 'the 9.5 commandments'.

[4] 'Severe narrowing'? Virtual elimination (by about 99%), even taking into account the repetition of the ten commandments!

three bits: 'moral', 'ceremonial' and 'judicial'.[5] *Christ has not only abolished these last two bits of the law, but his work covers the believer's failure in the first. But, since Scripture never divides the law like this, never sets out which commandment (or part of a commandment) is moral or ceremonial, how is the believer supposed to determine which part of any particular law is moral (and is, therefore, obligatory) and which is ceremonial (and is, therefore, abolished)? This vexed question applies particularly to the fourth commandment.*[6] *So what should believers do? In effect, the Reformed answer amounts to this: 'Consult your chosen Reformed pope. Let him tell you what's what. Grit your teeth and get on with it. And learn to live with the endless conundrums you will inevitably have to face as a consequence'.*[7]

Needless to say,[8] all this is unscriptural, and, for those involved, spells bondage and sadness, and raises one dilemma after another.

Now for Scripture.

Apostolic authority for new-covenant use of the law

Christ promised his disciples that he would not leave them without guidance in all matters of the faith:

The Holy Spirit, whom the Father will send in my name... will teach you all things, and bring to your remembrance all things

---

[5] These constructs cannot be justified from Scripture. They are medieval, almost certainly stemming from Thomas Aquinas. See my *Christ* pp100-104,392-400.

[6] Is the fourth commandment entirely moral, entirely ceremonial, or partly both? If the latter, what constitutes the moral part, and is therefore obligatory on believers, and which part is ceremonial and has therefore been abolished? How do the Reformed decide? On what biblical grounds do they decide? And what about the sabbath commandments (of which there are many examples) outside the ten? The assorted answers given to such questions demonstrates that hardly any two Reformed teachers agree over the practicalities of their system.

[7] If any reader thinks this is a caricature, he should read Reformed works on the sabbath. For a sample, see my *Sabbath Notes* pp137-156.

[8] At least, I hope it is! If not, for my arguments, see my *Christ*.

that I said to you... The Spirit of truth... will guide you into all truth... He will glorify me, for he will take of what is mine and declare it to you. All things that the Father has are mine. Therefore I said that he [the Spirit] will take of mine and declare it to you (John 14:26; 16:13-15).

Having been given the law of Christ from their Redeemer, their lawgiver in the new covenant, and having received the promised Holy Spirit who brought to their remembrance *all* things which Christ had said to them, and who guided them into *all* truth (John 14:26; 16:13), the apostles spelled out Christ's law for all Christ's disciples for all time. The apostolic writings are replete with the concept: 'Be mindful of the words which were spoken before by the holy prophets, and of the commandment of us, the apostles of the Lord and Saviour' (2 Pet. 3:2). The gospel, 'the way of righteousness', is called 'the holy commandment' (2 Pet. 2:21). The apostles taught 'the law of Christ' (Gal. 6:2), 'this rule' which is to be observed by the Israel of God (Gal. 6:16),[9] commanding believers to 'walk by the same rule' (Phil. 3:16),[10] and to 'consent to wholesome words, even the words of our Lord Jesus Christ, and to the doctrine which accords with godliness' (1 Tim. 6:3; Tit. 1:1).[11] The apostles commanded Christ's people to

---

[9] Is 'this rule' of Gal. 6:16 the law of Christ? I think so. It is the believer's norm, the principle of Gal. 6:15. It is not the law of Moses. Gal. 5:25 does not support the claim that it is; that law is not even mentioned. But by 'rule' we must not think in old-covenant mode. See below and my *Christ* pp212,247,503-504.

[10] Is 'the same rule' of Phil. 3:16 the law of Christ? I think so. Although 'rule' probably was not in the original, even so it is clearly implied. We could use 'principle', or (NASB) 'standard', or 'precept', 'doctrine of Christ', 'the rule of faith as opposed to works'. But by 'rule' we must not think in old-covenant mode. See below and my *Christ* pp212,247,503-504.

[11] Are these 'wholesome words' the law of Christ? I think so. Leaving aside the first 'even' (supplied by the NKJV), consider the 'and' in 'the words of our Lord Jesus Christ, *and* to the doctrine'. This 'and' is *kai* which – see discussion in my *Christ* pp315,552-553 – may be translated 'even'. If so, 'the words of our Lord Jesus Christ, *even* the doctrine which accords with godliness' form the law of Christ. In other words, Christ's teaching is that which leads to and promotes godliness. And

be sanctified, instructing them in the matter (1 Cor. 14:37; 1 Thess. 4:1-12; 2 Thess. 3:4-15). They gave instructions about family life (Eph. 5:22-33; 6:1-4; Col. 3:18-21), the work place (Eph. 6:5-9; Col. 3:22-25; 4:1), church life (1 Cor. 11:17-34; 1 Tim. 3:14-15), the way believers should conduct themselves in the State (Rom. 13:1-7; 1 Pet. 2:13-17), and so on. They also commanded other teachers to do the same on the authority of the apostles and their instructions (1 Tim. 4:11; 5:7; 6:2,17; 2 Tim. 2:2,14; 4:1-5; Tit. 2:1-15; 3:1-2,8,14). And all was in the name of Christ himself: 'Now I plead with you, brethren, by the name of our Lord Jesus Christ...' (1 Cor. 1:10).

In particular, the apostles laid down the ground rules for the way believers should read and apply the law.

Now to answer my original question. How should believers read, quote and use the law? All they have to do is ask the apostles how they used the law, and walk in their boots. So how did they use the law? In one way. Always. With every law. With all the law. And that way was... what? They never used the law in an old-covenant way, as a rule by which believers are to be governed, but *they always used the law as a paradigm for them.*[12]

An objection

'Whoa! If, as you claim, believers are not under the law, why does the New Testament appeal to the ten commandments? And why do the apostles press the ten commandments on believers?'

Christ's teaching includes the apostles' teaching, of course. See my *Christ* pp212,247,503-504.

[12] As for Christ, in the Sermon on the Mount, he not only took some principles from the Mosaic law and made them more intense, he upheld others – in particular the love commandment (Lev. 19:18) – and made others redundant. In this sermon, Christ was not renewing the Mosaic covenant, but, right at the start of the new age, he was instituting his own law for the new covenant. He was setting out a new law, under a new covenant, in a new age, for new men. See my *Christ* especially pp236-241,493-500.

The Reformed have no problem with this, of course. It is just what would be expected.

But wait a minute! Is it? The New Testament does use the ten commandments when addressing believers, yes. But how does it do it? And how often does it do it? Surely, if the Reformed view is right, the New Testament should always – always! – be drawing the attention of believers to the ten commandments; 'as the ten commandments say' should be a constant refrain. After all, the Reformed say that the ten commandments are the believer's perfect rule. If so, shouldn't the New Testament be always pointing believers to the ten commandments – to that which is their 'perfect' rule? But we do not find it so. Nor do we find the apostles pressing the law on believers, do we? Where? When?

Let us clear away some loose thinking. And there is need! We meet plenty of sloppy – not to say, shoddy – exegesis when the Reformed turn to these passages, and try to make their case. For instance: Paul did not *impose* the fifth commandment on the believers at Ephesus (Eph. 6:1-3). Christ and the apostles did not *always* refer believers to the law when they wanted to speak of godliness. Nor does the New Testament show that *frequently* meditating upon the law is the *best* way to live a sanctified life, or to be stirred to it. Nor does it repeat and enforce *all* the ten commandments. These things are claimed. Do we get the impression that believers in the New Testament were turning to the law and *frequently* meditating upon it as the *best* way to discover God's will for their lives, and stirring them to godliness? I think not! What evidence do we have that Gentile believers in that time had, or had even seen, a copy of the ten commandments?[13] To think Gentile believers had (let alone pored over) a copy of the law (in Greek or Hebrew) is wildly fanciful.

The truth is, reader, where does Paul *ever* tell believers they are under Moses' law? Where does he *ever* tell believers they must regard the law of Moses as their norm, their rule? Which commandment of the ten does Paul *ever* tell believers they must

---

[13] See my *Christ* p481 regarding most Diaspora Jews and their lack of the Hebrew Scriptures.

obey? The silence is deafening. These significant facts cannot be ignored. Yes, Paul *used* the law when *exhorting* believers – though even this is rare – but he never commanded believers to obey the Mosaic law.

Having cleared the ground in general, let me now go on to consider those particular places where Paul does appeal to the ten commandments when writing to believers. There are three. Only three. But let us look at all three of them.

Consider Romans 13:8-10

Owe no man anything except to love one another, for he who loves another has fulfilled the law. For the commandments: 'You shall not commit adultery, you shall not murder, you shall not steal, you shall not bear false witness, you shall not covet' – and if there is any other commandment – are all summed up in this saying; namely: 'You shall love your neighbour as yourself'. Love does no harm to a neighbour; therefore love is the fulfilment of the law.

The love Paul spoke of is love for men – particularly, if not expressly, believers – not love for God. As to the 'law' in question, there can be no doubt. Both the wider context – Paul's overwhelming use of the word throughout Romans – and especially the immediate context – in which some of the ten commandments are quoted (Rom. 13:9) – make it clear that Paul, writing to believers, was here speaking about the Mosaic law,[14] the ten commandments in particular. The upshot is, Paul undoubtedly quoted some of the ten commandments when writing to the believers at Rome. This is agreed.

But notice what Paul did not do. He did not make the law the be-all and end-all of his teaching. He did not make the law its climax. *Notice further what Paul did not say.* He did not tell the believers – nor remind them of what, according to Reformed teaching, they are supposed to have been fully aware of – that they are, of course, under the law of Moses. Strange silence! Not exactly a proof that Calvin's third use of the law is wrong, I grant you, but from the Reformed point of view, certainly odd! Rather, the apostle said that love fulfils the law (Rom. 13:8,10; Gal.

---

[14] He quoted Lev. 19:18. See below for more on this point.

5:14). 'Fulfil'! How many times we meet this word in this context (Matt. 5:17-18; Rom. 8:4; 13:8-10; Gal. 5:14-16; 6:2; Jas. 2:8, for instance)! Love, said Paul, *fulfils* the law. And we know that, in this regard, old-covenant regulations do not count: 'For in Christ Jesus, neither circumcision nor uncircumcision avails anything, but faith working through love' (Gal. 5:6). I realise that Paul was speaking of justification in this last verse, but the point is justifying faith will show itself by love – not by trying to keep the law of Moses! It is by faith a believer is justified, and it is as his faith works by love that he shows his sanctification.

While love does not dispense with the law – rather it fulfils it – Paul certainly did not say the law of Moses is the regulative norm for believers; he did not impose it upon them. He did not say it is their rule. He did not say believers must strive to keep it. *Nor did he imply it.* He simply cited examples from the ten commandments, making the point that love is the real end, the 'fulfilment', of the law. And in order to drive the point home, Paul says it twice in this brief paragraph (Rom. 13:8,10). *This*, I say, is the point. Furthermore, if the apostle's citing of the ten commandments really does prove that the law is the believer's perfect rule, does the same apply to nature and pagan poets? After all, see Acts 17:28-29; 1 Corinthians 11:14; Titus 1:12-13. No! Paul briefly quotes the ten commandments to say that love fulfils them.

'Fulfil' is a strong word. What does it mean? It does not here mean 'sum up'. Rather, we are, once again, in the realm of the eschatological. It also reminds us of something Paul said earlier in Romans: God has done a work through his Son in order 'that the righteous requirement of the law might be fulfilled in us who do not walk according to the flesh but according to the Spirit' (Rom. 8:3-4). I refer you, reader, to chapter 10 and my remarks on those verses. Linking that passage and this, both in the same book, remember, with no chapter/verse divisions, Paul, it is evident, is speaking of believers, those who are redeemed by Christ, who are indwelt by the Spirit, who belong to the new age of the Spirit, who are no longer under 'law', 'but now' are in Christ – the one who is the 'end of the law' (Rom. 10:4). And what does Paul say of these believers? Believers, who love one another, have satisfied, fulfilled the demands of the law as far as their conduct towards their fellow-men is concerned.

But, I hasten to add, as the context also makes clear, this does not mean that love has replaced the commandments; love *fulfils* the law, it does not replace it. Believers still need the written word, including the law of Moses – but they need all the word, including all the law, not merely the ten commandments. The entire word teaches them, reproves them, corrects them, instructs and trains them (2 Tim. 3:16-17). And this word, I repeat, includes the Mosaic law in all its entirety – properly nuanced in line with the New Testament, of course. But it also includes apostolic commands. And love is the fulfilling of it. Love is the purpose of the commandment – whether we understand it to refer to the precise command Paul gave Timothy (1 Tim. 1:5), or to the whole of Scripture, including the law. The law is 'all summed up' in love (Rom. 13:9). The believer, one of God's people, a member of the new covenant, is no longer under the law of Moses, the law for Israel, the old-covenant people of God. On the contrary, he is under a new law, 'the law of Christ' (1 Cor. 9:19-21; Gal. 6:2). And at the heart of Christ's new law lies that commandment of Moses – namely, the commandment to love our neighbour as ourselves (Lev. 19:18; Gal. 6:2 with 5:13-14).

There is not a hint of a suggestion that Romans 13:8-10 is a list of rules for believers. Indeed, such a thing would have destroyed what the apostle is, in fact, saying. Consider the context. Paul has been dealing with practical godliness right from Romans 12:1. We can go back even further. From Romans 6:1, he has been dealing with sanctification.[15] On reaching Romans 13:9, Paul cites several of the ten commandments to illustrate the point that love is the great fulfiller of the law. Love is the great motive and spur for godliness. Love is both its test and standard: 'He who loves another has fulfilled the law... Love is the fulfilment of the law' (Rom. 13:8,10). And how does the apostle go on? By sundry commands and exhortations. Ah, but why? Why 'do this' and 'do that'? Because the law says so, because we are under regulation, because otherwise we might get lashed with

---

[15] See my *Christ* pp158-177,448-468.

Calvin's whip?[16] Not at all! Why should we be godly? Because Christ is coming, because our salvation is getting daily nearer (Rom. 13:12). Avoid carnality, Paul demands. But how? By this:

> Put on the Lord Jesus Christ, and make no provision for the flesh... the Lord... the Lord... the Lord... the Lord... the Lord... the Lord... Whether we live or die, we are the Lord's... Christ... Lord... We shall all stand before the judgment seat of Christ... the Lord Jesus... Christ... joy in the Holy Spirit... Christ... Christ... Christ Jesus... glorify the God and Father of our Lord Jesus Christ... just as Christ... Jesus Christ... by the power of the Holy Spirit... Jesus Christ... sanctified by the Holy Spirit... Christ Jesus... Christ... the Spirit of God... Christ... Christ... Christ... I beg you, brethren, through the Lord Jesus Christ, and through the love of the Spirit... in the Lord... in Christ Jesus... in Christ... in Christ... in the Lord... in Christ... in Christ... in the Lord... in the Lord... in the Lord... in the Lord... Christ... Lord Jesus Christ... The grace of our Lord Jesus Christ be with you. Amen... the Lord... The grace of our Lord Jesus Christ be with you all. Amen (Rom. 13:11 onwards).

Otherwise you 'do not serve our Lord Jesus Christ' (Rom. 16:18). In conclusion:

> Now to him who is able to establish you according to my gospel and the preaching of Jesus Christ, according to the revelation of the mystery kept secret since the world began but now[17] made manifest, and by the prophetic Scriptures made known to all nations, according to the commandment of the everlasting God, for obedience to the faith – to God, alone wise, be glory through Jesus Christ for ever. Amen (Rom. 16:25-27).

If this does not set Romans 13:8-10 in its proper context, nothing will. The suggestion that Paul is imposing the law of Moses upon believers is incredible. The sense of anticlimax – to return to Moses after nearly thirteen chapters of teaching on the glory of Christ in the gospel – would be intolerable. Paul does not go back to Moses. Of course not! In contrast, he rises to the Lord Jesus Christ. 'Christ' is what he leaves ringing in their ears. Christ!

---

[16] The very word Calvin used in his third use of the law.

[17] Note the 'now'.

Let me summarise the passage. As I have already said, the argument runs from Romans 12:1. Paul, having reached Romans 13, lays the foundation and measure of sanctification, 'love' (Rom. 13:10), and then moves on to the eternal hope believers have in Christ (Rom. 13:11-12), and the consequent holiness of life this must produce, both in a negative sense – things to 'cast off' (Rom. 13:12) – and in a positive sense – 'let us put on... put on the Lord Jesus Christ, and make no provision for the flesh' (Rom. 13:12-14). Paul then takes up the issue of 'things indifferent' (Rom. 14:1-23; 15:1-7). Notice the absence of a list of rules and regulations – the law approach. And not only an absence of regulations! Observe how the apostle gives believers an *overall principle* by which to order their lives. And what is this principle? It can be summed up as the law of Christ. Note the references to Christ. In addition to references to 'the Lord', it is Christ and his work which are specifically and repeatedly used as the believer's motive and touchstone (Rom. 14:6-10,14-15,18; 15:1-3,5-7). And Moses is not mentioned once! Above all, notice Paul's final word on the subject: 'Therefore receive one another, *just as Christ also received us*, to the glory of God' (Rom. 15:7). As in the previous chapter, I draw attention yet again to this paramount comparison, this staggering comparison: 'Just as...'! Is this what Reformed critics mean by 'wishy-washy'?[18]

Thus the believer has to take a far more spiritual stance than merely looking up a code of practice and seeking to obey it. How mistaken it is, therefore, to say that Paul, at the start of Romans 12, takes up the law and wields it to teach believers their duties. By his use of 'the will of God', the apostle does not mean 'the law of God'. Certainly, 'the will of God' cannot be confined to the ten commandments, a mere sixteen verses (thirty-two, with the repeat) of Scripture. It is the entire revealed will of God – 'all Scripture' (2 Tim. 3:16-17). As Christ prayed for his people: 'Sanctify them by your truth. Your word is truth' (John 17:17). 'Your word' – your entire word! The apostle does not tell the

---

[18] See my *Christ* pp156,219,222,248,280-281,285,287,488-489,528-529,535.

believer to keep the law. He does not say the law is the rule, the norm, the standard of the Christian life. That could not be right.

Paul, in Romans 13:8-10, shows that he is not against the law. He does not attack Moses. He is not an antinomian. The work of Christ in the gospel fulfils the law in the believer. But this does not mean that Paul here re-issues the law. How could he? He has already taught that believers, living by the Spirit, are enabled by him to love one another – and that this is what the law wanted to produce but could not. Paul is not making the law the rule for believers in Romans 13:8-10, and thus going back on what he set out a few pages before (Rom. 6:14; 7:1-6). Believers have died to the law!

Consider Galatians 5:13-14

Here is another place where Paul, when writing to believers, quotes the Mosaic law, or a kind of summary of it – but not, in fact, one of the ten commandments:

> You, brethren, have been called to liberty; only do not use liberty as an opportunity for the flesh, but through love serve one another. For all the law is fulfilled in one word, even in this: 'You shall love your neighbour as yourself'.

Paul does not here destroy what he has so carefully established in the rest of his letter to the Galatians. Of that we may be sure. After all that he has said, he is not at this late stage putting forward 'the moral law', the ten commandments, as the believer's rule. And if he is, he chooses a singularly inept way of doing it, since he quotes from Leviticus.[19] The law here is, without question, the Mosaic law. Consequently, if Reformed teachers want to use this passage to say the moral law is binding on believers as their perfect rule, it proves too much for them. They must extend their view of the law far beyond the ten commandments. 'The law', in Galatians 5:14, is the law of Moses.[20] It is, literally in the Greek, 'the whole law'.

---

[19] See above for Paul's use of Lev. 19:18 in Rom. 13:8-10. See also below.

[20] Not the law of Christ. See my *Christ* pp116-157,412-447.

But why did Paul quote from Leviticus? Why this emphasis upon 'love your neighbour'? We have met this reference to Leviticus 19:18 before, and will meet it again. This is noteworthy. Whereas before Christ's use of it, and Paul wrote his letters to the churches, there are no explicit references to the verse in Jewish writings, in clear contrast, in the New Testament this verse is the most frequently quoted passage from the Pentateuch (Rom. 13:9; Gal. 5:14; Jas. 2:8). This can only mean that the emphasis on Leviticus 19:18 is particularly and specially a gospel emphasis, and must have come from Christ himself, who first used it in this way (Matt. 5:43; 19:19; 22:39; Mark 12:31; Luke 10:27).

Notice Paul's emphasis upon 'fulfilled' once again. Paul is certainly not establishing the Mosaic law as the believer's rule, the commandments of which are to be obeyed in every particular. Love is the fulfilment of the law, and this love is possible only to those who have the Spirit. To try to establish Calvin's third use of the law from this passage is to miss the point of what Paul is saying, and to miss it badly. He is not exhorting believers to keep the law. He is stating a fact. By their life of love, he declares, all the law is fulfilled. And he puts it in the passive, 'the law is fulfilled'. I am not word-spinning. Paul is not commanding them to 'fulfil the law'; he is telling them 'the law is fulfilled' – two very different things. Paul speaks of believers and the fulfilment of the law in three places (Rom. 8:4; 13:8-10; Gal. 5:14), and in none of them does he command believers to fulfil the law. Rather, as believers walk according to, by or in the Spirit, the law is fulfilled, he says. We have already met this important passive. Paul says the righteous requirement of the law is *fulfilled* in believers (Rom. 8:4), but never says believers have to *do* or *keep* the law.

So what is the issue? It is no accident that 'fulfilled' (Gal. 5:14) and 'fullness' (Gal. 4:4) come from the same root word (which is, significantly, the same word as in Matt. 5:17), *plēroō*. The truth is, Paul is expounding the theme he has stressed so much in this letter; namely, the eschatological. The age of the law is over. The 'fullness' of the time has come (Gal. 4:4). Christ has come. The faith, the gospel, has come. And this has huge consequences for the individual. 'All the law is fulfilled' in believers by their obedience to Christ and his law in this new age. They are a new creation. And this is what Christ said he came to accomplish (Matt. 5:17).[21] And this is the issue in Galatians 5:13-14.

Paul, it must not be forgotten, is directing his remarks to those 'who desire to be under the law' (Gal. 4:21).[22] To Paul, such a desire is unthinkable, the stock-in-trade of false teachers, the Judaisers. He stresses the believer's freedom from the law (Gal. 4:21-31; 5:1,13), and this context of Galatians 5:13-14, both narrow and wide, must not be forgotten or ignored. It is the eschatological point all over again, worked out in individual experience. Paul is speaking of the believer's freedom (Gal. 5:1), the freedom he has by the work of the Holy Spirit. The believer has been rescued from this present evil age (Gal. 1:4).

As for 'all the law', Paul meant 'the whole law', the entire law of Moses; that is, not so much individual commands, but the law in its entirety and purpose. Compare Romans 8:4. The literal Greek, 'the all law', is 'odd' in that Paul put the 'all' in a peculiar place, and this is significant. Moreover, Paul put the definite article – 'the' – in a strange position too. None of this would have been lost on the original readers; 'the all law' is 'the entire law', 'the heart of the law', the fulfilment of the law's purpose.[23]

---

[21] See my *Christ* pp96,170,236-244,498-500.

[22] The Reformed get caught in this net.

[23] What of the seeming contradiction between Gal. 3:10-12; 5:3 and Gal. 5:14? See my *Christ* pp536-537 for my views. In brief, in Gal. 5:3, Paul was speaking of the attempt to earn justification by 'doing the law', which can be only by 'doing the whole law', 'the observance of all that the law requires' (Gal. 3:12; 5:3). This is impossible for fallen man. *Hence the negative overtones.* In Gal. 5:14, however, Paul was speaking of the new-covenant provisions Christ brought in, by which he gives people grace to 'fulfil the whole law', giving them his Spirit to enable them to live a sanctified life which expresses love (see Rom. 8:3-4). 'The love of God' – the sense of God's love to his people – 'the love of God has been poured out in our hearts by the Holy Spirit who was given to us' (Rom. 5:5). Thus the Spirit enables believers to love in return (Luke 7:36-50; 1 John 4:7-11,19) and so 'fulfil the whole law'. *Hence the positive overtones.*

As I have pointed out, 'loving one's neighbour' is not a soft option, not a lowering of the standard of the law. To dismiss the thesis of my book by such a device is too tempting for some; they wave it away as something vague and hazy – 'imprecise ethics'.[24] Not at all! The very imprecision in defining 'love' and 'neighbour', and how this can vary according to time and circumstance (Gal. 6:10),[25] makes Christ's law *all the more demanding* than Moses' law. While Christ does not call for conformity to rules, a ticking-of-the-boxes approach to sanctification – which, in truth, is no sanctification at all – neither does he call for a warm, vague feeling towards other believers. He wants, he demands, a real, practical and concentrated love, the sharing of goods and money, even – wait for it – even to the laying down of one's life for the brethren, all because Christ laid down his life for us (Rom. 15:1-3; 1 John 3:11-18)! And we are to have the mind of Christ in this (Phil. 2:5)! Think of that! I hesitate, I shrink back, even as I write the words and cite the passages! How do they strike you, reader, as your read them? 'Soft option', indeed!

Galatians 6:2 is apposite here. The law of Christ is that law of love which Christ taught in John 13:34-35; 15:12, and so on. In bearing one another's burdens, believers are obeying the law of their Lord. When they fail to do this, they break his law. Believers keep the law of Christ, the essence of which is love, and they do so out of gratitude to him for his love to them. To break his law, therefore, is to show gross ingratitude to him for his love. Clearly, the law of Moses and the law of Christ are in contrast. Paul was saying the bearing of one another's burdens, under Christ's law, is infinitely better than keeping the external Moses' law.

Of course, an emphasis upon the believer's freedom, unless accompanied by the equally biblical emphasis on the all-

---

[24] See my *Christ* pp156,219,222,248,280-281,285,287,488-489,528-529,535.

[25] Because the 'neighbour' in Lev. 19 referred to a fellow-Israelite, it is probable that the focus here is love to fellow-believers. Leaving aside Gal. 6:10, is there any reference in Galatians as to how believers should relate to unbelievers?

embracing law of Christ, can be turned into an excuse for all sorts of carnal behaviour. This, it goes without saying, is utterly wrong. In declaring that 'all the law is fulfilled in one word' (Gal. 5:14), in declaring that 'all are summed up in this saying, namely: "You shall love..."' (Rom. 13:9), Paul was not jettisoning the Mosaic law, saying it no longer had any place or value. Nor was he replacing the Mosaic law by a warm feeling. Certainly he was not abandoning all restraint. But nor was he imposing the law of Moses upon believers.

To sum up: the comments made above on Romans 13:8-10 apply with equal validity here. In Galatians 5:14, Paul was not imposing the Mosaic law on believers. Rather, he was continuing his theme of the epoch of the Spirit having superseded the epoch of the law, and the relevance of this triumphant 'but now' to the believer. It is tragic, it is a travesty, to reduce such a momentous argument by trying to claim Paul was making the ten commandments the believer's rule.

Consider Ephesians 6:1-3
Children, obey your parents in the Lord, for this is right. 'Honour your father and mother', which is the first commandment with promise: 'that it may be well with you and you may live long on the earth'.

Paul, clearly addressing godly children, here commanded them to obey their parents in the Lord; he said this is right. And he backed up his command by referring to, alluding to the law. *But he did not quote the law as the rule under which believers live.* Rather, he used the law as a paradigm, a model of good behaviour for believers, not as a rule which he imposed upon them. He simply reminded his readers that the Jews had this fifth commandment with its associated promise of possession of the land of Canaan – which promise he stressed. He was challenging his readers: If the Jews had this commandment, and this promise, how much more should believers live a sanctified family-life! What greater benefits are promised to them than to Israel of old! If the Mosaic law spoke of Canaan, how much more does Christ promise to his people today! This is what he was saying.

But if it is still maintained that the commandment must come over unchanged as part of the believer's perfect rule, *then so must the promise*. We cannot pick-and-mix! In other words, we shall have to admit that we have made a serious mistake in dismissing the 'prosperity gospel'. In the new covenant, obedience, after all, does bring huge material benefit, here and now. Mind you, depending on how strictly we interpret the promise, we might all have to move to the Middle East and settle in 'the land'. Hmm! A bit far-fetched? Surely, the apostle was using the commandment as an illustration or paradigm to encourage sanctified family-life among believers. This is what he was doing. He was certainly not imposing the commandment on them, nor was he promising them material prosperity for obedience!

And this is made all the more evident if we bear in mind that the issue of family life – here, the attitude of godly children to their parents – is but one example of the apostolic call for sanctification among many. This stands out all the more if the entire passage concerning practical godliness, the three chapters, Ephesians 4 – 6, is read in one sitting. Paul's total argument, its overall force, must be kept in mind. Which is? The believer must obey – he will obey – the gospel, and do so in practice, not by thinking he is under the rule of the law of Moses, but by thinking of his calling as a believer, imitating God his Father, living as a child of light, and being filled with the Spirit, and so on; above all, by thinking of Christ – I estimate that 'Christ' or 'Jesus' appears some nineteen times in these three chapters. And what is at the heart of these chapters? 'Christ... loved the church and gave himself for her, that he might sanctify and cleanse her with the washing of water by the word, that he might present her to himself a glorious church, not having spot or wrinkle or any such thing, but that she should be holy and without blemish' (Eph. 5:25-27). The cross! The cross leading to the believer's holiness! This is what Paul says to the believer. As the believer walks by the Spirit, living out the life of Christ, keeping his eye and heart on Christ and his cross, so he fulfils the law, fulfils it as it were indirectly. True, in addressing this particular topic, Paul quotes the fifth command to illustrate and enforce his call for godly children to be sanctified at home, but the apostle does not impose the command on believers; he simply uses the law as a paradigm for this godly behaviour.

What am I talking about? What is this 'paradigm' business? I have noted it on several occasions. Now is the time to establish and develop what I mean by it.

But before I do, I need to make a vital point. Believers, being in the new covenant, are not under the law of Moses (Rom. 6:14-15; 7:4-6; 8:1-4; 10:4; 2 Cor. 3:6-11; Gal. 2:19-20; 5:18; Eph. 2:14-15; Heb. 7:18-19; 8:13). They are under the law of Christ. But – and this is the vital point – although the word 'law' is used in both covenants (Mosaic and new), the law of Christ is a very different entity to the law of Moses.

The use of 'law' in the old covenant and in the new

It all hinges on the word 'law'. 'The law of Moses' and 'the law of Christ' are (in the common parlance) very different beasts; that is, they are very different 'entities', 'systems', 'regimes'. And they are poles apart, not only in content, but in their whole basis, approach, ethos, outlook, attitude and mindset. It is all to do with 'Moses' and 'Christ' (John 1:17). The two laws belong to two distinct, contrasting ages, and are very different 'laws'. The law of Moses is a list of specific rules – the decalogue is *ten* commandments, after all. The law of Christ, however, is far wider, far bigger. And I am not thinking of a hundred commandments instead of ten! (Or, rather, a thousand commandments instead of the more-than six hundred in the Mosaic law!) The law of Christ is not a list at all. This is the point I am striving for. The law of Christ is a principle, an all-embracing principle. Anything more different to a list of rules, especially a list of 'do nots', would be hard to imagine. Christ's law is inflexible, but there is a certain flexibility within it. Within limits, differences of judgment are allowed under Christ (see Rom. 14:1 – 15:7; Phil. 3:15-16, for instance). This is a remarkable aspect of the law of Christ. In general, law allows no room for conscience. In particular, the Mosaic law allows none. Summarising the essential difference between the two 'laws', the law of Moses and the law of Christ, we may put it this way: we are talking about the difference between precept and principle.

We are now ready to get to the question I posed. How should believers read, quote and use the law?

The law is a paradigm for believers

The apostles never used the law in the old-covenant way. This needs stating, and stating with force, because, as I have said, law mongers have a hybrid – pick and mix – way of using the law. Sometimes they speak of it as a command binding on believers. At other times they speak of it as a paradigm. And sometimes they use it as a mixture of the two, turning to medieval constructs such as the threefold use of the law or 'the moral law' as opposed to 'the ceremonial law', and play one off against the other. Such goings on are shoddy. Worse, they are unscriptural. And, alas, they thoroughly confuse believers. The solution is the apostolic way of using the law; namely as a paradigm, and always as a paradigm.

While Paul did not make the law the rule under which believers live, he did not go to the other extreme and ignore the law or say it is of no use whatsoever. From the rich treasury of the entire Old Testament, Paul drew various lessons, types, illustrations, analogies and examples. In particular, he cited the Mosaic law, quoted it, illustrated and supported his doctrine with it, and gave examples from it. Of course he did – the New Testament quite rightly treats the Old Testament as the Scriptures, pointing to Christ, foreshadowing him (Col. 2:17; Heb. 8:5; 10:1). In Hebrews 8:5, two words are used, 'copy' and 'shadow'. A copy is not the real or original, but it shows what the real thing is like; inadequately, yes, but nevertheless usefully. A shadow bespeaks the existence of the real, solid thing. True, a shadow is colourless, blurred and flat, but this does not detract from the glory of the original. In fact, it adds to it. Shadows are vital to an artist in conveying a sense of reality and solidity. In 'pure' water-colours, the lights are formed by painting in the darks, and deepening the darks enhances the lights. The Old Testament may be shadow, but how greatly it highlights the New!

Paul, therefore, used the entire old covenant, including the law, to enforce his doctrine: 'Christ, our Passover, was sacrificed for us' (1 Cor. 5:7), for instance. But this is not to say he preached Moses, or that he imposed Moses on believers. He preached Christ, making use of Moses to preach Christ.

This is what I mean by using the law as a paradigm – which is what Paul did, and what we should do. But the law must be used lawfully, properly nuanced[26] under the new covenant. The law, a component of 'all Scripture', has its role to play in the life of the believer, and part of that role is as a paradigm. But this is not the same as saying that every part of the Old Testament, down to its minutest detail, has authority over the believer, nor that the law is his perfect rule. The New Testament *uses* the Old, but its system of sanctification is not based upon it. The basis of new-covenant ethics is Christ, not the ten commandments. The law of Christ *uses* all the law of Moses to illustrate its claims. It *borrows* from it – but that only *occasionally*. Above all, it is not *based* upon it.

Take 1 Corinthians. In that book, Paul several times alludes to the Mosaic law. I emphasise this. He alludes to the law, the whole, all the law – not just the so-called 'moral law'. Paul draws on the entire law, including the Passover (1 Cor. 5:6-8), the removal of offenders from Israel (1 Cor. 5:9-13), the non-muzzling of the ox while treading the grain (1 Cor. 9:8-12), people and priests eating the sacrifices (1 Cor. 9:13-14; 10:18), Israel's sins in the wilderness (1 Cor. 10:1-11), the use of foreign languages (1 Cor. 14:21), and woman's submission (1 Cor. 14:34). But not once does Paul tell believers they are under the law. Never once does he tell them that they must keep Moses' precepts. Not once does he speak of the law as a list of rules which govern the life of the believer. Instead, he uses the law to give the believer a paradigm, an example, an illustration of the Christian life. 'These things happened to them as examples and were written down as warnings for us, on whom the fulfilment of

---

[26] What I am setting out is very different to those who say the law is binding in every detail, but at the same time 'modify' it by cutting out its punishment, or in splitting it into three, and so on. I am simply doing what the New Testament does with the law. It never plays Reformed 'ducks and drakes' with it. See my *Christ* pp99-110,154,392-408.

the ages has come' (1 Cor. 10:11, NIV). That is to say, the apostle uses the Old Testament in general, and the law in particular, as a pattern, a model, an illustration of his teaching, to help his readers understand his instructions for godliness, and to encourage them in obedience – including the need for purity, for proper financial support of gospel teachers, warning against sin, against the misuse of foreign languages in meetings, showing the right way for a woman to show her submission, and so on. Certainly this is the main way in which Paul uses the law in, say, 1 Corinthians. He appeals to the law as a paradigm for godliness. The same goes for 2 Corinthians. Paul uses the law as a paradigm in the matter of holiness (2 Cor. 6:14 – 7:1), the giving of money (2 Cor. 8:15), and the need for two or three witnesses to confirm a case (2 Cor. 13:1). But, as before, never does he turn the law into the believer's rule. In short, he takes his own medicine and uses the law lawfully (1 Tim. 1:8). He is *not* dividing the law into three bits, disposing of two, and setting up 'the moral law' as a rule; rather, he uses the entire law to illustrate new-covenant principles for believers. While the law of Moses very usefully serves as an illustration of the believer's behaviour, or an allusion to it, it cannot be the believer's perfect rule.

So, for instance, on not muzzling the ox, Paul takes the law but makes it say something different to what it originally said, applying it to the present circumstances of the believer, showing how the new covenant uses the old as a paradigm for the proper financial support for those who labour in the gospel (1 Cor. 9:1-18). Paul backs his argument by reference to the law: 'Do I say these things as a mere man?' he asks. 'Or does not the law say the same also?'[27] Reader, where did 'the law say the same also'? Where did it say that a gospel preacher needs and must receive financial support to do his work? It said it in the new-covenant reading of Deuteronomy 25:4. Listen to Paul: 'For it is written in the law of Moses: "You shall not muzzle an ox while it treads out the grain"'. Pause, reader! A literalist, an old-covenant reader, has to argue that Deuteronomy says nothing about financial support

---

[27] In writing to Timothy, he used the same paradigm, saying 'the Scripture says' (1 Tim. 5:17-18).

for a preacher of the gospel. And he is quite right – on *old-covenant* principles; the verse is concerned with allowing an ox to eat some corn as it works the treadmill, and that is all. But listen to Paul, reading the law through new-covenant eyes:

> Is it oxen God is concerned about? Or does he say it altogether for our sakes? For our sakes, no doubt, this is written, that he who ploughs should plough in hope, and he who threshes in hope should be partaker of his hope. If we have sown spiritual things for you, is it a great thing if we reap your material things?... Do you not know that those who minister the holy things eat of the things of the temple, and those who serve at the altar partake of the offerings of the altar? Even so the Lord has commanded that those who preach the gospel should live from the gospel (1 Cor. 9:9-14).

The Jews, no doubt, should have realised that the principle applied to more than oxen. All who labour ought to partake of the benefit of their labour. Surely oxen should not be treated better than men! Even in the old covenant, the humane treatment of oxen served as a paradigm for labour-relations. But it is only in the full light of the gospel that the spiritual point is made clear. This is the way the old covenant serves as a paradigm for the new. This is the way believers should use the Mosaic law, not as a binding rule down to its last Jewish detail.[28]

There are many such examples. In that same section, Paul cited temple-practice (1 Cor. 9:13-14; 10:18). Before that, he had raised the Passover. I know, like the sabbath, the Passover slightly anticipated Sinai (Ex. 12 and 16), but, again, like the sabbath, the Passover was in fact an integral part of the Sinai covenant. In any case, both came very heavily into the law, and both played an enormous part in the life of Israel under the law. Now then, what did Paul command the Corinthians? 'Purge out the old leaven, that you may be a new lump, since you truly are unleavened. For indeed Christ, our Passover, was sacrificed for us. Therefore let us keep the feast, not with old leaven, nor with

---

[28] I am not supporting the Puritan way of making the law teach every new-covenant matter in advance. There is all the difference between *that*, and looking back, through the gospel to the law and seeing an illustration.

the leaven of malice and wickedness, but with the unleavened bread of sincerity and truth' (1 Cor. 5:7-8). Let us think about that for a moment. Believers must get rid of yeast, and keep the feast of Passover. Hang on a minute! Do believers keep the feast as Moses stipulated? Do they keep the feast at all? They do not! If they did, it would be anathema to the Lord, would it not – since it would be an offence against the person and finished work of Christ? It would be tantamount to saying he had not died, and had not, by the shedding of his blood, redeemed his people. The truth is, of course, Paul was not talking about keeping any literal feast! Nobody in their right mind would think it![29] He was telling believers to get rid of all worldly contamination, and live godly lives for Christ, live sincerely and scripturally for the glory of their Redeemer. The apostle simply used the Passover as a paradigm to drive home his point. What he was not doing was to make the law the believer's rule.

And so it goes on, everywhere, throughout the apostolic writings. Look, for instance, at the thrilling use Paul made of the clash between Sarah and Hagar (Gal. 4:21-31), and the lessons he drew from it. Listen to his punch line. Let it sink in: 'Stand fast therefore in the liberty by which Christ has made us free, and do not be entangled again with a yoke of bondage' (Gal. 5:1). How relevant this is to the question in hand!

Then again, take the sabbath. Compare the Reformed approach with the apostolic. The Reformed pound out their old-covenant talk of sabbath observance in terms of a day on which

---

[29] But the unthinkable does happen. I know of a professing believer, once Judaisers had got a toehold, religiously get rid of yeast products, eat unleavened bread for the requisite number of days, and then, on the 'right' day, eat roast lamb while standing up, deliberately-timed at sunset. I know of another who seriously contemplated smearing blood on the front door – with hyssop, I wonder? How long will it be before such people, staff in hand, sandals on feet, cloak tucked in, eat the whole lamb, innards and all, burning the remains the next morning, and doing it all in a rush? And what about the Feast of Tabernacles, the New Moon, and all? Bizarre! And sad. And worse. For Christ has fulfilled all the Jewish shadows, and abolished them! Heb. 7 – 10 is categorical; in particular, Heb. 9:10; 10:9,18.

*this **cannot*** be done, and *that **ought*** to be done, all being couched in terms of a law which is attended by the direst of punishments for disobedience,[30] and all the rest of it. Contrast that with the writer to the Hebrews and his treatment of the subject (Heb. 3:7 – 4:11). Christ is the believer's sabbath. Christ gives the believer rest. Christ *is* the believer's rest.[31]

Similarly, old-covenant worship had an altar. So does the new: 'We have an altar from which those who serve the tabernacle have no right to eat' (Heb. 13:10; compare 1 Cor. 10:14-22). This verse – and its context – encapsulates precisely the right way for Christians to apply old-covenant terms. The altar of the new covenant is spiritual. Only the regenerate can partake of its sacrifices. The kingdom of God is spiritual; it does not consist of foods (Heb. 13:9); 'the kingdom of God is not eating and drinking, but righteousness and peace and joy in the Holy Spirit' (Rom. 14:17). When we are told 'to go forth to [Christ], outside the camp' (Heb. 13:13), who thinks we are to make a move to a physical place? Likewise, who (apart from the revivalist with his 'altar-call') thinks that in order to obey Christ's command to 'come to me' (Matt. 11:28), a person has to leave his seat and make a physical movement? Again, the city we seek in the new covenant is not the physical Jerusalem (Heb. 13:14). It is the heavenly, spiritual Jerusalem (Gal. 4:25-26); believers 'have come to Mount Zion and to the city of the living God, the heavenly Jerusalem' (Heb. 12:22). The saints of the Old Testament[32] were conscious of the very same thing (Heb. 11:10,13-16).

---

[30] Though the Reformed always offer their followers the panacea that the curse has, in truth, been removed for them. For more on this clever-but-groundless device of 'pulling the law's teeth', see my *Christ* pp107-108,404-408. I am not denying, of course, that Christ bore the curse of the law, sin and death for the elect (Rom. 8:1-4; 2 Cor. 5:21; Gal. 3:10-14; 1 Pet. 3:18), but Reformed shenanigans have nothing in common with apostolic doctrine on this vital point.

[31] See my *Sabbath Questions* pp71-83. Also, put 'sabbath' in the Keyword box on my sermonaudio.com page.

[32] Who were, of course, in the new covenant.

Yes, I know the Reformed have their answer ready. 'Believers are under the moral law. All that stuff is ceremonial'. Oh? I have already shown how that technique only works as long as you are willing to do what Scripture never does, and break the law into convenient bits. The Bible will never warrant it; it always treats the law as indivisible. In any case, it misses my point. I am simply showing that Paul (along with the other apostles) would use anything and everything from the law to enforce his doctrine on believers – the ten commandments (including, therefore, the sabbath), feasts, whatever. But never once did he impose any of those things upon believers as their perfect rule. He simply used anything and everything from the law as a paradigm. *That* is my point. So, whether or not any particular example comes from the ten commandments or any other part of the law (allowing, for argument's sake, such a division to exist), the Reformed gloss is utterly irrelevant.

Furthermore, Paul would use any source to enforce his teaching, not only the law. Moses, of course, was in a different league to the following, but the apostle was prepared to cite nature (Acts 14:15,17; 17:24-29; Rom. 1:20; 1 Cor. 11:14), history (Acts 14:16; 17:30; 1 Cor. 10:1-13), superstitious pagan and idolatrous practices (Acts 17:22-23; Rom. 1:21-23; 1 Cor. 10:18-22), and the writings of pagan poets, prophets and philosophers (Acts 17:28; Tit. 1:12-13), common sense and every-day practice (1 Cor. 9:7,10-12), the facts of life (1 Cor. 11:11-12; 12:12-31), and so on. But he made none of these the basis for his teaching, nor was he saying these constituted a norm for believers. Rather, he was making use of all these resources to draw analogies, and thus illustrate his doctrine.

In short, when addressing believers, the New Testament sometimes quotes and draws lessons from the whole law, yes, but this is a far cry from saying that the ten commandments are binding on believers as their rule of life. Paul never adopts the Reformed threefold division to limit 'the law' to 'the moral law', and so make the ten commandments the believer's perfect rule. On the contrary, the apostle makes the commands of the entire law to serve as a paradigm or example, illustration, specimen, instance or model of the behaviour which is required of believers.

And that is all! I say again: new-covenant men use all the law – we do not select a mere 1% or less of it! No! The Reformed may call us antinomians. Let them! They need to use the mirror. For, unlike them, we use all the law – *but we only use it the way the New Testament does when it applies it to believers.* And never does it make the law the believer's rule.

Let me confirm that this *is* the right way to read those places in the New Testament where the law is so used. Take 1 Peter 1:15-16: 'As he who called you is holy, you also be holy in all your conduct'. Why? 'Because it is written'. Where is it written? In the law (Lev. 11:44-45; 19:2; 20:7). What is written in the law? 'Be holy, for I am holy'. If the Reformed view is right, then it follows that since believers must be holy because God in the law told the Jews they had to be holy, then it follows that *that very law therefore is binding on believers as their rule.* Will the advocates of Calvin's third use of the law call upon this passage in 1 Peter for support? I doubt it. Although Peter quoted from the law, he did not quote from that part of the law which Reformed writers like to say is binding upon the saints. The fact is, turning to Leviticus, the apostle quoted from a passage (Lev. 11:1-47, especially verses 44-45) which commanded the Jews as to what kind of animals, fish, reptiles and insects they could or could not eat. He also quoted from another passage (Lev. 19:1-37, especially verse 2) which commanded the Jews to keep the fifth commandment; to keep the sabbaths (note the plural, reader; it was *all* the sabbaths they had to keep); to keep the second commandment; and to keep listed regulations for eating the sacrifices, reaping at harvest time, and so on. And he quoted from yet another passage (Lev. 20:1-27, especially verse 7) which commanded the Jews to stone idolaters, to execute all who cursed a parent or committed adultery, and so on. Is *this* law binding upon believers? Is it authoritative over them in every minute detail?

Of course not! It is the principle which counts. *As* the Jews had to be holy because God is holy, *so* believers must be holy. But this is not to say that the law, which God imposed upon the Jews, now forms the rule for believers! Rather, it serves as an illustration, exemplar or paradigm: *as* God never changes, and is always holy, and always requires holiness in his people, *so* believers must be holy. As I have shown more than once, this is the vital principle and demand. *As* God has forgiven his people, *so* they must forgive (Eph. 4:32). 'As... so' is the key here. Compare also Matthew 18:23-35.

For another instance of the use of the law in this way, see Romans 12:19-21, where believers are instructed: 'Beloved, do not avenge yourselves, but rather give place to wrath'. Why? 'For it is written'. What is written? 'Vengeance is mine, I will repay'. So says the Lord (Rom. 12:19; see also 1 Thess. 4:6; Heb. 10:30). But, reader, *where* did the Lord say this? In the law. Ah! but, I ask every Reformed reader, in which of your three categories of the law did God put it? You will not find it in what you like to call 'the moral law'! The original you will find in Deuteronomy 32:35, among the last words of Moses to the Jews before his death. Does *this* constitute the believer's rule?

The fact is, the New Testament is its own interpreter in all these matters: 'Whatever things were written before were written for our learning' (Rom. 15:4), and 'these things became our examples... All these things happened to [the Jews] as examples, and they were written for our admonition, upon whom the ends of the ages have come' (1 Cor. 10:6,11). 'Whatever things'! In short: 'All Scripture is given by inspiration of God [better, God-breathed, God breathed them out], and is profitable for doctrine, for reproof, for correction, for instruction [training] in righteousness' (2 Tim. 3:16). 'All Scripture'! But this is a far cry from asserting – as the Reformed want to assert – that what they call 'the moral law' is binding on believers as their rule of life. I say again, it is 'whatever things, all these things, all Scripture', not just the ten commandments. The Old Testament does not give us all we need. If it does, why the New Testament?

In saying this, I do not say believers may be less holy than the Jews. Far from it: 'Unless your righteousness exceeds the righteousness of the scribes and Pharisees, you will by no means enter the kingdom of heaven'. And Jesus spelled out what he meant: 'You have heard that it was said to those of old... But I say to you...' (Matt. 5:20-22). If you have any suspicion that I am teaching believers to be lawless, reader, I ask you to read my *Christ Is All* pp279-298,528-542; *passim*. I assure you I am not.

Nor am I saying a word against the law. Paul never argues that 'the Mosaic law is a bad thing'. Quite the opposite! But the fact is the time of the law of Moses is over. It has had its day. No doubt the child-custodian was good for the child (Gal. 3:24; 4:1-2), but hardly appropriate for a grown man! The law is not the norm of the Christian life. The law must be viewed through the new covenant.[33] While the law still has relevance for the believer, it is not Moses but Christ who is his people's lawgiver (Deut. 18:15-19; John 5:46-47; Acts 3:22-23; Heb. 3:5-6). The believer reads Moses, and gains from him, but it is Christ, the one of whom Moses prophesied, the one who fulfilled the law of Moses, whom believers are under. Christ is Lord, even of Moses. This is how and why Paul speaks as he does in 1 Corinthians 9:20-21. And he speaks for all believers everywhere and at all times. It is Christ, not Moses, who is his people's lawgiver. John 1:17 really must be given its full weight: 'The law was given through Moses, but grace and truth came through Jesus Christ'.

---

[33] For the Anabaptist position on this, and their citation of various laws no longer applicable to believers, see my *Christ* pp77-78,374-378. I quote just one paragraph (sources may be found in my *Christ* p378): 'Menno Simons: "To swear truly was allowed to the Jews under the law; but the gospel forbids this to Christians". Sebastian Franck complained of "wolves, the doctors of unwisdom, apes of the apostles, and antichrists [who] mix the New Testament with the Old... and from it prove [the legitimacy of]... [the] power of magistracy... [the] priesthood; and praise everything and ascribe this all forcibly to Christ... And just as the popes have derived all this from it, so also many of those who would have themselves called evangelicals hold that they have nobly escaped the snare of the pope and the devil, and have nevertheless achieved... nothing more than that they have exchanged and confounded the priesthood of the pope with the Mosaic kingdom... If [that is, since] the priesthood cannot be re-established out of the old law, neither can [Christian] government... be established according to the law of Moses". In all this, Franck listed the sabbath along with circumcision, kingship, temple and sacrifices, as old-covenant externals'. For my own modest contribution, listen to my short discourse: 'No Mixture! Separation'.

In short, while the New Testament uses the old covenant in general, and makes very occasional use of some of the ten commandments (never all of them), in order to illustrate the law of Christ, it never once tells believers that they are under the law of Moses as the rule of life. Certainly not! Believers are not under that killing, condemning ministry, now made obsolete by Christ who fulfilled it in every particular (Rom. 6:14-15; 7:4-6; 8:2-4; 10:4; 2 Cor. 3:6-9; Gal. 2:19-20; Heb. 7:18-19; 8:7,13). The old covenant, as a shadow, illustrated and pointed to Christ and his work, but its days are now well and truly over. The shadows have fled away. The Sun of Righteousness (Mal. 4:2), has arisen. The law remains, as part of the old covenant – indeed, as a part of the word of God – and it serves as an illustration or paradigm of the glorious new covenant. This is how believers should use the law. They should read the law as a collection of insights into the work of Christ, as illustrations of how they should walk in the law of Christ, but not as a list of rules which they cannot sort out and which, in any case, they are unable to keep. They are, after all, the children of Romans 8:2-4:

> For the law of the Spirit of life in Christ Jesus has made me free from the law of sin and death. For what the law could not do in that it was weak through the flesh, God did by sending his own Son in the likeness of sinful flesh, on account of sin: he condemned sin in the flesh, that the righteous requirement of the law might be fulfilled in us who do not walk according to the flesh but according to the Spirit.

The Law on the Believer's Heart

We know that the law is written on a believer's heart in the new covenant, written by the Spirit in regeneration.[1] The terms and promises of the new covenant, prophesied in Jeremiah 31:31-34, and set out in Hebrews 8:6-13 and 10:16-17, are these:

> Behold, the days are coming, says the LORD, when I will make a new covenant with the house of Israel and with the house of Judah – not according to the covenant that I made with their fathers in the day that I took them by the hand to lead them out of the land of Egypt, my covenant which they broke, though I was a husband to them, says the LORD. But this is the covenant that I will make with the house of Israel after those days, says the LORD: I will put my law in their minds, and write it on their hearts; and I will be their God, and they shall be my people. No more shall every man teach his neighbour, and every man his brother, saying: 'Know the LORD', for they all shall know me, from the least of them to the greatest of them, says the LORD. For I will forgive their iniquity, and their sin I will remember no more.

How should we interpret and apply such prophecies? What are the general principles? Specifically, of what time was Jeremiah speaking? To whom does this prophecy apply? And to what law does it refer?

As to the time in question, in the first instance, of course, Jeremiah was speaking to the people of his own day; his words had relevance for them in their particular circumstances. But *that* does not exhaust the import of the passage – not by a long chalk. Jeremiah was clearly speaking of what he called 'the days [which] are coming', 'after those days'. What 'days' are these?

Next, he addressed 'the house of Israel and... the house of Judah', saying God would make 'a new covenant' with *them* in those 'days'. Of whom was he speaking? There are two main views. Some think he was speaking of the spiritual blessing of

---

[1] This article is taken from my *Christ* pp299-301,312-321,543-555, lightly edited.

national Israel at the end of the gospel age; namely, a general conversion of the Jews, and a covenant which God will make with the Jewish nation in those days. Others, however, think the prophecy refers to the church, the new or spiritual Israel, and speaks of the new covenant with every child of God throughout this gospel age. Some believe both.

Then there is the 'law' of which Jeremiah prophesied. In Jeremiah's day, of course, 'the law' was the entire law of Moses, just as 'Israel and Judah' in Jeremiah's day meant 'the nation of Israel'. But Jeremiah was a prophet, and his words were a prophecy. What does 'the law' mean in the days of which he was speaking, the days of this new covenant? *That* is the question. As above, there are two main views, dividing in precisely the same way as over the first question. Many think Jeremiah's prophetic use of 'law' refers to the law of Moses, the ten commandments in particular; others think it is the law of Christ. But there is a great deal of inconsistency. As I will show, many want to regard the 'Israel and Judah' as spiritual Israel, but keep the law as the law of Moses.

Whatever answers to these questions we arrive at, three things must be borne in mind.

First, we must not assume our answers, but work them out scripturally. We must not assume, for instance, that 'law' must mean the law of Moses. The 'law' does not automatically mean that. I have already dealt with this. 'The law of faith' (Rom. 3:27), 'the law of the Spirit of life in Christ Jesus' (Rom. 8:2), 'the law of liberty' (Jas. 2:12) and 'the law of Christ' (Gal. 6:2) – these are not the law of Moses! In any case, is it not possible – to put it no stronger – that a prophecy of a *new* covenant might be concerned with something other than the law of the *old* covenant, the law of Moses? We must not assume that 'the law' for this new-covenant people is the same as for the old-covenant people of God. Nor must we assume the people are the same. Might not a new covenant speak of a new law for a new people? And it is a *new* covenant: 'I will make a *new* covenant... *not according to* the covenant that I made with their fathers in the day that I took them by the hand to lead them out of the land of Egypt'.

306

Secondly, we must be consistent. If Jeremiah's use of 'Israel and Judah' is a prophecy of a new Israel, then a similar conclusion and 'change' of meaning must apply to 'law'. It will not do to say that one part of the passage – 'Israel and Judah' – becomes 'new' in the prophecy, but the other – 'the law' – does not. A new Israel requires a new law.

Thirdly, if it is the law of Moses that is written on the heart in the new covenant, then it is the law of Moses – all of it! It is quite wrong to whittle this down to the ten commandments, blithely assuming it is so. If it is the law of Moses, the complete law, that is written on the heart of every believer, the consequences will have to be lived with![2]

Clearly, all this raises a very important point of biblical interpretation. Did Jeremiah prophesy the law of Moses would be written on the hearts of the Jews? Or did he prophesy the law of Moses would be written on believers' hearts? Or did he prophesy the law of Christ would be written on the hearts of Jews at the end of the age? Or did he prophesy the law of Christ would be written on believers' hearts now? In other words, how should we read Old Testament prophecies such as this? That is, should we read them as predicting old or new-covenant blessings to old or new-covenant people? Naturally, the prophecies were delivered, in the first instance, to Jews in old-covenant language and terms, but are they to be understood in that way in the days of the new covenant?

What tools has God given us so that we might do the job – and come to a definitive, biblical answer to such questions? It is high time we looked at the key passage, namely 1 Peter 1:8-12, leading to an overview of all the prophets. And that is precisely what I did in: 'The Prophets and the New Covenant'. If you have not read that article, reader, I respectfully ask you to do so at this point. It is vital background material for what follows.

---

[2] Consequences? Every believer will have heart love for, and devote heart obedience to, the sacrifices, observance of the festivals, dietary laws, and so on.

Assuming that you have, I now go on to consider the major Old Testament prophecy of the new covenant; namely Jeremiah 31:31-34.

A look at Jeremiah 31:31-34

Let me start by retracing my steps. The law *is* written on a believer's heart in the new covenant, written by the Spirit in regeneration. The terms and promises of the new covenant, prophesied in Jeremiah 31:31-34, and set out in Hebrews 8:6-13 and 10:16-17, are these:

> Behold, the days are coming, says the LORD, when I will make a new covenant with the house of Israel and with the house of Judah – not according to the covenant that I made with their fathers in the day that I took them by the hand to lead them out of the land of Egypt, my covenant which they broke, though I was a husband to them, says the LORD. But this is the covenant that I will make with the house of Israel after those days, says the LORD: I will put my law in their minds, and write it on their hearts; and I will be their God, and they shall be my people. No more shall every man teach his neighbour, and every man his brother, saying: 'Know the LORD', for they all shall know me, from the least of them to the greatest of them, says the LORD. For I will forgive their iniquity, and their sin I will remember no more.

After all we have seen, we know how we should interpret this prophecy. We need be in no doubt. Jeremiah was predicting the coming of Christ and the setting up of the new covenant. God was announcing that in that new covenant, he would write his law – the law of Christ – upon the hearts of believers.

Moving from the general, to the specific, the New Testament directly quotes this prophecy, and interprets and applies it. I refer, of course, to Hebrews 7:18-19,22; 8:6-13; 9:24-28; 10:1-18. How does the writer of the letter to the Hebrews interpret this prophecy? Literally or spiritually? The literal interpretation of Jeremiah's prophecy and its context would entail the setting up of David's kingship once again (Jer. 30:9), the rebuilding of Jerusalem (Jer. 30:18; 31:38-40), its establishment for ever (Jer. 31:40), and the reinstatement and immense enlargement of the priesthood with its sacrificial ministry (Jer. 31:14; 33:17-18,21-22). Did the writer to the Hebrews speak of such things? Certainly not! That there was a physical restoration of the Jews to their land after their captivity in Babylon, I do not deny, but we are left in no doubt as to the New Testament fulfilment of Jeremiah's prophetic words; which is, the gospel, the new covenant (Heb. 8:6-13).

In a lengthy extract drawn from the prophet, and a detailed exposition of that extract, the writer to the Hebrews is explicit as to how we should read, interpret and apply Jeremiah. May I suggest, reader, that you read Hebrews 7:18-19,22; 8:6-13; 9:24-28; 10:1-18, and do so out loud? If you do, I think things will soon become exceedingly clear. Having already spoken of a change of law under the gospel, and that change a 'necessity' (Heb. 7:12), the writer to the Hebrews contrasts the new 'law' with the Mosaic law, which he called 'old', 'obsolete', and 'ready to vanish away', 'disappear' (NIV) (Heb. 8:10,13). Note how he speaks of 'now... now... now, once at the end of the ages' (Heb. 8:6; 9:24,26). Note the 'us' and 'we' (Heb. 7:19; 9:24; 10:10,15). Note the utter lack of a whiff of a suggestion that there will be another fulfilment – a greater fulfilment – of the prophecy, which will come in some future Jewish kingdom. In fact, the whole context is that the prophecy was being fulfilled there and then – even as the writer was penning his letter. It was the present experience of the early believers. And it is ours, now, as believers. The passage speaks for itself. On its own, it is conclusive.

In short, Jeremiah's prophecy of Israel and Judah (Jer. 31:31-34) is to be understood spiritually, of believers. The law of which he prophesied, and which is fulfilled in the new covenant, is not the law of Moses, but the law of Christ, the gospel. The hill of Zion, Jerusalem, spiritually, is the church (Gal. 4:24-26; Heb. 12:22-23; Rev. 14:1-5) – which is called the *new* Jerusalem (Rev. 21:2); the temple is the church (Eph. 2:19-22; see also 1 Cor. 3:9,16; 2 Cor. 6:16; and I would include 2 Thess. 2:4).

All this, of course, is a hammer blow to those who object to the case I made out for the believer's rule in my *Christ Is All* on the grounds that, in the new covenant, the law is written on the believer's heart. It is no objection at all. Jeremiah's prophecy is, in fact, the strongest biblical proof for the rebuttal of Calvin's third use of the law. For 'the law' in Jeremiah's prophecy is nothing other than the law of Christ. It *cannot* be the law of Moses. It *is not* the law of Moses; no, not even the limited Reformed view of the law – 'the moral law', as they call it. Neither Jeremiah, nor any other prophet, nor, come to that, any New Testament writer, ever used the phrase. They would not know what it meant! The truth is, God, through Jeremiah, promised that with the coming of his Son, he would set up the new covenant and, by his Spirit, write Christ's law in the hearts of all his people. Indeed, as I showed in 'The Prophets and the New Covenant', the law of Christ is Christ himself, *for the new covenant is Christ himself.*

All this is further strengthened when we consider that most intriguing of phrases, 'the Israel of God', coined by Paul in Galatians 6:16.

'The Israel of God' (Gal. 6:16)

> As many as walk according to this rule, peace and mercy be upon them, and upon the Israel of God.

In my *Christ Is All* (pp211-278,481-527), I gave my reasons for regarding 'this rule' as the law of Christ, but I now ask: Who or what is 'the Israel of God'? The verse is unique, and presents several difficulties, punctuation – which has to be supplied – being one of them. Without getting involved in a convoluted discussion, let me say that, along with the majority, I take the punctuation as above, placing the comma after 'rule' and before 'peace'.[3] But what of 'the Israel of God'? This is the only time

---

[3] The two possibilities are: 'As many as by this rule shall walk, peace upon them and mercy, and upon the Israel of God'; in other words, 'peace' and 'mercy' both belong to 'as many as shall walk by this rule'. That is one possibility – the one I accept. Or: 'As many as by this rule shall walk, peace upon them, and mercy [and] upon the Israel of God'; in other words, 'peace' belongs to 'as many as shall walk by this rule', but 'mercy' belongs to 'the Israel of God'. That is the other – the one I

Paul used the phrase. Indeed, as I have said, it is unique in the whole of Scripture. What did the apostle mean by it? Above all, what of the 'and' in '*and* upon the Israel of God'? And why did Paul pen a piece of such remarkable, if not awkward, Greek? And why did he do it here – at the end of Galatians?

Let me tackle the 'and' first. When Paul said '*and* the Israel of God', was he using 'and' as 'and also'? In other words, was Paul speaking of two distinct groups – on the one hand, those who were living according to Christ's rule, *and also*, on the other, the Israel of God? If so, the Israel of God could not have been walking according to Christ's rule. Therefore, they were unbelievers; in fact, they were unbelieving Jews. But what an odd way of expressing it! 'The Israel of God', apparently, counter-balances 'as many as walk according to this rule'. This is not convincing. Quite the reverse! It is hard – for me, impossible – to accept that Paul called unbelieving Jews 'the Israel of God'. Why did he not use 'the circumcised' or 'the circumcision', his usual terminology (Rom. 3:30; 4:9; 15:8; Gal. 2:7-9,12; Eph. 2:11; Tit. 1:10, for instance), and which would have aptly fitted the context? What is more, if he was speaking of unbelieving Jews, it means that Paul desired peace and mercy upon them, every bit as much as he did upon those who belong to Christ. This is unthinkable. Why would Paul wish peace and mercy for those who did not see eye to eye with him on Galatians 6:14-15, who were not believers? For their salvation, he would pray, yes (Rom. 9:1-3; 10:1), but a desire for 'peace and mercy' does not translate into a desire 'that they might be saved'. In any case, concern for the salvation of unbelieving Jews is foreign to the context, both immediate and throughout the letter. And if he was including the Judaisers in 'the Israel of God' – as he ought, if he was speaking of unbelieving Jews – I cannot see how Galatians 6:16 can be made to fit with Galatians 5:12.

---

reject. There is a second point; 'peace' and mercy' are in reverse order to every other occasion of their conjunction in Scripture (1 Tim. 1:2; 2 Tim. 1:2; Tit. 1:4; 2 John 3; Jude 2). The order in Gal. 6:16 is 'illogical', although it occurs in the Nineteenth Benediction in the liturgy of the synagogue, which Paul might have been using. But this does not explain the structure of Gal. 6:16.

Not only is it very unlikely (it is unthinkable!) that Galatians 6:16 teaches that Paul prayed for 'peace and mercy' for both believers and unbelievers, it is hard to see how the verse teaches that Paul prayed for two sorts of believers – Gentile and Jewish.[4] The idea that the people of God can be divided into Gentile believers and Jewish believers is utterly foreign to Galatians,[5] and is surely eliminated by John 10:16; 11:52; 17:20-23; Ephesians 2:11-22.[6] Paul never does such a thing. So this kind of division cannot be the meaning of 'and the Israel of God'.

The fact is, Paul was not praying for two groups at all. The 'and', *kai*, can be translated 'namely', 'even' or 'that is', and this is how it should be read here: 'Peace and mercy to all who follow this rule, even to the Israel of God' (NIV).[7] Indeed, the word is sometimes best left untranslated. The upshot is, Paul prayed that 'peace and mercy be upon them, [that is, namely, even] upon the Israel of God'. In other words, he desired peace and mercy upon all who walk according to Christ's law; that is, all believers. 'The Israel of God', therefore, is an all-encompassing term for all believers, for all – for 'as many as', whether Jews or Gentiles – for all who live according to Christ's law.

But why did Paul choose the term 'the Israel of God'? Why did he not say 'the elect', or 'the saints', or 'the church', or some such? Why did he use 'Israel'? This is the most interesting question of all. We find its answer by re-considering our parallel

---

[4] Nor was Paul thinking of ministers, on the one hand, and private believers, on the other. I have not made up these 'explanations'. As always, they are seriously suggested by various writers.

[5] Moses, through his law, divided men, whereas Christ unites. This is a vital part of Galatians.

[6] See also Ezek. 34:23-31; 37:24-28.

[7] There is scriptural warrant for it, not least in Galatians. For instance: 'But even (*kai*) if we, or an angel from heaven, preach any other gospel to you than what we have preached to you, let him be accursed' (Gal. 1:8). 'And the rest of the Jews also played the hypocrite with [Peter], so that even (*kai*) Barnabas was carried away with their hypocrisy' (Gal. 2:13). 'Knowing that a man is not justified by the works of the law but by faith in Jesus Christ, even (*kai*) we have believed in Christ Jesus' (Gal. 2:16). 'Even (*kai*) so we' (Gal. 4:3).

discussion,[8] of Paul's choice (and in the same context – and, as always, the context must be king) of the word 'law' in 'the law of Christ' (Gal. 6:2). When thinking about *that*, I asked why Paul did not use another, neutral word for 'law', saying he must have had good reason for his use of the old Jewish word. It could only have been deliberate. I called 'the law of Christ' a staggering phrase, a breathtaking paradox, and noted how intriguing was Paul's choice of such a loaded term as 'law'. I also commented on his word play over 'law'. Above all, I noted the important part played by the eschatological aspect of law and grace.

All this applies equally to Paul's use of 'Israel' here and elsewhere. His word play, for instance, is clearly at work in his astounding statement that 'they are not all Israel who are of Israel' (Rom. 9:6). At once the spotlight shines upon 'Israel'. Paul, there can be no question of it, meant his readers to sit up and take notice. We know that 'Israel', as a word, had enormous resonance for the Hebrew people. It was peculiarly their own name, their self-designation as the covenant people of God; outsiders called them Jews. This is significant. Whenever we come across 'Israel', we have something noteworthy, something precious. 'The Israel of God' (Gal. 6:16), therefore, must be exceedingly significant; not only 'Israel', but '*the* Israel', even 'the Israel of *God*'!

Then again, it is clear that in leading up to his use of 'the Israel of God' (Gal. 6:16), Paul has had 'Israel according to the flesh' in mind. Note his emphasis on law, circumcision, flesh and boasting (Gal. 6:12-13). This is what I meant by the context. Then comes his thunderous: 'But God forbid that I should boast except in the cross of our Lord Jesus Christ, by whom the world has been crucified to me, and I to the world' (Gal. 6:14), which prepares the way for his shattering statement: 'For in Christ Jesus, neither circumcision nor uncircumcision avails anything, but a new creation' (Gal. 6:15) – an unmistakable echo of Galatians 5:6. I say shattering, and so it is in light of the context. Paul could not have picked a more emotive topic to make his point for those tempted to go to the law – circumcision, of all

---

[8] See my *Christ* pp214-218,481-483.

things. How often he has spoken of it in this letter in one way or another (Gal. 2:3,7-9,12; 5:6,11-12; 6:12-13,15). The truth is, 'the circumcision' or 'the circumcised' was a euphemism for 'Israel' (Acts 10:45; 11:2; Rom. 3:30; 4:9,12; 15:8; Gal. 2:7-9,12; Eph. 2:11; Col. 4:11; Tit. 1:10). But circumcision, or lack of it, is of no concern, says Paul. All that matters is to be 'in Christ', to be a new creation, to boast in nothing but his cross. 'And as many as walk according to *this* rule, peace and mercy be upon them'. *They* are 'the Israel of God' (Gal. 6:16). Furthermore, in his use of 'peace and mercy', unmistakable Jewish overtones are evident once again. As I say, Paul's readers would not have missed all this emphasis upon Israel; 'the Israel of God' would have assumed enormous significance for them. The phrase was no idle choice, one grabbed out of the air, but was deliberate, calculated to produce maximum effect.

And not the least aspect of the phrase's fascination lies in the fact that 'the Israel of God' is virtually impossible to express in Hebrew. It is entirely a New Testament phrase and concept. All this indicates that Paul had a special purpose in coining[9] 'the Israel of God', every bit as much as when he coined 'the law of Christ'. As with 'law', so with 'Israel'; the significance of both lies in the eschatological period we are talking about.[10] Which Testament are we in? Which covenant are we talking about? 'The law of Moses' was for 'Israel after the flesh' (1 Cor. 10:18) in the old covenant. 'The law of Christ' is for 'the Israel of God' in the new. Both 'law' and 'Israel' have been taken over and transformed in the change of covenants. Paul, in the same

---

[9] As before, I deliberately use the word 'coin'.

[10] By eschatological, I do not mean some supposed restoration of national Israel in the millennium, which is utterly foreign to Galatians (and everywhere else, as far as I can see). As I have explained at large, Paul has been speaking about the eschatological 'but now'. 'Once at the end of the ages, [Christ] has appeared to put away sin by the sacrifice of himself' (Heb. 9:26). 'The ends of the ages have come' upon us (1 Cor. 10:11). 'Now', 'but now' (Rom. 3:21; 5:9,11; 6:22; 7:6; 8:1; 11:30; 11:31 (second 'now' in NIV, NASB); 16:26; see also John 15:22,24; Acts 17:30; 1 Cor. 15:20; Gal. 4:9; Eph. 2:12-13; 5:8; Col. 1:26; Heb. 8:6; 9:26; 12:26; 1 Pet. 2:10). I cannot stress too much the 'but now'.

context, using the two weighty Jewish words, pregnant with meaning, 'law' and 'Israel', coined two new-covenant phrases, 'the law of Christ' and 'the Israel of God'. It is a classic demonstration of how the New Testament writers (Paul in particular) use the language, rites and titles of the old-covenant people, Israel, and apply them to the new-covenant people, the church. 'Passover', 'circumcision', 'sabbath', 'altar', 'sacrifice', 'priest', 'temple', *etc.* have all come over and been transformed.[11] Likewise with 'law' and 'Israel'. The law of Christ is the new law for the new people. As the Israel of the Old Testament had its law, the law of Moses – so the Israel of the New Testament has its law, the law of Christ.

Linking this with Jeremiah's prophecy of the new covenant, we can, once again, face up to the two questions. Who are the 'Israel' and 'Judah'? What is the law? These two questions are inextricably linked through the historic change of epoch in redemption history. The law of Moses gave way to the law of Christ (Gal. 6:2), and Israel after the flesh gave way to the Israel of God (Gal. 6:16). Let me use the despised word, 'replacement'; I am not ashamed of it: 'the law of Christ' has replaced 'the law of Moses', and 'the Israel of God' has replaced 'Israel after the flesh'. There is a contrast between the 'Israel of God' and the 'Israel after the flesh' (1 Cor. 10:18) The 'Israel of God' is the spiritual Israel, the whole body of believers whether Jew or Gentile, those who are governed by this rule. On them, peace and mercy abide, since they are the true Israel of God. All this, of course, was fully determined in God's decree, accomplished by Christ, and is being applied by the sovereign Spirit.

This is confirmed by other scriptures. 'We are the circumcision, who worship God in the Spirit, rejoice in Christ Jesus, and have no confidence in the flesh' (Phil. 3:3). 'He is not a Jew who is one outwardly, nor is circumcision that which is outward in the flesh; but he is a Jew who is one inwardly; and circumcision is that of the heart, in the Spirit, not in the letter; whose praise is not from men but from God' (Rom. 2:28-29; see also Rom. 4:12; 9:6-8; Gal. 3:7,9,28-29; 5:6; 6:15). In Christ, all

---

[11] For more in this vein, see my *Psalm 119*; *Sabbath Questions*.

believers, Jew and Gentile, are 'circumcised with the circumcision made without hands, by [better, in] putting off the body of the sins of the flesh, by the circumcision of Christ' (Col. 2:11). Such are now 'a holy nation, his own special people... now the people of God' (1 Pet. 2:9-10; see also Tit. 2:14; Heb. 2:17). Note the 'now' – '*now* the people of God'. Before conversion, Gentile unbelievers 'were without Christ, being aliens from the commonwealth of Israel and strangers from the covenants of promise, having no hope and without God in the world'.[12] But after conversion, Gentile believers (and Jewish, of course) 'have been brought near by the blood of Christ' (Eph. 2:11-13). Christ has reversed all the negatives. Gentile (and Jewish) believers are in Christ, they are one body in Christ, citizens of the true Israel, they partake of the covenants of promise, have hope and God in the world. I underline, in particular, the fact that the saints are Israelites indeed (see John 1:47; Rom. 9:6). They form 'one new man', 'one body', one 'household', 'one 'building', one 'temple', one 'dwelling place' of and for God (Eph. 2:14-22). All believers – Jew and Gentile – are Abraham's children (Rom. 4). In truth, they are the 'children of promise' (Gal. 4:28), God's adopted children, no less (Rom. 8:14-17; Gal. 4:5-7). They are, in short, the Israel of God.

'As many as walk according to this rule, peace and mercy be upon them, and [even] upon the Israel of God', therefore, is the climax – and a fitting climax, at that – to Paul's letter to the Galatians. It is not a mere add-on. Moreover, Paul is not at this late stage introducing a new subject – such as some future blessing for the Jews. Far from it. He is summing up his letter, drawing the threads together. 'The Israel of God'! All through his letter, Paul has been working towards, not the 'Israel after the flesh', but the 'Israel of God'; 'peace and mercy be upon *them*'. And, coupled with this, of course, he has been defending his readers – stirring his readers – against the attacks of the Judaisers, showing believers that holiness is not by the law of Moses (Gal. 3:2-5), but by the law of Christ.

---

[12] Jewish unbelievers, of course, although Israelites, were without Christ, and so on, but Paul is addressing Gentiles at this point.

Galatians 6:16 is not sufficient, on its own, to come to a clear decision about the believer and the law, especially in connection with Jeremiah 31:31-34. No! For that, I can only refer you, reader, to the abundant biblical evidence I have already cited. Galatians 6:16 is only one part of this, I accept. Nevertheless, it is a part! And it is all very well to say what we *cannot* deduce from the verse, but what *was* Paul saying? After all, he used the phrase, 'the Israel of God'! He must have meant something by it! If he was not thinking of what I have said, then what was he thinking of? I contend that both parts of Jeremiah's prophecy – 'the law' and 'Israel and Judah' – are transformed by the epochal change of covenant. The parallel use of eschatological terms in Galatians and Hebrews concerning the replacement of the law by the Spirit, to my mind clearly establishes that 'the Israel of God' (Gal. 6:16) is not 'Israel after the flesh'. I do not agree with the suggestion that 'the Israel of God' are the elect Jews, not the church. Nor do I think that Justin Martyr (*c.* AD160) was the first to call the church 'the Israel of God'. I am convinced Paul used 'Israel' in this way in Galatians 6:16. And it is all of a piece with the rest of the New Testament teaching about the eschatological 'but now'.

Christ has come. It is the age of the Spirit; the age of the Mosaic law is over. No more is it Israel according to the flesh, but Israel according to the Spirit. No longer is it the bondage of Mount Sinai in Arabia, but the liberty of the spiritual Zion. The law of God is now the law of Christ.

And all this confirms the view of Jeremiah 31:31-34 which I have set out. The prophet was not speaking of the law of Moses being written on the hearts of Jews. Nor was he saying that the law of Moses would be the believer's rule under the gospel. The new covenant, of which Jeremiah prophesied, is an inward covenant, inward through the indwelling Christ, he himself being the new law, by his Spirit, 'written on the heart' of the believer. The law within the believer is nothing less than Christ living and formed within him (John 14:23; 17:23; 2 Cor. 6:16; Gal. 4:19; Eph. 3:17; Rev. 3:20; 21:3). Indeed, Christ himself is the believer's covenant. As the apostle could declare to the Colossians: 'I became a minister according to the stewardship from God which was given to me for you, to fulfil the word of God, the mystery

317

which has been hidden from ages and from generations, but now has been revealed to his saints. To them God willed to make known what are the riches of the glory of this mystery among the Gentiles: which is Christ in you, the hope of glory' (Col. 1:25-27).

Nor was Jeremiah the only prophet to speak of the new covenant. Take God's promise through Isaiah: 'All your children shall be taught by the LORD' (Isa. 54:13; John 6:45). Again, through Ezekiel: 'I will give them one heart, and I will put a new spirit within them, and take the stony heart out of their flesh, and give them a heart of flesh, that they may walk in my statutes and keep my judgments and do them; and they shall be my people, and I will be their God... I will sprinkle clean water on you, and you shall be clean; I will cleanse you from all your filthiness and from all your idols. I will give you a new heart and put a new spirit within you; I will take the heart of stone out of your flesh and give you a heart of flesh. I will put my Spirit within you and cause you to walk in my statutes, and you will keep my judgments and do them' (Ezek. 11:19-20; 36:25-27; see also Ezek. 16:59-63). Nor, for obvious reasons, is the doctrine of the new covenant confined to the Old Testament![13]

The *doctrine* of the new covenant (despite its relative rarity as a *phrase*) is written large throughout the entire Bible. It pervades everything; it is a major concept in Scripture. Take Isaiah 42, where God was addressing the Messiah, Christ (Matt. 3:17; 12:17-21; 17:5): 'Behold! My servant whom I uphold, my elect one in whom my soul delights' (Isa. 42:1). God commanded the people to 'sing to the LORD a *new* song', having addressed Christ thus: 'Behold, the *former* things have come to pass, and *new* things I declare; before they spring forth I tell you of them' (Isa. 42:9-10). This was a foretelling of the *new* covenant which would be established by Christ. 'Do not remember the *former* things, nor consider things of old. Behold, I will do a *new* thing' (Isa. 43:18-19; Jer. 31:22). God described this *new* thing: 'I will even make a road in the wilderness, and rivers in the desert... waters in the wilderness and rivers in the desert, to give drink to

---

[13] See also my *Psalm 119*.

my people, my chosen' (Isa. 43:19-20), and 'a woman shall encompass a man' (Jer. 31:22), something unheard of! God assured his people that they would 'hear *new* things', things they had not known (Isa. 48:6), 'be called by a *new* name' (Isa. 62:2), and eventually live in a '*new* heavens and a *new* earth' (Isa. 65:17; 66:22). The *new* song to be sung by the elect is a repeated theme of the Psalms (Ps. 33:3; 40:3; 96:1; 98:1; 144:9; 149:1). No wonder, since God promised to 'give... a *new* heart [to] and put a *new* spirit within' his people (Ezek. 36:26; 11:19-20), fulfilling his command that they should 'get [themselves] a *new* heart and a *new* spirit' (Ezek. 18:31).[14]

When the Psalmist spoke of the godly man, and recorded that 'his delight is in the law of the LORD, and in his law he meditates day and night' (Ps. 1:2), naturally, he was thinking of the law of Moses. Of course he was, since he was living in the days of the old covenant. But as a prophet, was he saying that the believer in the age of the Spirit would delight in, and day and night meditate upon, the law of Moses? Or, as so many (mis)define the law, the ten commandments? Reader, if you are a believer, does this describe you? When you ask God: 'Open my eyes, that I may see wondrous things from your law' (Ps. 119:18), and tell him: 'Oh, how I love your law! It is my meditation all the day' (Ps. 119:97), are you thinking only – or primarily – of the Mosaic law? Or do you read, delight in and meditate upon the entire Scripture, and especially the gospel of our (your) Lord and Saviour, Jesus Christ? 'Consider *him*' (Heb. 12:3)! Surely the staunchest advocate of Calvin's third use of the law would not spend *all* his time in the law, would he? Nor would he spend *more* time in the Old Testament than the New, would he? And when reading and interpreting the Old, would he not do so in terms of the New? Reader, when you cite, sing or otherwise use, say, Psalm 3:4; 5:7; 18:6; 20:2-3; 24:3; 27:4-6; 48:9,12; 50:5; 51:18-19; 54:6; 65:4; 122; 128:5; 134; 141:2, what is going through your mind? If you were to be washed up on a desert island, and could have only one leaf of Scripture, would you

---

[14] See my *Christ* p228 for the importance of 'new' and 'heart'.

select Exodus 20 or Romans 8? To ask such questions is to answer them.[15]

In all this, please do not forget this vital distinction I drew when setting out the believer's rule in my *Christ Is All* (pp218-219,483-486). This is what I said:

> When, in Scripture, we meet 'the law of God', we must ask ourselves which covenant we are talking about. If it is the old covenant, then 'the law of God' is the 'the law of Moses'. If it is the new covenant, then 'the law of God' is 'the law of Christ'.

Here is where it comes into its own.

Conclusion

Calvin's third use of the law is wrong! The ten commandments cannot sanctify. The ten commandments do not form the believer's perfect rule. The ten commandments are not written on the believer's heart in the new covenant. The gospel is. The law of Christ is. Christ himself is.

God demands heart obedience, heart experience, heart worship, but man cannot provide it. The good news is that God, by his grace, through Jeremiah (and others) promised that he would set up a new covenant and do this very thing, writing his new law, the law of Christ, upon his people's hearts. More than that, even better than that, at the appointed time God sent his Son into the world to establish this new covenant, to die for his people in order to redeem them, and to earn the gift of the Holy Spirit for them, and so write his law upon their hearts.

Thus the new-covenant man inevitably delights in obedience, and gives God heart worship and service, not a grudging conformity to irksome rules imposed from without. To any who object to my use of 'irksome', I can only suggest they re-read passages such as Acts 15:5,10,24; Galatians 2:4-5; 3:21-25; 4:21

---

[15] Believer, have you not found that you can open the New Testament anywhere and turn it into prayer without adjustment? Do you find you can do the same with, say, Deut. 28:58-68; 1 Kings 8:14-53; Ps. 18:20-24; 109:1-20? What about Isa. 58:13-14 with Ex. 35:2-3; Jer. 17:21-27? See my *Psalm 119*.

– 5:1,13, noting words such as 'trouble', 'slavery', 'bondage', 'locked up', and 'prison' which are coupled with the law, and words such as 'freedom' and 'liberty' which are associated with the new covenant. The truth is, the believer serves God in Christ in glorious freedom. Why? How? Because God's Spirit enables the believer to *delight* in the law (the entire word of God, especially the gospel) from his heart, where the Spirit writes it (Ps. 1:2; 19:7-8; 37:31; Jer. 31:33; Rom. 7:22; Heb. 8:10; 10:16).

Take just one example. God commands his people to 'love one another fervently with a pure heart'. How can they do it? What grace and power does God give them to enable them to obey? Let the new covenant speak: 'Since you have purified your souls in obeying the truth through the Spirit in sincere love of the brethren, love one another fervently with a pure heart, having been born again, not of corruptible seed but incorruptible, through the word of God, which lives and abides for ever' (1 Pet. 1:22-23). That's how believers can do it – 'having been born again'. They can do it, they will do it, because they are regenerate, because they have the Spirit of God, because they are 'partakers of the divine nature' (2 Pet. 1:4), and because they are newly 'created to be like God in true righteousness and holiness' (Eph. 4:24, NIV).

So, while believers are under a far more searching regime in the new covenant, far more incisive than the Jews under the old covenant,[16] while the law of Christ is far more penetrating, far more demanding than the law of Moses, Christ provides so much more than Moses. God demands all. God promises all. Christ accomplished all. Christ is all. Christ gives grace to enable his people to love and obey his law from the heart, by his Spirit, and thus glorify God.[17]

---

[16] See my *Christ* pp232-236,508-509.

[17] In saying this, I do not imply that there were no regenerate people in the Old Testament. While the position of Old Testament believers is 'somewhat anomalous', Abraham (before the law was given), Moses (who was given the law), and David (after the law had been given), are typical of those who lived and died trusting in the coming Messiah, and are rightly counted among the men and women of faith (John 8:56; Heb. 11). The Psalmist spoke for all new-covenant people of both ages when

'The law was given through Moses' – BUT – 'grace and truth came through Jesus Christ' (John 1:17).

---

he said: 'Oh, how I love your law!' (Ps. 119:97). 'Love' is a heart word. Throughout Psalm 119, note the connection between 'law', 'precepts', 'judgments', and so on, and such words as 'heart' or 'whole heart', 'rejoice', 'delight', 'longing', 'love', and the like. The man who prefers the law above 'thousands of shekels of gold and silver' shows us where his heart is (Matt. 6:21). See also Ps. 1:2; 40:8. The fact that there were new-covenant people living in the Old Testament, of course, is why I can quote their words! There is no difference between David and Paul: 'I delight in the law of God according to the inward man' (Rom. 7:22). As I have made clear, it is all 'the law of God', but in the old covenant it is 'the law of Moses', while in the new it is 'the law of Christ'. In saying this, of course, I am not going back on my comments on Rom. 7:14-25; I am deliberately not defining the man in question. In all this, see my *Psalm 119*.

The Penetrating Law of Christ

Many ill-informed and dismissive comments are made about those who advocate the law of Christ, and not the law of Moses, as the believer's rule. Speaking for myself, I do not merely resent this. It is a travesty. It hinders many in making a fair assessment of new-covenant theology. Worse, it is a direct offence against the Lord Christ himself. Christ's law is *not* foggy sentiment.[1] Christ is *not* content with a woolly obedience, a vague profession of some sort of 'love'. He demands total, unstinted, constant and continual obedience, out of the highest possible motives – because he loved me, because of all that he is, because of all he has done for me, because he has taught me to love him, because he has written his law on my heart, because he himself has been formed within me, and because he has given me his Spirit, the one who moves me to live in increasing conformity to my Redeemer's likeness to the glory of God:

> My brothers, you... have died to the law through the body of Christ, so that you may belong to another, to him who has been raised from the dead, in order that we may bear fruit for God. For while we were living in the flesh, our sinful passions, aroused by the law, were at work in our members to bear fruit for death. But now we are released from the law, having died to that which held us captive, so that we serve in the new way of the Spirit and not in the old way of the written code... There is therefore now no condemnation for those who are in Christ Jesus. For the law of the Spirit of life has set you free in Christ Jesus from the law of sin and death. For God has done what the law, weakened by the flesh, could not do. By sending his own Son in the likeness of sinful flesh and for sin, he condemned sin in the flesh, in order that the righteous requirement of the law might be fulfilled in us, who walk not according to the flesh but according to the Spirit... For those whom he foreknew he also predestined to be conformed to the image of his Son, in order that he might be the firstborn among many brothers. And those whom he predestined he also called, and those whom he called

---

[1] See 'Fuzzy Sentiment' in my series: 'New-Covenant Theology Made Simple'.

he also justified, and those whom he justified he also glorified...
I appeal to you therefore, brothers, by the mercies of God, to
present your bodies as a living sacrifice, holy and acceptable to
God, which is your spiritual worship. Do not be conformed to
this world, but be transformed by the renewal of your mind, that
by testing you may discern what is the will of God, what is good
and acceptable and perfect (Rom. 7:4-6; 8:12-4,29-30; 12:1-2).

This Christ-likeness in the believer is both an inevitable and
essential consequence of the new covenant. Anything less
'wishy-washy' could not be imagined. In this short article, I want
to explore these things a little.[2]

Now there are two vital principles to make clear before we go
any further. The law of Christ is not the law of Moses. It is not
even a 'law' in the Mosaic sense. Since I have set all this out in
detail elsewhere, I will not develop my line of reasoning here.
Nevertheless, these two points are not trivial, and I urge you to
read and weigh my supporting arguments.[3]

In saying that the law of Christ is not a list of rules, and in
stressing that 'we serve in the new way of the Spirit and not in the
old way of the written code', however, I am not implying that the
believer is not under the rule of the entire Scripture (John 17:17;
2 Tim. 3:16). Nor am I saying that God's demands under the
gospel are easier than the demands of the law. Far from it. Why,
the new covenant is more searching than the old. As the letter to
the Hebrews makes crystal clear, to sin against Christ's law is far
worse than sinning against Moses. That letter was written, not to
inform its readers that it would be a pity if they went back from
Christ to the old covenant, but to tell them bluntly that it would
be fatal! Don't do it! Don't even think of it! And that is what the
sacred writer is saying to us, and saying to us now. We must not
leave Christ.

---

[2] For this article, I have lightly edited certain sections from my *Christ*
pp162-163,232-236,252-253,494-495,508-509,535-536.
[3] 'The Law on the Believer's Heart'; 'The Law the Believer's Rule?';
'What is the Law?'; '"The Law" in "the Law of Christ"'.

The warning passages in Hebrews

Let me start with this:

> Anyone who has rejected Moses' law dies without mercy on the testimony of two or three witnesses. Of how much worse punishment, do you suppose, will he be thought worthy who has trampled the Son of God underfoot, counted the blood of the covenant by which he was sanctified a common thing, and insulted the Spirit of grace? (Heb. 10:28-29).

Clearly, it is more culpable to sin under the new covenant than the old.

Furthermore, *ekklēsia* life plays a vital role in the law of Christ; in particular, the discipline of church life. Take the case of incest at Corinth, over which the believers were – yes – boasting! Paul rebuked them. They should have 'been filled with grief' (NIV) over it, and removed the offender. The apostle went on, setting out the way in which the law of Christ must be applied in such cases:

> In the name of our Lord Jesus Christ, when you are gathered together, along with my spirit, with the power of our Lord Jesus Christ, deliver such a one to Satan for the destruction of the flesh, that his spirit may be saved in the day of the Lord Jesus. Your glorying is not good. Do you not know that a little leaven leavens the whole lump? Therefore purge out the old leaven, that you may be a new lump, since you truly are unleavened. For indeed Christ, our Passover, was sacrificed for us. Therefore let us keep the feast, not with old leaven, nor with the leaven of malice and wickedness, but with the unleavened bread of sincerity and truth. I wrote to you in my letter not to keep company with sexually immoral people. Yet I certainly did not mean with the sexually immoral people of this world, or with the covetous, or extortioners, or idolaters, since then you would need to go out of the world. But now I have written to you not to keep company with anyone named a brother, who is sexually immoral, or covetous, or an idolater, or a reviler, or a drunkard, or an extortioner – not even to eat with such a person. For what have I to do with judging those also who are outside? Do you not judge those who are inside? But those who are outside God judges. Therefore 'put away from yourselves the evil person' (1

Cor. 5:1-13; see also Matt. 18:15-19; Acts 5:1-11; 8:18-23; 2 Thess. 3:6-15).

Do not miss the references to the old covenant, the law – the Passover and the extract drawn from several repeated Deuteronomy passages. The law of Christ knows how to make full – but properly nuanced – use of the law of Moses, the Mosaic covenant – as a paradigm.[4] Do not miss the reference to leaven – echoes of Galatians 5:9. And while the severity aspect of the law of Christ stands out a mile, do not forget that its application at Corinth had a reforming effect, and all was put right (2 Cor. 2:5-11). This, too, is another heart-warming aspect of Christ's law. But the point at issue stands. The law of Christ is anything but hazy sentimentalism, vague ethics, however often such dismissive terms are used by its ill-informed critics. Iron sits within the velvet.

The fact is, however, here we have what seems to be a contradiction. How can the new covenant be *more searching* than the old, and to sin against Christ's law be *far worse* than sinning against Moses' law (Heb. 10:28-29), and yet at the same time the 'law' of Christ, his 'yoke', his 'burden', be 'easy' and 'light' (Matt. 11:30)?

How do Reformed teachers, covenant theologians, deal with this?[5] They say the law of Christ is the law of Moses shorn of its condemnation. I call this 'pulling the law's teeth'. The new law, according to this, is something *less* than the old, *less* severe. It is the old law *minus* the difficult part. Reader, how can this be reconciled with the fact that the new covenant is more penetrating than the old? Instead of explaining the problem, this approach explodes it! How ironic, it is, therefore, that the Reformed are so free with their accusations of fuzzy sentiment, woolly concept, and all the rest, when dismissing new-covenant theology! Glass houses and the throwing of stones comes to mind. Who's the real antinomian, after all?[6]

---

[4] See my 'The Law the Believer's Rule?'
[5] See my 'The Law: Reformed Escape Routes'.
[6] See my video: 'Antinomianism!'.

The question remains: How can the law of Christ be more severe than the law of Moses? What is the biblical answer? How can the new covenant be more penetrating than the old, and yet be easy and light? Clearly, although the Bible states the seeming contradiction, there can be none. As to the severity aspect of Christ's law, contrary to the Reformed approach, no teeth are to be pulled. The warnings of the new covenant *are* to be taken seriously and given their full weight. There must be no getting round them by semantics. The warning passages are real.

The fundamental sin of the new covenant is to depart from Christ. I have just quoted Hebrews 10:29. What sin does the verse warn against? Nothing less than the deliberate, wilful (Heb. 10:26) forsaking of Christ, the bitter rejection of him and his Spirit.[7] Whoever breaks Hebrews 10:29 'has trampled the Son of God underfoot, counted the blood of the covenant by which he was sanctified a common thing, and insulted the Spirit of grace'. 'Worse punishment' than under Moses awaits such a man! And this warning note is sounded again and again throughout the letter to the Hebrews (Heb. 2:1-3; 3:12-14; 4:1,11; 6:4-8; 10:26-39; 12:14-17,25-29). Take also Romans 8:6,13: 'To be carnally minded [to have the mind of the flesh] is death... If you live according to the flesh you will die'. And Galatians 6:8: 'He who sows to his flesh will of the flesh reap corruption, but he who sows to the Spirit will of the Spirit reap everlasting life'. I stress the reality of the warning passages. They are not hypothetical. They are not put in Scripture as 'bogey men'. They are unfeigned. They mean what they say, and they say what they mean. I do not think they can be 'relegated' to dealing with the believer's reward. The believers who received the letter to the Hebrews were in danger of forsaking Christ.

Perseverance under Christ, holding to him and his law, is a sure mark of grace, the ultimate proof of spirituality. To depart from Christ is the worst of all sins. We are Christ's 'house... *if* we hold fast the confidence and the rejoicing of the hope firm to the end' (Heb. 3:6). 'For we have become partakers of Christ *if* we hold the beginning of our confidence steadfast to the end... And

---

[7] Do Matt. 12:31-32; Mark 3:29; Luke 12:10 speak of this?

we desire that each one of you show the same diligence to the full assurance of hope until the end... See that you do not refuse him who speaks' (Heb. 3:14; 6:11; 12:25). 'The gospel... by which... you are saved, *if* you hold fast' to the apostolic word, the gospel (1 Cor. 15:1-2). 'He who endures to the end shall be saved' (Matt. 24:13).

Is the punishment under the new covenant severe? It is indeed. To break the law of Christ – to reject Christ, to turn back from him, to forsake him – leads to: 'I never knew you; depart from me, you who practice lawlessness' (Matt. 7:23; see verses 13-29). How harrowing, then, is Christ's question: 'Do you also want to go away?' There is only one satisfactory reply: 'Lord, to whom shall we go? You have the words of eternal life. Also we have come to believe and know that you are the Christ, the Son of the living God' (John 6:67-69). The ultimate testimony which counts is this: 'I have fought the good fight, I have finished the race, I have kept the faith' (2 Tim. 4:7). Believer, Christ will 'present you holy, and blameless, and above reproach in his sight – *if* indeed you continue in the faith, grounded and steadfast, and are not moved away from the hope of the gospel' (Col. 1:22-23).

But just a moment! Surely all believers sin? Sadly, they do! Well, when a believer sins, does he bring condemnation upon himself? Does he lose his salvation? Certainly not! Let me explain. The law of Christ is far more than a list of rules. 'We serve in the new way of the Spirit and not in the old way of the written code' (Rom. 7:6). Of course, as I have said, the believer is under Scripture (John 17:17; 2 Tim. 3:16), but, I repeat, he does not serve God in the old way of the letter (2 Cor. 3:6). The law of Christ is not a sort of re-vamped law of Moses! In truth, it is not that at all. It is an entirely new system. To submit to the law of Christ is to yield to him, to receive him as Lord and Saviour, to honour and obey him, to learn of him, to cleave to him, to abide in him, to continue in him, to have him formed within, to have his Spirit, to walk according to his Spirit. Now although a believer may stumble into sin, this is a far cry from deserting the

Redeemer.[8] While I would not excuse the least sin, there is a world of difference between *failing* Christ and *forsaking* him. The believer sins; sadly, it is so. But God has made abundant provision for such (1 John 1:5-10; 2:1-2, for instance). Nevertheless, the warnings are real. If professing believers do turn their back upon Christ, and abandon him, they will come under the severest of all judgments: 'For if, after they have escaped the pollutions of the world through the knowledge of the Lord and Saviour Jesus Christ, they are again entangled in them and overcome, the latter end is worse for them than the beginning. For it would have been better for them not to have

---

[8] The believer cannot go back to the old slavery, and sin. He dare not, it is unthinkable: 'What then? Shall we sin because we are not under law but under grace? Certainly not!' (Rom. 6:15). So thunders the apostle. Before his conversion, the believer was a slave of sin, but now he is not; he is a slave of righteousness (Rom. 6:17-18). In his former slavery to sin he produced sin and death (Rom. 6:19-21). Now, being the slave of God, the slave of righteousness, he produces holiness (Rom. 6:22-23). I am not preaching sinless perfection. I do not say that a believer cannot sin. Of course not! But there is all the difference between 'sinning', and 'living in' or 'being a slave' to sin; between 'being in the flesh', and 'the flesh being in you'; between 'a sense of desertion', and 'living without God'; between 'a sense of darkness', and 'living in the kingdom of darkness'. I am not – *not* – teaching sinless perfection, I repeat. But I am restating Paul's doctrine: the unbeliever is a slave to sin; the believer is not. In Scripture, no believer is ever addressed as a sinner. John said: 'Whoever abides in [Christ] does not sin. Whoever sins has neither seen him nor known him. Little children, let no one deceive you. He who practices righteousness is righteous, just as he is righteous. He who sins is of the devil... Whoever has been born of God does not sin, for his seed remains in him; and he cannot sin, because he has been born of God' (1 John 3:6-9). NASB has 'sins... sins... practices sin... practices sin... sin'; NIV has 'keeps on sinning... continues to sin... does what is sinful... continue to sin... go on sinning'. He does not 'sin wilfully' (Heb. 10:26), 'sin deliberately' (NIV). He does not live in the *realm* of sin. Above all, although I talk as though *I* am saying this or that, all I have done is quote the apostle and try to enforce what *he* is saying! And at the heart of Paul's doctrine is this glorious statement: 'For sin shall not have dominion over you, for you are not under law but under grace' (Rom. 6:14).

known the way of righteousness, than having known it, to turn from the holy commandment delivered to them' (2 Pet. 2:20-21). This, it goes without saying, is far worse than under Moses.

This, then, is the biblical answer to the seeming contradiction. I realise that this, in itself, raises other problems, problems connected with God's sovereignty, his purpose and decree. One the one hand, I know that God will bring all his elect to everlasting glory. I rejoice in it. But I also know that each one of the elect has to come individually to faith in Christ and has to continue in Christ. I do not try to reconcile these two. I believe them both because I find them both revealed in Scripture. However much I explored these matters, I would still end up with a seeming contradiction, something beyond my wit to understand or explain. But this happens so often with me, I do as I always do: after trying to reconcile the paradox as far as I can within biblical parameters, I accept the remaining tension, and press on by faith. And it not just me! All believers find the same. Of course they do! Unless, that is, they are prepared to trim Scripture to fit their system![9] Which they are!

So, although there is much that can be said – and must be said – about the gentle, kindly aspect of Christ's law,[10] its severity aspect is real. We must take the warnings seriously. In the final analysis, to break the law of Christ is to depart from Christ, to desert him, to live according to the flesh. And the consequences are indescribably bad. But the law of Christ is far from negative. Although I have spent a little time on this negative aspect of it in order to tackle a seeming contradiction, there is far more to be said on the positive side. 'But you, beloved, building yourselves up on your most holy faith, praying in the Holy Spirit, keep yourselves in the love of God, looking for the mercy of our Lord Jesus Christ unto eternal life... Now to him who is able to keep you from stumbling, and to present you faultless before the presence of his glory with exceeding joy, to God our Saviour,

---

[9] On the seeming contradiction or paradox between God's sovereignty and the free offer, and between human inability and duty faith, see my *Offer*, especially pp75-152.

[10] That is, there is more to be said about the 'easy' (the opposite of burdensome) and 'light' (easy to be kept) aspect of Christ's law.

who alone is wise, be glory and majesty, dominion and power, both now and for ever. Amen' (Jude 20-21,24-25).

Nevertheless, I say again, the letter to the Hebrews was written, not merely to inform its readers that it would be a pity if they went back from Christ to the old covenant, but to make sure they persevered to the end. Departing from Christ would be fatal! Don't do it! Don't even think of it! That is what the sacred writer is saying to us, and saying to us right now: Do not leave Christ for anything or anybody!

The law of Christ as spelled out by Christ himself

As I have said, Christ's law is *not* foggy sentiment. He is *not* content with a woolly obedience, a vague profession of some sort of 'love'. Christ demands total, unstinted, constant and continual obedience, out of the highest possible motives – because he loved me, because of all that he is, because of all he has done for me, because he has taught me to love him, because he has written his law on my heart, because he himself has been formed within me, and because he has given me his Spirit, the one who moves me to live in increasing conformity to my Redeemer's likeness to the glory of God.

Having glanced at Hebrews, let me now go directly to Christ himself. We know what he declared in the Sermon on the Mount. Addressing his disciples, Christ took the Mosaic law for his springboard or starting point, saying again and again: 'You have heard that it was said... but I say to you' (Matt. 5:21-22,27-28,31-32,33-34,38-39,43-44). Christ always cut deeper than Moses. Instead of making obedience an external matter, Christ made (his) law-keeping a matter of the heart, which is far more penetrating and searching. He could not have made it any clearer: 'Unless your righteousness exceeds the righteousness of the scribes and Pharisees, you will by no means enter the kingdom of heaven' (Matt. 5:20).

At the highest pitch of all, the believer, as Christ declares, has to 'keep my [Christ's] commandments... just as I [Christ] have kept my Father's commandments' (John 15:10). Note the 'just as'. This is what Christ requires. This is what pleases him. He demands the same quality of obedience from his people as that which he himself gave to his Father. Let *that* sink in! Moreover, such obedience not only pleases Christ, this is what makes his people truly happy: 'If you know these things, blessed [happy, AV] are you if you do them' (John 13:17).[11] More, obedience is essential; it is no option. And if anyone dares to dismiss this obedience to the gospel as sentimental vagueness, I urge him to think seriously about what he is doing. On a coming day, he will have to explain his words to Christ, the one who commands his people to show their love to him by obedience to his commandments, his law, and to do so with the same quality of obedience as he himself, while he lived on earth, showed to his Father.

Hear the word of Christ:

If you keep my commandments, you will abide in my love, *just as* I have kept my Father's commandments and abide in his love. These things I have spoken to you, that my joy may remain in you, and that your joy may be full. This is my commandment, that you love one another *as* I have loved you (John 15:10-12).
Receive one another, *just as* Christ *also* received us, to the glory of God (Rom. 15:7).
Be kind to one another, tender-hearted, forgiving one another, *even as* [*just as*, NIV] God in Christ [*also*, NASB] forgave you. Therefore be imitators of God as dear children. And walk in love, *as* Christ *also has* loved us and given himself for us (Eph. 4:32 – 5:2).
Husbands, love your wives, *just as* Christ *also* loved the church and gave himself for her... *just as* the Lord does the church (Eph. 5:25,29).

In light of biblical commands of this nature and weight, all foolish, dismissive talk – cheap talk! – about the so-called inadequacy or vagueness of the law of Christ should cease forthwith. Such scorning of the law of Christ verges on the blasphemous.

---

[11] This is more than a warm feeling, of course. Such people are truly blessed in God's eyes.

Extracts with brief comments

Robert Govett:

> Let us now turn to another field in which the loftiness of the new rule of life is more fully exhibited. I refer to the Sermon on the Mount, in which the Saviour's doctrine is compared with that of Moses in many and most important points. The main difference between the two systems consists in this – that Moses' law embodies the spirit of JUSTICE; the teaching of our Lord, the spirit of MERCY. It is from this fundamental distinction that the superiority of the new rule of life flows... Jesus came in no hostile spirit against the law or the prophets. Both were sent by his Father; both must receive their entire fulfilment ere they passed away, as it was designed that they should. But... there is no 'unseemly opposition' here...
>
> The Saviour begins to compare his new standard with the old. He takes the second table of the decalogue, and shows how much more he requires than Moses demanded of old. The Saviour announces his commands with the most studied contrast to the law: a contrast which has been blunted to English readers by our translation. We read [in the AV of Matt. 5:21]: 'You have heard that it was said *by* those of old time', instead of '*to*', which beyond just question is the correct rendering; and which is given in the margin [of the AV, and is the translation in the NKJV, NIV; the NASB has 'the ancients were told']. [Christ] begins with the sixth command. The law forbade murder, and announced to the murderer the judgment of the appointed court. Jesus assures his disciples that even anger between brethren would come before his future court; and that a malicious word would expose the utterer to the danger of hell-fire. Here is a heightening indeed of the offence and of the penalty. That which was no misdeed against the law of Moses is now to be visited with a sentence greater than that belonging to the highest crime under the law (Matt. 5:21-22).
>
> When he speaks of the seventh command, there is a similar raising of the standard. That which was no misdeed at all as reckoned by Moses is by Jesus announced to be adultery, and exposed to the visitation of Gehenna. With like words does Jesus exalt the rule of life concerning theft, false witness and coveting a neighbour's goods (Matt. 5:27-30).
>
> But he does not halt at the decalogue. That was not the Jew's entire rule of life.

Let me break in. What a very important point Govett is making. It must not be missed. The ten commands comprised only a part of the rule for Jews. So, if the Reformed are right, believers, who according to the Reformed have only the ten commandments as their rule, have a lesser regime than the Jews! The Jews had 613 commands, whereas believers have only ten! Remarkable.

And that's not all. Govett:

> The Saviour therefore shows how his new commands rise above and set aside the law. He forbids divorce in cases permitted by Moses. Moses allowed oaths and vows... the Saviour forbids them... Moses' general doctrine was that goodness and kindness were to be exhibited towards men, specially towards the holy nation of Israel; but it admitted of two exceptions – criminals and enemies... Criminals... pity was forbid (Deut. 13:8; 19:21). The enemies of Israel might be smitten to death with the sword. The priests with the trumpets of God were to encourage and bless their warfare. Now [under the law of Christ] this is forbidden. The law of grace is to encircle even the cases excepted by Moses. The disciple is not to prosecute the offender; nor is he permitted on any occasion to take the sword against a foe. His Father in heaven is sparing criminals and enemies; he is to resemble him (Matt. 5:38-48).
>
> Jesus next drops a word of warning. He confesses the extreme difficulty to fallen man of a rule of life so high and heavenly as this. 'Tis a narrow gate and a strict way indeed! But he tells us not to imagine that he was asking of disciples born of God only conduct such as might be exhibited by the lowest of mankind. Was such a life difficult indeed? Yes, but an especial reward was also promised thereto. Were they born again of God? Let them show it by grace like that of the Father in heaven.
>
> In regard of religious service, the Saviour next exalts the standard greatly beyond the law. Moses... required only that the offerer should be a circumcised Jew, not ceremonially unclean, and that the offering... should be without blemish. But now our Lord brings into view the motives of the worshipper... (Matt. 6:1-18).
>
> The law promised, and gave as its blessing, treasures on earth. Filled barns and overflowing storehouses were the sign of Jehovah's favour. Now the disciples were to give up these for treasures in heaven, and for a recompense at the resurrection of the just (Matt. 6:19-34). Under the law, to be a magistrate and ruler was an honour, rightly desired by an Israelite... The

Saviour now forbids this to his disciples... (Matt. 7:1-2). The law admitted to its sacred rites every circumcised descendant of Abraham. No matter how sensual, bloodthirsty, deceitful and unbelieving a Jew might be, he had a right to partake of the Passover. Judas the betrayer had as good a right to the Paschal lamb as our Lord. Wicked as a high priest might be, if he were not ceremonially unclean, he had a right to enter the holiest. But that defect is removed in the Saviour's new scheme. His disciples were to exclude from the sacred rites appointed by our Lord all the unclean and unrenewed in spirit (Matt. 7:6).

Thus I have rapidly gone over the Sermon on the Mount, and have exhibited our Lord as indeed the author of a new doctrine, affecting all the Christian's life, and standing in constant contrast with the commands of the Mosaic law. Jesus is no mere expounder of Moses.

What a vital point this is. Govett went on:

Most would make Jesus only a land-surveyor, pointing out afresh the old boundaries of the fields, scraping from the surface the stones, the moss and lichens which in the course of ages had covered them; or rooting from their neighbourhood the brambles that concealed them. But now evidence in plenty has been adduced to prove that this view is mistaken. Moses brought LAW: Jesus brought GRACE (John 1:17). The prophet who was to come, according to God's own promise, was not merely one who was to recall attention to the words spoken by Moses. He was to bear a new doctrine ['his law' (Isa. 42:4)]: and woe to him that refused it! The two schools of doctrine taught by Moses and by Christ, respectively, have been briefly presented. You, my reader, must decide by which you will be led. Some, as the Saviour foresaw, would prefer the old and easier rule of life. For them, he draws the consequence of such a choice... (Matt. 5:20).[12]

Let me emphasise this last point. As Govett rightly shows, the law of Christ is more penetrating than the law of Moses, and its punishment ultimately more severe. The warning passages are real! Please remember Jesus' words about judgment were largely delivered to his disciples and for them. Most evangelicals today

---

[12] Robert Govett: *Is The Law The Christian's Rule Of Life?*, Fletcher and Son, Norwich, Third edition, 1874, pp48-53.

are quite content to forget the context and apply them to unbelievers. So, taking up Govett's expression, those who opt for the Mosaic law as the way of progressive sanctification have actually opted for the 'easier rule of life' – the wrong one, but easier!

John G.Reisinger as editor of *Sound of Grace* in an 'Open Letter to Dr Sproul':

Dr Sproul, please explain why your magazine labels new-covenant theology as antinomian when we not only affirm just as strongly as you that the Christian is not only under clear objective ethical commandments in the new covenant, but we also insist those new-covenant laws are even higher than those written on stone. How is it possible for our belief in a *higher* law to be turned into *anti* law? Your September [2002] issue of *Tabletalk* condemns us as heretics simply because we believe that our Lord Jesus Christ is a true lawgiver in his own right and, as such, gives higher and more spiritual laws that anything Moses ever gave. Why do we deserve the odious label of 'antinomian' simply because we believe that Christ replaces Moses as the new lawgiver in exactly the same way he replaces Aaron as high priest?[13]

James D.G.Dunn, commenting on Galatians 5:14, quashed the notion that the biblical call for 'love' is 'imprecise':

On the contrary, just because it is less prescribed beforehand what love of the neighbour demands, and depends on who the neighbour is and his/her situation in each particular instance, *it is all the more demanding*. Moreover, the demand is open-ended: we do not know beforehand who our neighbour might be at any one time (see also... Gal. 6:10)... It is a call for a practical love, a concentrated love, not a vague feeling for humankind stretched so thin as to be non-existent.

I agree, further, with Dunn when he once again observed how an emphasis upon 'the freedom of the Spirit can easily degenerate' into all sorts of carnal behaviour, unless it is accompanied by the equally biblical emphasis on the all-embracing law of Christ. As Ben Witherington likewise observed, carnal behaviour 'is the lot

---

[13] John G.Reisinger: 'An Open Letter to Dr R.C.Sproul', *Sound of Grace*, Frederick, Vol.9 number 4, February 2003, p3, emphasis his.

of those who throw over the law without a principle as penetrating as love of neighbour to guide them, and without a genuine commitment to serve one another. Without that, the call to freedom can open a floodgate which sweeps away every foundation'.[14]

Conclusion

So, paradoxically, Christ's law is both more penetrating and yet easy (Matt. 11:30). I see both in Scripture, I state both with equal vehemence, and, by God's Spirit, I seek to apply both with equal fervour, beginning with myself. The is the new-covenant theology I espouse.

I praise God for his grace, and I use all necessary means to hold on my way by his Spirit. Oliver Cromwell's 'trust in God my boys and keep your powder dry' is an excellent dictum.

No, I am not teaching that any of the elect can be lost. But the warning passages (the Gospels, *Hebrews*) are real, not hypothetical. My works don't save or keep me. Only God's grace does that. But I have to persevere:

> For if you live according to the flesh you will die, but if by the Spirit you put to death the deeds of the body, you will live (Rom. 8:13).
> Therefore, my beloved, as you have always obeyed, so now, not only as in my presence but much more in my absence, work out your own salvation with fear and trembling, for it is God who works in you, both to will and to work for his good pleasure (Phil. 2:12-13).
> If then you have been raised with Christ, seek the things that are above, where Christ is, seated at the right hand of God. Set your minds on things that are above, not on things that are on earth. For you have died, and your life is hidden with Christ in God. When Christ who is your life appears, then you also will appear with him in glory. Put to death therefore what is earthly in you: sexual immorality, impurity, passion, evil desire, and

---

[14] James D.G.Dunn: *The Epistle to the Galatians*, A & C Black, London, 1993, pp289,292-293, emphasis mine; Ben Witherington III: *Grace in Galatia: A Commentary on... Paul's Letter to the Galatians*, T.&T.Clark, Edinburgh, 1998, pp384-385.

covetousness, which is idolatry. On account of these the wrath of God is coming. In these you too once walked, when you were living in them. But now you must put them all away: anger, wrath, malice, slander, and obscene talk from your mouth. Do not lie to one another, seeing that you have put off the old self with its practices and have put on the new self, which is being renewed in knowledge after the image of its creator. Here there is not Greek and Jew, circumcised and uncircumcised, barbarian, Scythian, slave, free; but Christ is all, and in all. Put on then, as God's chosen ones, holy and beloved, compassionate hearts, kindness, humility, meekness, and patience, bearing with one another and, if one has a complaint against another, forgiving each other; as the Lord has forgiven you, so you also must forgive. And above all these put on love, which binds everything together in perfect harmony. And let the peace of Christ rule in your hearts, to which indeed you were called in one body. And be thankful. Let the word of Christ dwell in you richly, teaching and admonishing one another in all wisdom, singing psalms and hymns and spiritual songs, with thankfulness in your hearts to God. And whatever you do, in word or deed, do everything in the name of the Lord Jesus, giving thanks to God the Father through him (Col. 3:1-17).

His divine power has granted to us all things that pertain to life and godliness, through the knowledge of him who called us to his own glory and excellence, by which he has granted to us his precious and very great promises, so that through them you may become partakers of the divine nature, having escaped from the corruption that is in the world because of sinful desire. For this very reason, make every effort to supplement your faith with virtue, and virtue with knowledge, and knowledge with self-control, and self-control with steadfastness, and steadfastness with godliness, and godliness with brotherly affection, and brotherly affection with love. For if these qualities are yours and are increasing, they keep you from being ineffective or unfruitful in the knowledge of our Lord Jesus Christ. For whoever lacks these qualities is so nearsighted that he is blind, having forgotten that he was cleansed from his former sins. Therefore, brothers, be all the more diligent to confirm your calling and election, for if you practice these qualities you will never fall. For in this way there will be richly provided for you an entrance into the eternal kingdom of our Lord and Saviour Jesus Christ (2 Pet. 1:3-11)

Therefore, beloved, since you are waiting for these, be diligent to be found by him without spot or blemish, and at peace. And count the patience of our Lord as salvation, just as our beloved brother Paul also wrote to you according to the wisdom given him, as he does in all his letters when he speaks in them of these matters. There are some things in them that are hard to understand, which the ignorant and unstable twist to their own destruction, as they do the other Scriptures. You therefore, beloved, knowing this beforehand, take care that you are not carried away with the error of lawless people and lose your own stability. But grow in the grace and knowledge of our Lord and Saviour Jesus Christ. To him be the glory both now and to the day of eternity. Amen (2 Pet. 3:14-18).

The Law Written

There are several places in the New Testament where the law in its *written* aspect is spoken of, where it is described as 'the law of commandments contained in ordinances', 'the letter', 'the written code', and so on.[1] This written law, Scripture explains, is at enmity with those it holds in its grip. It is a 'ministry of condemnation', a 'ministry of death' for those who are under it. Above all, these New Testament passages declare that, for his people, Christ has dealt with this 'letter', this 'law of commandments contained in ordinances', this 'written and engraved' law which was against them. He has removed it. They are no longer under it. In short, these passages concerning the written law teach the very same as Romans 6:14; 7:4,6; 8:4, Galatians 3:25-26; 5:18, and elsewhere.

Here are the passages in question:

> But now we have been delivered from the law, having died to what we were held by, so that we should serve in the newness of the Spirit and not in the oldness of the letter [the written code (ESV)] (Rom. 7:6).
> God... made us sufficient as ministers of the new covenant, not of the letter but of the Spirit; for the letter kills, but the Spirit gives life. But if the ministry of death, written and engraved on stones, was glorious, so that the children of Israel could not look steadily at the face of Moses because of the glory of his countenance, which glory was passing away, how will the ministry of the Spirit not be more glorious? For if the ministry of condemnation had glory, the ministry of righteousness exceeds much more in glory. For even what was made glorious had no glory in this respect, because of the glory that excels. For if what is passing away was glorious, what remains is much more glorious (2 Cor. 3:5-11).
> [Christ]... having abolished in his flesh the enmity; that is, the law of commandments contained in ordinances... putting to death the enmity (Eph. 2:14-16).

---

[1] This article is taken from my *Christ* pp200-207,478-480, lightly edited.

[Christ] having wiped out the handwriting of requirements that was against us, which was contrary to us. And he has taken it out of the way, having nailed it to the cross (Col. 2:14).

These four passages speak about the same thing, making the same point to the same sort of people. They speak to believers, teaching them the truth about their past and present relationship to the law. These passages tell us that the law was the *letter*, the *written code*, the law *written* and *engraved* on stones, the law of commandments contained in *ordinances*, the *handwriting*. And addressing believers, these passages all say this written law was a ministry of *condemnation*, at *enmity* with or *against* them. And they all say the written law, which was against them, was by Christ's work and gift of the Spirit *passing away*, *abolished*, or *wiped out*, so that believers are *delivered from* it.

Let me deal with the words I have just emphasised.[2]

The Greek for *delivered from*, *passing away* and *abolished* means 'to cause to cease, to put an end to, to do away with, annul, abolish, to make invalid'. Thus Romans 7:6, 2 Corinthians 3:11 and Ephesians 2:15 all speak of the same thing; namely, of the end of the law, of its being abolished, of its being done away with, of its being put away, its being made to cease. In other words, believers are released from the law by the work of Christ. He has done away with it. The word is used elsewhere in the New Testament, to speak of making the law *void*, of *destroying* the body, of *putting away* childish things and of *abolishing* death

---

[2] *katargeō*: 'To cause to cease, to put an end to, to do away with, annul, abolish, to make invalid'. *exaleiphō*: 'To wipe off, wipe away, obliterate, erase, blot out, remove, destroy'. *entolē* is used of 'the commandments of the Mosaic law, that which God prescribed in the law of Moses, particular precepts as distinguished from the body or sum of the law'. *nomos* refers to 'the Mosaic law – the volume or its contents'. *dogma* means 'the rules and requirements of the law of Moses' (Joseph Henry Thayer: *A Greek-English Lexicon of the New Testament*, Baker Book House, Grand Rapids, Ninth Printing 1991; William Arndt and F.Wilbur Gingrich: *A Greek-English Lexicon of the New Testament and Other Early Christian Literature*, The University of Chicago Press, Chicago, Illinois, and The Syndics of the Cambridge University Press, London, 1957).

(Rom. 3:31; 1 Cor. 6:13; 13:11; 2 Tim. 1:10).[3] This makes the meaning of our passages very clear. The law, for believers, has been abolished, put away, destroyed, made invalid, brought to an end, made void.

A different word is used in Colossians 2:14, translated *wiped out*. It means 'to wipe off, wipe away, obliterate, erase, blot out, remove, destroy'. Hence it speaks with a similar voice to the other passages; Christ has obliterated the law for believers, wiped it away, erased it. Note the three steps. He 'blotted it out'. Is that enough? No! 'He took it out of the way'. Is *that* enough? No. He 'nailed it to his cross'. It is finished, over and done with, for ever.

Ah! But what is the 'it'? What, precisely, has been abolished, done away with, removed by Christ? What have believers been delivered from? *This* is the issue. It is the law (Rom. 7:6; Eph. 2:15), the killing letter, the ministry of death and condemnation written on stones (2 Cor. 3:6-7,9), 'the handwriting of requirements' (Col. 2:14). It is the law which is blotted out, not the law in 'so far as it was against us and cursed us'. The law! Sadly, however, there is a great deal of confusion over this. Let me look at it in more detail.

Take the Ephesian passage. Paul spoke of 'the law', 'the law of commandments', 'the law of commandments contained in ordinances'. What did he mean? He was speaking of the law of Moses written on stones and written in Scripture, the Mosaic law in its entirety. The same goes for the Corinthian and the Colossian passages.[4] There is no difference between 'the letter' which 'kills... the ministry of death, written and engraved on stones... the ministry of condemnation' (2 Cor. 3:5-11), 'the enmity; that is the law of commandments contained in ordinances... the enmity' (Eph. 2:14-16), and 'the handwriting of requirements that was against us, which was contrary to us' (Col. 2:14).

---

[3] While I recognise that Rom. 3:31 states that the gospel establishes the law and does not make it 'void', I am drawing attention to the use of the word 'abolish', which is used of the law in the other texts. As for Rom. 3:31 see my video and audio clips under David H J Gay Ministry, 'New-Covenant Theology Made Simple'.

[4] But see below.

In 2 Corinthians 3, Paul was certainly referring at least to the ten commandments given at Sinai. *They* were written on stones (Ex. 34:28; Deut. 4:13; 5:22; 10:4). Moreover, the Greek word for *letter* or *writing* in Romans 7:6 and 2 Corinthians 3:6, is the same as in Romans 2:27; namely, the written code, the written law of Moses, 'his writings' (John 5:47). And this, it goes without saying, is the law, including the ten commandments. Furthermore, in Romans 7:7, Paul quoted the tenth commandment. In addition, the Greek word for *commandments* in Ephesians 2:15 is used in Ephesians 6:2, speaking of the fifth commandment. So 'the law of commandments' (Eph. 2:15) must include the ten *commandments*. Furthermore, it is the word which is used repeatedly in Romans 7:8-13, where Paul undeniably was speaking of the decalogue, the commandments of the law, that law which God gave to Moses. In the Ephesian passage, Paul declares that the law of Moses itself is the dividing wall of hostility between Jews and Gentiles, and that Christ made peace between Jews and Gentiles by destroying this hostility, the dividing wall, by abolishing the law of commandments in ordinances itself – that which gave rise to the hostility. This is further confirmed by the Greek word for *law* which is used in Ephesians 2:15 and many other places, including Romans 7; Galatians 3 and 4; and 1 Timothy 1:8-9. It refers to 'the Mosaic law – the volume or its contents', including the ten commandments. It is the whole of the Mosaic law, the ten commandments in particular, which 'passes [fades] away' (2 Cor. 3:11,13; Heb. 8:13).[5] What is more, the Greek word for *ordinances*, which is used in Ephesians 2:15 and Colossians 2:14, means 'the rules and requirements of the law of Moses', and is linked as above with *commandments*. There is no doubt, therefore, that these four passages – in Romans 7, 2 Corinthians 3, Ephesians 2 and Colossians 2 – speaking of the written law, all refer to the Mosaic law including the ten commandments.

Exodus 34:27-28 is a crucial passage, showing that 'the ten commandments' and 'the words of the covenant' are one and the

---

[5] Note the comparison with man's likeness to a temporary and vanishing 'vapour' in Jas. 4:14 and associated passages.

same. The Reformed tripartite division of the law founders on this passage.[6] The Mosaic law given at Sinai is one indivisible law, and this statement (Ex. 34:27-28) paints the background for Paul's declaration about its abolition. It is the law of Moses as a whole, and in all its parts, which has passed away, and this includes the ten commandments. 'The whole law' is embraced in Paul's declaration.

It is abundantly plain, therefore, that the four passages in question speak about one and the same thing; namely, the Mosaic law, that same law as is spoken of in Romans 6:14; 7:1-12; 8:2-4 and Galatians 3:10-25; 4:21-25; 5:14,18. If you have any doubt, reader, please read these passages, and compare them with the passages in question in this article. They all speak of the same law – the Mosaic law, including the ten commandments – and they consistently speak of it in terms of its rule, bondage, curse, enmity, requirements, and so on, and they consistently speak of its removal for believers by the work of Christ. So the believer – the person who has the Spirit of the Lord – is no longer in bondage, because in Christ 'there is liberty' (2 Cor. 3:17).[7] 'For freedom Christ has set us free; stand firm therefore, and do not submit again to a yoke of slavery' (Gal. 5:1).

In 2 Corinthians 3:3-18, Paul was contrasting the glory of the gospel with that of the Mosaic economy, contrasting the ministries of the old and new covenants, contrasting their relative

---

[6] I have repeatedly dealt with this fundamental mistake of covenant theologians; namely, dividing the law into three, thus enabling them (they think) to jettison everything but the ten commandments, their so-called 'moral law'. In particular, see my 'Reading The Bible'.

[7] Now a question might suggest itself. Since the law was given to the Jews and not to the Gentiles, how were these Gentiles ever under this 'handwriting' in the first place? How were they under the law? The answer is Rom. 2:14-15. Gentiles have 'the work of the law written in their hearts'. See my *Christ* pp38-48,342-347 for an examination of Rom. 2:14-15. This same difficulty arises elsewhere of course; Rom. 7:1-6, for instance. One thing is certain, however. If any Reformed writer wants to limit 'the law' in these passages to the ceremonial law, he needs to explain how the Gentiles were ever under the ceremonial law. See below.

glories.[8] The old covenant was to do with the flesh; the new covenant is the covenant of the Holy Spirit (verses 3,6,8). The old covenant was an outward covenant, written on stones; the new covenant is an inward covenant, written on the heart (verses 2-3,7). The old covenant killed; it spelled death; the new covenant spells life (verses 3,6-7). The old covenant was deliberately temporary, designed by God to be so; the new covenant is permanent; it remains (verses 11,13). The old covenant had glory, but its glory was lesser and fading; the new covenant has a glory which exceeds, excels, being so much greater than the glory of the old covenant (verses 7-11). The old covenant condemned; the new covenant is justifying (verse 9).[9] The old covenant spelled bondage; the new covenant, liberty (verses 12,17). Note the new/old contrast; the new is established, the old is abolished; the new has power, the old was useless and ineffective.

The enmity of the law in Ephesians 2:14-16 came about because of its divisive nature. God built this separation into the law, making it a fundamental aspect of the law. God gave the law to Israel, and only to Israel, as a special mark to separate the Jews from the rest of mankind (Deut. 4:1 – 6:25; Ps. 147:19-20; Rom. 3:1-2; 9:4-5, and so on).[10] The law separated Jew and Gentile, and both were separated from God (Rom. 3:19-20; 4:15; 5:20; 7:7-11). And this law can be none other than the law of Moses, the whole of it. The same goes for Colossians 2:14. Christ abolished the law, by fulfilling it. By his death, he has freed believers from the law. They are no longer under the law but under grace (Rom. 6:14). The word 'ordinances' must not be misunderstood. Paul was not talking about what Reformed people call the ceremonial law – he was talking about the whole law

---

[8] See my *Christ* pp178-184,469-470.

[9] Although the apostle spoke of 'justification' in 2 Cor. 3:9, he was encompassing much more; indeed, the whole of salvation. No sinner was saved by keeping the law. To clutch at a straw here, and try to use this verse to limit the passage – and all the other passages – to the law for justification is simply not worthy of serious teachers. If John Calvin's third use of the law depends on such puerile exegesis, its case must be desperate. See below for more on Calvin's threefold use of the law.

[10] See my *Christ* pp27-37,337-341.

expressed in particular rules, regulations, commands and ordinances. It certainly included the fourth commandment – the sabbath. After all, the sabbath was a principal dividing marker between Jew and the rest of mankind (Ex. 31:12-18; Neh. 9:13-14; 13:14-22; Ezek. 20:5-26).[11]

As for Romans 7:6, 'the oldness of the letter' is the law. It is called 'the letter' simply because it was an external written code, written on the two tablets of stone, and then in Scripture. Both the old and new covenants were (are) written; the old, externally on stone and in the pages of Scripture; the new, in Scripture and, above all, in the heart. The old was a killing covenant; the new brings life. 2 Corinthians 3:6 is a parallel passage. Christ has set believers free from the law.

In short, these four passages on the written law, Romans 7:6, 2 Corinthians 3:5-11, Ephesians 2:14-16 and Colossians 2:14, teach the same doctrine as we have seen in many other places of Scripture; namely, Christ has set his people free from the law of Moses. It cannot be, therefore, the believer's perfect rule of godliness.

Sadly, it is not unknown for Reformed writers to gloss these passages. Let me give some examples.

Some say the law in question is the ceremonial law

This is a frequent claim, but inconsistently made. Some argue for instance that Ephesians 2:14 refers to 'the ceremonial law', but Romans 7 is the entire Mosaic law. And yet these two passages, as I have shown, speak of precisely the same law. Some argue that it was only the ceremonial law which divides Jew and Gentile. Yet they also admit that the ten commandments, like the ceremonies, were given to Israel. Some make much of the word 'ordinances' in Ephesians 2:14-16, deducing Paul was not talking about the ten commandments. But this is a mistake. Even in the ten commandments, there are ordinances, 'rules and regulations'. Were these not an integral part of 'the Mosaic code' and its 'stipulations'? Does Colossians 2:14 not refer to the Mosaic law,

---

[11] See my *Sabbath Questions*.

including the ten commandments? Who wrote the handwriting in Colossians 2:14? and where did he write it? In other words, what or whose is 'the handwriting of requirements' which has been 'wiped out'? I have answered all these questions. There can be no doubt that the writing and law of commandments which was against us includes the ten commandments, not merely the so-called 'ceremonial law'. Ephesians 2:14-15 is 'the law with its commandments and regulations'; not the *ceremonial* law. If anybody should try to argue that the 'that is' of Ephesians 2:15 proves Paul was referring to the ceremonial law, they should bear in mind that the translators have added the 'that is'; Paul didn't write it!

As for the ordinances in the ten commandments, take the fourth. Sabbath law was full of ordinances – ordinances about work, the family, servants, animals and immigrants. And the number of sabbath ordinances contained in the rest of Moses' writings is, I might say, legion. So even if Paul had been speaking about the ordinances which flesh out the commandments, and not the commandments themselves, he would have destroyed the Reformed case: Christ, apparently, has delivered us from the sabbath *because he has delivered us from all its ordinances*. And if he has delivered us from the fourth commandment, he has delivered us from the entire system (Jas. 2:10-11). Since Reformed sabbatarians claim Christ has removed all ceremonial laws for his people, how can they argue for the retention of a commandment so obviously ceremonial?

And, reader, do not forget, when Paul was writing to the Ephesians and Colossians, he was writing to Gentiles. Were they ever under the ceremonial law (allowing the term) with all its Jewish fasts, feasts, foods, offerings and circumcision? Were the Ephesians labouring under such things before conversion? Was that their problem? No Reformed writer – as far as I am aware – has ever suggested that Gentiles were under what the Reformed call the ceremonial law. Where and when did God ever command and require – I use the word 'require' advisedly in light of 'handwriting of *requirements*' (Col. 2:14) – where did he command and require Gentiles to observe the fasts, feasts, offerings and circumcision? Did Christ die to release Gentiles from *Jewish* feasts and rituals? Paul was not saying that Christ abolished the law of ceremonies, destroying its binding power. I am glad Christ has done far more than that for his people.

The Ephesian passage teaches us that the Jews were distinguished from the Gentiles, separated from them, that there was 'a middle wall of division between' them. This barrier, this wall of division, this demarcation line between the two, primarily comprised 'the law of commandments contained in ordinances'. True, circumcision had become in the Jewish mind the great divider, the most visible, the most obvious, divider (Eph. 2:11),[12] the one the Jews boasted of more than any, but the fact is the Gentiles 'at that time... were without Christ, being aliens from the commonwealth of Israel and strangers from the covenants of promise, having no hope and without God in the world' (Eph. 2:12). Especially were they separated from the Jews – and from God – by the fact that God gave his law, 'his word... his statutes and his judgements', 'the law of commandments contained in ordinances', to the Jews and not to them (Ps. 147:19-20). They were not under the pedagogue of the law as were the Jews (Gal. 3:23-25). As I have shown, God gave his law to Israel and to no others.[13] What law was this, which distinguished the Jews from the Gentiles? The law of Moses. All attempts to restrict this to a part of the law are very wide of the mark.

Some say the law in question is the judicial law

Disagreeing with those who think it was the ceremonial law which divided Jew and Gentile, some think it was 'the judicial law' which did it; it was the 'civil regulations' which comprised 'the wall of partition'. Oh? How is it then that we are told (Ex. 31:12-18; Neh. 9:13-14; 13:14-22; Ezek. 20:5-26) that the sabbath[14] was given to the Jews as a sign to mark them out from all other nations, that it was a central part of his covenant with

---

[12] Not only was circumcision an obvious separating mark, so were the sabbath and dietary laws.
[13] See my *Christ* pp27-37,337-341 for more on the law as the wall of partition.
[14] See my *Sabbath Questions*.

Israel, his special people (Deut. 4:1-8,44-45; 5:1-3; 29:1,10-15,25,29)? I mention this because the sabbath is not, of course, according to Reformed writers, part of the judicial law, but the moral! What is more, if Christ shed his blood to remove the handwriting of the *judicial or social* law, he must have died to grant his people liberty to eat pork, wear garments of mixed yarns, and so on.[15] The idea is preposterous. And, as before, who will claim that the Gentiles were ever under the *Jewish* civil law?

Some show a reluctance to take the passages seriously, especially in their works on the sabbath

I have detected a seeming unwillingness on the part of some, or an inadequate examination of the passages, in their works on the law or the sabbath, to face up to John 1:17, 2 Corinthians 3:6-11, Ephesians 2:15 and Colossians 2:14, passages of high significance in this debate. Why is it that, in their works on the sabbath, so many Reformed writers seem reluctant to tackle these passages?[16] And, even when they do, they frequently introduce (contradictory) glosses to circumvent them. Why?

Various other escape routes

Romans 7:6, Ephesians 2:15 and Colossians 2:14 clearly teach that the law is abolished; the believer is free of it. Christ did not abolish the entire law *except* the ten commandments. He abolished the law. Paul did not say that the believer is free of the law only in the sense of obtaining justification by it, that he is no longer under its curse. Christ has wiped out the law for the believer. Above all, Paul was not speaking only of justification when writing to the Ephesian and Colossian believers. The context of Colossians 2 is not justification but progressive sanctification.[17] The letter starts with justification, but Paul's aim

---

[15] Or does this come under the *ceremonial* law?

[16] Take, for instance, Joseph A.Pipa: *The Lord's Day*, Christian Focus, Fearn, 1997. He did not mention any of these passages.

[17] The sinner, on coming to faith, is united to Christ and is justified and positionally sanctified. Thus, in God's sight, in Christ he is accounted or

was his readers' progressive sanctification. By reading the letter through in one sitting, this becomes very clear. See especially Colossians 1:9-14; 2:6-10,16 – 4:18. In particular, in his letter, the apostle was not only telling the Colossians that there is no justification by law work – he was telling them there is no progressive sanctification by the law, either. He was speaking of justification leading to progressive sanctification. See Ephesians 4:1 – 6:24; Col. 1:10,22-29; 2:6,16-23; 3:1 – 4:18. Reader, you may verify this from Ephesians 2, for instance. Note how justification (Eph. 2:8-9) leads to progressive sanctification (Eph. 2:10) which leads directly to Ephesians 2:11 and on, beginning with the word 'therefore' (Eph. 2:11-22).

The ten commandments were written by the finger of God on two tablets of stone (Ex. 31:18; 32:14-15; 34:1,28; Deut. 5:22) – and it was *precisely* this system, the temporary ministry of death, written on stones, which was abolished when Christ fulfilled the law (2 Cor. 3:7,11). It is not only the glory of the law which was done away with – it was the law itself. 2 Corinthians 3:11,13 proves it. Yes, the glory of the old covenant was fading – but only because the old covenant itself was fading! It was temporary (Gal. 3:19,23-25); it was being annulled (Heb. 7:18); it was 'becoming obsolete and growing old' and was 'ready to vanish away' (Heb. 8:13). But, please note, it was *the entire system of law* which Christ abolished, not merely its glory. It was not merely the glory of the law which was becoming obsolete, growing old and ready to vanish away – it was the law *itself.* Indeed, only the covenant could be said to be 'abolished', not its glory. In any case, the evasion is the merest quibble. If the law has lost its glory, it has lost everything! For those who think it is just the glory of the law which is gone, what now of the suggestion that we are to think that Christ leads his people back

---

made righteous, free of sin and condemnation, and perfectly separated unto God. See, for instance, 1 Cor. 1:2,30; 6:11; Eph. 5:25-27; Heb. 10:10-18; 13:12. In his Christian life, he has to work out his perfection in Christ, and he will be moved to do so by the Spirit under the direction of Scripture; this is his progressive sanctification or holiness of life. But this, alas, is imperfect. The believer will only be absolutely sanctified in the eternal state. See my *Fivefold.*

to Moses? If this is so, it means that the law, far from losing its fading glory, has greater glory under Christ than ever it had under Moses! But Christ took away the first – law – to establish the second – grace (Heb. 10:9). Moses has given way to Christ. Christ has superseded him. Christ is better: 'For this one has been counted worthy *of more glory* than Moses... Moses indeed was faithful in all his house as a servant, for a testimony of those things which would be spoken afterwards [that is, Christ and the gospel], but Christ...' (Heb. 3:1-6). See John 1:17.

Christ and his covenant have more glory than Moses and his covenant. Therefore, if the Reformed are right, and sinners, on conversion, are taken under Moses for their progressive sanctification, then they are taken under a covenant that has less glory than the new covenant Christ established for them. This, it seems to me, can only mean that the Reformed end up with a system that gives Moses more glory than Christ. Nonsense!

Nor will it do to try to argue that the law *as a piece of writing*, independent of the Spirit, was done away with, and *that* was the old, obsolete thing which was abolished, not the law itself. Such a view, of course, prepares the way for asserting John Calvin's third use of the law,[18] in which the Spirit takes up that same law and uses it as the perfect rule in the believer's life. In plain English, it is not done away with after all! Rather, it is made stronger! No! 'The letter' means 'the law in its written aspect'. 'The letter' is contrasted with 'the Spirit' (Rom. 2:29; 7:6; 2 Cor. 3:6), as is 'the law' (Rom. 7:6; Gal. 5:18). 'The letter' therefore is 'the law', not the law without the Spirit.

The four passages we have looked at in this article, which all concern the written law, Romans 7:6, 2 Corinthians 3:5-11, Ephesians 2:14-16 and Colossians 2:14, all teach the same doctrine as we have seen in many other places of Scripture;

---

[18] Calvin had three uses for the law. 1. To prepare sinners for Christ. 2. To restrain sin. 3. As the motive, spur, whip to beat believers into progressive sanctification, 'the moral law' being their standard, their perfect rule. I have fully documented this, and challenged it, in many of my works. In particular, see my *Christ* pp51-74,348-368.

namely, Christ has set his people free from the law of Moses. It therefore cannot be the believer's perfect rule of godliness.

True, the old covenant had a glory. But the new covenant is better, superior, and its glory, therefore, is all the greater. The old covenant of death and condemnation, which was temporary, has gone. The new covenant, of Christ, of the Spirit, brings justification, and is permanent. What is more, it brings progressive sanctification leading to glorification. Beyond all doubt, the new covenant is more glorious than the old. Notice how Paul, in 2 Corinthians 3, takes his argument on to progressive sanctification, the transformation of believers. It is as Christ is preached, believed and looked to – in other words, as the new covenant is declared and received – that believers, having and realising their freedom in Christ, are transformed more and more into his image:

> Behold what manner of love the Father has bestowed on us, that we should be called the children of God... Beloved, now we are children of God; and it has not yet been revealed what we shall be, but we know that when he [Christ] is revealed, we shall be like him, for we shall see him as he is. And everyone who has this hope in him purifies himself, just as he is pure (1 John 3:1-3).

If that is not 'the law of Christ', what is it? If such passages do not tell us the motive, the spur, the way, and the aim of progressive sanctification – with no mention whatever of 'the law' – what do they tell us?

Extracts and comments

I start with Samuel Bolton, the great Puritan advocate of Calvin's view on the law:

> By the 'handwriting of ordinances', I conceive is not meant the ceremonial law alone, but the moral law also... We can here observe the successive steps which the apostle sets out. 'He has blotted out'. But lest this should not be enough, lest any should say, It is not so blotted out, but [that] it may [still] be read, the apostle adds, 'he took it out of the way'. But lest even this should not be enough, lest some should say: 'Yes, but it will be found again and set against us afresh', he adds, 'nailing it to his

cross'. He has torn it to pieces, never to be put together again for ever.[19]

First-rate! But Bolton put a fly in the ointment – adding his own gloss; namely, 'so far as it was against us and bound us over to the curse'. Bolton simply failed to get the point the apostle was making! Or, did he get it, but simply had to trim (that is, expand!) the apostle to make him fit his system? Let's get back to Paul!

D.Martyn Lloyd-Jones on Romans 7:

> What law is this?... [Some] say that this is a reference only to the law as given through Moses... Some even go further and say that it refers to the ceremonial part of [the Mosaic] law alone, and to nothing else... It would be quite unprofitable to spend time in refuting these false expositions. [What Paul said] is true of the Mosaic law, certainly, but not only of the Mosaic law... [Paul] is referring, of course [please note], to the written moral law that was given through Moses to the children of Israel. They referred to it as the 'writing' because God wrote it on the tables of stone which he gave to Moses.[20]

I must say, I like Lloyd-Jones' 'of course', although I wish he had not introduced the unnecessary 'moral law'. Nevertheless, bearing in mind what the Reformed mean by it, I am rather glad he did, and I find I now like Lloyd-Jones' 'of course' very much indeed! Do the Reformed?

Colin G.Kruse: In the Ephesian passage:

> Paul says that it is the law of Moses itself which gives rise to the dividing wall of hostility between Jews and Gentiles... Christ made peace between Jews and Gentiles by destroying the dividing wall (that is, the hostility), and by abolishing the law of commandments [expressed – Kruse's addition] in ordinances which gave rise to the hostility.[21]

---

[19] Samuel Bolton: *The True Bounds of Christian Freedom*, The Banner of Truth Trust, London, 1964, pp31-32.

[20] D.Martyn Lloyd-Jones: *Romans: An Exposition of Chapters 7:1 – 8:4. The Law: Its Function and Limits*, The Banner of Truth Trust, Edinburgh, 1973, pp15,92.

[21] Colin. G.Kruse: *Paul, The Law and Justification*, Hendrickson Publishers, Peabody, Massachusetts, 1997, pp263-264.

Fred G.Zaspel:

> It is the Mosaic legislation in its entirety and the decalogue
> specifically that Paul said 'fades away' (*katargesas*, 2 Cor. 3:11;
> *cf. exaleipsas*, Col. 2:14)... [Ex. 34:27-28 is a passage] of critical
> significance... where God identifies 'the ten commandments' as
> 'the words of the covenant'. No dividing of Moses will fit here'.
> Nor anywhere else! 'The legislation of Sinai is an inseparable unit,
> and this statement (Ex. 34:27-28) must inform the apostolic
> declaration of its abolition. It is the Mosaic code as a whole and in
> all its parts that has passed away, and the apostolic declarations to
> that end must therefore be seen to embrace even the decalogue...
> 'The whole law' stands or falls together as an indivisible unit. It
> would be wrong to forget this stated, essential unity of the old
> covenant/decalogue when reading New Testament statements of
> the covenant's/law's abolition... The statements are as broad and
> inclusive as they appear.[22]

'It would be wrong to forget this...', I agree, but that is precisely
what the Reformed do when they force Scripture to support their
system. In fact, they more than 'forget' the apostolic statements;
they gloss them to make them say the opposite!

On 2 Corinthians 3:7-18, Kruse:

> Paul had occasion to compare and contrast the glory of the
> apostolic ministry with that of Moses... Here Paul compares and
> contrasts the ministries of the old and new covenants... [He] was
> contrasting the lesser splendour of the ministry of the law to the
> greater splendour of the ministry of the gospel.[23]

Richard Sibbes, in his 'considerable volume' on 2 Corinthians
3:17-18, spoke of three 'distinct properties and prerogatives of
the gospel in which it excels the law, [following which,] by
inferences drawn from these properties... the apostle more largely

---

[22] Fred G.Zaspel: 'Divine Law: A New-Covenant Perspective',
Reformation & Revival Journal, editor John H.Armstrong, Reformation
& Revival Ministries, Inc., Carol Stream, Vol.6, Number 3, Summer
1997, pp154-155.
[23] Kruse pp151-153,155.

illustrates the transcendent glory of the gospel, and how far it exceeds the glory of the law'.[24]

On Ephesians 2:14-15, M.R.Vincent:

> The enmity was the result and working of the law regarded as a separative system; as it separated Jew from Gentile, and both from God. See Rom. 3:20; 4:15; 5:20; 7:7-11... Law is general, and its contents are defined by *commandments*, *special injunctions*, which injunctions in turn were formulated in definite *decrees*.[25]

On the same passage, Patrick Fairbairn: 'The law of commandments in ordinances is but another name for the Sinaitic legislation, or the old covenant'. On Colossians 2:14: 'What here is meant by the handwriting in ordinances... there can be no doubt, was the law, not in part but in whole – the law in the full compass of its requirements'.[26]

On Ephesians 2:14-15, Charles Hodge:

> Christ abolished the Mosaic law by fulfilling all its types and shadows... the abolition of the Mosaic law removes the wall between the Jews and Gentiles. This is what is here taught... This was done by abolishing the law... He abolished the law... Having by... his death abolished the law... Christ by his death has freed us from the law. We are no longer under the law but under grace, (Rom. 6:14)... The law which Christ has thus abolished is called "the law of commandments in ordinances". This may mean the law of commandments with ordinances... or it may refer to the

---

[24] Richard Sibbes: *The Excellency of the Gospel Above the Law*, in *Works of Richard Sibbes*, Vol.4, The Banner of Truth Trust, Edinburgh, 1983, pp202-205. Sibbes worked this out over the next 100 pages or so.

[25] M.R.Vincent: *Word Studies in the New Testament*, Macdonald Publishing Company, Florida, Vol.2 p852.

[26] Patrick Fairbairn: *The Revelation of Law in Scripture*, Alpha Publications, Indiana, 1979, pp458,466-467. Yet in his *The Typology of Scripture Viewed in Connection With The Whole Series of... The Divine Dispensations*, Evangelical Press, Welwyn, 1975, Vol.2 pp175-177, Fairbairn contradicted himself, calling 'the handwriting of requirements that was against us' (Col. 2:14) 'the ceremonial law', 'those ceremonies', 'the purifications of the law', 'the Old Testament ceremonies', 'the ceremonies of Moses'. No! 'The law' is the law.

form in which the precepts are presented in the law... as commands... giving the contents of the law... The idea is probably the law in all its compass, and in all its forms, so far as it was a covenant prescribing the conditions of salvation, is abolished. The law of which the apostle here speaks is not exclusively the Mosaic law... it is the law of God in its widest sense... not merely the law of Moses... [But] (in the passage before us), special reference is had to the law in that particular [that is, the Mosaic] form... The doctrine of the passage... is that the middle wall of partition between the Jews and Gentiles... has been removed by Christ having, through his death, abolished the law in all its forms.[27]

Do the Reformed agree with Hodge here? If so, how can the 'abolished' law, which 'Christ by his death has freed us from', be the believer's perfect rule for progressive sanctification?

On Romans 7:6, John Murray:

'The oldness of the letter' refers to the law, and the law is called the letter because it was written. The writing may refer to the two tables of stone on which the ten commandments were written or to the fact of the law as contained in Scripture. It is law simply as written that is characterised as oldness, and the oldness consists in the law. This is apparent not only from the context where the apostle has been dealing with the powerlessness of the law to deliver from sin, and the confirmation it adds to our servitude, but also from the parallel passage in 2 Corinthians 3:6. The contrast there between the letter and the Spirit is the contrast between the law and the gospel, and when Paul says 'the letter kills, but the Spirit makes alive', the letter is shown by the context to refer to that which was engraven on stones, the law delivered by Moses.[28]

Charles Hodge, like Murray, rightly called 2 Corinthians 3:6 one of the 'parallel passages... The letter [refers to] the law [which] is so designated because the decalogue, its most important part, was originally written on stone, and because the whole law, as

---

[27] Charles Hodge: *A Commentary on the Epistle to the Ephesians*, The Banner of Truth Trust, London, 1964, pp130-131,134-136.

[28] John Murray: *The Epistle to the Romans...*, Two Volumes in One, Marshall Morgan and Scott, London, 1974, Vol.1 p246.

revealed to the Jews, was originally written in the Scriptures, or writings... Believers then are free from the law, by the death of Christ'.[29] I repeat the questions I asked above. Do the Reformed agree with Hodge here? If so, how can the 'abolished' law, which 'Christ by his death has freed us from', be the believer's perfect rule for progressive sanctification?

Richard C.Barcellos: 'The middle wall of separation was the law of the old covenant... the old or Mosaic covenant'.[30] Of course, the law is used in the new covenant as a paradigm for believers,[31] but, as Paul said, the law divided Jew and Gentile before the coming of Christ. Barcellos spoiled his comment by qualifying 'law' by adding 'as old-covenant law',[32] a redundant phrase since that is precisely what the Mosaic law was! Let me illustrate. Take these two statements: *First*, the levitical sacrifices were old-covenant sacrifices. *Second*, the spiritual sacrifices of believers are new-covenant sacrifices. The first, as it stands, is a tautology. Linked with the second,[33] however, it is a powerful statement, emphasising the fundamental contrast of the two covenants, the oldness of the old covenant and the newness of the new covenant, and the radical difference in the nature of the sacrifices. So it is with Barcellos' phrase: 'old-covenant law'. The law of Moses is the old-covenant law. The law of Christ is the new-covenant law. And these two 'laws' are utterly different – not only in content, but in nature. I do not for a moment think that Barcellos meant *that*. Thus his phrase was redundant.

Gordon D.Fee, linking Romans 6:14 and 7:6 with Romans 2:29 and 2 Corinthians 3:6:

The contrast between Spirit and 'letter' has nothing to do with the several popularisations of this language [euphemism for

---

[29] Charles Hodge: *A Commentary on Romans*, The Banner of Truth Trust, London, 1972, p219.
[30] Richard C.Barcellos: *In Defense of the Decalogue: A Critique of New-Covenant Theology*, Winepress Publishing, Enumclaw, 2001, p67.
[31] See 'The Law the Believer's Rule?'
[32] Barcellos pp67-68.
[33] See my *The Priesthood*.

'Reformed glosses']; *e.g.*, between 'the spirit and letter' of the law, or between 'internal and external', or between 'literal and spiritual'... [The language of the biblical text] is eschatological and covenantal language. 'Letter' has to do with the old covenant that came to an end through Christ and the Spirit... The new has thus replaced the old, which was ratified by Moses and Israel on Sinai and characterised by 'written regulations requiring obedience'.[34]

---

[34] Gordon D.Fee: *God's Empowering Presence: The Holy Spirit in the Letters of Paul*, Hendrickson Publishers, Peabody, Massachusetts, 1994, pp507-508.

Made in the USA
Las Vegas, NV
27 June 2021

25543404R00199